Living & Working in
ITALY

● A Survival Handbook ●

Edited by Caroline Prosser

D1417481

Survival Books ● London ● England

First Edition 2001
Second Edition 2003
Third Edition 2007
Fourth Edition 2011

Copyright © Survival Books 2001, 2003, 2007, 2011
Cover photograph: Portofino © Borodaev (🖥 www.shutterstock.com)
Illustrations, cartoons and maps © Jim Watson

Survival Books Limited
9 Bentinck Street, London W1U 2EL, United Kingdom
☎ +44 (0)20-7788 7644, 🖨 +44 (0)870-762 3212
✉ info@survivalbooks.net
🖥 www.survivalbooks.net

British Library Cataloguing in Publication Data
A CIP record for this book is available
from the British Library.
ISBN: 978-1-907339-30-1

Printed and bound in Singapore by Stamford Press

Acknowledgements

The publisher would like to thank all those who contributed to the successful publication of the 4th edition of *Living and Working in Italy*, in particular Caroline Prosser for updating, Marta Vigneri, Caterina Pikiz Gattinoni, and Giovanni Amalfitano. We would also like to acknowledge the help provided by Geoffrey Watson (British Embassy in Rome, press department), John Murphy (The Informer) and Susan Jarman (The Grapevine).

Thanks are also due to Robbi Forrester Atilgan for editing; Lilac Johnston for proofreading and research; Peter Read for final checking; Di Bruce-Kidman for desktop publishing and photo selection; and Jim Watson for the cover design, cartoons and maps. Also a special thank you to the many photographers (listed on page 350) – the unsung heroes – whose beautiful images add colour and bring Italy to life.

What Readers and Reviewers Have Said About Survival Books:

"It's everything you always wanted to ask but didn't for fear of the contemptuous put down – The best English language guide – Its pages are stuffed with practical information on everyday subjects and are designed to complement the traditional guidebook."

Swiss News

"A must for all future expats. I invested in several books but this is the only one you need. Every issue and concern is covered, every daft question you have but are frightened to ask is answered honestly without pulling any punches. Highly recommended."

Reader (Amazon)

"Let's say it at once. David Hampshire's Living and Working in France is the best handbook ever produced for visitors and foreign residents in this country; indeed, my discussion with locals showed that it has much to teach even those born and bred in l'Hexagone. It is Hampshire's meticulous detail which lifts his work way beyond the range of other books with similar titles. This book is absolutely indispensable."

The Riviera Reporter

"Covers every conceivable question that might be asked concerning everyday life – I know of no other book that could take the place of this one."

France in Print

"It was definitely money well spent."

Reader (Amazon)

"The ultimate reference book – Every conceivable subject imaginable is exhaustively explained in simple terms – An excellent introduction to fully enjoy all that this fine country has to offer and save time and money in the process."

American Club of Zurich

Important Note

Italy is a diverse country with many faces, a variety of ethnic groups, languages, religions and customs, and continuously changing rules, regulations (particularly regarding business, social security and taxes), interest rates and prices. Note that a change of government in Italy, which happens frequently, can have an influence on many important aspects of life. We cannot recommend too strongly that you check with an official and reliable source (not always the same) before making any major decisions or taking an irreversible course of action. However, don't believe everything you're told or read – even, dare we say it, herein!

Useful addresses and references to other sources of information have been included in all chapters and in **Appendices A** to **C** to help you obtain further information and verify details with official sources. Important points have been emphasised, in **bold** print, some of which it would be expensive, or even dangerous, to disregard. **Ignore them at your peril or cost!**

NOTE

Unless specifically stated, a reference to a company, organisation or product in this book doesn't constitute an endorsement or recommendation. None of the businesses, products or individuals listed have paid to be mentioned.

Contents

Publisher's Notes

◆ Frequent references are made in this book to the European Union (EU), which comprises Austria, Belgium, Bulgaria, Cyprus, the Czech Republic, Denmark, Estonia, Finland, France, Germany, Greece, Hungary, Ireland, Italy, Latvia, Lithuania, Luxembourg, Malta, the Netherlands, Poland, Portugal, Romania, Slovakia, Slovenia, Spain, Sweden and the UK. The European Economic Area (EEA) includes the EU countries plus the European Free Trade Association (EFTA) countries of Iceland, Liechtenstein and Norway. Switzerland is also included in the EEA agreement but isn't a member.

◆ Names of the major Italian cities are written in English, which include Florence (Firenze in Italian), Milan (Milano), Naples (Napoli), Padua (Padova), Rome (Roma), Turin (Torino) and Venice (Venezia).

◆ Times are usually shown in Italy using the 24-hour system, where 11am is 1100 and 11pm is 2300. In Italian, am (ante meridiem) is indicated as *di mattina* and pm (post meridiem) as *del pomeriggio* (from around 1pm to 4pm) or *di sera* (from around 5pm to late pm). See also **Time Difference** on page 298.

◆ Prices should be taken as guides only, although they were mostly correct at the time of publication. Unless otherwise stated, all prices quoted usually include value added tax (*imposta sul valore aggiunto/IVA*) at 4, 10 or 20 per cent (see page 220). To convert from other currencies to euros or vice versa, see 🖥 www.xe.com.

◆ His/he/him also means her/she/her (please forgive us ladies). This is done to make life easier for both the reader and the editor, and isn't intended to be sexist.

◆ The Italian translation of many key words and phrases is shown in brackets in *italics*.

◆ All spelling is (or should be) British and not American English.

◆ Warnings and important points are printed in **bold** type.

◆ The following symbols are used in this book: ☎ (telephone), 🖹 (fax), 🖥 (Internet) and ✉ (email).

◆ Lists of **Useful Addresses**, **Further Reading** and **Useful Websites** are contained in **Appendices A**, **B** and **C** respectively.

◆ For those unfamiliar with the metric system of **Weights & Measures**, conversion tables are included in **Appendix D**.

◆ A physical map of Italy is shown inside the back cover and a maps showing the regions and communications (rail, roads, airports and ports) are included in **Appendix E**.

Ponte Saint'Angelo & St Peter's Basilica, Rome

Introduction

Whether you're already living or working in Italy or just thinking about it, this is **THE BOOK** for you. Forget about all those glossy guide books, excellent though they are for tourists; this amazing book was written particularly with you in mind and is worth its weight in truffles. Furthermore, this fully revised and completely re-designed 4th edition is printed in colour. *Living and Working in Italy* is intended to meet the needs of anyone wishing to know the essentials of Italian life – however long your intended stay in Italy, you'll find the information contained in this book invaluable.

General information isn't difficult to find in Italy (provided you speak Italian) and a multitude of books is published on every conceivable subject. However, reliable and up-to-date information in English specifically intended for foreigners living and working in Italy isn't so easy to find, least of all in one volume. This book was written to fill this void and to provide the comprehensive practical information necessary for a trouble-free life. You may have visited Italy as a tourist, but living and working there's a different matter altogether. Adjusting to a different environment and culture and making a home in any country can be a traumatic and stressful experience – and Italy is no exception.

Living and Working in Italy is a comprehensive handbook on a wide range of everyday subjects and represents the most up-to-date source of general information available to foreigners in Italy. It isn't, however, simply a monologue of dry facts and figures, but a practical and entertaining look at life.

Adapting to life in a new country is a continuous process and, although this book will help reduce your beginner's phase and minimise the frustrations, it doesn't contain all the answers. (Most of us don't even know the right questions to ask!) What it will do, however, is help you make informed decisions and calculated judgements, instead of uneducated guesses. **Most importantly, it will help save you time, trouble and money, and repay your investment many times over.**

Although you may find some of the information in this book a bit daunting, don't be discouraged. Most problems occur only once and fade into insignificance after a short time (as you face the next half a dozen!). The majority of foreigners in Italy would agree that, all things considered, they love living there. A period spent in Italy is a wonderful way to enrich your life and hopefully please your bank manager. We trust this book will help you avoid the pitfalls of life in Italy and smooth your way to a happy and rewarding future in your new home.

Buona fortuna!

Survival Books
January 2011

Galleria Vittorio Emanuele II, Milan

1.
FINDING A JOB

Finding a job in Italy isn't always as difficult as the unemployment figures may suggest, particularly in Rome, Milan and other large cities, depending of course on your qualifications and Italian language ability. However, if you don't qualify to live and work in Italy by birthright or as a national of a European Union (EU) country, obtaining a work permit (*permesso di soggiorno per motivi di lavoro* – **see page 59**) may be more difficult than finding a job. Americans and other nationalities without the automatic right to work in Italy must have their employment approved by the Italian Ministry of Labour and need an employment visa before arriving in Italy.

The hiring of non-EU workers is a sensitive and emotive issue in some regions. Restrictions on the employment of non-EU nationals have been strengthened in recent years due to the high unemployment rate (around 8.4 per cent in July 2010). The government has imposed a quota system since 2002, restricting the number of non-EU workers allowed into the country with the quota being decided each year. Non-EU workers are admitted into Italy only if they have an employment contract (*contratto di soggiorno*), with an employer paying for accommodation, travel and other expenses. There are no restrictions as yet for skilled workers.

The regulations have been criticised by both trade unions and employers' associations, particularly those in the north, where thousands of non-EU nationals are employed due to a severe shortage of semi-skilled and skilled workers (in the northeast in particular). Employers are putting pressure on the government for immigration quotas to be handled by the regions, according to local employment needs, while the politicians would prefer to create jobs for southern Italians. The employment of non-EU nationals must be approved by the Italian labour authorities, who can propose the employment of an EU national in place of a foreigner (although this is rare).

Despite the difficulties, foreigners are found in large numbers in almost every walk of life, particularly in the major cities. Italy has a long tradition of welcoming immigrants, particularly political refugees. In 1972, for the first time, it registered more people entering the country than leaving, although many of these were Italians returning home from northern Europe and the US. Italy has received an increasing number of migrants from Asia, Africa and Latin America in the last few decades and its recent rapid economic growth has attracted further immigrants to the country, mainly from North and sub-Saharan Africa, but also from the Philippines, China, South America and, most recently, from Eastern European countries newly admitted to the European Union. In 2010, the foreign population was estimated to be 4.3m (around 7 per cent of the population), most from outside the EU, including some living there illegally (*clandestini*).

The majority of foreigners settle in the centre and north, in the major conurbations of Milan, Rome, Turin and Genoa, although Florence and Palermo are also popular, particularly among African immigrants.

EMPLOYMENT PROSPECTS

Being attracted to Italy by its weather, cuisine, wine and lifestyle is laudable but doesn't rate highly as an employment qualification.

You should have a positive reason for living and working in Italy; simply being fed up with your boss or the weather isn't the best motive (although thoroughly understandable). It's extremely difficult to find work in rural areas and isn't easy in cities (even Rome or Milan), especially if your Italian isn't fluent. You shouldn't count on being able to obtain employment in Italy unless you have a firm job offer or special qualifications or experience for which there's a strong demand. If you want a good job, you must usually be well qualified and speak fluent Italian. If you intend to arrive in Italy without a job, it's wise to have a plan for finding employment on arrival and to try to make some contacts before you arrive.

There's a huge difference between northern and southern Italy in terms of wealth and job opportunities. The *Mezzogiorno* (the name given to the southern area of the country, comprising the regions of Abruzzo, Molise, Campania, Calabria, Puglia and Basilicata and the islands of Sicily and Sardinia), which constitutes some 40 per cent of Italy's total land area and 35 per cent of its population, creates only around 25 per cent of its gross domestic product (GDP). Unemployment in the south is around three times the northern rate and wages are some 40 per cent below the national average.

Many people turn to self-employment or starting a business to make a living, although this path is strewn with pitfalls for the newcomer. If you're planning to start a business in Italy, you must also do battle with the notoriously obstructive Italian bureaucracy – *buona fortuna*!

⚠ **Caution**

Most foreigners don't do sufficient homework before moving to Italy. While hoping for the best, you should plan for the worst and have a contingency plan and sufficient funds to last until you're established.

UNEMPLOYMENT

Italy's unemployment rate was officially running around 8.5 per cent in mid-2010; having slowly reduced during the 21st century down to just over 6 per cent in 2008, it climbed again in the wake of the recent economic crisis. Unemployment varies according to the region, and in the impoverished south it's as high as 50 per cent in some areas, where young people have traditionally migrated to the north or abroad in search of work. Unemployment is endemic among Italy's youth; some 30 per cent of people under 25 are unemployed, many of whom have little prospect of finding a job. It's difficult for young Italians to get a foothold on the employment ladder due to lack of experience and many young people, even university graduates, attend vocational schools or special programmes to gain work experience.

Although unemployment has hit manufacturing industries the hardest, no sector has been unaffected, including the flourishing service industries. Some of the hardest-hit industries have been construction, electronics, communications, the media and banking – all traditionally strong sectors. Many companies have periodic bans on recruitment and expect many employees to accept short-term contracts rather than life-long security (Italian job security had traditionally been among the best in Europe). Over a quarter of Italy's working population has short-term contracts.

Unemployment benefits are very limited in Italy; less than 25 per cent of the country's unemployed are eligible for any form of unemployment compensation, and families have traditionally been expected to support their unemployed members. There's no national scheme or assistance for the long-term unemployed in Italy, although there's a limited degree of support for low-income families in the south.

ECONOMY

Italy has Europe's fourth-largest economy (after the UK, Germany and France) and is around 4th out of the 27 EU countries in terms of GDP per head. The country had an estimated per capita GDP in 2009 of US$35,435 (projected to be US$35623 in 2011), compared with US$35,334 in the UK, US$40,875 in Germany and US$42,747 in France. However, Italy has huge extremes of wealth and poverty, and there's a vast difference in incomes between the rich northern region and the poor southern *Mezzogiorno* – an imbalance that vast injections of central government and EU cash have done little to correct.

Not surprisingly, given Italy's woeful fiscal 'management', the rules to allow Italy entry to the euro in 1999 were fudged (Italy had a public debt well above the level specified in the Maastricht Treaty) and it remains one of the weaker links in the Eurozone.

Italy was badly hit by the recession in the post-2007 credit crunch and, although the economy is slowly recovering, unemployment remains relatively high, the cost of living has increased in recent years and per capita personal debt has risen considerably.

The percentage of the working population engaged in agriculture is around 5 per cent, compared to some 30 per cent in industry and around 65 per cent in the service sector. The fast-growing service industry is the most important and includes tourism, the hotel industry, restaurants, transport and communications, domestic workers, financial services, and public administration. Factors that have contributed to the growth of the service sector in recent years include the rise in the standard of living in Italy (and Europe in general), leading to an increase in mobility, financial transactions, business, demand for leisure activities and tourism.

Industrial production in Italy is typified by the many small and medium-size companies engaged in sectors such as the clothing, mechanical engineering and textile industries.

However, there are also many multi-national companies, a number of which are still family-dominated, such as Benetton, Fiat and Pirelli. Italy is also at the forefront of many hi-tech industries such as aviation, computing, electronics and telecommunications. Olivetti is one of the world's leading suppliers of computers and software products. Other prominent Italian industries include ceramics, glass, furniture, household goods and leather articles, which are world renowned for their design and quality. The country's most significant industries are based in the northern cities of Milan and Turin and in the Veneto Region.

Industrial Relations

There has been a reduction in strikes (*scioperi*) in recent years, as the power of the trade unions has lessened, although Italy still has the worst industrial relations in the EU (a day's holiday is jokingly referred to as *un giorno di sciopero*). At one time, strikes were so frequent that a space was reserved in newspapers for announcements about public services that wouldn't be operating (nowadays you can obtain the latest information via the TV televideo service or online at 🖥 www.televideo.rai.it). The majority of strikes are in the public sector and the transportation industries.

ITALY & THE EUROPEAN UNION

Italy was one of the six founding members of the EU in 1957 along with Belgium, France, Germany, Luxembourg and the Netherlands, and the original Common Market agreement was signed in Italy and dubbed the 'Treaty of Rome'. Since then a host of other countries have joined, increasing the number of members to 27. The EU countries plus Iceland, Liechtenstein and Norway also make up the European Economic Area (EEA). Nationals of EU (and EEA) countries have the right to work in Italy or any other member state without a work permit, provided they

have a valid passport or national identity card and comply with the member state's laws and regulations on employment. EU nationals are entitled to the same treatment as Italian citizens in matters of pay, working conditions, access to housing, vocational training, social security and trade union rights, and their families and immediate dependants are entitled to join them and enjoy the same rights.

The Single European Act in 1993 created a single market, and made it easier for EU nationals to work in other EU countries. Nevertheless, there are still barriers to full freedom of movement and the right to work within the EU; for example some jobs require applicants to have specific skills or vocational qualifications. In most trades and professions, member states are required to recognise qualifications and experience obtained elsewhere in the EU, although this isn't always the case in Italy (see **Qualifications** below). There are also restrictions on employment in the civil service, where the right to work may be limited in individual cases on the grounds of public policy, security or public health.

QUALIFICATIONS

If you aren't experienced, Italian employers expect you to have studied a relevant subject and to have undertaken work experience. Professional or trade qualifications are necessary to work in most fields, and qualifications are also often needed to be self-employed or start a business. It isn't just a matter of hanging up a sign and waiting for the stampede of customers to your door.

The most important qualification for working in Italy is the ability to speak Italian. Once you've overcome this hurdle, you should establish whether your trade or professional qualifications and experience are recognised in Italy.

Under EU regulations, when a qualified professional from another European member state wishes to pursue his career in Italy, all qualifications and professional experience are to be taken into consideration. If the diplomas held are equivalent to those required under national legislation for working in a specified field, a qualified professional is authorised to set up a practice. Italy defines the rules and

regulations to be followed when setting up a practice, and rights concerning trade unions, working conditions and employee contracts are the same as for Italian nationals. You must apply to the relevant professional body for permission to set up a practice and to have your qualifications recognised.

Theoretically, qualifications recognised by professional and trade bodies in one EU country should be recognised in Italy. However, recognition varies from country to country and in some cases foreign qualifications aren't recognised by Italian employers or professional and trade associations. All academic qualifications should also be recognised, although they may be given less prominence than equivalent Italian qualifications, depending on the country and the educational establishment. A ruling by the European Court in 1992 declared that where EU examinations are of a similar standard with just certain areas of difference, individuals should be required to take exams only in those particular areas. In some trades and professions, you must prove that you've been practising as a self-employed person for a certain period, generally five or six years.

In order to set up and operate a professional practice, you must produce (in Italian) a certificate of equivalence (*certificato di equipollenza*) document from the relevant government ministry in your home country, stating that your qualifications are equivalent to Italian qualifications. You must provide evidence that you satisfy the requirements regarding character and repute, and haven't been declared bankrupt. You need a residence permit (*certificato di residenza* – see page 63) and a national identity document, and are informed within 30 days if further documents are required. In certain cases, you may be required to take an aptitude test or in exceptional cases undergo a period of training.

The recognition of your qualifications entitles you to register in the professional rolls and to practise your profession according to the requirements of the Italian state. If your profession isn't regulated in Italy, you don't need to apply for recognition of your qualifications and can begin practising under the same conditions as Italian nationals.

Italy (and other EU states) may reserve certain posts for their nationals if the jobs involve the exercise of powers conferred by public law and the safeguarding of the general interests of the state or local authorities, for example in the diplomatic service, police, judiciary and the armed forces. However, most public sector jobs in the areas of health, education, the provision of commercial services and research for civil purposes are open to all EU nationals and aren't subject to any restrictions on the grounds of nationality. Access to public sector jobs varies from one country to another and you should contact the Italian authorities for information regarding specific jobs.

All EU member states publish occupation information sheets containing a common job description with a table of qualifications. These cover a large number of trades and are intended to help someone with the relevant qualifications look for a job in another EU country. You can obtain a direct comparison between any EU qualification and those recognised in Italy from the Italian branch of the National Academic Recognition Information Centre (NARIC). For information about equivalent academic and professional qualifications in Italy, contact CIMEA, Fondazione Rui, Viale Ventuno Aprile, 36, 00162 Rome (☎ 06-8632 1281) or the Presidenza Consiglio Ministri, Ministerio Coordinamento Politiche Comunitarie, Via Giardino Theodoli, 66, 00186 Rome (☎ 06-6779 5322).

In the UK, information about academic qualifications can be obtained from UK NARIC, Oriel House, Oriel Road, Cheltenham, Glos GL50 1XP (☎ 0871-330 7033, 🖥 www.naric.org.uk). NARIC can also issue a certificate of experience detailing your qualifications and experience in a particular profession which should be accepted in other EU countries; see their Certificate of Experience website for more details (🖥 www.certex.org.uk).

> You can also check which trades and professions in Italy require specific qualifications on the European Commission's Regulated Professions database (🖥 http://ec.europa.eu/internal_market/qualifications/regprof/index.cfm).

STATE EMPLOYMENT SERVICES

Job seekers in Italy should register with an employment office (*ufficio di collocamento*) run by the government employment service, the Sezione Circoscrizionate per l'Impiego. You can register without being a resident (and should be given the same help as Italian nationals and residents), but non-EU citizens require a permit to stay (see page 60). Employment offices provide information about registration, agricultural jobs, residence, apprenticeships, and benefit applications and payments. They organise seminars about job hunting and have trained counsellors to help you find an appropriate job. Many centres have internet access.

Regional employment agencies are operated by the Ministry of Labour and Social Welfare (Ministero del Lavoro e Della Previdenza Sociale) and there are local employment centres (*centri di iniziativa locale per l'occupazione/CILO*) in cities and large towns, which provide help and advice about work-related problems and self-employment.

information regularly on job vacancies, and EURES offices have access to information on how to apply for a job, and living and working conditions in each country. The international department of your home country's employment service can put you in touch with a EURES Advisor who can provide advice on finding work in Italy. EURES Advisors have permanent links with EURES services in other member states and also have permanent access to two databases. One contains details of job offers in all member states and the other provides information on living and working conditions, and a profile of the trends for regional labour markets.

EURES Advisors can also arrange to have your details forwarded to the Italian employment service (Sezione Circoscrizionale per l'Impiego) but given the high level of unemployment in Italy, this is rarely the fastest or the most efficient method for finding a job there, particularly from abroad. National employment services give priority to their own nationals, and jobs aren't generally referred to EURES or other national agencies until after prospective local candidates have been considered. For further information contact the Ministero del Lavoro e Della Previdenza Sociale (🖳 www.lavoro.gov.it).

PRIVATE RECRUITMENT AGENCIES

There are two main kinds of recruitment agency in Italy, temporary agencies (*lavori ad interim*) and executive search companies (*ricerca personale*).

Temporary Jobs

Under Italian law, a temporary agency can place workers with an employer only to satisfy a temporary demand. A temporary contract (*contratto per prestazioni di lavoro temporaneo*) is a fixed-term contract or an open-ended contract, where an agency must pay compensation to a worker for the periods when he isn't working. The agency must pay

There are also information centres for the unemployed (*centro informazione disoccupati*) in major cities, run by the larger trade unions. Here you can obtain information about job vacancies, finding work and employment regulations; some offices also offer advice on job interviews, writing application letters, setting up a business, self-employment, income tax and social security.

Young people can obtain information about jobs and training at local information centres (*informagiovani*), found in most towns and cities. These centres have situations vacant boards for temporary jobs (*lavoro interinale*) and part-time jobs (*lavoro a tempo parziale* or *lavoro part-time*) such as baby-sitting, teaching children, gardening and domestic work. They maintain job listings (you can also place a 'work wanted' advertisement) and distribute leaflets, flyers and booklets about finding work in Italy. They provide help and advice on finding temporary work, information about courses and training, evening classes, scholarships, enrolment at university, cultural events and hobbies. You can lodge your curriculum vitae (CV) on the Informagiovani website (🖳 www.informagiovani.it), check job offers, contact agencies offering part-time work and apply directly to companies offering employment. There's also a section listing employment laws, working conditions and employment contracts.

Another source of job services is the European Employment Services (EURES, 🖳 http://ec.europa.eu/eures) network, members of which include all EU countries plus Norway and Iceland. Member states exchange workers' social security contributions and work accident insurance. Temporary workers have pro-rata rights to annual and public holidays, a 13th month's salary and any other payments which other workers employed by the same company are entitled to.

To sign up with an agency you need a permit to stay which allows you to work, a fiscal (tax) code (*codice fiscale*) and a CV or work record (translated into Italian). You're required to complete a form in Italian and must supply a passport-size photograph. You'll be interviewed by the agency and probably again by a prospective employer. Temporary work is most common in the secretarial, computer and industrial fields, and work in other sectors is limited, although it may still be worth enquiring and registering with agencies. Always ensure that you know exactly how much, when and how you'll be paid. Because of the long annual holidays in Italy and generous maternity leave, companies often require temporary staff, and a temporary job can frequently be used as a stepping stone to a permanent position (companies often hire temporary workers for a 'trial' period before offering them a full-time contract).

Temporary agencies with offices in most Italian cities include Adecco (🖥 www.adecco.it), ALI (🖥 www.alispa.it), Eurointerim (🖥 www.eurointerimservizi.it), Kelly (🖥 www.kellyservices.it), Manpower (🖥 www.manpower.it), Sinterim (🖥 www.sinterim.it) and Vedior (🖥 www.cambiolavoro.com/vedior/welcome.html).

You can also find local agencies in the *Yellow Pages* under *Lavoro Interinale e Temporaneo*.

Executive Positions

Executive recruitment and 'head-hunting' companies are common in the major cities and are mainly used by large Italian companies to recruit staff, particularly executives, managers and professionals. Agents place advertisements in daily and weekly newspapers and trade magazines, but don't usually mention the client's name, not least to prevent applicants from approaching a company directly, thus depriving the agency of its fat fee. Recruitment agencies have been hard hit by the recent recession, particularly those dealing with executives and senior

managers, and many Italian companies now do their own recruiting or promote in-house. Unless you're a particularly outstanding candidate with half a dozen degrees, are multi-lingual and have valuable experience, sending an unsolicited CV to an agent is usually a waste of time. There are also recruitment agencies in many countries that specialise in recruiting executives, managers and professionals for employers in Italy.

Working for the United Nations

The United Nations (UN) has its Food and Agriculture Organisation (FAO) in Rome, and offers varied-term contracts, with general service and administrative positions in human resources, finance and information technology, plus expert and professional positions in the fields of agriculture, fisheries, forestry and related areas. Applicants are often required to have working knowledge of two of the following languages: English, Spanish, French, Chinese and Arabic. See the UN's FAO website (🖥 www.fao.org) and the UNJobs website (🖥 http://unjobs.org/duty_stations/italy) for vacancies in other UN programmes in Italy, e.g. UNICEF.

Online Agencies

The rapid development of the internet has led to a huge increase in the number of online recruitment agencies and job search websites. Some sites charge a fee to access their vacancy listings, but many allow job seekers to review and respond to listings free of charge. It's also possible to submit your CV online (usually free), but it's wise to consider the security implications of this move. By giving your home address or phone number, you could lay yourself open to nuisance phone calls or worse. A number of websites that list vacancies in Italy are listed below:

www.alispa.it
www.altamira.it
www.craigslist.com
www.easyjob.it
www.executivenetwork.it
www.fionline.it (for jobs in Florence)
www.informagiovani.it

www.insidersabroad.com/
englishyellowpages
www.joblitz.com
www.job-net.it
www.kangaroo.it (for jobs in information
technology)
www.lavorare.net
www.mondolavoro.it
www.monster.it
www.stepstone.it
www.wantedinrome.com

You may not find any information in English
on Italian websites (those which end .it). But
if your Italian skills are poor, you can obtain
a rough translation using the (free) Babel
Fish translator provided by the search engine
company Alta Vista. Enter 💻 http://babelfish.
altavista.com in your browser, and then enter
the address of the website that you wish to visit
in the Babel Fish dialogue box that appears.
You will be presented with an instant translation
of the web page in question into the language
selected. Google has a similar translation tool.

SEASONAL JOBS

Seasonal jobs (*lavoro stagionale*) are available
throughout the year in Italy, the vast majority
in the tourist industry. Many jobs last for the
duration of the summer or winter tourist season
– May to September and December to April
respectively – although some are simply casual
or temporary jobs for a number of weeks.
Italian fluency is required for all but the most
menial and worst-paid jobs, and is as important
as or more important than experience and
qualifications (although fluency in Italian
alone won't guarantee you a well-paid job).
Seasonal jobs include most trades in hotels
and restaurants, couriers and travel company
representatives, a variety of jobs in ski resorts,
sports instructors, jobs in bars and clubs, fruit
and grape pickers, and various jobs in the
construction industry.

If you aren't an EU national, it's essential
to check whether you're eligible to work in
Italy before making plans and you may also
be required to obtain a visa (see page 57).
Check with an Italian embassy or consulate
in your home country well in advance of your
visit. Foreign students in Italy can obtain a

temporary work permit (*autorizzazione di
lavoro provvisoria*) for part-time work during the
summer holiday period and school terms (see
page 126). The main seasonal jobs available in
Italy are mentioned below.

If you're a sports or ski instructor, tour guide
or holiday representative or are involved in any
job that gives you responsibility for groups of
people or children, you should be extremely
wary of accepting an illegal job without a
contract, as you won't be insured for injuries
to yourself, the public or accidents while
travelling. Bear in mind that seasonal workers
have few rights and little legal job protection
in Italy, and can generally be fired without
compensation at any time.

There are many books for those seeking
holiday jobs, including *Summer Jobs
Worldwide* and *Work Your Way Around the
World* both published by Vacation Work
(💻 www.crimsonpublishing.co.uk) and *A Year
Off, A Year On*, published by Hobsons PLC,
Challenger House, 42 Adler Street, London E1
1EE, UK (💻 www.hobsons.com).

Holiday Company Representatives

The duties of holiday representatives include
ferrying tourist groups to and from airports,
organising excursions and social events,
arranging ski passes and equipment rental,
and generally ensuring that holidaymakers
enjoy themselves. A job as a representative is
tough and demanding, and requires resilience
and resourcefulness to deal with the chaos
associated with the package holiday business.

> **☑ SURVIVAL TIP**
>
> The majority of representative jobs in Italy
> are available during the winter ski season
> with British ski-tour companies and school
> ski-party organisers (see Ski Resort Jobs on
> page 26).

The necessary requirements include the ability
to answer many questions simultaneously
(sometimes in different languages), to remain
calm and charming under extreme pressure
and, above all, to resolve problems. Lost

passengers, tickets, passports and tempers are everyday occurrences. It's an excellent training ground for managerial and leadership skills, pays well and often offers opportunities to supplement your earnings with tips and commission.

Representatives are required by many local and foreign tour companies in both winter and summer resorts. Competition for jobs is fierce and local language ability is usually required, even for employment with British tour operators. Most companies have age requirements, the minimum usually being 21, although many companies prefer employees to be a few years older.

Many of the large tour operators have summer and/or winter programmes in Italy, and representatives are also required for summer camps organised for both adults and children. Employees are required to speak good Italian. Tour operators in Italy include Thomas Cook (🖳 www.thomascook.com/recruitment), TUI (🖳 www.tuitraveljobs.co.uk) and Club Med (🖳 www.clubmedjobs.com), while smaller companies include camping holiday specialist Canvas Holidays (🖳 www.canvasholidaysrecruitment.com), educational tour companies for high school students, e.g. NETC (National Educational Training Council, 🖳 www.educationaltravel.com), and older travellers' tour companies, e.g. 50plus Expeditions (🖳 http://50plusexpeditions.com). It's advisable to apply to a company based in your home country well before the start of the season, as they generally arrange work permits and flights.

Hotel & Catering Staff

Hotels and restaurants are the largest employers of seasonal workers, from hotel managers to kitchen hands. Experience, relevant qualifications and fluent Italian are required for all the best and highest paid positions, although a variety of jobs is available for the untrained and inexperienced. Ensure that your salary is sufficient to pay for accommodation, food and other living expenses, and to hopefully save some money. If accommodation with cooking facilities or full board isn't provided with a job, it can be expensive and difficult to find. The best way to find work is to contact hotel chains directly (see **Hotels** on page 231), preferably at least six months before you wish to start work.

Tour Guides

There are plenty of mostly British or American-owned companies that employ English speakers to guide groups of tourists around city attractions or popular areas of archaeological importance in Italy. Prospective guides must be lively speakers and have a degree in art history, archaeology or a related subject to train with a reputable company. Be aware, though, that the only way to practice legally (and to be protected from fines) is to obtain a licence by passing the stiff exams (in Italian) set by city authorities. Some authorities will now make concessions and give licences to holders of relevant degrees. See city governmental websites: for example, Rome (☎ 060606, 🖳 www.comune.roma.it), and the Rome Tourism Professions Association (Ufficio Professioni Turistiche della Provincia di Roma, ☎ 06-6766 7324, 🖳 www.provincia.roma.it).

Fruit & Vegetable Pickers

To find a fruit or vegetable picking job, visit the local youth information centre (*informagiovani*) which will provide you with a list of farms in the area taking on temporary workers for the harvest season. Local employment offices (*uffici di collocamento*) and agricultural co-operatives (Sezione Circoscrizionale per l'Impiego Collocamento in Agricola/SCICA) may also be helpful, although it's generally best to contact farms directly. You may not be provided with accommodation but workers usually camp. Pay is usually on a piece-work basis (*lavoro a cottimo*) where the more you pick, the more you earn.

One of the most popular summer jobs in Italy is grape picking. Goodness knows why, because it's boring and badly paid and involves hard physical work, although a surprising number of young people find it appealing. Occupational hazards include mosquito and other insect bites, cuts from secateurs, rashes on arms and legs caused by chemical sprays, and incessant back pain from bending all day long. Accommodation and cooking facilities can be primitive, and the cost of food and accommodation is usually deducted from your pay. The main grape-picking areas are Emilia Romagna, Lazio, Marche, Piedmont, Puglia, Trentino-Alto Adige, Tuscany and Veneto, where the harvest (*vendemmia*) is in September or October. The seasons and regions for some other crops are shown below:

♦ **apples & pears:** Emilia Romagna, Trentino and Veneto from August to October;

♦ **cherries, peaches, plums & strawberries:** Emilia Romagna and Piedmont from May to August;

♦ **flowers:** Liguria and Tuscany, year round;

♦ **olives:** southern Italy, Marche, Sardinia, Sicily, Tuscany, Umbria and Veneto, from November to January;

♦ **tobacco:** Campania, Puglia and Umbria from November to December;

♦ **vegetables:** Emilia Romagna and Veneto from spring to late autumn.

Ski Resort Jobs

Ski resorts require an army of temporary workers to cater for the annual invasion of winter sports enthusiasts. As well as the jobs in the hotel and catering trades already mentioned, a variety of other jobs is available, including resort representatives, chalet girls, ski technicians, ski instructors and guides. A seasonal job in an Italian ski resort can be rewarding and a lot of fun, but it's wise to find out the kind of clients you're likely to be dealing with, particularly if you're allergic to children or yuppies (young urban professionals – similar to children but less mature). You will get fit, improve your Italian and make some friends and may even save some money. However, although a winter job may be

a working holiday to you (with lots of skiing and little work), to your employer it means exactly the opposite! As a general rule, the better paid the job, the longer the working hours and the less time there is for skiing – though employment in a winter resort usually entitles employees to a discounted ski-pass.

☑ **SURVIVAL TIP**

Useful resources for job hunters include ski magazines which contain regular listings of tour companies showing who goes to which resorts. UK job hunters can check out the recruitment website for Crystal, First Choice and Thomson winter sports holidays (see 🖳 www.jobsinwinter.co.uk).

Sports Instructors

Sports instructors are required for a variety of sports, including badminton, canoeing, diving, golf, gymnastics, hang-gliding, horse riding, mountaineering, parachuting, rock-climbing, sailing, squash, sub-aquatic sports, swimming, tennis and windsurfing. Whatever the sport, it's probably played and taught somewhere in Italy. Most jobs are available in the summer months. If you're a qualified winter sports instructor, you should contact Italian ski resorts. Ski instructors and guides should also contact tour operators, large luxury hotels, and ski rental and service shops.

You should start applying for work from May onwards. Interviews usually take place from early September through to early November and successful candidates are on the job by mid-December. If you miss the May deadline, you should still apply, because many applicants who have been offered jobs drop out at the last minute.

TEMPORARY & CASUAL WORK

Temporary work (*lavoro temporaneo*) and casual work (*lavoro occasionale*) is usually for a limited or fixed period, ranging from a few hours to a few months, or intermittent. It differs from part-time work (*lavoro a tempo parziale* or *lavoro part-time*), which may be a

temporary or permanent job but with reduced working hours, e.g. up to 20 hours per week. Casual workers are often employed on a daily, first-come, first-served basis. Anyone looking for casual unskilled work in Italy must usually compete with Albanians, North Africans and other unemployed foreigners, who are usually prepared to work for less money than anyone else, although nobody should be paid less than the minimum wage (see page 43). Many employers illegally pay temporary staff in cash without making deductions for social security (see **Illegal Working** on page 36). Temporary and casual work usually includes the following:

♦ office and secretarial work, which is well paid if you're qualified and the easiest work to find in cities and large towns;

♦ work in the building trade, which can be found by applying at building sites and through industrial recruitment agencies (such as Manpower);

♦ jobs in shops, which are often available over Christmas and during sales periods;

♦ gardening jobs in private gardens (possibly working for a landscape gardener), public parks and garden centres, particularly in spring and summer;

♦ selling ice cream, cold drinks and fast food in summer, e.g. on beaches;

♦ working as a deck-hand on a yacht operating from one of Italy's fashionable coastal resorts;

♦ a wide variety of jobs on board ships – most cruise and some ferry companies are happy to take on foreign staff, although you stand a better chance if you can speak another European language fluently;

♦ writing and translating – suitably qualified people can find work with Italian businesses wishing to do business with the English-speaking world;

♦ market research, which entails asking people personal questions, either in the street or door to door;

♦ modelling at art colleges – both sexes are usually required and not just the body beautiful;

♦ work as a security guard (long hours for low pay);

♦ nursing and auxiliary nursing in hospitals, clinics and nursing homes;

♦ newspaper, magazine and leaflet distribution;

♦ courier work (own transport required – motorcycle, car or van – and a driving licence valid in Italy);

♦ driving jobs, including coach and truck drivers, and ferrying cars for manufacturers and car hire companies;

♦ miscellaneous jobs such as office cleaners, baby-sitters and labourers, which are available from a number of agencies specialising in temporary work;

♦ summer camps run by language schools sometimes need young teaching staff, although they usually require them to have a TEFL qualification (see below).

Temporary jobs are advertised in employment offices, on notice boards in expatriate clubs, churches and organisations, and in expatriate newsletters and newspapers. See also **Private Recruitment Agencies** on page 22.

ENGLISH TEACHING & TRANSLATING

There's a high demand for English teachers, translators and interpreters in the major cities, particularly in Rome and the north of the country. There's a high turnover of teachers in language schools and a constant demand for translators (and sometimes writers) from Italian companies.

Language Schools

There are literally hundreds of language schools (*scuole di lingua*) teaching English, many of which expect teachers to have a TEFL (Teaching English as a Foreign Language) certificate or its equivalent, although this isn't always the case. Some schools employ anyone whose mother tongue is English provided they've had experience in teaching, while others have their own teaching methods and prefer to train teachers to their own standards. Many of the best schools are members of the Italian Association of English Language Schools (Associazione Italiana Scuole di Lingua Inglese/ AISLI), a list of which is available from the Cambridge Centre of English, Via Rainusso Elia, 144, 41100 Modena (☎ 059-822 370, 🖳 www. cambridgecentre.biz).

Language schools generally pay less than you can earn giving private lessons, but they may provide a contract and pay your taxes and social security. You may be able to obtain only a short-term contract or freelance work. You're usually paid by the hour and therefore should ensure that you have a guaranteed number

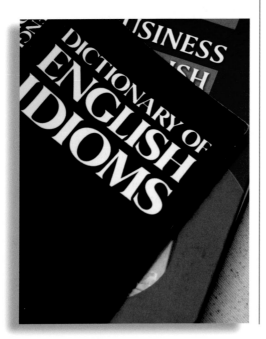

of hours per week. Schools are listed under *Scuole di Lingua* in the *Yellow Pages*.

International Schools

Qualified primary and secondary school teachers may be able to find work in bilingual international schools where many classes are given in English. Typically, the same requirements for teachers that apply in the UK or US also apply in Italy, i.e. a degree or postgraduate certificate in education. However, experienced TEFL teachers may find an opening, teaching primary-level English classes.

Private Lessons

Italians tend to favour learning lots of grammar, therefore if you aren't up-to-date with grammar and you want to teach privately, you should stick to teaching conversation or children. (You also find that students know a lot about English literature but cannot ask the time correctly!) Work is generally easy to find, particularly in university cities and towns, as students must usually study English as part of their course work.

Many foreigners teach English privately and are paid cash-in-hand by students; much of their income is never declared. Most people find that when they have a few students they spread the word and before you know it you have as much work as you can handle. You could also try placing an advertisement in local newspapers and magazines offering private English lessons, although if you're female, replies may be received from Italian men who think that 'English lessons' implies something other than learning a language! The going rate for private lessons varies, but averages around €30 per hour and is usually higher in major cities.

Translating & Interpreting

Professional translators and interpreters are in huge demand and are usually employed by agencies. Translators are paid by the page (or line) and the average rate is €22 per page, although this varies according to the kind of translation; rates are higher in Rome and the northern cities than in the south. Translating can be a tedious business; you must usually work to stringent deadlines, the subject matter can be highly technical (requiring specialised vocabulary) and translations must be precise. If you translate medical notes, legal papers or business documents inaccurately, it can have serious consequences! Interpreters are employed mainly for exhibitions, congresses and seminars. You may be paid a flat rate for the day, e.g. between €75 and €150, or by the hour, e.g. €15.

University Teaching

English is taught in most universities in Italy and positions for assistants (*lettori*) in the English-language departments of Italian universities are open to foreigners with university degrees. Applications should be made directly to the Rector of the University, followed by the name of the town or city, e.g. '*Al Magnifico Rettore, Università di …*'. The same procedure should be followed for the Libera Università di Lingue e Comunicazione (Liberal University of Languages and Communication, 🖥 http://iulm.it) which has two campuses, in Feltre, Veneto, and in Milan, and also for the Università Cattolica del Sacro Cuore di Milano and the Istituto Universitario Orientale di Napoli.

Further Information

An excellent source of information is *Teaching English in Italy* by Martin Penner (McGraw-Hill). For a more general overview you could try *Teaching English Abroad* by Susan Griffith (Vacation Work). Another useful resource for English teachers is the monthly *El Gazette* published in the UK (☎ 020-7481 6700, 🖥 www.elgazette.com). Finally, make use of the British Council (🖥 www.britishcouncil.org), which recruits English teachers and supervisory staff for placements in its language centres.

☑ SURVIVAL TIP

It's necessary to have an RSA diploma in TEFL or a PGCE and two years' experience for most teaching positions. For managerial posts, postgraduate qualifications and a minimum of five years' experience are required.

JOB HUNTING

When looking for a job in Italy, it's best not to put all your eggs in one basket – the more jobs you apply for, the better your chances are of securing one. Contact as many prospective employers as possible, by writing to them, telephoning them or calling on them in person. Your approach will largely depend on the kind of job or position you're seeking. For example, the recruitment of executives and senior managers is handled almost exclusively by executive search companies, which advertise in the Italian 'national' press and trade magazines. At the other end of the scale, manual jobs requiring no previous experience may be advertised at local employment offices (*uffici di collocamento*), in local newspapers and on notice boards, and the first suitable applicant may be offered the job on the spot. The following resources may be useful in your job hunt:

Newspapers

Most national, regional and local newspapers (see page 273) contain a 'situations vacant' or jobs section (*Offerte di Lavoro* or *Offerte di Collaborazione*) on certain days of the week. The Milan daily newspaper, *Corriere della Sera*, publishes a *Corriere Lavoro* jobs and careers supplement on Fridays (🖥 http://lavoro.corriere.it) and the financial newspaper, *Il Sole 24 Ore*, publishes *Cerco Lavoro – Giovani* for college graduates seeking work, on Mondays, and a general *Lavoro & Carriere* supplement on Fridays. There are also specialised local and national newspapers for job seekers such as *Il Posto* ('the job') and *Il Concorso* (which lists civil service and local government jobs) in Naples, *Trova Lavoro* ('find a job') and *Bollettino Del Lavoro* (🖥 www.bollettinodellavoro.it), a monthly publication available at employment offices and libraries. Jobs are also advertised in industry and trade newspapers and magazines. Ask the locals which publications and days are best for job advertisements in your area.

Most major newspapers and magazines have websites where you can usually access their 'situations vacant' sections free of charge, and local and national newspapers are available in libraries, bars and cafes in

Italy, so you don't always need to buy them. Italian newspapers are also available abroad from international news agencies, trade and commercial centres, expatriate organisations and social clubs (although they don't always contain the 'appointments' or 'situations vacant' sections).

Most professions and trade associations publish journals containing job offers (see *Benn's Media Directory Europe*) and jobs are also advertised in various English-language publications, including the *International Herald Tribune*, *Wall Street Journal Europe*, *Wanted in Rome* and other local publications (see **Appendix B**). You can also place an advertisement in the 'situations wanted' section of a local newspaper in Italy in an area where you would like to work. If you're a member of a recognised profession or trade, you could place an advertisement in a newspaper or magazine dedicated to your profession or industry. It's best to place an advert in the middle of the week and avoid the summer and other holiday periods.

☑ SURVIVAL TIP

Most Italian newspapers have websites containing job ads (see 💻 www.onlinenewspapers.com/italy.htm).

Information Centres & Libraries

Local youth information centres (*informagiovani*) are useful for information about jobs, job hunting, and education and training; for more details visit their website (💻 www.informagiovani.it). Main libraries also provide a range of resources for job seekers, although they don't specifically provide advice and assistance for the unemployed, as in some other countries.

Employment Offices

Visit local employment offices (*uffici di collocamento*) and other offices in Italy . Jobs on offer are mainly non-professional, particularly in industry, retailing and catering.

Recruitment Agencies

Apply to international recruitment agencies acting for Italian companies and foreign companies in Italy. These companies chiefly help to recruit executives and key personnel, and many have offices worldwide, including in many Italian cities. Some Italian agencies may find positions only for Italian and EU nationals or foreigners with a residence permit.

Chambers of Commerce

Foreign chambers of commerce (*camera di commercio*) in Italy maintain lists of their member companies doing business (or with subsidiaries) in Italy. British nationals can join the British Chamber of Commerce for Italy, Via Dante, 12, 20121 Milan (☎ 02-877 798 or 8056 094, 💻 www.britchamitaly.com) for between €50 and €3,000, for a range of different memberships and benefits. Italian chambers of commerce abroad are also a useful source of information, as are Euro Info Centres (EIC) found in the major cities of EU countries. Infoimprese (💻 www.infoimprese.it) is a useful website set up by Italian chambers of commerce with information on companies.

The Internet

The internet provides access to hundreds of sites for job-seekers, including corporate websites, recruitment companies and newspaper job advertisements (you can use a search engine such as Google to find them).

Networking

Networking involves getting together with like-minded people to discuss business. It's particularly useful in Italy, where people use personal contacts for everything from looking for jobs to finding accommodation. In fact, a personal recommendation (*raccomandazione*) is often the best way to find employment in Italy, where nepotism and favouritism are rife. When looking for a job in Italy, it isn't necessarily **what** you know but **who** you know that counts. It's difficult for most foreigners to make contacts among Italians and therefore many turn to the expatriate community, particularly in Rome and Milan. If you're

already in Italy, you can contact or join local expatriate social clubs, churches, societies and professional organisations (see also **Appendix A**). Finally, don't forget to ask your friends and acquaintances working in Italy if they know of an employer seeking someone with your experience and qualifications.

Written Applications

Apply to American, British and other multi-national companies with offices or subsidiaries in Italy, and make written applications to Italian companies. Companies are listed by products, services and province in *Kompass Italy* and similar directories, available at libraries in Italy and main libraries and Italian chambers of commerce abroad. Making unsolicited job applications is naturally a hit-and-miss affair. It can, however, be more successful than responding to advertisements, as you aren't usually competing with other applicants. Some companies recruit a large percentage of employees through unsolicited applications.

When applying for jobs, address your letter to the personnel director (*capo del personale*) and include your CV (in Italian), and copies of references and qualifications. If possible, offer to attend an interview and say when you're available. Letters should be tailored to individual companies and professionally translated if your Italian isn't perfect. Some Italian companies require hand-written letters from job applicants and may submit them to graphologists. When writing from abroad, enclosing an international reply coupon may help to elicit a response.

Personal Applications

Your best chance of obtaining certain jobs in Italy is to apply in person, when success is often simply a matter of being in the right place at the right time. Many companies don't advertise at all, but rely on attracting workers by word of mouth and by their own vacancy boards. Shops and supermarkets often put vacancy notices in their windows or have notice boards where employers can advertise jobs, although these are generally for temporary and part-time posts only.

It's recommended to leave your name and address with a prospective employer and, if possible, a telephone number where you can be contacted, particularly when a job may become vacant at a moment's notice.

References

When leaving a job in Italy, it's wise to ask for a written reference (which isn't usually provided automatically), particularly if you plan to look for further work in Italy or you think your work experience will help you find work in another country.

SALARY

It isn't usually difficult to determine the salary you should command in Italy, where salaries in most industries are decided by collective bargaining between employers and unions. Agreements specify minimum wage levels for each position in each main employment category in a particular industry or company. When there's a collective agreement, employers must offer at least the minimum wage agreed, although these are exceeded by most major companies and salaries vary considerably for the same job in different regions of Italy.

Those working in Milan and other northern cities are generally the highest paid, primarily due to the high cost of living, particularly accommodation. Women are generally paid less than men, even when they're doing the same job.

In 2009, Italy ranked 72 (one of the lowest among European countries) in the World

Economic Forum's annual Gender Gap Index, which assesses how countries divide their resources and opportunities among their male and female populations.

Most employees in Italy receive an extra month's salary at Christmas, known as the 13th month's salary (*tredicesima mesilità*) or Christmas bonus (*gratifica natalizia*), and many employees also receive a 14th month's salary (*quattordicesima mesilità*) before the summer holiday period. Some employees, such as those in the banking and petroleum industries, even receive a 15th and 16th months' salary!

If you're able to negotiate your own salary you should ensure that you receive the salary and benefits commensurate with your qualifications and experience, i.e. as much as you can get! If you have friends or acquaintances working in Italy or who have worked there, ask them what an average or good salary is for your trade or profession. When comparing salaries you must take into account compulsory deductions such as tax and social security, and also the cost of living (see page 211). Italian salaries for executives and managers compare favourably with those in other developed countries and are among the highest in Europe, although wages are below average for many other workers. Salaries are generally similar to those in France or Spain, for example, but lower than those in the UK or US. In recent years, university graduates and school-leavers have had to accept almost any wage in order to get a foot on the career ladder.

In the managerial category, staff may receive from €3,550 per month, office staff from around €1,800 per month, manual workers from €1,400 and agricultural workers around €1,750 before tax and social security payments are deducted.

For many employees, particularly executives and senior managers, their remuneration is much more than what they receive in their monthly pay packets. Many companies offer a range of benefits for executives and managers that may include a company car (although rare in Italy), private health insurance and health screening, expenses-paid holidays, private school fees, inexpensive or interest-free home and other loans, rent-free accommodation, free or subsidised public transport tickets, a free or subsidised company restaurant, sports or country club membership, a non-contributory company pension, stock options, bonuses and profit-sharing schemes, tickets for sports events and shows, and 'business' conferences in exotic places.

SELF-EMPLOYMENT

If you're an EU national or a permanent resident with a *certificato di residenza,* you can be self-employed (*lavoro autonomo* or *lavoro in proprio*), freelance (*lavoro indipendente* or *libero professionista*) or a sole trader (*commerciante in proprio*, *imprenditore* or *ditta individuale*) in Italy.

If you wish to be self-employed in a profession or start a freelance business in Italy, you must meet certain legal requirements and register with the appropriate organisations. For example, you must be included on the Register of Enterprises (*Registro delle Imprese*) maintained by the local chamber of commerce (*camera di commercio*) and obtain a certificate of registration (*certificato di iscrizione*). Before starting work you must also register with the local tax office (*intendenza di finanza*) and be registered for VAT (*imposta sul valore aggiunto/ IVA* – see page 220). Furthermore, many foreign artisans and traders are required to undergo a 'business' course before they can start work in Italy.

Under Italian law, a self-employed person must have an official status and it's illegal to simply hang up a sign and start trading. Members of some professions and trades must have certain qualifications and certificates recognised in Italy. You should **never** be tempted to start work before you're registered, for which there are stiff penalties which may include a large fine, confiscation of machinery or tools, deportation and even a ban from entering Italy for a number of years.

If you operate as a sole trader, you must register with the local tax office and are taxed in the same way as any other individual. The liabilities of a sole trader aren't deemed to be separate from his personal debts, and should you become insolvent, you would be declared bankrupt. Therefore you may find it advantageous to operate as a limited company, e.g. a *società a responsabilità limitata* (*Srl*) or *società per azioni* (*SpA*). Always obtain professional advice before deciding whether to operate as a sole trader or form a company, as it has far-reaching social security, tax and other consequences.

Self-employed people may wish to join the Camere di Commercio (⌨ www.unioncamere. gov.it) which provides a range of information and assistance for the self-employed and those running their own businesses, including supplementary health insurance and help in dealing with Italian bureaucracy, taxation and social security.

Whatever people may tell you, working for yourself isn't easy and requires a lot of hard work (self-employed people generally work much longer hours than employees), a sizeable investment and sufficient operating funds (most new businesses fail due to a lack of capital), good organisation (e.g. bookkeeping and planning), excellent customer relations, and a measure of luck – although generally the harder you work, the more 'luck' you have.

☑ **SURVIVAL TIP**

Don't be seduced by the apparently laid-back way of life in Italy – if you want to be a success in business, you cannot play at it. Bear in mind that some two-thirds of all new businesses fail within three to five years and that the self-employed enjoy far fewer social security benefits than employees.

RUNNING A BUSINESS

The bureaucracy associated with starting a business (*azienda*) in Italy is horrendous and rates among the most pernicious in the world. Italy is an almost impenetrable red tape jungle and Italian civil servants (*impiegati*) can be inordinately obstructive, endlessly recycling bits of paper to create 'employment' for themselves. It's an even worse nightmare for foreigners who don't speak Italian, as you'll be inundated with official documents and must be able to understand them. It's only when you come up against the full force of Italian bureaucracy that you understand what it **really** means to be a foreigner! You should expect to spend most of your time battling with civil servants when establishing a new business. However, despite the red tape, Italy is traditionally a land of small companies (there are over 3m businesses which employ fewer than 50 people) and individual traders, and the culture and economic philosophy encourage and even nurture the creation of small businesses – once you get past the paperwork.

Legal Advice

Before undertaking any business transactions in Italy, it's important to obtain legal advice to ensure that you're operating within the law. There are severe penalties for anyone who ignores the regulations and legal requirements. For example, non-EU nationals require a licence to start a business in Italy and no commitments should be made until permission has been granted. It's also important to obtain legal advice before establishing a limited company. Among the best sources of help and information are local chambers of commerce and town halls (*municipio*).

Professional Assistance

On account of the difficulties in complying with (or understanding) Italian laws and bureaucracy, there are agencies (colloquially called *galoppini*) that specialise in obtaining documents and making applications for individuals and businesses; they're listed in the *Yellow Pages* under *Certificati, Agenzie*. They act as a buffer between you and officialdom, and register your business with the tax registrar's office (*ufficio registro*), registrar of enterprises (*registro delle imprese*), registrar of companies (*ufficio delle ditte*) at the local chamber of commerce and local tax office (*intendenza di finanza*), and obtain a value added tax (*imposta sul valore aggiunto/IVA*) number from your local VAT office (*ufficio IVA*). A notary (*notiao*) can also do this but is much more expensive.

It's best not to start a business until you have the infrastructure established, including an accountant, lawyer and banking facilities. There are various ways to set up a small business and it's essential to obtain professional advice regarding the best method of establishing and registering a business in Italy, which can dramatically affect your tax position. It's also important to employ an accountant (*commercialista*) to do your books.

If you're a professional, you may need to take a routine examination before you can be included on the professional register (*albo professionale*) with the chamber of commerce.

There are business consultants and relocation agencies in many areas that provide invaluable local assistance. International accountants such as PricewaterhouseCoopers and Ernst & Young have offices throughout Italy, and are an invaluable source of information (in English) on subjects such as forming a company, company law, taxation and social security. Many countries maintain chambers of commerce in Italy, which are also a good source of information and assistance.

Italian Trade Organisations

There are a number of Italian trade organisations, including the Istituto Nazionale per il Commercio Estero (ICE), Via Lizst, 21, 00144 Rome (☎ 06-59921, 🖳 www. ice.it), which is a public organisation (with over 30 offices in Italy and some 80 abroad) that promotes Italian trade throughout the world. The Italian General Confederation of Enterprises, Professional Activities and Self-Employment, Confcommercio, Piazza G. G. Belli 2, 00153 Rome (☎ 06-58661, 🖳 www.confcommercio.it) specialises in certain industries, such as construction, computers (hardware and software), cosmetics, fashion, retailing, and import and export; organises trade fairs and other promotional activities, and

provides free financial and legal advice to its members.

Grants & Incentives

Many grants and incentives are available for new businesses in Italy, particularly in rural areas and the south of the country (the *Mezzogiorno*). Grants include EU subsidies, central government grants, regional development grants, redeployment grants, and grants from provincial authorities and local communities. Grants may include assistance to buy buildings and equipment (or the provision of low-cost business premises), research and technological assistance, subsidies for job creation, low-interest loans and tax incentives (lasting ten years for new companies established in the *Mezzogiorno* regions). Contact Italian chambers of commerce and embassies for information (see **Appendix A**).

Information about chambers of commerce in Italy and a list of offices can be found on the Italian Chambers of Commerce web portal (🖳 www.camcom.gov.it).

Experience

Generally speaking you shouldn't consider running a business in Italy in a field in which you don't have previous experience (with the possible exception of 'businesses' such as bed and breakfast, where experience isn't really necessary). It's often wise to work for someone else in the same line of business in order to gain experience, rather than jump in at the deep end. Always thoroughly investigate an existing or proposed business before investing any money. As any expert will tell you, Italy isn't a country for amateur entrepreneurs, particularly amateurs who don't speak fluent Italian!

Many small businesses in Italy exist on a shoe-string and certainly aren't what would be considered thriving enterprises. As in many countries, most people are self-employed for the lifestyle and freedom it affords (no clocks or bosses), rather than the financial rewards. It's important to keep your plans small and manageable, and stay well within your budget,

rather than undertaking some grandiose scheme.

Avoiding the Crooks

To add to your problems with the Italian authorities, you may come into contact with assorted crooks and swindlers who will try to relieve you of your money. You should have a healthy suspicion of the motives of anyone you do business with in Italy, particularly your fellow countrymen. (It's a sad fact that foreigners who prey on their fellow countrymen are commonplace in Italy.) In most cases you're better off dealing with a long-established Italian company with roots in the local community (and therefore a good reputation to protect), rather than your compatriots. It's also generally best to avoid partnerships, as they rarely work and can be a disaster. In general, you should trust nobody and shouldn't sign anything or pay any money before having a contract checked by a lawyer. If things go wrong, you may be unprotected by Italian law, the wheels of which grind extremely slowly – when they haven't fallen off completely!

Buying a Business

It's much easier to buy an existing business in Italy than to start a new one and it's also less of a risk. The paperwork for taking over an existing business is simpler, although still complex. Buying a business that's a going concern, however, is difficult as Italian businesses are usually passed down from generation to generation and offered for sale only when they fail. If you plan to buy a business, obtain an independent valuation (or two) and employ an accountant to audit the books. Never sign anything that you don't understand fully and, even if you think you understand everything, obtain unbiased professional advice, e.g. from local experts such as banks and accountants, before buying a business.

Starting a Business

Most people are far too optimistic about the prospects for a new business in Italy and overestimate income levels (it often takes years to make a profit). Be realistic or even pessimistic when estimating your income, and overestimate the costs and underestimate the revenue (then reduce it by 50 per cent!). While hoping for the best, you should plan for the worst and have sufficient funds to last until you're established (under-funding is the major cause of business failures). New projects are rarely, if ever, completed within budget and you need to ensure that you have sufficient working capital and can survive until a business takes off. Italian banks are extremely wary of lending to new businesses, particularly businesses run by foreigners, and it's almost impossible for foreigners to obtain finance in Italy.

If you wish to borrow money to buy property or for a business venture in Italy, you should carefully consider where and in what currency to raise the finance.

Location

The location for a business is even more important than the location for a home. Depending on the type of business, you may need access to motorways and railways or to be located in a popular tourist area or near major attractions. Local plans regarding communications, industrial development and major building work, e.g. housing complexes and new shopping centres, may also be important. Plans regarding new motorways and railways are usually available from local town halls.

Type of Business

The most common businesses operated by foreigners in Italy include holiday accommodation, caravan and camp sites, building and allied trades (particularly restoring old houses in Tuscany and Umbria), farming, catering, hotels, shops, franchises, estate agencies, translation and interpreting bureaux, language schools, landscape gardening, and holiday and sports centres. The majority of businesses established by foreigners are linked to the leisure and catering industries, followed by property investment and development. Many professionals, such as doctors and dentists, have set up practices in Italy to serve the expatriate community. There are also opportunities in import and export, e.g. importing foreign foods for the Italian and expatriate market and exporting Italian handicrafts and clothing. You can also find niche markets in providing services for expatriates and Italians that are unavailable in Italy.

Limited Companies

Companies cannot be purchased 'off the shelf' in Italy and it usually takes a number of months to establish one. Incorporating a company in Italy takes longer and is more expensive and more complicated than in many other European countries. There are many kinds of business entity in Italy and choosing the right one is important. The most common types of limited company in Italy are a *società a responsabilità limitata* (*Srl*) and a *società per azioni* (*SpA*), with a minimum share capitalisation of around €10,000 and €120,000 respectively.

Always obtain professional legal advice regarding the advantages and disadvantages of different types of company.

Hiring Employees

The hiring of employees shouldn't be undertaken lightly in Italy and must be taken into account before starting a business. You must enter into a contract under Italian labour law and employees enjoy extensive rights. If you buy an existing business, you may be required to take on existing (possibly inefficient) staff who cannot be dismissed, or be faced with paying high redundancy compensation. It's **very** expensive to hire employees, because, in addition to salaries, you must pay around 35 per cent in social security contributions, a 13th (and possibly 14th) month's salary, five or six weeks' paid annual holiday, plus pay for public holidays, sickness, maternity, etc.

ILLEGAL WORKING

Illegal working (*lavoro in nero*) thrives in Italy, particularly in the south of the country and among expatriate and immigrant communities. It has been estimated that the black economy (*economia sommersa/nera*) is equal to as much as 30 or even 40 per cent of the country's official GDP, and that up to 50 per cent of all incomes in the south of the country are hidden from the taxman! An employer may even ask you whether you want to be paid officially, with tax and social security deducted (*in regola*) or unofficially, i.e. in cash! This is most common in industries that employ itinerant workers, such as catering, construction, farming, tourism and textile manufacture, and in jobs such as domestic work and language teaching.

In many areas, officials turn a blind eye, as the black economy keeps many small businesses alive and the unemployed in 'pocket money'. (The government doesn't pay unemployment benefits to the long-term unemployed and any other benefits paid are usually too low to live on.) Moonlighting by employees (i.e. taking second or third jobs) is also widespread, particularly among those in the public sector, who are generally low paid. However, unscrupulous employers also take advantage of those who are prepared to work illegally in order to pay low wages (below the minimum wage) for long hours and poor working conditions.

> ☑ SURVIVAL TIP
>
> It's strictly illegal for non-EU nationals to work in Italy without a work permit. If you work illegally, you have no entitlement to social security benefits such as insurance against work injuries, public health care and a state pension.

A foreigner who works illegally in Italy is liable to a heavy fine and deportation, while businesses employing people illegally can be fined, or closed down and the owners imprisoned.

LANGUAGE

Although English is the *lingua franca* of international commerce and may help you secure a job in Italy, the most important qualification for anyone seeking employment is the ability to speak fluent Italian. English is the second language of young Italians and the ability to speak English confers prestige, and it's widely spoken in the major cities such as Florence, Milan, Rome and Venice, which attract millions of foreign visitors each year; however, it's unlikely to be spoken in the far south of the country or rural areas, and most Italians expect anyone living or working in Italy to speak Italian.

Italian is one of the romance languages and is a beautiful tongue that's relatively easy to learn, particularly if you already know some French or Spanish (or Latin) – and are good with your hands. Modern Italian is a descendant of 'vulgar' spoken Latin and was standardised in the 14th century by the literary triumvirate of Boccaccio, Dante and Petrarch, who wrote mainly in the Florentine dialect, which subsequently became the basis for today's standard Italian (*italiano standard*). This is the language taught in schools and used in the media, although it's often mixed with dialects. Standard Italian has been in widespread use only since the unification of Italy in the 1860s and Italians were slow to adopt the language of the new nation-state, identifying much more strongly with their regional dialects.

If you don't already speak good Italian, don't expect to learn it quickly, even if you already have a basic knowledge and take intensive lessons. It's common for foreigners still not to be fluent after a year or more of intensive lessons in Italy. If your expectations are unrealistic you'll become frustrated, which can affect your confidence. It takes a long time to reach the level of fluency needed to be able to work in Italian and understand the various accents – let alone dialects (see below). If you don't speak Italian fluently, you should begin Italian lessons on arrival and consider taking a menial or even an unpaid voluntary job, as this is one of the quickest ways of improving your Italian.

If necessary you should have Italian lessons before arriving. A sound knowledge of Italian will not only help you find a job and perform your job better, but also make everyday life much simpler and more enjoyable. If you come to Italy without being able to speak Italian, you'll be excluded from local life and will feel uncomfortable and alienated. The most common reason for negative experiences among foreigners in Italy, both visitors and residents, is because they cannot or won't speak the language. However terrible your Italian, your bad grammar, limited vocabulary and excruciating accent will be much better appreciated than your fluent English. Italians will usually encourage you and greet your butchered attempts with appreciation and good humour. You **must** learn Italian if you wish to have Italian friends.

When doing business in Italy, communications should always be in Italian. Many Italians have a phobia about writing letters (most are unable to write grammatically correct Italian) and postpone replying to letters for as long as possible. But if you write a letter to an Italian company applying for a job, you should ensure that it's grammatically correct, even if it means employing a professional translator. When stating your Italian-language ability, it's important not to exaggerate, as it's easy to confirm the truth. If you state that your Italian is very good or fluent, you'll almost certainly be interviewed in Italian (which is also possible even if you have only a little knowledge). Overstating your fluency is a waste of your and a prospective employer's time.

Those interested in the Italian language may like to check the Italian Language website (🖳 www.italianlang.org) and the About.com guide (🖳 http://italian.about.com). See also **Learning Italian** on page 137.

Foreign Languages & Dialects

Foreign languages are spoken exclusively by around 15 per cent of the population. Italy is home to a number of linguistic minorities, some of which have been granted special privileges in autonomous or semi-autonomous regions, and their language given equal status with Italian; these include French (Valle d'Aosta), German (Alto Adige) and Slovene (Friuli-Venezia Giulia), which are all official languages taught in state schools in these regions. Most German-speaking minorities (some 300,000 speak the Bavarian-Austrian dialect) live in the province of Bolzano, while Slovenes are generally restricted to the Val di Resia in Udine province, the upper Torre and Natisone valleys, Val Canale, the eastern part of Gorizia province and most of the province of Trieste (a total of about 80,000).

Several groups speaking Serbo-Croat are found in Molise, while Croatian, the smallest minority language and spoken by some 4,000 people, has survived in Campobasso province in Molise. Albanian-speaking colonies are concentrated mainly in Sicily and Calabria, but are also found in Molise, Abruzzo, Campania, Puglia and Basilicata, some of which (descended from 15th-century Albanian mercenaries) speak a dialect of Albanian known as Arbëresh. There are Catalan-speaking groups in the town of Alghero in the northwest of Sardinia, dating from the island's capture by the crown of Aragon in 1354. Greek dialects are spoken in some parts of Calabria and Puglia. There are also gypsies who speak the *Sinti* dialect in the north and the *Rom* dialect in the centre and south of the country.

Dialects are used by some 60 per cent of Italians, although most of them speak *italiano standard* when travelling outside their home region or speaking to foreigners. *Franco-Provençal* or *Arpitano* French dialects are spoken in Valle d'Aosta, and in certain Piedmont valleys; and in the upper Val Argentina, in Imperia Province, *Provençal* or *Occitanian* dialects are spoken. The main Italian dialects are *Sardo* (around 1,350,000 speakers), *Friulano* (700,000) and *Ladin* (40,000). *Sardo*, spoken in Sardinia, is virtually a different language, similar to Catalan and dating back to Spanish rule. Other dialects are *Ligurian* (which employs a mixture of Italian, Catalan and French), *Neapolitan* and *Sicilian*.

The Catholic Church still uses Latin as the official liturgical language, and it's still taught in Italian schools from the 6th grade upwards (with the exception of technical establishments).

Siena, Tuscany

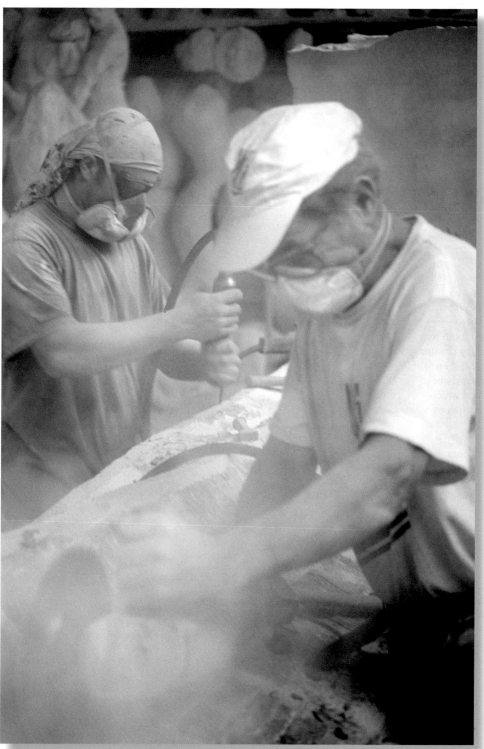

marble workers

2.
EMPLOYMENT CONDITIONS

Employment contracts (*condizioni di lavoro*) in Italy are generally good, always provided you receive one – black-market working is widespread (see Illegal Working on page 36). Legal employees are well protected by extensive social and labour laws (*statuto dei lavoratori*). Italian labour law is protective of an employee's welfare (particularly regarding dismissal) and tends to favour job security, although to a lesser extent than in the past. In recent years, the need for 'flexibility' in the job market has become more widely accepted, and both temporary and part-time jobs are increasingly common. Nevertheless, Italians enjoy greater job security than almost any other people; in Europe, only the Swiss have greater security. Italians also enjoy a wide range of benefits, which may include assistance towards housing, free transport, company canteens, children's nurseries and kindergartens, all of which are provided by many medium-size and large companies. Women are entitled to extensive maternity benefits, which are among the most generous in the world.

Labour relations in various trades, industries and professions are governed by collective bargaining agreements (*contrattazione collettiva* or *contratto collettivo di lavoro*) negotiated between trade unions and employers' organisations. These cover about 75 per cent of the workforce and specify the rights and obligations of employers and employees in a particular industry or occupation. Collective bargaining agreements may be national (*contratto collettivo nazionale del lavoro/CCNL*), provincial or local in scope. Agreements are binding on all parties and establish the various categories of employee and the criteria and minimum limits for wages and benefits. Large enterprises usually have their own agreements or contracts (*accordi/contratti integrativi aziendali*), which operate within the framework of collective agreements adopted at national level, but often improve upon the minimum requirements and take into account local circumstances.

If an employer doesn't abide by the laws or the regulations in a particular industry, employees can report him to unions or work syndicates. Where there's no union, a case is heard before an industrial tribunal (*tribunale del lavoro*) comprising employer and syndicate representatives (elected by the workforce).

Employment conditions are often dependent on the region where you work and the local economic conditions. In some regions – particularly the south of the country, where there's high unemployment – there's a tendency for employers to use the black market. Although legislation requires employees to be given a contract, this can often be difficult to obtain.

EMPLOYMENT CONTRACTS

Under Italian law every employee must have an employment contract (*contratto di lavoro*) for a job for which he expects to be paid. Although some employers are less than keen to provide one, you should insist on a written contract. You and your employer are obliged to follow the rules and regulations established under Italian law and to abide by the conditions laid down in your contract.

There are usually no hidden surprises or traps for the unwary in an Italian employment contract. Nevertheless, as with any contract, you should know exactly what it contains before signing it. If your Italian isn't fluent, try to obtain an English translation, as your language ability would need to be excellent to understand the legal jargon that goes into some contracts. Italian employers seldom provide foreigners with contracts in English, irrespective of the number of English-speaking foreigners employed.

☑ SURVIVAL TIP

If you cannot obtain a written English translation of your contract, you should at least have it translated orally so that you don't receive any nasty surprises later – such as discovering you're required to give six months' notice.

There are two main kinds of contract: for employees (*dipendenti*) and for apprentices or those in work-training. Apprenticeship contracts (*contratto di appredistato* /*tirocinio*) are for people between the ages of 16 and 24 and cover a training period during which employees have reduced benefits and low pay compared with full employees. The duration of an apprenticeship cannot be less than 18 months or over four years. When the contract expires, the employer must offer you a permanent contract if he wishes to retain your services. Employers often take on staff using this type of contract to avoid paying taxes and certain benefits, which are instead paid by the state.

'Work-training' contracts (*contratto di formazione e lavoro*) were introduced to make it easier for young people to obtain jobs, and only workers between 16 and 32 years of age are eligible. There are two kinds of work-training contract, neither of which is renewable: a one-year contract and a two-year contract

leading to an intermediate or high professional level. One of the advantages (to employers) of these contracts is reduced social security contributions, which vary according to the type of enterprise and region of the country, mainly favouring the depressed southern areas.

Employee contracts may be for a fixed term (*contratto a termine* or *contratto a tempo determinato*) or permanent (*contratto a tempo indeterminato*), which is more common. Contracts for a fixed term are possible only in certain cases provided for in collective agreements or by law, e.g. seasonal or unusual occupations or replacements for temporarily-absent workers. A fixed-term contract lasts for a specified period and terminates automatically without requiring either party to give notice. A fixed-term contract may be renewed, but if it's renewed a second time it automatically becomes an unlimited duration contract and your job is then permanent. A third type of contract is the short-term or project contract (*contratto a progetto*). This contract can be renewed, but your employer is not entitled to provide sick, maternity, or holiday pay.

In most fields of employment in Italy, standard employment contracts are drafted by a professional body, based on collective labour contracts or legislation. These are usually applicable unless both employer and employee agree otherwise in writing. A contract should state your salary, holiday dates, pay details, sick pay entitlement and any bonuses, and make reference to a national collective bargaining agreement if appropriate. At the top of each contract there's a list of all the workers' union's agreement abbreviations, next to which is the word *stipula*, which means the date you were hired. *Decorrenza* means 'with effect from', under which will be the date you start work. Your employment contract may also contain your:

♦ job title;

♦ department name and manager;

♦ main duties;

♦ relationships with other departments;

♦ responsibility to the employer;

♦ place(s) of work;

♦ salary details, including any extra month's salary and any agreed increases;

♦ probationary and notice periods.

Other kinds of employment contract include those for positions such as seasonal work (*lavoro stagionale*) and temporary replacement (*lavoro interinale*) to cover maternity leave, illness, military service, etc., when it's necessary to hire temporary staff.

In addition to a contract, you should obtain a copy of your employer's general terms and conditions (*condizioni di impiego*), which govern such things as staff regulations and benefits, and apply to all employees unless otherwise stated in individual contracts of employment. General conditions are usually referred to in employment contracts and employees usually receive a copy on starting a job (or, in some cases, beforehand).

Employment contracts (particularly temporary contracts) sometimes come under review and you should check the latest legislation before signing a contract.

SALARY & BENEFITS

Your salary (*stipendio*) is stated in your employment contract, and details of salary reviews, planned increases and cost of living rises may also be included. Salaries in job contracts are usually stated gross (*lordo*), i.e. before all deductions and withholdings for benefits, taxes and social security. Salaries are generally paid monthly, although they may be quoted in contracts on an hourly (*orario*), monthly (*mensile*) or annual (*annuale*) basis, depending on the type of job or position. If a bonus is paid, such as a 13th or 14th month's salary, it's stated in your employment contract. Details such as the method of payment of your salary into a bank or post office account and the date of salary payments are usually included in general terms and conditions. You receive a pay slip (*busta paga*) with your salary detailing your gross pay and deductions.

Minimum Wage

Minimum salaries (*paga base*) are fixed under collective agreements between unions and employers for each category of worker. This basic wage may, however, be adjusted downwards for apprentices. Inexperienced employees may earn the minimum basic wage, although most employees are paid much more, particularly in the north of the country (wages are lower in the south). The basic salary may be supplemented by an 'above base payment' (*superminimo*), a seniority increase (*scatti di anzianità*), overtime (*straordinari*) and bonuses (*premi e gratificazioni*). Minimum wages are not set by law but collectively bargained on a sector-by-sector basis and reviewed every few years, and there's also a wage increase for inflation every two years. The government publishes a salary rate book (*tabella professionali*) for each category of employee, including operatives (*operai*), staff employees (*impiegati*) and managers (*dirigenti*).

13th Month's Salary & Bonuses

Many employees in Italy are entitled to an additional month's remuneration – the so-called 13th month's salary (*tredicesima mesilità*), usually paid in December before Christmas and referred to as a Christmas bonus (*gratifica natalizia*) when it applies to factory or manual workers. In addition, salaried employees in the commerce industry, managers, executives, and those who have worked for many years in the same company usually receive a 14th month's salary (*quattordicesima mesilità*) during the summer, generally in June.

Some employees, such as those in the petroleum and banking industries, receive 15th and even 16th months' salaries. Extra months' salaries are guaranteed bonuses and aren't pegged to the company's performance. In your first and last years of employment, your extra months' salaries and other bonuses should be paid pro rata (calculated in twelfths or *dodicesimi*) if you don't work a full calendar year. Senior and middle managers often receive extra bonuses (*premi e gratificazioni*), perhaps linked to profits, equal to around 10 to 20 per cent of their annual salary.

Education & Training

Employee training (*formazione professionale*) isn't taken as seriously as in many other EU countries, and Italian employers aren't obliged to provide employee training programmes, such as seminars, conferences, technical courses or language lessons. If you need to learn or improve your Italian or another language in order to perform your job, however, the cost of language study is usually paid by your employer. Employers who are keen to attract the best employees, particularly those engaged in hi-tech fields, usually allocate extra funds and provide excellent training schemes, although not all employees benefit equally from training, which is decided by the employer. It's in your interest to investigate courses of study, seminars and lectures that you feel will be of direct benefit to you and your employer.

Most employers will give reasonable consideration to a request to attend a course during working hours, provided you don't make it a full-time occupation.

RELOCATION & TRAVEL EXPENSES

Travel and relocation expenses (*spese per viaggio e trasferimento*) to Italy depend on your agreement with your employer and are usually included in your employment contract or conditions. If you're hired from outside Italy, your air ticket and other travel costs to Italy are usually booked and paid for by your employer or his local representative, although this doesn't usually apply to seasonal workers. In addition you can usually claim incidental travel costs, e.g. the cost of transport to and from airports. If you travel by car to Italy, you can usually claim a mileage rate or the equivalent air fare.

An employer may pay a fixed relocation allowance based on your salary, position and size of family, or he may pay the total cost of removal; you may be required to sign a contract stipulating that if you leave the employer before a certain period (e.g. five years), you must repay a percentage of your removal costs. The allowance should be sufficient to move the contents of an average house (castles aren't usually catered for) and you must usually pay any excess costs yourself. If you don't want to bring your furniture to Italy or have only a few belongings to ship, it may be possible to purchase furniture locally up to the limit of your allowance. Check with your employer. When a company is liable for the total cost of relocation, they may ask you to obtain two or three removal estimates.

Generally, you're required to organise and pay for the removal in advance. Your employer usually reimburses the equivalent amount in local currency **after** you've paid the bill, although it may be possible to have him pay the bill directly or give you a cash advance. If you change jobs within Italy, your new employer may pay your relocation expenses when it's necessary for you to move house. Don't forget to ask; they may not offer to pay unless prompted (it may depend on how desperate they are to employ you).

WORKING HOURS

Under European Union law, you may not work more than eight hours per day or 48 hours per week. In general, Italians tend to work 40 hours per week divided into eight hours per day from Mondays to Fridays – the average working week comes to just under 41 hours. Official working hours in most organisations are from 8.30am to 1pm and from 3 to 7pm, although some companies

(including many foreign-owned businesses) work from 9am to 6pm with only an hour for lunch. This is more common in the north of the country than in the south. Managers and executives generally work long hours, even allowing for their occasionally long lunch breaks. Senior staff in the south work shorter hours than those in the north, particularly on hot summer days (when they sensibly go home early and jump in the swimming pool!).

Weekends are sacrosanct and almost nobody works on Saturdays and Sundays unless it's part of their normal job, e.g. shop staff. Employees cannot be obliged to work on Sundays unless collective agreements state otherwise. Official authorisation is usually required for employees to work on Sundays and time off in lieu must be granted during the normal working week.

There are usually no scheduled breaks for coffee or tea in Italy, although drinks can usually be taken at an employee's work station at any time. Many companies traditionally have a two-hour lunch break, particularly in the provinces, although this is no longer standard practice. Nevertheless, taking a long lunch break, perhaps for a game of tennis or a swim, isn't frowned upon, provided you put in the required hours and don't neglect your work.

> ☑ **SURVIVAL TIP**
>
> It may come as a nasty surprise to some foreigners to discover that many Italian employers (including most large companies) require employees to clock in and out of work. If you're caught cheating the clock, you can be dismissed.

Flexi-time

Many employers operate flexi-time working hours (*orario flessibile*), particularly in the north of the country and in the civil service. A flexi-time system usually requires all employees to be present between certain hours, known as the core or block time, e.g. from 9 to 11.30am and from 1.30 to 4pm. Employees may make up their required

working hours by starting earlier than the required core time, reducing their lunch break or working later. Most business premises are open from around 7am to 6pm and smaller companies may allow employees to work as late as they wish, provided they don't exceed the maximum permitted daily working hours (see above).

Overtime

Overtime (*lavoro straordinari*) earns you up to 130 per cent of your basic pay for daytime work and up to 150 per cent for work on public holidays or at night. Overtime must not exceed two hours per day, or 80 hours per quarter or 250 hours per year. Some companies have a limit of 200 overtime hours per year, and some unions don't permit overtime at all. Executives and managers aren't generally paid overtime, although this depends on their employment contracts.

HOLIDAYS & LEAVE

Annual Holidays

The amount of annual holiday (*ferie*) you're entitled to depends on your length of service, although employees in Italy are usually entitled to five or six weeks' paid holiday per year, which must usually be taken during the year in which it's earned. Most people take a month in the summer (virtually the whole country closes down from 20th July to 20th August, except for the leisure industry) and two weeks around Christmas and the New Year. If your company closes in August, you **must** take holiday at that time. If you don't take all your holiday allowance, you may be paid in lieu, although some companies insist that employees take all the holiday they've accrued.

Before starting a job, you should check that any planned holidays will be honoured by a prospective employer. This is particularly important if they fall within your probationary period, when holidays may not be permitted.

Public Holidays

Most collective agreements include the ten Italian national holidays (*feste nazionali*), which are as follows:

Public Holidays

Date	Holiday
1st January	New Year's Day (*Capodanno* or *Primo dell'Anno*)
6th January	Epiphany (*La Befana* or *Epifania*)
March or April	Easter Monday (*Lunedì di Pasqua*)
25th April	Liberation Day (*Festa della Liberazione*)
1st May	Labour Day (*Primo Maggio* or *Festa del Lavoro*)
15th August	Feast of the Assumption (*Ferragosto*)
1st November	All Saints' Day (*Ognissanti* or *Tutti i Santi*)
8th December	Immaculate Conception (*Immacolata Concezione*)
25th December	Christmas Day (*Natale*)
26th December	Boxing Day (*Santo Stefano*)

Republic Day (*Festa della Repubblica*) and Armistice Day (*Caduti di Tutti le Guerre*), on the first Sundays in June and November respectively, aren't official national holidays but are widely allocated as paid holidays for staff who generally work on a Sunday. Employees generally also receive a day off on the local saint's day. The following are the saints' days in the major cities:

Saints' Days

City	Date
Bologna	4th October (St Petronio)
Florence, Genoa & Turin	24th June (St John)
Milan	7th December (St Ambrose)
Naples	9th September (St Gennaro)
Palermo	11th July (St Rosalia)
Rome	29th June (St Peter)
Venice	25th April (St Mark)

There are usually also a number of half-day holidays, which vary from region to region but may include Easter Friday, Christmas Eve, New Year's Eve and a spring festival in April.

When a holiday falls on a Saturday or Sunday, another day's holiday is usually granted in compensation. If a public holiday falls on a Tuesday or Thursday, the day before or after (i.e. Monday or Friday respectively) may also be declared a holiday, depending on your employer – a practice known as making a bridge (*ponte*). If a holiday falls on a Wednesday, employees may take the two preceding or succeeding days off.

All public offices, banks, post offices, schools and most shops and businesses are closed on public holidays, when only essential work is carried out. Public transport remains in service, although schedules may be reduced. Foreign embassies and consulates in Italy usually observe Italian public holidays **plus** their own country's national holidays.

Sick Leave

Employees in Italy don't receive a quota of sick days and there's no limit on the amount of time you may take off work due to sickness or accidents, although you only receive sick pay for a limited amount of time. Sick leave for workers in commerce and industry is paid by the employer and the National Institute for Social Security (INPS), to which contributions are automatically deducted from your salary (see **Sickness Benefit** on 199). Some employers pay the full salary of sick employees for up to six months.

An application for sickness benefit must be made by your employer to an INPS office with a doctor's medical certificate (*certificato medico*) showing the diagnosis and how long you'll be unable to work. Benefit is payable only after the certificate is received, therefore you should register immediately or get someone to do so on your behalf. If you're still unable to work after the date given on the original medical certificate, you must provide another certificate within two days.

Parental Leave

Expectant mothers can work until their eighth month of pregnancy (subject to medical approval) and are entitled to five months' paid maternity leave (*congedo per maternità*), including at least one month before the birth, on 80 per cent of their salary. Fathers usually receive a few days' paternity leave when a child is born and can obtain a three-month leave of absence after a child is born if the mother is deceased or seriously ill. Parental leave doesn't affect your state pension. See also **Maternity Benefit** on page 199.

A woman cannot be dismissed from her job from the beginning of her pregnancy (fixed at 300 days before the date when the baby is due) through to the baby's first birthday – except for gross misconduct. If she is dismissed, she has the right to reinstatement (*il ripristino del rapporto di lavoro*), provided she presents the appropriate certificate of pregnancy or birth to her employer within 90 days of dismissal. A woman wishing to regain her job should take this step immediately, as she won't be paid for the interim period between dismissal and reinstatement.

Compassionate & Special Leave

Most companies provide additional days off for certain occasions, e.g. moving house, your own or a family marriage, the birth of a child, or the death of a family member or close relative. Grounds for compassionate leave (*congedo per gravi motivi* or *congedo straordinario*) are usually defined in collective agreements, and the number of days' leave granted varies with the reason.

Employees who have worked for a company for a certain number of years may be entitled to take a sabbatical of up to a year (usually without pay).

Notification of Sickness or Accident

You're usually required to notify your employer as soon as possible of sickness or an accident that prevents you from working, i.e. within a few hours of your normal starting time. Failure to do so may result in your not being paid for that day's absence. You're required to keep your boss or manager informed about your illness and when you expect to return to work.

For more than a few days' sickness, you're usually required to provide your employer with a doctor's certificate (*certificato medico*); the period will be specified in your employment conditions. An employer cannot terminate an employee's contract during a period of sickness or when he's recovering from an accident.

INSURANCE

Social Security

Italian and foreign employees of Italian companies and the self-employed must usually contribute to the Italian social security (*previdenza sociale*) system. Exceptions include some nationals of countries with a reciprocal social security agreement with Italy, which allows social security payments to be made abroad for a limited period. Social security covers you for sickness and maternity, accidents at work and occupational diseases, and provides limited unemployment cover, plus family allowances, and old age, invalidity

and survivor's pensions. It doesn't include the contributions to Italy's national health service (Servizio Sanitario Nazionale/SSN), which is funded separately from general taxation.

Contributions (*contributi*) are calculated as a percentage of your gross income and are deducted at source by your employer. Employees pay around 10 per cent of their gross earnings, while the employer pays around 35 per cent of an employee's salary, making a total of some 45 per cent. See **Social Security** on page 199 for details.

Health Insurance

Residents in Italy are eligible for healthcare under the Servizio Sanitario Nazionale (SSN) but many people have supplementary private health insurance. Many foreigners have an international private health insurance policy, which covers their families both in Italy and elsewhere. Most companies provide private health insurance policies for employees transferred to Italy, and some employers, particularly foreign companies, provide comprehensive private health insurance for all executives and senior managers and their families. For further information see **National Health Service** on page 183 and **Health Insurance** on page 203.

Unemployment Insurance

Employees in Italy make obligatory contributions to the state unemployment fund in their monthly social security contributions. If you become unemployed, you're

entitled to ordinary unemployment benefits (*indennità di disoccupazione*) but only if you've worked for at least a year and made contributions in the preceding two years. Reduced benefits are available in certain circumstances. For details see **Unemployment Benefits** on page 200.

Accident Insurance

Accident insurance (*assicurazione contro gli infortuni*) is mandatory for all employees in Italy. It's paid for by employers and provided by the Instituto Nazionale per l'Assicurazione Contro gli Infortuni sul Lavoro (INAIL). It covers accidents or illness at work and accidents that occur while travelling to and from work and on company business. Although the primary responsibility for safety rests with the employer, employees are required by law to ensure that they co-operate with their employers and that they don't endanger themselves or anyone else by their actions or negligence. There are usually specific regulations for activities involving high risks, e.g. when operating electrical equipment and certain classes of machinery, and when using chemicals.

When an accident occurs at work, an employee must inform his employer immediately and complete a report (*denuncia*). If recovery takes longer than three days, employers must inform INAIL within two days; in the case of death, INAIL must be informed within 24 hours.

There are various kinds of compensation to which employees (or their survivors in the case of death) are entitled, depending on whether an accident results in temporary or permanent disability (see **Disability Benefits** on page 199). If an employee or self-employed person dies as a result of an accident at work or an illness caused by work, a survivor's pension is paid to his family based on a percentage of the deceased's last annual salary (see **State Pensions** on page 201).

Salary Insurance

Salary insurance (*assicurazione di stipendio*) pays employees' salaries during periods of sickness or after accidents and is provided under social security. All workers are compulsorily enrolled with the relevant national institutions. After a certain number of consecutive sick days (the number varies with the employer, although it's usually three), a percentage of your salary is paid by your employer and by social security, although employees in industry usually have their salary paid entirely by their employer. For information see **Sickness Benefit** on page 199.

RETIREMENT

Your employment conditions may be valid only until the official Italian retirement (*pensionamento*) age, which is 65 for men and 60 for women in most trades and professions, although some employees can retire on a full pension earlier. If you wish to continue working after you've reached retirement age, you may be required to negotiate a new employment contract.

All employees in Italy are obliged to contribute to a state old age pension fund (*pensione di vecchiaia*), to which payments are included in your monthly social security contributions. Almost every trade and occupation has its own pension scheme. Management employees usually make additional contributions to a supplementary managerial company pension fund run by National Security for Managers of Commercial Concerns (INPADAC) or National Social Security for Managers of Industrial Concerns (INPDAI). For further information see **State Pensions** on page 201.

UNION MEMBERSHIP

The Italian constitution establishes the right to organise trade unions (*sindacali*), which are active (at least 40 per cent of the Italian workforce is unionised) and powerful. In fact, one of the main reasons many employers take on workers illegally is that legal employees are heavily protected by unions and employers often find it almost impossible to sack them, even for poor time keeping, theft and other offences. The right to strike is also guaranteed by the constitution, and it remains a potent weapon in the hands of the trade unions. Nevertheless, union membership isn't obligatory.

There are three major unions in Italy, each with different political or religious alignments. The Confederazione Generale Italiana del Lavoro (CGIL) is closest to the left and was formerly dominated by the Italian Communist Party; the Confederazione Italiana Sindacati Lavoratori (CISL) is closest to the Catholic church with links to the Christian democrats; and the Unione Italiana del Lavoro (UIL) is closest to the secular parties and associated with the Socialists. A number of independent unions are also active, particularly in the public-service sector; these are quite militant and increasingly challenge the monopoly of the three confederations on national contractual negotiations.

Collective bargaining contracts between unions and employers regulate employees' employment conditions, and employment contracts are reviewed and new minimum wages fixed every few years. Unions also negotiate with the government on policies concerning the economy and welfare.

In addition to trade unions, Italy has numerous workers' associations (*ordine*) for different professions, which have branches in major Italian cities; you can obtain a list of associations from your local town hall or chamber of commerce.

In companies with over 40 employees, employee delegates must be elected to the board of directors and a labour management committee formed. In addition to dealing with matters relating to the terms and conditions of employment, the committee must be consulted on proposed major changes relating to the operation, organisation and management of a company before they can be initiated. However, a company isn't usually required to act on the opinion of the labour management committee.

OTHER CONDITIONS
Acceptance of Gifts

Employees are usually forbidden to accept gifts of more than a certain value from customers or suppliers. Many suppliers give bottles of wine or small gifts at Christmas, and businessmen often exchange small gifts, e.g. a watch or pen, when they close a deal or sign a contract. These don't breach the rules, but providing a 'sweetener' (e.g. cash) to oil the wheels of bureaucracy, obtain a contract or receive better treatment in a hospital is illegal, although part of everyday life in Italy.

Changing Jobs & Confidentiality

Companies in a hi-tech or highly confidential business may have restrictions on employees moving to a competitor in Italy or elsewhere within a certain period of resigning, or restrictions regarding starting a company in the same line of business. You should be aware of these restrictions, as they're enforceable under Italian law, although it's a complicated subject and disputes often need to be resolved by a court. Italian laws regarding industrial secrets and general employer confidentiality are strict. If you breach this confidentiality you may be dismissed and could be unable to find further employment in Italy.

Probationary & Notice Periods

For most jobs in Italy there's a probationary period (*periodo di prova*) of one to three months, depending on the type of work, the employer and your contract (three months is usual for permanent positions). A probationary period isn't required by law, although there's no law forbidding it. The length of a probationary period is usually stated in collective agreements, which impose restrictions on the maximum period. During the probationary period, either party may terminate the employment contract without notice or any financial penalty, unless otherwise stated in a collective agreement.

Notice periods (*periodo di preavviso*) usually vary with length of service and are governed by law and collective agreements. The minimum notice period is usually a month for clerical and manual workers, two months for foremen and supervisors, and three months for managerial and senior technical staff. The minimum notice period for employees with over two years' service is two months. If you resign, your employer can decide whether you should work to the end of your notice period or be paid in lieu of notice (*indennità di mancato preavviso*),

while if you've been dismissed, you can choose to be paid in lieu of notice. Compensation must also be paid for any outstanding annual holiday entitlement up to the end of the notice period. See also **Dismissal & Redundancy** below.

Dismissal & Redundancy

Employees are entitled to a severance payment on the termination of their employment, for whatever reason, depending on their salary and number of years' service. Dismissal (*licenziamento*) is permitted only if it's given in writing for a 'just cause' (*giusta causa*) or a 'justifiable reason' (*giustificato motivo*). Just cause includes any event that renders the continuation of employment impossible, such as non-performance of contractual obligations, repeated failure to turn up for work, violence against a colleague or employer, or theft from an employer; dismissal is immediate and requires no notice. Justifiable reason, which includes redundancy due to a general reduction of the workforce or an employee's position being abolished, must be negotiated with a trade union and requires an employer to give notice.

If no cause or reason for a dismissal is given, an employee is entitled to compensation and to be reinstated if the unit from which he was dismissed employed over 15 people or the employer has over 60 employees in Italy. If you're fired or made redundant, you have two months in which to lodge an appeal and, if you've been dismissed unfairly, you can reclaim your old job with compensation for any lost wages.

> If you lose a contracted position, you're entitled to state unemployment benefit (see page 201), although your eligibility for benefits depends on your contributions, and the amount you receive is based on your salary at the time of your dismissal.

Uniquely, if you're made redundant, fired (for any reason!) or resign voluntarily from a job in Italy, you're entitled to a termination payment (*trattamento di fine rapporto/TFR* or *liquidazione*) based on your average salary and calculated according to your length of service.

(Your average monthly salary is reckoned to be a twelfth of 13.5 months' wages.) You also receive any compensation payments agreed under trade union rules and any holiday pay due. This termination payment is yours by right and isn't a voluntary payment on the part of the employer; any severance incentives, e.g. for taking voluntary redundancy, are paid in addition to this. Employees can even obtain an advance of up to 70 per cent of their termination payment to buy a home or pay for urgent medical expenses, provided they've worked for a company for at least seven years. Part of your termination payment can be converted into securities and lodged with a private pension fund.

Medical Examination

Many Italian employers require prospective employees to have a pre-employment medical examination (*esame medico*) performed by a doctor nominated by the employer. An offer of employment is usually subject to a prospective employee being given a clean bill of health. However, this may be required only for employees over a certain age (e.g. 40) or for employees in certain jobs, e.g. where good health is of paramount importance for safety

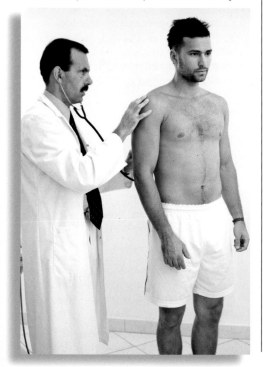

reasons. Thereafter a medical examination may be required periodically, e.g. every one or two years, or may be requested at any time by your employer. A medical examination may be necessary as a condition of membership of a company health, pension or life insurance scheme. Some companies insist on certain employees having regular health screening, particularly executives and senior managers.

Part-time Job Restrictions

Restrictions regarding part-time work (*lavoro a tempo parziale* or *lavoro part-time*) may be detailed in your contract or general terms and conditions. It's common for people to have second or even third jobs, although most Italian companies don't allow full-time employees to moonlight for another employer in the same line of business. Much part-time employment is done illegally (i.e. without declaration to the authorities), particularly as part-time employment involves complying with more stringent requirements and formalities with regard to contracts.

CHECKLISTS

When negotiating your conditions of employment, you'll find the checklists on the following pages useful. The points listed under **General Positions** (below) apply to most jobs, while those listed under **Executive Positions** (on page 53) usually apply to executive and senior managerial appointments only.

General Positions

Employer

♦ What are the employer's prospects?

♦ Does he have a good reputation?

♦ Does he have a high staff turnover?

Contract

♦ Do you have a written list of your job responsibilities?

♦ Have your employment conditions been confirmed in writing?

♦ If a dispute arises over your salary or working conditions, under the law of which country will your employment contract be interpreted?

Salary

◆ Is the salary adequate, taking into account the cost of living? Is it index-linked?

◆ Is the total salary (including expenses) paid in euros or is it paid in another country in a different currency, with expenses for living in Italy?

◆ When and how often is the salary reviewed?

◆ Does the salary include a 13th month's salary and annual or end-of-contract bonuses?

◆ Is overtime paid or time off given in lieu of extra hours worked?

Relocation Expenses

◆ Are removal expenses or a relocation allowance paid?

◆ Does the allowance include travelling expenses for all family members? Is there a limit and is it adequate?

◆ Are you required to repay relocation expenses (or a percentage) if you resign before a certain period has elapsed?

glass blower

◆ Are you required to pay for your relocation in advance? This can run to several thousand euros for normal house contents.

◆ If employment is for a short period only, will your relocation costs be paid by the employer when you leave Italy?

◆ If you aren't shipping household goods and furniture to Italy, is there an allowance for buying furnishings locally?

◆ Do relocation expenses include the legal and agent's fees incurred when moving home?

◆ Does the employer use the services of a relocation consultant (see page 73)?

Accommodation

◆ Does the employer pay for a hotel or pay a lodging allowance until you find permanent accommodation?

◆ Is subsidised or free temporary or permanent accommodation provided? If so, is it furnished or unfurnished?

◆ Must you pay for utilities such as electricity, gas and water?

◆ If an employer doesn't provide accommodation, is assistance given to find a home? If so, what sort of assistance?

◆ What will accommodation cost?

◆ Are your expenses paid while looking for accommodation?

Working Hours

◆ What are the weekly working hours?

◆ Does the employer operate a flexi-time system? If so, what are the fixed working hours? How early must you start? Can you carry forward extra hours worked and take time off at a later date, or carry forward a deficit and make it up later?

◆ Are you required to clock in and out of work?

◆ Can you choose whether to take time off in lieu of overtime or be paid?

Leave

◆ What is the annual holiday entitlement? Does it increase with length of service?

♦ What are the paid public holidays? Is Monday or Friday a free day when a public holiday falls on a Tuesday or Thursday respectively?

♦ Is free air travel to your home country or elsewhere provided for you and your family and, if so, how often?

Insurance

♦ Is extra insurance cover provided besides obligatory insurance (see **Chapter 13**)?

♦ Is free life insurance provided?

♦ Is private health insurance provided for you **and** your family (see page 203)?

♦ For how long will your salary be paid if you're sick or have an accident?

Company or Supplementary Pension

♦ What percentage of your salary must you pay into a pension fund?

♦ Are you required or able to pay a lump sum into the fund in order to receive a full or higher pension?

♦ Is the pension transferable to another employer?

Other Terms

♦ Are free or subsidised Italian lessons provided for you and your spouse?

♦ Is travel between your Italian residence and your place of work paid for or subsidised?

♦ Is free or subsidised parking provided at your place of work?

♦ Is a free or subsidised company restaurant provided? If not, is an allowance paid or are luncheon vouchers provided? (Some companies provide excellent staff restaurants that save employees both money and time.)

♦ Will the employer provide or pay for professional training or education, if necessary abroad?

♦ Are free work clothes or overalls provided? Does the employer pay for the cleaning of work clothes?

♦ Does the employer provide any fringe benefits, such as subsidised banking services, low interest loans, inexpensive petrol, employees' shop or product discounts, sports and social facilities, and subsidised tickets?

Executive & Managerial Positions

The following points generally apply to executive and top managerial positions only:

♦ Is private schooling for your children financed or subsidised? Will the employer pay for a boarding school in Italy or abroad?

♦ Is the salary index-linked and protected against devaluation? This is particularly important if you're paid in a foreign currency that fluctuates wildly or could be devalued. Are you paid an overseas allowance for working in Italy?

♦ Is there a non-contributory pension fund besides the supplementary company scheme? Is it transferable and, if so, what are the conditions?

♦ Are the costs incurred by a move to Italy (e.g. the cost of selling your home or employing an agent to let it for you and storing household effects) reimbursed?

♦ Will the employer pay for domestic help or contribute to the cost of a servant or cook?

♦ Is a car provided? With a chauffeur?

♦ Are you entitled to any miscellaneous benefits, such as membership of a social or sports club or free credit cards?

♦ Is there an entertainment allowance?

♦ Is there a clothing allowance? For example, if you arrive in Italy in the winter from the tropics, you'll probably need to buy new winter clothes.

Redundancy

Is extra compensation paid if you're made redundant or fired? Redundancy or severance payments (see page 50) are compulsory for employees in Italy (subject to length of service), but executives often receive a generous 'golden handshake' if they're made redundant, e.g. after a takeover.

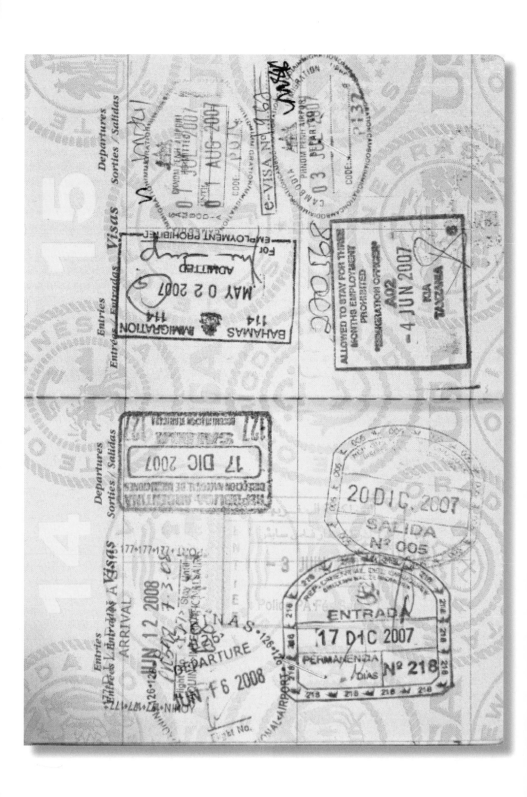

3.
PERMITS & VISAS

Before visiting or moving to Italy, you must ensure that you have the necessary documents and permits. These will depend on your country of origin, the length of your intended stay and the purpose of your visit or stay.

While in Italy, you must always carry your passport, permit to stay or residence permit (as applicable) as an identity card (*carta d'identità*); all Italians must carry ID by law. You can be asked to produce your identification papers at any time by the police or other officials, and if you don't have them you can be taken to a police station and interrogated. Keep photocopies of these documents in a safe place, in case the originals are lost or stolen.

Immigration is a sensitive issue in Italy, which in recent years has been flooded with refugees and illegal immigrants (*clandestini*) from Africa, Eastern Europe (particularly Albania, Turkey and the former Yugoslavia) and Asia (particularly China). Italian immigration laws change frequently and new legislation may alter some of the information contained in this chapter. You shouldn't base any decisions or actions on the information contained herein without confirming it with an official and reliable source, such as an Italian consulate.

Permit infringements are taken seriously by the authorities and there are penalties for breaches of regulations, including fines or even imprisonment for flagrant abuses. In 2009, Silvio Berlusconi's government introduced a package of anti-immigration laws, which included making it a criminal offence for someone to enter or stay in Italy without a visa or authorisation, punishable by a fine of €5,000-10,000, with immigration officials allowed to detain illegal immigrants for up to six months. Other new measures involved criminalising those who rent or offer accommodation to someone without the correct papers – carrying a jail term of up to three years – and obliging civil servants (including doctors and medical staff) to alert the authorities if they receive information about illegal immigrants.

BUREAUCRACY

Although Dante didn't know it at the time, he perfectly described the labyrinth of Italian government offices and bureaucracy when he wrote 'Abandon hope all ye who enter here'. Italian bureaucrats love red tape and have invented official papers and stamps for every possible occasion and purpose. Just finding the right office is a challenge and when you finally locate it, it's invariably closed (many offices open on a few days a week for a couple of hours only). You even need documents to obtain other documents, and the laws governing the issue and use of these documents are frequently incomprehensible. For example, in what other country can your birth certificate be printed with varying information, on two kinds of official paper, have varying costs, and expire if you fail to renew it?

Once you have the correct documents, they must be officially translated and numerous copies made. Wander into any post office, police headquarters or government office and you hear a symphony of stamping and banging while long lines of confused Italians pray that they're in the right place and the right queue for the document required. If all this bureaucracy is bewildering for Italians, just imagine how frightening it is for foreigners!

The situation isn't helped by the fact that the Italian judicial system is based upon a simple premise: *La Legge non ammette l'ignoranza* (The Law doesn't admit ignorance). Laws have been created to govern everything under the Italian sun, but there's no official process of communicating or explaining them to the general public. This leaves the responsibility of gathering information entirely to the individual with little or no help from the state. A plethora of documentation is necessary to obtain a visa, permit to stay or residence or work permit. Unfortunately, not all the official information explaining how to obtain this documentation is readily available or interpreted in the same way, making the tortured road to obtaining visas and permits fraught with dead ends and U-turns. Due to the difficulties in conforming to Italian laws and documentation, there are official 'document agencies' which can obtain documents and make applications on your behalf (listed in the *Yellow Pages* under *Certificati*, *Agenzie*).

When dealing with Italian bureaucracy, try to remain composed and polite (even when you feel like strangling the person behind the counter) and if your Italian isn't excellent, take someone with you who's fluent (most officials speak only Italian). Never take anything for granted where Italian civil servants (*servitori civili*) are concerned, and make sure that you understand all communications. If in doubt, have someone translate them for you.

In the last few years, many official documents have been abolished and substituted by a simple auto-certification process, usually a printed form (*modulo*) available in public offices. Meanwhile, the government is trying to reduce bureaucracy and provide more access to information, particularly via the internet, e.g. 🖥 www.governo.it.

VISITORS

European Union (EU) nationals don't require a visa and are at liberty to live and work freely within the EU. Citizens of the following countries don't require a visa for short stays (up to between 30 and 90 days depending on the country; check with your local Italian embassy or consulate): Andorra, Antigua & Barbuda, Argentina, Australia, Barbados, Benin, Bolivia, Bosnia-Herzegovina, Brazil, Brunei, Burkina Faso, Canada, Chile, Colombia, Costa Rica, Croatia, Cyprus, Ecuador, El Salvador, Fiji, Guatemala, Guyana, Honduras, Hong Kong, Iceland, Israel, Ivory Coast, Japan, Kenya, (South) Korea, Liechtenstein, Macau, Macedonia, Malaysia, Maldives, Malta, Mauritius, Mexico, Monaco, New Zealand, Nicaragua, Niger, Norway, Panama, Paraguay, Samoa, Saint Kitts& Nevis, San Marino, Seychelles, Singapore, South Korea, Switzerland, Togo, Trinidad and Tobago, Uruguay, the US, Vatican City and Venezuela. All other nationalities require a visa to visit Italy for any period (see **Visas** below).

Citizens of many EU countries can visit Italy with a national identity card, while all others require a full passport. However, while identity cards are accepted at all points of entry to Italy, the Italian authorities may not accept them when you're applying for a residence permit (see page 63). If you're an EU national and wish to remain in Italy for longer than 90 days, it's therefore highly recommended to enter with a full passport.

The *permesso di soggiorno* (permit to stay) no longer applies to EU nationals living in Italy. However, they're required to take out a residence permit at the registry office (*ufficio anagrafe*) within three months, by providing some proof of employment or financial resources, which can be in the form of bank statements, tax returns or a work contract.

If you're a non-EU national, it isn't possible to enter Italy as a tourist and change your status to that of an employee, student or resident, and you must return to your country of residence and apply for the appropriate visa.

When you stay with friends in Italy (rather than, for example, at a hotel or campsite) for longer than three days, you're officially required to register with the local police. Although few short-stay visitors comply with this requirement, failure to register is punishable by a fine of up to around €220.

VISAS

EU nationals don't require visas for visits to Italy. Some non-EU nationals need a visa to enter Italy for any length of time (see **Visitors**, above) and all non-EU nationals require a 'residence visa' (*visto per ragioni di dimora*) to enter Italy if they plan to stay more than 90 days.

Italy has been a signatory to the Schengen Agreement since 1998 and can issue a 'Schengen visa' which allows the holder to move freely between Schengen countries (Austria, Belgium, Czech Republic, Denmark, Estonia, Finland, France, Germany, Greece, Hungary, Iceland, Italy, Latvia, Luxembourg, Malta, the Netherlands, Norway, Poland, Portugal, Slovakia, Slovenia, Spain, Sweden and Switzerland).

If you aren't a national of a Schengen member country or a country on the Schengen visa-free list (see 🖵 http://italy.visahq.com/requirements), you'll need a Schengen visa (costing €60) to visit Italy. To obtain a Schengen visa, you must hold a passport or travel document recognised by all Schengen member states and valid for at least three months beyond the validity of the visa. You can apply for a Schengen visa, which is valid for 90 days within a six-month period, from the consulate of the country that's your main destination or the one you intend to visit first.

Schengen visa holders aren't permitted to live permanently or work in Italy (or any Schengen member country); business trips aren't considered to be employment. Foreigners who intend to take up employment or a self-employed activity in Italy may require an employment visa (see below), even if they're listed on the Schengen visa-free list.

A Schengen visa isn't the appropriate visa if you wish to remain in Italy (or any member state) for longer than 90 days, to study, take up employment or establish a trade or profession.

If you decide to stay longer than 90 days, you must obtain an extension of your Schengen visa from the local police headquarters, although this isn't a right and cannot be taken for granted (you need a good reason and proof of financial resources) and must obtain a permit to stay.

Application for a visa should be made at an Italian consulate abroad well in advance of your planned departure date. It can take up to a month to obtain a routine visa or up to 90 days in 'difficult' cases. Visas are usually valid for 60 days from the date of issue and may be valid for a single entry only or for multiple entries within a limited period. A visa is in the form of an adhesive sticker (not a stamp) inserted in your passport, which must be valid until at least three months **after** the visa expires.

Visas are issued for many reasons, each of which has its own abbreviation (*sigla*). These include tourism (A), business (B), religion (C), diplomatic service (D), domicile (DM), joining family (F), dependent work (L-1), self-employment (L-2), artistic work (L-3), medical care (M), mission (MS), study (S), sporting activity (SP), re-entry (R), transit (T), airport transit (TA) and visiting family (V).

The type of visa issued depends on the purpose of your visit and the length of your stay, and determines the type of permit to stay that's issued after you arrive in Italy. If you plan to stay in Italy for longer than six months, you must ensure that you obtain a visa that's valid for at least a year; otherwise you'll be able to obtain a permit to stay for only six months and won't be able to renew it.

Au pairs wishing to work in Italy are generally advised to obtain a study rather than a work visa if they're planning to stay in the country for longer than 90 days. Because the 'pocket money' they receive isn't considered a salary, the au pair agencies say that technically there's no need for them to obtain a work visa.

Some of the documentation you may need to apply for a visa, mainly concerning permission to work, must be obtained in Italy. Although your prospective employer usually handles this on your behalf, your presence in Italy can help to speed up the process. If you plan to start a business or work freelance, you must also register at the local tax office (*intendenza di finanza*) and chamber of commerce (*camera di commercio*) or professional registrar (*albo dei professionisti*), and present the documents from these agencies together with your visa application. This can be a costly and time-consuming process, as once the documentation is obtained you must return to your country of residence to apply for the visa. Nevertheless, it may be worthwhile.

Another reason you may decide to visit Italy to obtain documents in connection with a visa application is simply to obtain proof that you've been in Italy. This evidence may be important, as the Italian government is continually changing the immigration laws. For example, a law passed by the Italian government in 1998 included a remedy clause (*sanatoria*) stating that all non-EU citizens who could prove their presence in Italy before 27th March 1998 could apply for a permit to stay without having to obtain a visa from their country of residence. This wasn't the first time a new immigration law included this kind of clause, nor will it be the last.

Having obtained the necessary paperwork, an application for a visa must be made to your local Italian consulate with jurisdiction over your place of residence. It may be possible to make an application by post, but in other cases you're required to attend in person. If you decide to apply in person (or have no choice), bear in mind that there are invariably long queues at consulates in major cities (take a thick book).

The documentation required for a visa application depends on the purpose of your visit to Italy. All applicants require:

♦ a passport valid for at least three months beyond the validity of the requested visa, with a blank page to affix the visa sticker;

♦ a number of colour, passport-size photographs on a white background.

Depending on the purpose of your visit, you may also require some of the following (note that some consulates may require both originals and photocopies):

♦ proof of residence in the country from which you're applying;

♦ proof of travel arrangements showing your name and exact dates of entry into and exit from Italy (if applicable);

♦ proof of financial resources (see below);

♦ a health insurance certificate if you aren't eligible for health treatment under Italian social security or through your employer;

♦ an authorisation to work in Italy issued by the Italian Ministry of Labour if you're a non-EU national taking up employment (see below);

Mole Antonelliana, Turin

♦ proof of admission from an approved educational establishment if you're a student (see below);

♦ a marriage certificate (for non-EU nationals married to an Italian citizen or to a foreigner who's resident in Italy);

♦ written authorisation from a parent or guardian if you're under 18.

Many of the above documents must be translated into Italian. All translations must be done by a translator approved by your local consulate, a list of whom (*elenco di traduttori*) is provided by Italian consulates on request. Many documents need tax stamps (*marche da bollo*) affixed to them, and in many cases requests for official documents must be made on 'approved' lined paper (*carta da bollo*), to which a tax stamp must be attached. The standard stamp (*bollo*) for administrative documents (*atti civili*) costs around €11 and can be purchased from a tobacconist's shop (*tabaccaio*). There's also a fee for a visa, which can vary considerably.

If you require a visa to enter Italy and attempt to enter without one, you'll be refused entry. If you're in doubt as to whether you require a visa to enter Italy, enquire at an Italian consulate abroad before making travel plans.

Proof of Financial Resources

Proof of financial resources or financial support may take the form of bank statements, letters from banks confirming arrangements for the regular transfer of funds from abroad, or letters from family or friends guaranteeing regular support. Letters should be notarised. Students may submit a letter from an organisation or institution guaranteeing accommodation or evidence of a scholarship or grant. Retired people should take their pension book or copies of recent pension cheques. Proof of financial resources isn't required by someone coming to Italy to take up paid employment.

Authorisation to Work

Non-EU nationals intending to work in Italy require an 'entry visa for reasons of work' (*visto d'ingresso per motivi di lavoro*), which they must obtain from an Italian embassy or consulate in their home country or country of residence. However, work permits (*autorizzazione al lavoro*) are issued by the Ministry of Labour office (Ispettorato Provinciale del Lavoro) local to where you'll be working. These must in turn be authorised by the local police, who stamp them *nulla osta* (literally 'nothing hinders') on the back. A '*nulla osta*' must be obtained by your prospective employer in Italy and sent to you in your country of residence for presentation at an Italian consulate with your other documents. Be warned, however, that obtaining authorisation to work is a highly bureaucratic and time-consuming process. It can take a year or more, and unless you're employed by an Italian company in your own country, you're unlikely to find an employer in Italy who's willing to go to the trouble involved. See also page 17.

There's nothing to stop you visiting Italy as a tourist in order to find a job, but you cannot work without going home and applying for a work visa (which can take months to obtain). It's impossible to convert a tourist visa into a work visa, and therefore if you're a non-EU national and need a visa to work in Italy, you must obtain it before your arrival in the country.

Proof of Admission

Students require proof of admission from an approved school or university in Italy indicating when their studies start and end. The letter must either have the seal of the school or be notarised. If your studies are sponsored by an educational institution in your home country (or country of residence), you should also have a letter from the institution concerned confirming this. This, too, must contain the seal of the school or be notarised.

Family Members

If you're an EU national, members of your family, whatever their nationality, may go with you and live in Italy. Your family is defined as your spouse, children under 21 (or dependent on you), along with your parents and your spouse's parents, if they're also dependent on you. If you're a student, the right of residence is limited to your spouse and dependent children. If members of your family aren't EU nationals, they may, however, require an entry visa, which should be granted free of charge and without undue formalities.

There are two main types: the *visto per coesione familiare* and the *visto per ricongiungimento familiare*. The former is required when all family members are currently living outside Italy, while the latter is necessary when some family members are already living in the country. In the latter case, those living outside Italy must apply for a visa at an Italian consulate in their country of residence as usual, and their Italian relatives in Italy must also visit their local police headquarters to file an application for their relatives to join them. For both visas, in addition to the usual documents you also need documents proving your family connections, e.g. a marriage licence (*dispensa matrimoniale*).

☑ **SURVIVAL TIP**

Non-EU family members don't have the right to work in Italy unless they have their own work visa.

The right to travel enjoyed by non-EU members of your family under EU law isn't an independent right, and it applies only when they're accompanied by an Italian or EU national. Accordingly, they aren't entitled to the visa facilities available under EU legislation when they're travelling alone. On the other hand, non-EU members of your family don't require an entry visa if they wish to travel to another EU country, provided they're in possession of their identity document and residence permit (see page 63).

PERMIT TO STAY

Technically anyone visiting Italy for over a week who isn't staying in a hotel, boarding house or an official campsite should, by law, register at a local police station, although in practice this rarely happens. On the other hand, all (non-EU) foreigners (*extracomunitari*) planning to remain in Italy for longer than 90 days must apply for a 'permit to stay' at the local police headquarters (*questura*) within eight days of their arrival.

A permit to stay isn't a residence permit (see page 63), which must be applied for after you have your permit to stay if you wish to become a long-term resident. It can take up to three months to obtain a permit, which can be issued only for the purpose stated on your visa. There are many types of permit to stay, the most common of which include the following:

◆ *permesso di soggiorno per coesione familiare*: for the foreign spouse and children of an Italian or EU citizen when they move to Italy together;

◆ *permesso di soggiorno per lavoro*: a work permit for an employee (see **Employees** below);

◆ *permesso di soggiorno per lavoro autonomo/indipendente*: for independent or freelance workers (see **Self-employed** below);

◆ *permesso di soggiorno per studio*: for students (see **Students** below);

◆ *permesso di soggiorno per ricongiungimento familiare*: for the spouse, children (under 18) and dependent parents of foreigners married to Italian or EU citizens and also for family members from overseas who come to join others already in Italy (see **Family Members** above);

◆ *permesso di soggiorno per dimora*: for foreigners establishing residence in Italy who don't intend to work or study (see **Non-employed Residents** below).

There are also permits to stay for various other classes of person, including refugees and employees of religious missions. You may not apply for residence or study, take up employment or establish a business, trade or profession.

Unemployed EU nationals have the right to stay in Italy for a 'reasonable period' in order to look for a job. However, no matter how long you take to find a job, you cannot be asked to leave the country if you can prove that you're still seriously looking for employment and have a real chance of finding work (for example, you still have interviews to attend or tests to undergo). In certain circumstances, if you're receiving unemployment benefit in one EU country, you may continue to receive that benefit for up to three months in Italy. To do so, you must apply to the authorities in the country that pays your unemployment benefit.

Employees

If you're an EU national (your passport must show that you have the right of abode in an EU country), you don't require official approval to live or work in Italy, although you're still required to apply for a residence permit after three months.

Non-EU nationals require an 'entry visa for reasons of work' (*visto d'ingresso per motivi di lavoro*) – see **Authorisation to Work** on page 59.

Self-employed

If you're an EU national, you can be self-employed (*lavoro in proprio*) or a sole trader (*commerciante in proprio*) in Italy, although you must meet certain legal requirements and register with the appropriate organisations, e.g. the local chamber of commerce (*camera di commercio*). You must provide evidence of your status, such as membership of a professional or trade body, a VAT number, or registration on a trade register.

Students

Non-EU nationals wishing to study in Italy must prove that they're enrolled (or have been accepted) at an approved educational establishment for the principal purpose of following a course of education or vocational training. You must also prove that you're covered by health insurance and provide a declaration in writing that you have sufficient resources to pay for your studies and for living expenses for yourself and any members of your family accompanying you.

Foreign students wishing to attend university in Italy should apply to the Italian consulate in

their country of residence. You will be sent a list of the documents required, which include an application form; you're required to select four universities in order of preference. Once the consulate has received a completed application, it will send EU citizens an identity card stamped with a consul's visa, while non-EU students receive a student visa. You must present these documents to the police headquarters within eight days of arriving in Italy in order to obtain a student's permit to stay (*permesso di soggiorno per studio*) which is valid for a maximum of one year only.

Non-employed Residents

Retired and non-active EU nationals don't require a visa before moving to Italy, but must apply for a residence permit. All non-employed residents must prove that they have an adequate income (*reddito*) or financial resources to live in Italy without working. You're usually considered to have adequate resources if your income is at least equal to the basic Italian state pension of around €8,000 per year for each adult member of a family (although you're unlikely to be able to live on it!). This can be a regular income such as a salary or pension, or funds held in a bank account.

All foreign residents (including EU residents) who don't qualify for medical treatment under the Italian national health service (see page 183) must have private health insurance and be able to support themselves without resorting to state funds. EU nationals in receipt of a state pension are usually eligible for medical treatment under the health service, but require a European Health Insurance Card (EHIC) from their home country's social security administration as evidence (see page 208.

If you're an EU national and have lived and worked in Italy for over three years, you're entitled to remain there after you've reached retirement age, although if you retire before the official retirement age you won't be entitled to a state pension.

Frontier Workers

Frontier workers are defined as people working in Italy but residing outside the country and returning there at least once a week. Frontier workers don't require a permit to stay but must apply for a frontier worker's card at the police headquarters nearest to their place of employment and produce evidence of their employment status and residence abroad. EU rules on social security contain certain specific provisions for cross-border workers who are covered by EU social security legislation in the same way as all the other categories of people. You're entitled to receive sickness benefits in kind in either your country of residence or your country of employment, but if you're registered as unemployed you're entitled to claim unemployment benefit only in your country of residence.

Applications

All applications for permits to stay (for non-EU residents) must be made at the local police headquarters (*questura*). The validity of permits varies from six months to an indefinite period and they may or may not be renewable, depending on the original purpose.

The documents required for a permit application vary according to your circumstances and nationality, therefore you should check in advance and obtain a list;

however, don't believe anything unless it's official and in writing (and even then it may be wrong!).

All applicants require the following:

♦ a valid passport, with a visa if necessary, and a photocopy of the information pages, including the visa if applicable;

♦ a completed application form – IPS 209 (blue) for first time applications or IPS 210 (green) for a renewal – available from the local police headquarters;

♦ your previous permit (*permesso*) if you're renewing one;

♦ two or three colour (white background) passport-size photographs;

♦ a tax stamp (*marca da bollo*) to the value of €40 (non-EU nationals only).

The following are required for certain people, depending on their status (or at the whim of your local *questura*):

♦ a birth certificate (*estratto di nascita dell'Anagrafe*) for each child under 18 to be included on a permit;

♦ proof of residence, which may consist of a copy of a lease or purchase contract or an electricity bill; if you're a lodger, the owner must provide an attestation (*attestazione*) that you're living in his home;

♦ a photocopy of your spouse's permit if he's a foreigner or of his identity documents if he's Italian;

♦ proof of health insurance or a medical certificate (e.g. students) if you aren't

covered by Italian social security (or another country's social security system);

♦ an admission letter to an educational institution (for students);

♦ proof of financial resources (for non-employed or retired people);

♦ a family-status certificate (*stato di famiglia*), available from your town hall (*comune*) in Italy, or your marriage certificate (*certificato di matrimonio*) or divorce certificate (*sentenza di divorzio*) or other papers relating to your marital status; if you were married abroad you also need a consular declaration (translated and authenticated) to the effect that you're married;

♦ a criminal record (*fedina penale*) certificate – many countries don't issue these, although you should be able to get the police or a government bureau in your home country to issue a 'statement of good conduct', which may satisfy the Italian authorities;

♦ a declaration from a prospective employer stating his intention to hire you (or that you've started work, if permitted) and describing your professional capacity, and a stamped authorisation to work (see **Authorisation to Work** on page 59);

♦ a VAT number (*partita IVA*) or a letter of exemption and a chamber of commerce registration certificate (*iscrizione alla camera di commercio*) or a letter from the company where you're accredited if you're an independent worker.

> Certain documents must be notarised by a public notary (*notaio*) and all copies should be stamped 'official copy' (*copia ufficiale*) at the town hall or *questura*. Original documents must always be presented along with official copies.

If you don't have all the required documents, you'll be sent away to obtain them. Certain documents must be translated by a notarised translator (*traduttore autenticato*) and authenticated (*vidimato*). It isn't recommended to have documents translated in advance as it's expensive, and the requirements often vary according to the area or office and your nationality.

Renewal

An application for the renewal of a permit to stay (made on a green form) must be made well before its expiry date. When you renew a permit to stay, you must reconfirm your status and provide the same documentary evidence as for the original application. If you're self-employed, you need a photocopy of your latest tax return and the receipt for payment. If you're working in Italy, a renewal may be valid for one, two or four years, or even indefinitely (a so-called permanent permit to stay – *tempo indeterminato*), depending on how long you've been working there and other factors. There's a fee for the renewal of a permit to stay, and fines for late renewal or failing to renew your permit.

Moving House

When you move house, you must inform the *questura* with jurisdiction over your new place of residence and produce proof of your new address. Your permit to stay is updated with your new address. This is particularly important if you're in the process of renewing your permit to stay, as the change of address must be recorded before a new permit can be issued.

RESIDENCE PERMIT

Obtaining a permit to stay (see above) doesn't constitute registration as a resident (*residenza anagrafica*). For this you must apply to the registry office (*ufficio anagrafe*) at your local town hall (*comune*). To obtain a residence permit (*certificato di residenza*) you require a 'suitable' habitual residence (*dimora abituale*). Although all residences are potentially suitable, some rental contracts forbid you to use an apartment's address for this purpose. (Such rental contracts are mainly used with foreigners so that landlords can regain possession of their property more easily should they wish to do so. Eviction of any person from their legal residence is almost impossible in Italy and landlords don't want to take any unnecessary risks with foreigners.)

To apply for a residence permit you require the following documents:

- a valid passport with a relevant visa (if applicable);

- a valid permit to stay if applicable (see above);

- a completed declaration of residence (*dichiarazione di residenza*) form, which is available from your town hall (*comune*);

- a consular declaration (*dichiarazione consolare*) from your country's consulate in Italy containing your name and surname, father's name, mother's name, place and date of birth, civil status (with name of spouse if married), along with the date and place of the wedding, or the date of your spouse's death if you're a widow or widower), nationality, and details of other members of your family.

Once your application has been received, you're given a certificate stating that you've applied which is valid for three months and can be renewed if necessary. A decision on whether to grant you a residence permit must be taken within six months of your application. A city police officer (*vigile urbano*) will visit the address that you've given as your habitual residence to ensure that you actually live there. When your permit has been granted you receive a notification that it's ready for collection from the *ufficio anagrafe*. The fee for the issue (or renewal) of a residence permit is the same as that for the identity card issued to Italian nationals (currently €5).

A residence permit for an EU national is valid for at least five years and is automatically renewable, while a student's permit is valid for one year only but is renewable. Family members are issued with residence permits for the same period as the principal applicant. A residence permit remains valid even if you're absent from Italy for up to six months or if you're doing military service in your country of origin.

> **☑ SURVIVAL TIP**
>
> If you change residence within Italy, you must declare it at the police headquarters of your new residence within 15 days of moving home. Your new address is entered on your residence permit.

Despite the hassles, having the right of residence (*il diritto di soggiorno*) entitles you to ship your personal effects from abroad without paying duty or VAT, buy land or property, buy and register a car, open a resident bank account, apply for an Italian driving licence, obtain healthcare from the local health authority, and send your children to a state school.

Grand Canal, Venice

When you've been granted resident status, you're entitled to most of the rights and privileges accorded to Italian citizens, apart from the right to vote in Italian parliamentary elections. If you're staying in Italy for less than 90 days a year, you aren't legally required to apply for residence, but for anyone planning to stay in Italy for more than a few months, applying for residence is likely to be highly desirable. When you're resident in Italy, you need to show your residence permit for certain transactions such as converting your driving licence and obtaining a residential electricity contract.

Foreigners who have obtained a residence permit can obtain an Italian identity card (*carta di identità*) from their local registry office.

Renewal, Rejection & Cancellation

You may renew your residence permit by carrying out the same formalities as when you first applied (indicating any change in status), except that this time you don't need to produce a visa, medical certificate or proof of your ascendants'/descendants' relationship to you if you've already provided it. If, at the time of renewal, you've been involuntarily unemployed for more than 12 months in succession, your residence permit may be renewed for a limited period, which may not be less than 12 months. The authorities may refuse to renew your permit again if you're still unemployed when it next expires.

If your application for the issue or renewal of a residence permit is rejected or if a deportation order is served on you, you must be notified of the relevant decision and the reasons, except where considerations of state security prevent this. You cannot be refused a residence permit purely on the grounds that the identity documents with which you entered the country have expired.

If you're leaving Italy permanently, you must cancel your residence permit at the *sala dei certificati* section of the local police headquarters and receive confirmation. This permits you to export your personal effects from Italy without paying taxes.

36	6:10pm	On
34	7:14pm	On Ti
33	12:48pm	On Tim
20	6:05pm	On Tim
21	3:08pm	On Time
22	4:03pm	On Time
22	7:55pm	On Time
24	11:01am	On Time
37	7:06pm	LANDE
	11:11pm	LAN
	11:10am	Delay

4.
ARRIVAL

On arrival in Italy, your first task is to negotiate immigration and customs. Fortunately this presents few problems for most people, particularly nationals of EEA and 'Schengen' countries. However, visitors from many other countries require a visa (see page 57). Italy has many frontier crossing points, although entry for those with a visa is restricted to certain road/rail crossings and major airports only (as stated in a visa). A list is available from Italian consulates and embassies. Non-EEA foreigners planning to remain in the country for longer than 90 days must apply for a permit to stay within eight days of their arrival (see page 60).

IMMIGRATION

Italy is a signatory to the Schengen Agreement (named after a Luxembourg village on the Moselle River where it was signed), which came into effect on 26th March 1995 and introduced an open-border policy between member countries (most Western European countries). Under the agreement, immigration checks and passport controls take place when you first arrive in a member country, after which you can travel freely between other Schengen countries (see also **Visas** on page 57).

If you're a non-EU national and arrive in Italy by air or sea from outside the EU, you must go through immigration (*immigrazione*) for non-EU citizens. Officially, Italian immigration officials should check your passport, although this doesn't always happen. If you have a single-entry visa, it will be cancelled by the immigration official. If you require a visa to enter Italy and attempt to enter without one you'll be refused entry. Some people may wish to get a stamp in their passport as confirmation of their date of entry into Italy.

If you're a non-EU national coming to Italy to work, study or live, you may be asked to show documentary evidence, e.g. a return ticket, proof of accommodation, health insurance and financial resources, including cash, travellers' cheques and credit cards. The onus is on you to prove that you're who you say you are and won't violate Italy's immigration laws. Immigration officials aren't required to prove that you'll break the immigration laws and can refuse you entry on the grounds of suspicion only. Young people may be liable to interrogation, particularly long-haired youths with 'strange' attire.

> ☑ **SURVIVAL TIP**
>
> Italian immigration officials are usually polite and efficient, although they're occasionally a little over-zealous in their attempts to exclude illegal immigrants, and certain nationalities or racial groups (e.g. Africans and Albanians) may experience harassment.

CUSTOMS

The Single European Act, which came into effect on 1st January 1993, created a single trading market and changed the rules regarding customs (*dogana*) for EU nationals. The shipment of personal (household) effects to Italy from another EU country is no longer subject to customs formalities, although an

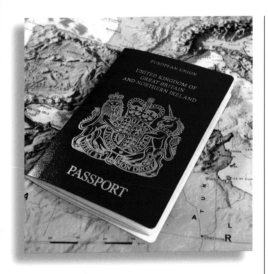

If you enter Italy by road, you may drive through a border post without stopping (most are now unmanned anyway). However, any goods and pets that you're carrying mustn't be subject to any prohibitions or restrictions. Customs officials can still stop anyone for a spot check, e.g. to check for drugs or illegal immigrants, anywhere in Italy. If you arrive at a seaport by private boat there are no particular customs formalities, although you must show the boat's registration papers on request. A vessel registered outside the EU may remain in Italy for a maximum of six months in any calendar year, after which it must be exported or imported (when duty and tax must be paid). Foreign-registered vehicles and boats mustn't be lent or rented to anyone while in Italy.

Visitors

Your belongings aren't subject to duty or valued added tax (VAT) when you visit Italy for up to six months (183 days). This applies to private cars, camping vehicles (including trailers or caravans), motorcycles, aircraft, boats and personal effects. Goods may be imported without formality, provided their nature and quantity doesn't imply any commercial aim (there may be limits on some items for non-EU nationals). Any means of transport or personal effects imported duty-free mustn't be sold or given away in Italy, and must be re-exported when you leave the country.

Residence

If you're an EU or non-EU resident planning to take up permanent or temporary residence in Italy, you're permitted to import your furniture and personal effects free of duty. These include vehicles, mobile homes, pleasure boats and aircraft. However, for non-EU residents to qualify for duty-free importation, articles must have been owned and used for at least six months. VAT (*IVA*) must be paid on all items owned for less than six months that weren't purchased in the EU. If goods were purchased in the EU, a VAT receipt must be produced.

All belongings should be imported within six months of the date of your change of residence, although they may be imported in a number of consignments (but it's best to have only one). If there's more than one shipment, subsequent consignments should

inventory must be provided. Anyone arriving in Italy from outside the EU (including EU citizens) is subject to customs checks and limitations on what may be imported duty-free.

There are no restrictions on the import or export of funds within the EU, but if you're arriving from or leaving for a country outside the EU, you may only import or export up to €10,000 in any combination of foreign or Italian currency and travellers' cheques. Amounts over €10,000 (e.g. to buy a home) must be declared in order to prevent money laundering (and provide statistical data for the Banca d'Italia). Information about duty-free allowances can be found on page 277 and pets on page 292.

Prohibited & Restricted Goods

The importation of certain goods is prohibited or restricted. This applies in particular to animal products, plants, wild fauna and flora and products derived from them, live animals, medicines and medical products (except for prescribed medicines), guns and ammunition, certain goods and technologies with a dual civil/military purpose, and works of art and collectors' items. If you're unsure whether any goods that you're planning to import fall into the above categories, you should check with Italian customs. Visitors arriving in Italy from 'exotic' regions, e.g. Africa, South America, and the Middle and Far East, may find themselves under close scrutiny from customs and security officials looking for illegal drugs.

be cleared through the same customs office. An inventory (in English and Italian) of all items to be imported must be approved by your local Italian consulate abroad (it will be stamped and a copy returned to you), together with proof of residence in your former country and proof of settlement in Italy (i.e. a permit to stay – see page 60). If you fail to follow the correct procedure, you may encounter problems and delays.

If you use a removal company to transport your belongings to Italy, it will usually provide all the necessary forms and take care of the paperwork.

☑ SURVIVAL TIP

Always keep a copy of all forms and communications with customs officials, both in Italy and in your previous country of residence. You should have an official record of the export of valuables from any country in case you wish to re-import them later.

EMBASSY REGISTRATION

Nationals of some countries are required to register with their local embassy or consulate after taking up residence in Italy. For other foreigners, registration isn't usually mandatory, although most embassies like to keep a record of their country's citizens resident in Italy (it helps to justify their existence). From your point of view, it makes it easier for them to find you in an emergency. For a list of embassies see **Appendix A**.

FINDING HELP

One of the most important tasks facing new arrivals in Italy is how and where to obtain help with essential everyday tasks such as buying a car and obtaining medical help and insurance. This book was written in response to this need. However, in addition to the comprehensive general information provided here, you'll require detailed local information. How successful you are at finding this depends on your employer (if applicable), the town or

area where you live (those who live in major cities are usually better served than those who inhabit small towns), your nationality, Italian proficiency and sex (women are usually better served than men, through numerous women's clubs). There's an abundance of information available in Italian, but little in English and other foreign languages. For example, bookshops may have some interesting publications about the local region, and tourist and information offices are also useful sources of information.

An additional problem is that much of the available information isn't intended for foreigners and their particular needs. Some companies may have a department or staff whose job is to help new arrivals settle in, or they may contract this task out to a relocation company. Unfortunately, many employers in Italy seem totally unaware of (or uninterested in) the integration problems faced by foreign employees, though some businesses (particularly multi-national companies) produce booklets and leaflets containing useful information about clubs or activities in the area.

You may find that other expatriates and work colleagues will offer advice based on their own experiences and mistakes. **But take care!** Although they mean well, you're likely to receive conflicting advice or information that's irrelevant to your particular situation. Your local community is usually an excellent source of reliable information, but you need to speak Italian to benefit from it.

If a woman lives in or near a major town, she is able to turn to many English-speaking women's clubs and organisations for help. The single foreign male must usually fend for himself, although there are men's expatriate clubs in some areas and mixed social clubs throughout the country. Among the best sources of information and help for women are the American Women's Clubs (AWC) located in major cities. AWC provide comprehensive information in English about both local matters and topics of more general interest, and many provide data sheets, booklets and orientation programmes for newcomers to the area. Membership of the organisations is sometimes limited to Americans or those with active links to the US, e.g. through study, work or a spouse who works for a US company or the US government, but most publications and orientation programmes are available to others for a small fee. AWCs are part of the Federation of American Women's Clubs Overseas (FAWCO), which can be contacted through its website (🖳 www.fawco.org). There are women's clubs for female foreigners in many cities, including Bari, Genoa, Naples, Padua (International Ladies Group), Rome (American Women's Association) and Turin.

There are many other social clubs and expatriate organisations for foreigners in Italy, whose members can help you find your way around. They may, however, be difficult to locate, as most clubs are run by volunteers and operate out of the president's or secretary's house and they rarely bother to advertise or take out a phone listing. If you ask around among your neighbours or colleagues, it's possible to find various Anglo-Italian 'friendship' clubs or English-speaking organisations. Finally, don't forget to check the internet, where local newspapers, government offices, clubs and organisations often have websites and there are expatriate sites with useful message boards or forums (see **Appendix C**). Contacts can also be found through expatriate magazines and newspapers such as *Wanted in Rome* and *The Informer* (Milan), an internet magazine (see **Appendix B** for a list).

Most embassies and consulates in Italy (see **Appendix A**) can provide their nationals with local information, including the names of lawyers, interpreters, doctors, dentists, schools, and social and expatriate organisations.

CHECKLISTS

You may find the following checklists helpful when planning your move to Italy.

Before Arrival

The following is a summary of the tasks that should (if possible) be completed before your arrival in Italy:

◆ Check that your family's passports are valid!

◆ Obtain a visa, if necessary, for you and all your family members (see **Chapter 3**). Obviously this **must** be done **before** your arrival in Italy.

◆ If applicable, visit Italy before your move to obtain permission to work there (see **Chapter 1**).

◆ If possible, visit Italy before your move to compare communities and schools and arrange for schooling for your children (see **Chapter 9**).

◆ Find temporary or permanent accommodation and buy a car if you'll need one. If you purchase a car in Italy, you need to register it and arrange insurance (see **Chapter 11**).

◆ Arrange the shipment of your personal effects to Italy (see **Chapter 5**).

◆ Arrange health (and travel) insurance for your family. This is essential if you aren't already covered by a private insurance policy and won't be covered by the Italian national health service (see **Chapters 12 & 13**).

◆ Open a bank account in Italy and transfer funds – you can open an account with some Italian banks from abroad or even via the internet. You may also find it convenient to obtain some euros before you arrive, which will save you having to change money immediately on arrival. (See **Chapter 14**.)

◆ Obtain an international driving permit, if necessary (see **Chapter 11**).

◆ Obtain an international credit or charge card, which will prove invaluable during your first few months in Italy (see **Chapter 14**).

◆ Obtain as many credit references as possible; for example, from banks, mortgage companies, credit card companies, credit agencies, companies with which you've had accounts, and references from professionals such as lawyers and accountants. These will help you obtain credit and a mortgage in Italy.

If you're planning to stay long term, you should also take all your family's official documents with you, plus certified copies, official translations and numerous passport-size photographs (students should take around a dozen). These may include birth certificates, driving licences, marriage certificate, divorce papers or death certificate (if a widow or widower), educational diplomas and professional certificates, employment references and curricula vitae, school records and student ID cards, medical and dental records, bank account and credit card details, insurance policies (plus records of no-claims' allowances), and receipts for any valuables. (See **Chapter 3** for more information.)

After Arrival

The following is a summary of the tasks to be completed after arrival in Italy (if not done before):

♦ On arrival at an Italian airport, port or border post, have your visa cancelled and your passport stamped, as applicable.

♦ If you aren't taking a car with you, you may wish to hire or buy one locally (see **Chapter 11**). Note that it's practically impossible to get around in rural areas without a vehicle.

♦ In the few days after your arrival, complete the following:

– Apply for a permit to stay (see page 60).

– Register with your local social security office if you're self-employed (see page 197).

– Apply for a fiscal code (*codice fiscale*) from your local tax office (see page 213).

– Register with your local embassy or consulate (see page 69.

– Open a post office or bank account (see pages 97 and 216 respectively) and give the details to your employer and any companies that you plan to pay by direct debit or standing order (such as utility companies).

– Register with a local doctor (see page 184).

– Arrange schooling for your children (see **Chapter 9**).

After arrival you should arrange whatever insurance is necessary, including health insurance, household insurance, car insurance and third party liability insurance (see **Chapter 13** and, for car insurance see page 162).

Isle of Procida, Gulf of Naples

Ostuni, Puglia

5.
ACCOMMODATION

In most areas of Italy, finding accommodation to rent or buy isn't difficult, provided your requirements aren't too unusual. There are, however, a few exceptions. For example, in major cities such as Rome and Milan, rented accommodation is in high demand and short supply, and rents can be high. Accommodation accounts for around 25 per cent of the average Italian family's budget, but can be up to 50 per cent in the major cities. Property prices and rents vary considerably according to the region and city, and have increased steadily in all major cities in recent years. For example, an apartment renting for €600 per month in Naples would cost up to €1,750 per month in Milan or Rome. In cities and large towns, apartments are much more common than detached houses, which are rare and prohibitively expensive.

The average Italian lives with his parents until the age of around 30. Over 80 per cent of Italian homes are owner-occupied (one of the highest rates in the world), around the same as in Spain, compared with some 70 per cent in the UK, 55 per cent in France and just 40 per cent in Germany and Switzerland. Many Italians also own second homes in the country (perhaps in their native village) or in a mountain or coastal resort.

TEMPORARY ACCOMMODATION

On arrival in Italy, you may find it necessary to stay in temporary accommodation for a few weeks or months, e.g. before moving into permanent accommodation or while waiting for your furniture to arrive. Some employers provide rooms, self-contained apartments or hostels for employees and their families, although this is rare and usually for a limited period only. Many hotels and bed and breakfast establishments cater for long-term guests and offer reduced weekly or monthly rates. In most areas, particularly in Rome and other main cities, serviced apartments are available. These are self-contained furnished apartments with their own bathrooms and kitchens, which are cheaper and more convenient than a hotel, particularly for families. Serviced apartments are usually rented on a weekly basis. In most provincial regions, self-catering holiday accommodation (see page 234) is available, although this is very expensive during the main holiday season (June-August).

For information about hotels, budget accommodation and self-catering, see **Accommodation** on page 231.

RELOCATION CONSULTANTS

If you're fortunate enough to have your move to Italy paid for by your employer, it's likely that he'll arrange for a relocation consultant to handle the details. There are fewer relocation consultants in Italy than in some other European countries and they usually deal exclusively with corporate clients with plenty of money to pay their fees. Fees depend on the services required, packages usually ranging from around €1,850 to €8,500. The main service provided by relocation consultants is finding

Rome

accommodation (either to rent or to buy) and arranging viewings.

Other housing services include conducting negotiations, drawing up contracts, arranging mortgages, organising surveys and insurance, and handling the move. Consultants also provide reports on local schools, health services, public transport, sports and social facilities, and other amenities and services. Some companies provide daily advice and help, and assistance in dealing with Italian officials, e.g. residence procedures. Finding rental accommodation for single people or couples without children can usually be accomplished in a few weeks, while locating family homes may take up to four weeks, depending on the location and requirements. You should usually allow two to three months between your initial visit and moving into a purchased property.

ITALIAN HOMES

Italian homes and living standards used to be fairly basic, particularly in rural areas, where many homes had no bathroom or toilet. However, with the huge rise in the standard (and cost) of living in the last few decades, Italian homes have been transformed and today's average Italian is better housed than many other Europeans. In cities, people generally live in apartments, houses being rare and excessively expensive. Italian apartments are usually surprisingly small and it's

unusual to find apartments with four or more bedrooms; even three-bedroom apartments aren't easy to find. Most do, however, have two bathrooms. New detached homes (called villas) are generally luxurious internally, but often have bland or even ugly exteriors. In contrast to modern homes, old buildings are an architectural delight and contain a wealth of attractive period features. Whether old or new, Italians take great pride in their homes and no expense is spared to make them comfortable and beautiful.

Homes are as varied as the climate and people, but one thing they have in common is sturdy building materials. The exterior may be made of wood, stone, brick or other (usually fire-resistant) materials. Interior walls are usually white *stucco* plaster (*intonaco*), which may be painted in pastel colours and makes a perfect backdrop for paintings and tapestries, while bedroom walls are often papered. Wood floors (*parquet*) are common in northern Italian homes, but are considered a luxury in the rest of Italy and therefore generally reserved for the master bedroom. Marble or *travertino* is often used in entrance halls (*ingressi*), corridors (*corridoi*) and living rooms (*saloni*), while kitchens (*cucine*) and bathrooms (*bagni*) are generally enhanced by beautiful ceramic tiles (for which Italy is famous). Bathrooms are fitted with a toilet (*gabinetto*), washbasin (*lavandino*), bidet (*bidé*) and shower (*doccia*) or bath (*vasca*), or perhaps a bath with a shower attachment. Luxury homes often sport a Jacuzzi (*idromassaggio*). When there's no separate utility or laundry room (*lavanderia*), the hot-water heater (*scaldabagno*) and washing machine (*lavatrice*) are usually stored in the main or 'service' (*servizio*) bathroom.

Italian homes are completely empty when purchased, except perhaps for the bathroom porcelain and the kitchen sink. All furnishings and appliances are chosen and bought by the new owner, who can have the kitchen fitted by a local carpenter-artisan or buy factory-produced units. Ovens can be electric or mains gas (which is available in most urban areas) and country properties may also have an outside pizza/bread oven (*forno a legna*) and sometimes a *tinello* or *taverna* that acts as a family room or a summer kitchen/dining room. Very few Italians use tumble driers (the sun and wind suffice), but washing machines are as common as televisions. If you live in a rural area, you may find a public washhouse (*lavatoio*), which is good for washing voluminous items such as curtains, in addition to being a good place to catch up on local gossip.

Country properties that haven't been restored rarely have central heating ('What you don't spend in wood, you spend in wool' is an old Italian saying), but numerous fireplaces. The stone walls of older homes (which may be over one metre thick) keep out the cold in winter, thus reducing heating (*riscaldamento*) costs, while in summer they act as insulation against the heat. In northern Italy and mountainous areas, double-glazing is common. Heating systems may consist of an oil-fired furnace, mains gas or gas bottles in rural areas. In apartments (*condominio*), hot water and heating are centralised and paid for along with other *condominio* fees, which may include the cleaning of common areas (*servizio di condomini*), a porter (*portiere*) and gardener (*giardiniere*).

In old rural homes, the fireplace (*camino*) plays an important role, being used for heating and cooking as well as for atmosphere. (Most city dwellers dream of having a fireplace, while

many country homeowners would like to have central heating!) Sometimes the fireplace surround is missing, as old buildings are often 'stripped' of architectural detail, although replacements can be bought from architectural salvage dealers. An old fireplace surround in marble or *peperino* costs between €1,500 and €5,500, but a local artisan can make a new one to order for much less. If you suspect that a room once had a fireplace, you can 'sound' the walls to find the flue, which can then be reopened. Windows are usually protected by shutters (*persiane*), which are often closed at night to keep heat in and prying eyes out. In city apartments they're known as *tapparelle* or *avvolgenti* (rolling shutters) and are made of metal, wood or plastic slats. They're raised and lowered manually with cords (that break frequently) or with an electric motor.

Vocabulary for Home-seekers

Italian	English
arredato/ammobiliato	furnished
ascensore	lift/elevator
camera doppia	twin bedroom
camera matrimoniale	double bedroom
camera singola	single bedroom
condizionato	air-conditioning
Monolocale	bed-sit/studio
no agenzia	private landlord
non-arredato/non-ammobiliato	unfurnished
partzialmente arredato	part-furnished
posto auto/moto (*coperto*)	(covered) parking
ultimo piano	top floor
vuoto	empty/unfurnished

BUYING PROPERTY

Italians aren't very mobile and move house much less frequently than the Americans and British. More Italians own their own homes than the inhabitants of most other EU countries, although they don't generally buy property as an investment, but as a home for life. Buying property in Italy is usually a good long-term investment and is preferable to renting. However, if you're staying only for a short period, you may be better off renting. It generally isn't worth buying a home in Italy unless you plan to stay for the medium to long term, say a minimum of five years and preferably 10 to 15, and you shouldn't expect to make a quick profit, although there's no capital gains tax on property.

Provided you avoid the most expensive areas, property is inexpensive compared with many other European countries, although the fees associated with a purchase add an average of around 12 per cent to the cost. Property experts tip prices in Italy's largest cities to increase by 0.6 per cent in the first six months of 2011 and 1.3 per cent in the following six months. The further south you go, the lower the prices are, while in the north property values seem to have risen by about 10 per cent in the more popular areas over the last ten years or so. Property prices rise faster than average in some fashionable areas, although this is generally reflected in higher purchase prices (in recent years, prices have risen quite sharply in the most popular major cities such as Rome, Milan and Florence).

As when buying property anywhere, it's never wise to be in too much of a hurry. Have a good look around your preferred area(s) and make sure that you have a clear picture of the relative prices and the kinds of property available. There's a huge variety of properties in Italy, ranging from derelict farmhouses requiring complete restoration to new luxury apartments and villas with all modern conveniences. Some people set themselves impossible deadlines in which to buy a property (e.g. a few days or a week) and often end up bitterly regretting their impulsive decision. Although it's a common practice, mixing a holiday with a property purchase isn't recommended, as most people are inclined to make poor business decisions when their mind is on play rather than work. To reduce the chance of making an expensive error when buying in an unfamiliar region, it's often prudent to rent for 6 to 12 months, taking in the worst part of the year (weather-wise). This allows you to become familiar with the region and the weather, and gives you plenty of time to look around for a permanent home at your

leisure. There's no shortage of properties for sale in Italy and whatever kind of property you're looking for, you'll have an abundance to choose from. Wait until you find your 'dream' home and then think about it for another week or two before signing a contract.

☑ **SURVIVAL TIP**

Once a purchase contract is signed, you may not be able to back out without losing your deposit.

To get an idea of property prices in different regions, check the prices of properties advertised in English-language property magazines and Italian newspapers, magazines and property journals (see **Appendix B**). Property price indexes for various regions are published by some Italian property magazines (e.g. *Ville & Casali*), although these should be taken as a rough guide only. Before deciding on the price, make sure you know **exactly** what's included, as it isn't unusual for Italians to strip a house or apartment bare when selling and remove the kitchen sink, toilets, light fittings and even the light switches! If applicable, have fixtures and fittings listed in the contract.

When you buy a home in Italy, you should go to the town hall (*municipio*) to register your ownership. After this date, all bills for local services are sent automatically and are payable at a post office or local bank (or by direct debit).

For anyone planning to buy a home in Italy, our sister publication, ***Buying a Home in Italy*** by David Hampshire, is essential reading. A comprehensive list of other books is contained in **Appendix B**.

RENTED ACCOMMODATION

If you're planning to stay in Italy for only a few years (say less than five), renting is usually advisable. It's also the answer for those who don't want the trouble, expense and restrictions associated with buying a property. In fact, if you're looking for a permanent home in Italy, it's prudent to rent for a period until you know exactly what you want, how much you wish to pay and where you want to live. This is particularly important for those who don't know Italy well, allowing you to become familiar with an area, its weather, amenities and the local people, to meet other foreigners who have made their homes in Italy and share their experiences, and not least, to discover the cost of living at first hand. This section is concerned with long-term rentals and not short-term holiday rentals (for information about holiday rentals see **Self-catering** on page 234).

Italy has a strong rental market and it's possible to rent every kind of property, from a tiny studio apartment (bedsit or *monolocale*) to a huge rambling castle (*castello*). Rental properties are mostly privately owned, but include properties owned by companies and public housing owned by local councils. If you're looking for a home for less than a year, you're better off looking for a furnished property. Most rental properties are let unfurnished (*non-ammobiliato*), particularly for lets longer than a year, and long-term furnished (*ammobiliato*) properties are difficult to find. Bear in mind that in Italy, unfurnished means completely empty, except perhaps for the bathroom porcelain and kitchen sink. There will be no kitchen cupboards, appliances, light fittings, curtains or carpets, although you may be able to buy these from the departing tenant. Semi-furnished apartments usually have kitchen cupboards and bathroom fixtures, and possibly a few pieces of furniture, while furnished properties tend to be fully equipped, including crockery, bedding and possibly towels.

Your success in finding a suitable property will depend on many factors, not least the kind of rental you're seeking (a one-bedroom apartment is easier to find than a four-bedroom detached house), how much you want to pay and the area where you wish to live.

Finding a Rental Property

There are a number of ways of finding a property to rent, including the following:

♦ Ask friends, relatives and acquaintances to help spread the word, particularly if you're looking in the area where you already live. A lot of rental properties are found by word

of mouth, particularly in major cities, where it's almost impossible to find somewhere with a reasonable rent unless you have connections.

♦ Check the small advertisements in local newspapers and magazines (see below).

♦ Look for properties with a 'to rent' (*affittasi* or *da affittare*) sign in the window.

♦ Visit accommodation and letting agents. Most cities and large towns have estate agents (*agenzie immobiliari*) who also act as letting agents. Look under *Agenzie Immobiliari* in the *Yellow Pages*. It's often better to deal with an agent than directly with owners, particularly with regard to contracts and other legal matters.

♦ Look for advertisements in shop windows and on bulletin boards in shopping centres, supermarkets, universities, colleges and company offices.

♦ Check newsletters published by churches, clubs and expatriate organisations, and their notice boards.

To find accommodation through small advertisements (*piccola pubblicità – affittasi appartamento*) in local newspapers you

Type of Property	Rome	Milan	Turin	Naples
Rental Costs				
Monthly Rental				
Studio/bedsitter (30m²)	€600 to €1,200	€550 to €600	€390 to €570	€510 to €540[3]
1 bedroom (50m²)	€850 to €1,250	€700 to €1,200	€450 to €750	€550 to €750
2 bedrooms (80m²)	€1,360 to €1,840	€1,040 to €1,360	€750 to €880	€880 to €1,200
3 bedrooms (100m²)	€1,700 to €2,300	€1,200 to €1,600	€800 to €1,000	€900 to €1,500

must usually be quick off the mark. Buy newspapers as soon as they're published and start phoning straight away. The best days for advertisements are usually Fridays and Saturdays. You can also view rental advertisements on the internet, and all major newspapers have websites (see **Newspapers, Magazines & Books** on page 273).

Other sources include expatriate publications published in major cities such as *Wanted in Rome* (see **Appendix B**) and small newspapers such as *Porta Portese* (Wednesdays and Saturdays) in Rome, *La Pulce* (Florence) and *Secondamano* (Milan) – there are equivalents in most cities. Some estate agents also provide apartment listings in their magazines, such as *Solo Casa* in Rome, although these may be out of date by the time they're published. Advertisers may be private owners, property investors or letting agencies (particularly in major cities).

You must be available to inspect properties immediately or at any time. Even if you start phoning at the crack of dawn, you're still likely to find a queue when you arrive to view a property in Rome or Milan. You can insert a 'rental wanted' (*cercasi appartamento* or *cercasi in affitto*) advertisement in many newspapers or place one on notice boards, but don't count on success using this method. Finding a property to rent in Rome is similar to the situation in London and New York, where the best properties are usually found through personal contacts. The worst time to look is during September and October, when Italians return from their summer holidays and students are looking for accommodation.

Rental Costs

Rental costs vary considerably according to the size (particularly the number of bedrooms) and quality of a property, its age and the facilities provided. However, the most significant factor affecting rents is the region of Italy, the city and the neighbourhood. Until recently, Italy had a 'fair rent' (*equo canone*) law that limited rents to levels set by local authorities. This resulted in a shortage of rental properties in some areas and owners are now permitted to set their own rents, which has encouraged more owners to let properties. Most rents are negotiable and you should try to obtain a reduction. Sometimes an agent will suggest offering a reduced rent and even tell you what to offer. The table above is a guide to current rents for furnished or part-furnished accommodation.

The above are average rents for properties in major cities; rents are considerably cheaper in rural areas and significantly more expensive in popular resorts, e.g. the Alps, Italian lakes and coastal hot spots such as the Italian Riviera.

If you rent a property through an agent, you must pay the agent's fee, typically around 10 per cent of a year's rent or one month's rental. Unless rent is paid more than two months in advance, a landlord can ask for a deposit equal to one to three months' rent. The deposit must be returned with interest within two months of the termination of the lease, less the amount due to the landlord for damages, redecoration, etc.

In addition to paying rent, tenants in an apartment must have insurance and pay service charges (*condominio*). Service charges usually include such things as heating, hot water, rubbish removal, upkeep of grounds and gardens, use of a lift, communal lighting and maintenance, and possibly a caretaker's services. Other utilities such as gas, electricity and water are usually paid separately by tenants. Always check whether rent is inclusive or exclusive of charges, which is usually stated in advertisements. Service charges are calculated monthly (payable with the rent) and are usually higher in a new building than an old one. They can vary considerably from as little as €25 to €300 or more per month. Ask to see a copy of the bills from the previous year.

You should also ask to see recent bills for services you must pay for individually, such as telephone and utilities (electricity, gas and water) and check that the previous tenant has paid bills up to date; otherwise you could be liable for any debts.

Tenants are also required to pay half of the contract registration tax, usually equivalent to 2 per cent of the annual rent and subject to a minimum amount of €51.65. On an apartment costing €400 a month, this tax would cost €96. Tenants must also pay a 'special tax' of €7.23 and 'stamp tax' of about €11.

Rental Contracts

There are two kinds of rental contract: a free market contract (*contratto atipico*) and a 'convention' contract (*contratto tipico*), containing set conditions. A contract should be registered with the local *ufficio del registro* to be valid.

The landlord and tenant decide the terms of a free market contract, but the rent may not be raised by more than 75 per cent of the rate of inflation. The minimum tenancy is four years and the tenant has the option to renew for another four years unless the landlord has given him six months' notice (*disdetta*) before the end of the contract that he wishes to sell the property, renovate it or move in himself or a family member (see below). During the second four years, the landlord can terminate the contract by serving six months' notice but need not invoke specific grounds. Subletting is allowed, but only if agreed to by the landlord.

A convention contract follows guidelines set by the national landlords' and tenants' association, the Sindicato Unitario Nazionale Inquilini ed Assegnatari (🖥 www.sunia.it). The tenancy is for not less than three years, with an option to renew for another two. Convention contracts have low maximum rentals and rent increases cannot exceed what is decided by the association. As a result, convention contracts usually only apply to cheaper accommodation, and to compensate for the low rents, there are tax incentives for landlords who choose them. The landlord cannot issue notice of cancellation during the first three years and subletting is prohibited. A convention contract can be used for short-term leases for university students and transitory workers.

A landlord may reclaim a property before the expiration of a free market contract under certain circumstances only. These include requiring the property for his own use, for a child who's getting married or for an elderly parent or in-law, or to make improvements or repairs prior to selling it. However, if within a year the property isn't used for the purpose stated in the notification, the landlord must renew the original rental contract with the same tenant or pay an amount equal to three years' rent as compensation. Otherwise a landlord can reclaim a property only by giving a tenant six months' notice prior to the end of the contract expiry date. If a landlord wishes to sell a property, the tenant has the first option to buy it.

Note that some rental contracts forbid you to use an apartment's address to obtain a residence permit. Such contracts are mainly

used with foreigners, so that a landlord can regain possession of his property more easily should he wish to do so. Eviction of a person from his legal residence is almost impossible in Italy and landlords don't want to take any unnecessary risks with foreigners.

When you rent a community property, there will also be a set of house rules and regulations (*regolamento*), of which you should obtain a copy.

MOVING IN

One of the most important tasks to perform after moving into a new home is to make an inventory of the fixtures and fittings and, if applicable, furniture and furnishings. When you've purchased a property, you should check that the previous owner hasn't absconded with any fixtures and fittings included in the price or anything which you specifically paid for, e.g. carpets, light fittings, curtains, furniture, kitchen cupboards and appliances, garden ornaments, plants or doors. It's common to do a final check when buying a new property, and this is usually done just before completion.

When moving into a long-term rental property, it's necessary to complete an inventory (*inventario*) of its contents and a report on its condition. This includes the condition of fixtures and fittings, the state of furniture and furnishings, the cleanliness and state of the decoration, and anything that's damaged, missing or in need of repair. An inventory should be provided by your landlord or agent and may include every single item in a furnished property (down to the number of teaspoons). The inventory check should be carried out in your presence, both when initiating and when terminating a rental agreement. If the two inventories don't correspond, you must make good any damages or deficiencies or the landlord can do so and deduct the cost from your deposit. Although Italian landlords are generally no worse than those in most other countries, some do almost anything to avoid repaying a deposit. If an inventory isn't provided, you should insist

on one being prepared and annexed to the lease. If you find a serious fault after signing the inventory, send a registered letter to your landlord and ask for it to be attached to the inventory.

Note the reading on your utility meters (e.g. electricity, gas and water) and check that you aren't overcharged on your first bill. Meters should be read by utility companies before you move in, although you may need to organise this.

It's wise to obtain written instructions from the previous owner regarding the operation of appliances and heating and air-conditioning systems, maintenance of grounds, gardens and lawns, care of special surfaces such as wooden, marble or tiled floors, and the names of reliable local maintenance men who know the property and are familiar with its quirks. Check with your local town hall regarding local regulations about such things as rubbish collection, recycling and on-road parking.

HOME SECURITY

When moving into a new home, it's often wise to replace the locks (or lock barrels) as soon as possible, as you have no idea how many keys are in circulation for the existing locks. This is true even for new homes, as builders often give keys to sub-contractors. In any case it's recommended to change the external locks or lock barrels periodically, particularly if you let a home. If not already fitted, it's best to fit high-security (double-cylinder or dead-bolt) locks. Many modern developments may have security gates and caretakers.

Modern properties may be fitted with high-security locks that are individually numbered. Extra keys for these locks cannot be cut at a local hardware store and you need to obtain details from the previous owner or your landlord.

In areas with a high risk of theft (e.g. most major cities and popular resorts), your insurance company will insist on extra security measures such as two locks on all external doors, internal locking shutters, security bars on windows less than 10m (33ft) from the ground and grilles on patio doors. An external door must usually be armoured (*porta blindata*) with a steel rod locking mechanism. An insurance policy may specify that all forms of protection must be employed when a property is unoccupied. If security precautions aren't adhered to, a claim may be reduced. It's usually necessary to have a safe for any insured valuables, which must be approved by your insurance company.

You may wish to have a security alarm fitted, which is usually the best way to deter thieves and may also reduce your household insurance (see page 205). It should be wired to all external doors and windows, and include internal infra-red security beams, and possibly a coded entry keypad (whose code can be frequently changed and is useful for clients if you let a home) and 24-hour monitoring (with some systems it's even possible to monitor properties remotely from another country). With a monitored system, when a sensor (e.g. smoke or forced entry) detects an emergency or a panic button is pushed, a signal is sent automatically to a 24-hour monitoring station. The duty monitor will telephone to check whether it's a genuine alarm and if he cannot contact you someone will be sent to investigate.

You can deter thieves by ensuring that your house is well lit and not conspicuously unoccupied. External security 'motion detector' lights (that switch on automatically when someone approaches), random timed switches for internal lights, radios and televisions, dummy security cameras, and tapes of barking dogs triggered by a light or heat detector may all help deter burglars. In remote areas, it's common for owners to fit two or three locks on external doors, alarm systems, grilles on doors and windows, window locks, security shutters and a safe for valuables. The advantage of grilles is that they allow you to leave windows open without inviting criminals in (unless they're **very** slim). You can fit UPVC (toughened clear plastic) security windows and doors, which can survive an attack with a sledge-hammer without damage, and external steel security blinds (which can be electrically operated), although these are expensive.

A dog can be useful to deter intruders, although it should be kept inside where it cannot be given poisoned food. Irrespective of whether you actually have a dog, a warning sign with a picture of a fierce dog may act as a deterrent. If not already present, you should have the front door of an apartment fitted with a spy-hole and chain so that you can check the identity of a visitor before opening the door. **Remember, prevention is better than cure, as stolen property is rarely recovered.**

Holiday homes are particularly vulnerable to thieves and in some areas they're regularly ransacked. No matter how secure your door and window locks, a thief can usually obtain entry if he is sufficiently determined, often by simply smashing a window or even breaking in through the roof or knocking a hole in a wall! In isolated areas, thieves can strip a house bare at their leisure and an unmonitored alarm won't be a deterrent if there's no one around to hear it. If you have a holiday home in Italy, it isn't wise to leave anything of value (monetary or sentimental) there.

If you vacate your home for an extended period, it may be obligatory to notify your caretaker, landlord or insurance company, and to leave a key with the caretaker or landlord in case of emergencies. If you have a robbery, you should report it immediately to your local police station, where you must make a statement (*denuncia*). You receive a copy, which is required by your insurance company if you make a claim.

Another important aspect of home security is ensuring that you have early warning of a fire, which is easily accomplished by installing smoke detectors. Battery-operated smoke detectors can be purchased from around €10 and should be tested weekly to ensure that the

batteries aren't exhausted. You can also fit an electric-powered gas detector that activates an alarm when a gas leak is detected.

ELECTRICITY

Most electricity in Italy is supplied by Ente Nazionale per l'Energia Elettrica (ENEL, 🖳 www.enel.it), which had a monopoly on providing electricity before being privatised in 1998; competition now comes from Edipower, Edison, Endesa and ENI, along with some smaller companies. Most electricity is generated by oil-burning power stations. Nuclear power is a controversial subject in Italy. The public voted to close all nuclear power plants in a 1990 referendum, but this decision was recently reversed and Italy now sources a tenth of its electricity from nuclear power and aims to increase this to 25 per cent by 2030. Italy imports around 15 per cent of its electricity from France and Switzerland. In major cities, electricity may be controlled by a local municipal energy board, e.g. the Azienda Energetica Municipale (AEM) in Milan. Electricity and

other utility offices are listed in telephone directories under *Numeri di Pubblica Utilità*.

After buying or renting a property (unless utilities are included in the rent), you must sign a new contract (*volturazione delle utenze*) at the local office of your electricity company. You need to take with you some identification (passport or residence permit), a copy of the deeds or rental contract, the registration number of the meter (*contatore*), the previous owner's or tenant's electricity contract or a bill paid by him and a good book, as queues can be long.

If you've purchased a home in Italy, the estate agent may arrange for the utilities to be transferred to your name or go with you to the office (no charge should be made for this service). Make sure all previous bills have been paid and that the contract is transferred to your name from the day you take over. If you're a non-resident owner, you should also give your foreign address or the address of a representative in Italy, in case there are any problems requiring your attention such as your bank refusing to pay the bills.

Power Supply

The electricity supply in Italy is generally 220 volts AC with a frequency of 50Hertz (cycles) and either two or three phases, although in some areas older buildings may still have 125 volt supplies. Not all appliances, e.g. televisions made for 240 volts, will function with a power supply of 220 volts. Power cuts are common in many areas of Italy (many lasting just a few micro-seconds – long enough to crash a computer), particularly in rural areas, and the electricity supply is also unstable, with frequent power surges. If you use a computer you should have an uninterrupted power supply (UPS) with a battery back-up, which allows you time to save your work and shut down after a power failure.

If you live in an area where cuts are frequent and rely on electricity for your livelihood, e.g. for operating a computer, fax machine and other equipment, you may need to install a back-up generator. Even more important than a battery back-up is a power surge protector for appliances such as TVs, computers and fax machines, without which you risk equipment being damaged or destroyed.

In remote areas you must install a generator or solar power system if you want electricity, as there's no mains electricity, although some people make do with gas and oil lamps (and without TV and other modern conveniences).

Wiring Standards & Connection

Most modern properties (e.g. less than 20 years old) in Italy have safe and efficient electrical installations. However, old rural homes may have no electricity or may need total rewiring. You should ensure that electricity installations are in good condition well in advance of moving house. The wiring in a new or renovated house (that has been rewired) must be approved by an ENEL inspector before a supply contract is issued and connection (*allacciato*) is made. If you have any electrical work done in your home you should ensure that you employ an electrician (*electtricista*) who's registered at the local chamber of commerce or a member of an official body such as Uane, which works to ENEL's standards. There are safety regulations for all domestic electrical and gas systems and appliances, which must be inspected annually. Householders must have a certificate of inspection and there are fines of over €5,000 for offenders who break the law.

If you buy a rural property without electricity and over 500 metres from the nearest electricity pylon, you must pay to have the service extended to the property. The cost of connecting a rural property to mains electricity can be prohibitive or connection may even be impossible, in which case you can install a generator or solar power system. In this case, wiring doesn't need to be installed to the high standard required by ENEL. A generator should be powered by diesel fuel and be secured against theft.

Meters

In an old apartment block there may be a common meter, with the bill shared among the apartment owners according to the size of their apartments. However, all new properties have their own meters, which for an apartment block or townhouse development may be installed in the basement or in a meter 'cupboard' in a stairwell or outside a group of properties. A meter should be located where it can be read by electricity company staff when you aren't at home.

Plugs

Depending on the country you've come from, you'll need new plugs (*spine*) or a lot of adapters. Plug adapters for most foreign electrical apparatus can be purchased in Italy, although it's wise to bring some adapters with you, including multi-plug extensions that can be fitted with Italian plugs. There's often a shortage of electricity points in Italian homes, with perhaps just one per room (including the kitchen), so multi-plug adapters may be essential. Electricity points don't usually have their own switches.

Most Italian plugs have two or three round pins (when present, the middle pin of three is for the earth or ground) and come in various sizes depending on the power consumption of the appliance. Low-wattage electrical appliances such as table lamps and TVs don't require an earth. However, plugs with an earth must be used for high-wattage appliances such as fires, kettles, washing machines and refrigerators, and must be used with earthed sockets. Electrical appliances that are earthed have a three-core wire and must never be used with a two-pin plug without an earth socket. Always make sure that a plug is correctly and securely wired, as bad wiring can be fatal.

Fuses

In modern properties, fuses (*fusibili*) are of the earth trip type. When there's a short circuit or the system has been overloaded, a circuit breaker is tripped and the power supply is cut off. If your electricity fails, you should suspect a fuse of tripping, particularly if you've just switched on an electrical appliance. Before reconnecting the power, switch off any high-power appliances such as a cooker, washing machine or heater.

Make sure you know where the electricity trip switches are located and keep a torch handy so you can find them in the dark (see also **Power Rating** below).

Bulbs

Electric light bulbs in Italy are of the Edison type with a screw fitting. If you have lamps requiring bayonet bulbs you should bring some with you, as they cannot be readily purchased in Italy. You can, however, buy adapters to convert from bayonet to screw fitting (or vice versa). Bulbs for non-standard electrical appliances (i.e. appliances that aren't made for the Italian market) such as refrigerators and sewing machines may not be available in Italy, so bring some spares with you.

Power Rating

If the power keeps tripping off when you attempt to use a number of high-power appliances simultaneously, e.g. an electric kettle, heater and cooker, the power rating of your property is probably too low. This is a common problem in Italy. If so, you may need to contact your electricity company and ask them to upgrade the power supply to your property (it can also be downgraded if the power supply is higher than you require). Bear in mind that it can take some time to get your power rating changed. The power rating to a private dwelling in Italy can be 3kw, 4kw or 6kw (incredibly, this is the maximum permissible – and even then, of the over 22m electrical service contracts in Italy, over 18m are for 3kw, including most apartments!). With a 3kw rating you're unable to run more than two or three high-powered appliances simultaneously. Consequently many people are now switching to 6kw. If you have a low supply, you can install a generator to increase it and use timers to ensure that no more than one high-powered apparatus is in operation at one time.

Your standing charge depends on the power rating of your supply, which is why owners tend to keep it as low as possible. A higher power rating also increases the cost per unit of consumption. For example, changing from 3kw to 6kw can cost €500 or more per year! The following table is an illustration of ENEL's tariffs for its 'Green Energy' electricity in 2010. The rates quoted apply to residents whose home has a 3kw power rating. For non-residents and those using a higher power rating, there's an additional charge of €9 a month.

Tariffs

The cost of electricity in Italy is high compared with many other EU countries. Your power rating (see above) determines your monthly standing charge, which is payable irrespective of whether you use any electricity during the billing period. Your actual consumption is charged per kilowatt hour (kWh) and the cost depends on the amount of usage: €0.26 per kWh for low consumption (around 3500 kWh /year) and €0.224 per kWh for high consumption (around 7500 kWh /year). In other words, the basic cost (standing charge) increases with the power rating, but the actual cost of electricity consumption is reduced the more you use.

A residence permit (*certificato di residenza*) is necessary to obtain a resident's electricity contract; ENEL charges non-residents a higher rate than residents.

You can buy 'energy-friendly' appliances that consume less energy than average and energy-saving devices can be installed in appliances such as washing machines, dishwashers and driers.

To compare electricity prices in European Union countries, see 🖳 www.energy.eu.

Bills

You're billed for electricity every two months. Bills (*conti* or *bollette*) are based on estimated consumption and adjusted twice per year when meters have been read. Consumption is usually estimated for four months (two bills) and then adjusted (*conguaglio*)

Power Rating Charges			
Tariff	Monthly usage	Monthly charge	Additional Kw
Small	Up to 100kw	€13.50	€0.25
Medium	Up to 225kw	€29.50	€0.27
Large	Up to 300kw	€46.50	€0.29
Extra large	Up to 375kw	€63.50	€0.30

GAS

Mains

Italy's major supplier of mains gas (*gas di città* or *mettano città*) is Eni Italgas (🖥 www.italgas. it), which is now deregulated; competition is provided by Edison and ENEL, among others. The country has the third-largest gas market in Europe (behind Germany and the UK) and gas provides some 30 per cent of Italy's total energy requirements. It's widely available in cities and large towns in the north of the country, but isn't available in the south or in rural areas (e.g. in Tuscany and Umbria). When moving into a property with mains gas, you must contact the supplier to have the gas switched on and the meter read, and then have the account registered in your name. You need to give the gas company the registration number of the meter and (if known) the name of the previous tenant. As with electricity, there are different contracts for residents and non-residents.

The average cost of mains gas depends on your usage. ENEL has a range of charge bands, based on usage measured in standard cubic metres (smc). Customers using up to 120m³ a year pay €11.40 per month, up to 480m³ a year costs €31 per month, up to 1,000m³ a year costs €58 per month, and up to 2,000m³ per year is charged at €109.60 per month. These are the charges for central and southern Italy; in the north, e.g. Lombardy, Trentino-Alto Adige, Veneto, Friuli-Venezia-Giulia and Emilia Romana, gas is slightly cheaper. You're billed every two months and bills can be paid at banks, post offices and supplier offices, or by direct debit (*domiciliazione*) from a bank account.

Mains gas is mostly used for central heating and cooking. All gas appliances must be approved by the supplier and installed by your local gas company. Old gas water heaters can leak carbon monoxide and have been the cause of a number of deaths in Italy and other countries, although this is unlikely with a modern installation. Gas water heaters must be regularly serviced and descaled annually. You can have a combined hot water and heating system installed (providing background heat), which is relatively inexpensive to install and cheap to run.

when a meter reading is taken. This may result in a larger than expected bill, and therefore if you're a non-resident, you should ensure that you have sufficient funds in your bank account. If you've overpaid, you receive a refund in the form of a postal order, which can be cashed at a post office or a payment directly into your bank account. Half the bill contains account information and how to pay the bill, the other half a payment slip and a receipt for your records. Bills show the account number (*numero utente*), amount payable (*importo*), due date (*scadenza*) and the utility company's account number (*conto corrente*).

Bills may be paid at banks, post offices and electricity company offices, although ENEL prefers to be paid by direct debit (*domiciliazione*) from a bank account (for which there's a small surcharge). Italian utility companies are notorious for over-charging, and internet forums reveal that extracting a refund can be a challenging process. It's recommended to check that your meters remain static when services are turned off and to learn to read your electricity bill and meter, and check your consumption to ensure that you aren't being overcharged.

Gas water heaters cannot be installed in bathrooms for safety reasons, although many people do so, often with fatal consequences.

To compare gas prices in European Union countries, see ⌨ www.energy.eu.

Bottled

Bottled gas is mostly used for cooking but can also be used to provide hot water and heating. The use of gas bottles (*bombole*) is common in rural areas and they're also frequently used for portable gas fires in cities. Cooking by bottled gas is cheaper than electricity and there's no standing charge (as with mains gas). Cookers often have a combination of electric and (bottled) gas rings (you can choose the mix). If your gas rings are sparked by electricity, keep some matches handy for use during power cuts.

You must pay a deposit on the first bottle and thereafter can exchange an empty bottle for a full one. The most common bottle sizes are 10kg and 15kg, which cost around €14 and €20 respectively plus €3-5 for delivery. Check when moving into a property that the gas bottle isn't empty. Keep a spare bottle or two handy and make sure you know how to change bottles (if necessary ask the previous owner or your estate agent to show you). Bottles are delivered in many areas and you can buy them from agents and supermarkets. A bottle used just for cooking lasts an average family around six weeks.

Some people keep their gas bottles outside, often under a lean-to. If you do, you must buy propane gas rather than butane, as it can withstand a greater range of temperatures than butane, which is for internal use only. Although bottled gas is very safe, if you use it you must inform your household insurance company as there's an extra premium to pay.

Tanks

If you live in a rural area, you can have a gas tank (*bombolone*) installed. Tanks come in various sizes and can be either leased or rented. If you buy a tank, you can buy gas from whichever supplier is cheapest. If you lease a tank from a gas company, you must sign a contract to purchase a minimum amount of gas per year, e.g. to the value of €500 to €1,000. Gas can officially be used only for heating and hot water, although many people also use it for cooking and gas fires. A gas tank usually holds between 750 and 1,500 litres of liquid gas (1,000 litres, or 1m³ is the most common size) and bulk gas costs around €5.5 per m³. The installation of gas tanks is strictly controlled and they must be at least 25m (82ft) from a house or road. If you have a gas tank installed on your property you must inform your insurance company, as it increases your home insurance premium.

WATER

Water, or rather the lack of it, is a major concern in many areas of Italy and the price paid for those long, hot summers. There's generally sufficient water in the north, but central and southern areas (and the islands) often experience acute shortages in the summer. Water shortages are exacerbated by poor infrastructure (up to 50 per cent is lost due to leaking pipes in some areas) and wastage due to poor irrigation methods.

Shortages

Water shortages are rare in towns but common in rural areas during the summer, when the water is periodically switched off. In areas with prolonged droughts, water may be switched off from 6pm to 6am daily to conserve supplies.

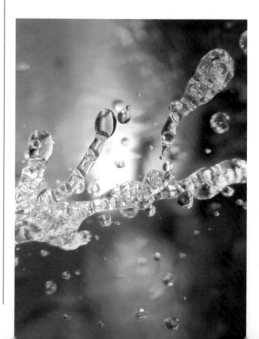

Water shortages are exacerbated in resort areas in summer, when the population may swell tenfold during the hottest and driest period of the year. The use of sprinklers and hose-pipes is banned in many areas in summer. In some areas, water shortages create low water pressure, which means that showers and hoses may not work.

If you plan to maintain a garden in a region with low rainfall, you need a reserve supply for dry periods (you can also use waste water). If you live in an area where cuts are common, you can have a storage tank (cassone) installed, which is topped up automatically when the water is switched on. A 500-litre tank is usually large enough for a family living in an apartment in a city or in a rural area that doesn't suffer water shortages. In a rural area without mains water, it may be necessary to install an underground tank of 500,000 or 1m litres (1,000m³), which is large enough to supply a family for up to six months. This is filled by tanker, which is expensive.

Quality

When water (e.g. from a public source) isn't drinkable it may be marked 'non-drinking' (acqua non potabile). Bear in mind also that water from wells and springs (see below) isn't always safe to drink. You can have well or spring water analysed by the public health department or the local water authority. It's possible to install filtering and cleansing equipment to improve water quality, but you should obtain independent advice before installing a system because not all equipment is equally effective. While boiling water kills any bacteria, it won't remove any toxic substances. Although mains water in Italy is usually drinkable, it may be contaminated by industrial chemicals and nitrates, although supposedly not enough to harm your health. However, many Italians consider it undrinkable and drink bottled water (when not drinking wine!).

In general, Italian water is hard (i.e. with a high calcium content). In some areas the iron, calcium and other minerals stain sinks and porcelain, which can be removed only by rubbing regularly with a soft pumice stone. Water may be fluoridated, depending on the area.

> **☑ SURVIVAL TIP**
>
> You can use a water softener to soften hard water and a filter to prevent the furring of pipes, radiators and appliances.

Wells & Springs

Rural homes with their own well (pozzo) or spring (sorgente) are at a premium in Italy and may be quaint, but both can dry up, particularly in parts of central and southern Italy, and neither may be suitable for consumption. Always confirm that a property has a reliable water source. If a property gets its water from a spring or well (possibly on a neighbour's land), make sure that there's no dispute over its ownership and your rights to use it, e.g. that it cannot be stopped or drained away by your neighbours. Well water is usually excellent (and free), although you may need a pump (manual or electric) to bring it to the surface. You can also create your own well if your land has water.

Dowsing (finding water by holding a piece of forked wood) is as accurate as anything devised by modern science and has an 80 per cent success rate. A good dowser or water diviner (rabdomante) can estimate the water's yield and purity to within 10 or 20 per cent. Before buying rural land without a water supply, engage an experienced dowser with a successful track record to check it.

Mains Water

Water is supplied by local companies, which may be called Società d'Acquedotto (SADA) or Azienda Comunale Energia e Ambiente (ACEA), and each commune has its own rules concerning the use of water. If you own a property in or near a town or village without mains water, you can usually be connected. However, connection can be expensive as you must pay for the digging of channels for pipes. Obtain a quotation (preventivo) from the local water company for the connection of the supply and the installation of a water meter. Expect the connection to cost at least €1,000 and possibly much more, depending on the type of terrain and soil (or rock!), which must be excavated to lay pipes. If you're thinking about buying a property and installing a mains water supply, obtain a quotation before signing the contract.

Mains water is usually metered (especially in northern Italy), meters being installed at the householder's expense. If water is metered, it's usual to have a contract for a limited number of cubic metres per household per year (e.g. 300m³), irrespective of the number of occupants. You're charged a higher rate for consumption above this limit. You cannot use this water for a garden or swimming pool, for which you need a different contract (called *uso vario*) and a separate meter. In rural areas, you may have access to 'agricultural' water for garden use. A *uso vario* contract can cost €500 to €1,000 per year. In some regions, the cost is prohibitive and therefore few residents have swimming pools, although you can have a pool filled by tanker (*autobotte*). In some areas, homeowners build a water basin (*vasca*) that fills with rainwater during the winter and can also be fed by a spring or well; with a lining and filtering system, a *vasca* can function as a swimming pool in summer.

The price of water varies considerably within each region according to its availability, and is among the most expensive in Europe. In central Italy, domestic water costs are the highest in the country (the average charge countywide is around €0.55 per m³). You receive a bill (*acquedotto comunale*) every six months after your meter has been read. When moving into a new home, ask the local water company to read your meter.

Like other utility bills, water bills may be paid by direct debit (*domiciliazione*) from a bank account, though your water is unlikely to be cut off if you're late paying a bill.

Most apartment blocks (*condomini*) have a single meter for the whole block, where the cost is shared equally between the owners and included in the fees or expenses (*spese*), which isn't recommended if you have a holiday home. Where no water meter is installed, water bills are calculated according to the size of a home. Charges vary significantly: a family of three living in a 200m² apartment in Florence can pay over €440 a year, whereas in Milan they would pay as little as €110.

Safety

Before moving into a new home you should check where the main stop-valve or stopcock is located, so that you can turn off the water supply in an emergency. If the water stops flowing for any reason, you should ensure that all the taps are turned off to prevent flooding when the supply starts again. In community (*condominio*) properties, the stopcock is usually outside the building. Note that water damage caused by burst pipes due to old age or freezing may be excluded from insurance policies and that under Italian law you're required to turn off the water at the mains if a property is left empty for more than 24 hours!

When leaving a property empty for an extended period, particularly during the winter if there's the possibility of freezing, you should turn off the main stopcock, switch off the system's controls and drain the pipes, toilets (you can put salt in the toilet bowls to prevent freezing) and radiators. It's also recommended to have your cold water tank and the tank's ball valves checked periodically for corrosion, and to check the hosing on appliances such as washing machines and dishwashers. It can be expensive if a pipe bursts and the leak goes undiscovered for a long time!

HEATING & AIR-CONDITIONING

Central heating systems in Italy may be powered by oil, gas, electricity, solid fuel (usually wood) or even solar power. Whatever form of heating you use, it's essential to have good insulation, without which up to 60 per cent of heating is lost through the walls and roof. Over half of Italian homes have central heating, which is necessary in northern Italy outside the summer months. Many people keep their central heating on a low setting during short absences in winter (which can be controlled via a master thermostat) to prevent freezing. Heating requirements in winter vary from six hours per day for around 14 weeks per year in the south to over 14 hours per day for six months or longer in the north.

Apartment blocks (*condomini*) usually have central heating (*riscaldamento*), which can be either autonomous (*autonomo*) or centralised (*centrale*). With *riscaldamento autonomo* you can control the heating independently and are billed according to use. With *riscaldamento centrale* the heating is turned on in autumn (October) and off in spring (March) and you have no control and must pay the same as other residents, even if you're a non-resident in winter.

Older buildings may have cast-iron radiators, which you should consider replacing. Aluminium radiators are preferable to cast-iron as they withstand extreme cold better and are less likely to leak or burst; more importantly, Italian insurance companies won't cover you for burst cast-iron radiators and the subsequent water damage.

Solid Fuel

Many people rely solely on wood-burning stoves or fireplaces for their heating and hot water, particularly in rural areas. Stoves come in a huge variety of sizes and styles, and may also heat radiators throughout a house and provide hot water. Most people burn wood, which needs to be seasoned for at least two years before burning, as it's less expensive than coal or coke. You can have it delivered cut and dried or can collect it free if you live in the country. The main disadvantages are the chores of collecting and chopping wood, cleaning the grate and lighting fires. Smoke can also be a problem and an open fireplace can be wasteful of heat and fuel. An enclosed hearth with a glass door is more effective and often has the advantages of a hot-air chamber that warms other parts of a home, a lower fire risk and less mess.

Electric

Electric central heating isn't common in Italy, as it's too expensive. However, many people with modern homes with good insulation and a permanent system of ventilation use electric storage heaters. Electric central heating isn't recommended for old properties with poor insulation. If you install an electric central heating system you may need to increase your electricity rating (see **Power Rating** on page 84) to cope with the extra demand.

Stand-alone electric (e.g. halogen) heaters are relatively expensive to run and are best suited to holiday homes.

Gas

Mains gas central heating is popular, relatively cheap to run and widely used in the north of Italy. Gas is clean, economical and efficient, and the boiler is usually fairly small and can be wall-mounted. In rural areas where there's no mains gas, you can have a gas tank (*bombolone*) installed on your property (see page 86).

Oil

Oil-fired central heating isn't common in Italy due to the high cost of heating oil and the problems associated with storage and deliveries. Italy is attempting to reduce its dependence on oil, especially for heating and generating electricity, and fuel oil consumption has decreased by 40 per cent since 1995. This may be due in no small part to the price of heating oil which is among the highest in Europe; it fluctuates with the price of crude oil but in mid-2010 was around €1.40 per litre.

An average family of four can expect to use around 1,700 litres per year (over some 120 days), which will cost around €2,380. You also need space to install a storage tank. If you have a tank with a 2,000-litre capacity or larger it must be buried in your garden or stored in a building sheltered from frost and away from the house. A smaller tank can be located in your home but needs to be refilled more often.

Solar Power

A solar power system can be used to supply all your energy needs, although it's usually combined with an electric or gas heating system, as solar power cannot be relied upon year-round for lighting, heating and hot water. The main drawback is the high cost of installation, which varies considerably according to the region and how much energy you require. A solar power system must be installed by an expert. The advantages are no maintenance or running costs and silent operation. A system should last 30 years (it's usually guaranteed for ten) and can be upgraded to provide more power in the future. Solar power can also be used to heat a swimming pool.

Continuous advances in solar cell and battery technology are expected to dramatically increase the efficiency and reduce the cost of solar power, which is forecast to become a major source of energy worldwide in the 21st century, along with other renewable energy resources such as wind and wave power.

☑ **SURVIVAL TIP**

A solar power system can also be used to provide electricity in a remote rural home, where the cost of extending electricity is prohibitive.

Costs

The cost of heating a property varies according to a number of factors, not least the fuel used, the size of your home, and the length of time your heating is switched on. You can have your home inspected by a heating engineer (*assistente tecnico del riscaldamento*), who assesses its heating requirements and cost, taking into account the insulation and equipment installed. The engineer produces a report detailing the most effective means of insulating and heating your home, and a number of cost estimates.

Humidifiers

Central heating dries the air and may cause your family to develop coughs; those who find the dry air a problem or unpleasant can purchase a humidifier to add moisture to the air. Humidifiers that don't generate steam should be cleaned occasionally with disinfectant (*disinfettante*) available from pharmacies (to prevent nasty diseases). Humidifiers may range from simple water containers hanging from radiators to expensive electric or battery-operated devices.

Air-conditioning

Few homes in Italy have air-conditioning (*condizionamento d'aria*), despite the fact that summer temperatures can exceed 40°C (104°F) in some areas. Although Italian properties are built to withstand the heat, you may find it beneficial to install air-conditioning, although there can be negative effects if you suffer from asthma or respiratory problems. You can choose between a huge variety of air-conditioners, fixed or moveable, indoor or outdoor installation, and high or low power. Air-conditioning units cost from around €400 (plus installation) for a unit that's sufficient to cool an average-size room. An air-conditioning system with a heat pump provides cooling in summer and heating in winter. Many people fit ceiling fans for extra cooling in the summer (costing from around €80), and these are standard fixtures in some new homes.

Elba island, Tuscany

6.
POSTAL SERVICES

I taly has a long history of organised postal service dating back to the *cursus publicus* of the Romans, although a national postal system wasn't established until 1862 after unification of the country. For many years it was part of the state-run post and telecommunications monopoly Poste, Telegrafi e Telefoni (PTT) until it became a limited company in 1998, although around 70 per cent of its shares are still owned by the government.

Today, the Italian post office (Poste Italiane) is proud of its service, and has made strenuous efforts to shed its reputation as the slowest and most inefficient postal service in Western Europe. An efficiency drive in the early 21st century has done much to improve standards. Other innovations include an increasing range of online services. However, while the standard postal service is acceptable for everyday items, many people in Italy prefer to send important letters and parcels by registered post (*posta raccomandata* – see page 96) or use a private courier service, as stories of post disappearing are legendary.

Although the reliability of Italy's postal service has increased considerably in recent years, registering items with proof of delivery is recommended for all important documents and items of value, including cheques. When cancelling contracts and subscriptions, some companies and organisations make it a requirement that letters are registered.

The (independent) Vatican City post office in Rome is the most efficient and reliable, as it sends all its international post via Switzerland (with colourful Vatican stamps!). Many companies and courier services in Italy also use the Swiss and other foreign post offices to deliver their international post, e.g. Deutsche Poste (⌨ www.deutschepost.de). The American company, Mailboxes, Inc., has franchises in Rome and other major cities.

The identifying colour of the Italian post office is currently yellow, and its logo is a distinctive *Poste Italiane* in blue on a yellow background, sometimes shortened to the initials 'PT'. In phone books, post offices are listed under *Poste Italiane*.

Information about all postal services is available from the post office's website (⌨ www.poste. it) and there are some English-language pages with information on letter, parcel and overseas mail options, and stamps (⌨ www.poste.it/en/ postali).

POST OFFICES

There's a post office (*ufficio postale*) in most towns and villages in Italy – a total of over 14,000 – providing a wide range of services. In main towns and cities there's a central post office for each district, as well as some smaller post offices (*agenzie*). Post offices in Italy are always operated by post office employees and there are (as yet) no post offices run by private businesses or located in shops.

In addition to the standard postal services, post offices offer facilities for telegram and fax transmissions, exchange of foreign currency, domestic and international cash transfers, and payment of utility bills, road tax and TV

licences. A range of financial and banking services is available, including cheque and savings accounts, investment plans, tax-paying facilities and the sale of post office shares and bonds. Telephone cards, lottery tickets, train and bus tickets, and pre-paid toll cards for Italian motorways are sold at post offices. The post office also acts as an agency for the payment of social security benefits such as state pensions. There are public telephones in main post offices.

Main post offices have separate counters (*sportelli*) for different services, which are divided between those dealing with post and those handling financial services, with sometimes a third counter for telegrams and faxes. New layouts in main post offices include a single-queue system with an electronic board showing the number of the next available window. When this system isn't in operation, you must ensure that you join the right queue (shown by a sign above the window or a sign near the entrance indicating the services provided at each window), or you'll need to start queuing all over again. If you require different services, you may need to queue at different counters at a main post office, although in rural towns and villages one or two counters usually provide all services.

Allow plenty of time if you need to visit a post office, as there are often very long queues, particularly in urban areas. One reason for this is that banknotes are regularly checked to see if they're forged.

Opening Hours

Post offices in towns and cities are generally open from around 8.30am to 6.30pm, Mondays to Fridays, and from around 8.15am to 12.30 or 1pm on Saturdays (with some larger post offices staying open all day) and the last day of each month (when they may close at noon). Main post offices in major cities often remain open until 8pm for postal transactions, although counters dealing with financial services are likely to close at around 5 or 6pm. Opening hours in rural towns and villages are limited, post offices usually opening from 8am until 1.30 or 2pm, Mondays to Fridays, and from 8 to 11.45am on Saturdays. There may be shorter hours on the last day of the month.

Address

On Italian letters, the surname often precedes the Christian name and the number of the house comes after the name of the street. If the person to whom you're addressing post isn't usually resident at that address, you must address your post 'care of' (c/o or *presso*) the person named on the post box or on the nameplate of the apartment itself. Otherwise you risk your letter being returned to the sender or simply not being delivered.

All letters to Italian addresses should bear a five-digit post code (*codice di avviamento postale* or *CAP*) which indicates the town and province. All provincial capitals use a different code for each street, the first two numbers indicating the town or city and the last three the street. The post code is written before the town or city, which is followed by the abbreviation for the province in brackets (this isn't required for post addressed to Rome, as *Roma* isn't abbreviated – see the list of provinces and abbreviations in **Appendix E**). If the first two numbers of the code are correct, your post will generally be delivered. All post codes with their corresponding towns, cities and provinces are listed in a *CAP* booklet, available free from post offices, and you can download it from the post office website (💻 www.poste.it/online/cercacap).

A typical Italian address is shown below:

> Bianchi Mario
> Via Cavour, 41
> I-10123 Torino (TO)
> Italy

Stamps

Stamps (*francobolli*) are available from tobacconists' (*tabacchi*), which are distinguished by a large black 'T' sign outside, and licensed bars (*bar tabacchi*), as well as from post offices. They're usually available only loose (not in booklets) and you must ask for them over the counter. It's generally much simpler and quicker to buy stamps at a tobacconist's or small post office than at a main post office. However, tobacconists' often run out of stamps (a few don't stock them) so it's recommended to buy a few at a time.

Fiscal stamps (*marche da bollo*) used for paying government taxes can be purchased at some post offices, but official document paper (*carta bollata*) used for legal communications is available only from tobacconists'.

If a letter has insufficient postage, it's usually returned to the sender. If it isn't, the postman insists on the addressee paying the postage due. If a letter isn't stamped, it's destroyed unless the sender's name is written on the envelope, in which case it's returned. You won't need to pay a fee in the latter case – merely face the postman's disapproval!

Commemorative stamps (*prodotti filatelici*) and coins are produced for collectors and can be ordered from dedicated windows at around 300 main post offices. For information about philatelic services, you can write to Poste Italiane S.p.A., Divisione Filatelica, Piazza Dante, 25, 00185 Rome, or to the person in charge of philatelic services (*sportelli filatelici*) at the central post office in your provincial capital. Information on collectors' stamps is available from the post office website (🖥 http://e-filatelia.poste.it/?lingua=english).

Post Boxes

Post boxes are red and either free-standing on a metal pole or attached to a wall. They're located outside tobacconists and post offices, as well as on platforms at main railway stations. It's recommended to post urgent letters at a main post office or railway station, as collections are more frequent. In cities and at main post offices there are often two boxes, one for local (*per la città*) post and one for all other destinations (*per tutte le altre destinazioni*),

including abroad. Alternatively, there's sometimes another slot for post going abroad (*all'estero*).

Latest collection times at main post offices are generally 5pm for ordinary post and 6pm for priority post, Mondays to Fridays, and noon for all post on Saturdays. At smaller post offices, collections are usually made at noon on all six days.

Collection & Delivery

There's one postal delivery per day, in the morning, from Monday to Saturday. If the postman is delivering to an apartment block, he presses the intercom of one of the apartments to gain access to the post boxes (*cassette postali*), which are situated in the entrance hall/foyer and accessible by key only. If a caretaker (*portiere*) lives in the block, he may be in charge of distributing post to individual boxes. In rural areas, a postman isn't obliged to deliver post to the front door unless it's located on a street; if it isn't, you must install a letterbox at the boundary of your property.

If a postman calls with post requiring a signature or payment of import duty or excess postage when you aren't at home, he'll leave a yellow collection form. Go to the address of the office stamped on the front of the form within the hours shown and present it, together with some identification (e.g. passport, identity card, residence permit or driving licence). If you cannot go in person, another person may go on your behalf provided you enter his name in the appropriate box on the back of the form and sign it. The post office will hold any item that needs collecting free of charge for three days, after which there's a daily charge of €0.26 for a maximum period of one month. This is a good reason to inform the post office if you're going to be away from home for more than a few days (see **Change of Address** on page 97), as they'll hold your post for you.

You can receive post at any post office in Italy via the *poste restante* (*fermo posta*) service. Letters should be addressed to your nearest main post office, as follows:

Smith, Marmaduke Cecil
Fermo Posta
I-65100 P.T. Pescara Centro
Italy

If you use one of the smaller post offices, you must specify the number of the post office (e.g. *agenzia numero 2*), **not** its street address. There's a charge of €0.26 for each letter received and you must produce an identity card, passport or driving licence as identification when collecting post. If you want to remain anonymous, you can have post addressed to you via a document number. The document number must be produced as proof of identity when collecting post. Post is kept at the post office for a maximum of 30 days, after which it's returned to the sender.

Another widely used service for receiving post, if you don't want it delivered to your home address, is to rent a post office box (*casella postale*), which are available at main post offices. There are two kinds of box: open (*aperta*) and closed (*chiusa*). The annual subscription for an open box is €100, but they're allocated only to companies that receive large amounts of post and prefer to use a post office box address. With this kind of box, post is collected from the appropriate post office window (usually *fermo posta*) by a representative of the company.

Smaller companies and private individuals are offered a closed box, for which there's an annual fee of €100-200. You're issued with a key to access your box, which is located inside the post office. The post office doesn't advise you of the arrival of any registered or express post in your box, therefore if you have a closed box it's wise to check it frequently.

LETTERS

There are four categories of letter post (mail) in Italy: priority post (*posta prioritaria*), express post (*postacelere1plus*), registered post (*posta raccomandata*) and insured post (*posta assicurata*), described below.

Priority Post

The priority service (*posta prioritaria*) usually provides next-working-day delivery within Italy

(although this isn't guaranteed), and delivery in two to three days for letters to all other EU countries, plus Norway and Switzerland. The priority service isn't available to other European countries or the rest of the world. The price for a standard letter (up to 23.5cm long, 12cm wide, 0.5cm thick and up to a weight of 20g) is €0.60.

Express Post

Express post (*postacelere1plus*) guarantees delivery within Italy of documents weighing up to 3kg in one working day for a fixed price of €10.

Registered Post

You can register post (*posta raccomandata*) with proof of delivery (*avviso di ricevimento*) or without (*semplice*) by completing a *raccomandata* form. The bottom half of the form, which is stamped by the post office clerk, is your receipt (*ricevuta*). The charge for registering a letter weighing up to 20g both within Italy and abroad is €3.30, in addition to the cost of postage. Fees then rise on a weight scale up to €9.85 to destinations within Italy and €19/29/34 (depending on the zone) to overseas destinations for letters weighing between 1 and 2kg. Proof of delivery costs an extra €0.60 (€0.65 overseas) and, in addition to the standard form, you must complete a yellow postcard, which is signed by the addressee and returned to you. For certain types of official correspondence (for example, judicial and tax correspondence and writing to the President of the Republic), you must use the same form but with red lettering (*raccomandata descritta*).

Insured Post

Insured post (*posta assicurata*) allows you to insure items up to a value of €3,000. You must use an envelope with a security seal for all items whose value exceeds €50 and for all items to be sent abroad. In order to send items, you must complete a form at a post office. Collection of an insured item within five days is free of charge; after that it costs €0.52 a day. After 30 days, items which haven't been collected are returned to the sender.

PARCELS

There are four services for parcel delivery within Italy:

♦ **Ordinary Parcel** (*pacco ordinario*): delivers parcels weighing up to 20kg within five working days for a fixed price of €7;

♦ **Express Courier 3** (*paccocelere3*): delivers parcels weighing up to 30kg within three working days for €9.10;

♦ **Express Courier 1** (*paccocelere1plus*): delivers parcels weighing up to 30kg in one working day for €15.30;

♦ **Express Business Courier** (*paccocelere impresa*): a fast business service for parcels weighing up to 30kg, with the option to pre-pay for a block of shipments.

There are three services for international parcel delivery:

♦ **International Express Courier** (*paccocelere internazionale*): for parcels weighing up to 30kg to over 220 countries, e.g. it costs €33.98 to send a 1kg package to the UK or Ireland, or €56.65 to send it to Hong Kong. Delivery to EU countries takes two working days, to non-EU European countries two or three working days and outside Europe three or four working days.

Items can be insured up to a value of €3,500 for €5.68.

♦ **Quick Pack Europe:** for parcels weighing up to 30kg to a selection of European countries (currently 15). Average delivery time is three working days and the cost varies between €27.20 and €65.35. Insurance is available as for International Express Courier (see above).

♦ **EMS Express Mail Service:** for items weighing up to 20kg and delivery within two to five working days. There's a three-tier system of rates (and 16 weight bands), the cost ranging from €28.80 to €406.25.

CHANGE OF ADDRESS

If you move house, you can have your post redirected to your new address (*cambio indirizzo*) by making a written request on plain paper (not *carta bollata*) to your local post office at least two days beforehand. The service is available for between 3 and 12 months, and the cost ranges from €8.40 to €15.60 for private customers, and around double the amount for business customers. There's no service for parcels to be redirected abroad (they're returned to the sender) and you're liable for any extra postage for letters redirected abroad.

Note that responsibility for redirecting your post falls to the local postman and therefore this service cannot be relied upon. If possible, it's better to ask the new occupants to forward mail or ask a neighbour or friend to visit your old home periodically to collect any post and forward it to your new address.

FINANCIAL SERVICES

The Italian post office offers a number of financial services. It's one of the largest single banking facilities in Italy and provides a variety of cheque and savings accounts. In rural areas, where the nearest bank is often many kilometres away, many people use the post office as their local bank.

POST OFFICE ACCOUNTS

Post office accounts provide most of the same services as bank accounts. In addition to the longer opening hours of post offices, one of the main advantages of a post office account over a bank account is that bills are debited free (with a bank, you usually pay a charge) and account charges are generally lower. The standard account (*conto bancoposta*) can be opened by any resident aged over 18 – non-residents may be able to open one but check the latest situation with your nearest post office. It offers the following services:

♦ automatic bill payment;

♦ direct debits;

♦ a cheque book;

♦ unlimited withdrawals (provided you have the money in your account!);

♦ confirmation of every transaction with a receipt sent through the post;

♦ an annual interest rate on your credit balance;

♦ money transfers;

♦ credit card facilities.

The account costs €2.59 per month with an annual maximum charge of €30.99, which covers deposits, post office cheques and regular transactions such as direct debits, although (as with most bank accounts in Italy) transactions made at the desk (*sportello*) are subject to a small extra charge, which is usually between €1 and €2.50. You can choose to receive monthly, quarterly or annual statements. There's no limit to the amount you can withdraw from your account using a cheque, although an overdraft isn't permitted. *Conto bancoposta* cheques may be used to pay for goods in shops but, like bank cheques, it's up to shopkeepers whether they accept cheques (or **your** cheques). If you're known to a shopkeeper he'll probably accept your cheque, but if you're new to the area (or the shop) you shouldn't rely on it. See page 217 for information about writing cheques in Italy.

For every payment into your account you must complete a paying-in slip (*bollettino di conto corrente*); your account is usually credited within four days. If you want your account to be credited the day after

the deposit, you can insert a cross in the appropriate box on the slip.

> A Postamat Maestro Card (*carta postamat maestro*) is currently available to all account-holders for paying bills and withdrawing cash. The card costs €10 annually.

Savings accounts (*libretto di risparmio postale*) are also available from the post office.

Postepay Card

One hugely popular initiative in Italy – where bank fees can be expensive – is the Postepay card. This works as a credit card surrogate for anyone (especially immigrant workers, minors or newly-arrived foreigners) without a credit rating or the necessary documents to set up a bank account. The pre-paid card, which can be topped up at any post office to a maximum of €3,000, can be used to make online purchases, ATM withdrawals and to pay bills online. The card is obtainable with a one-time fee of €5.

Bill Paying

The post office provides a service for paying bills (*pagamento delle bollette*) for utilities (telephone, gas and electricity), as well as road tax, television licence fees, university entrance fees and property rent. Most people pay their bills in cash at a post office, using the payment form included with every bill received by post. If the form is pre-printed (*bollettino premarcato*), it includes all the necessary payment details, including your name and address, and the payee's name and account number. If it isn't pre-printed, you must enter these details and must also state the reason for the payment (*causale*) on the reverse of the form. Post office payment forms must be completed in black or blue-black ink – if you make a mistake you must complete a new form, as you aren't permitted to make corrections.

Payment forms generally come in two parts. The larger, left-hand part is retained by the post office and sent to the company or individual being paid. The remaining part is your receipt (*ricevuta*), which is stamped by the post office clerk and given back to you (check that it has been stamped). If you need more than one receipt, you can complete a payment form in three or four parts, or photocopy your original receipt (the photocopy may, however, be used only for your records, as some organisations don't accept this as proof of payment).

You must complete a separate form for each bill and take them to the payments window (*bancoposta*). Payments may be made through a *conto bancoposta* account, in which case a cheque, the Postamat Maestro Card (see **Post Office Accounts** above) or a post office credit card can be used. It's wise to add up the total in advance so that you can confirm it (write it down if you don't speak Italian). If you don't have a *conto bancoposta* account, payment must be made in cash, as other forms of credit card and bank cheques aren't accepted. In all instances, you'll be charged a small transaction fee (see above).

If you choose to pay bills at a post office, it's wise to do so early in the morning, e.g. on your way to work. The deadline (*scadenza*) for paying many bills in Italy falls at the same time for everyone and therefore long queues are likely – even longer than usual! You can save time and your temper by setting up a direct debit through your bank, as this is usually free.

Other Services

Other financial products available at the post office include state bonds (*titoli di stato*), post office pension schemes (*postevita*) and post office bonds (*buoni ordinari*). Bonds pay from 0.55 per cent for the first year to 3.5 per cent from 15 to 20 years, but if you cash the bonds within the first year, you receive no interest.

Money transfers (*vaglia*) can be made within Italy and internationally and cost €6 per transaction, but they're limited to a value of €2,582.28 – this odd amount is a throwback to pre-euro times and is the equivalent of 5m Italian lire! A blue form must be completed for money transfers within Italy (*richiesta vaglia nazionale*) and a green-blue form for transfers abroad (*richiesta di trasferimento fondi verso l'estero*). They can be made in cash or by postcheque (if you have an account) and take a day to arrive at another Italian post office. International money transfers take 15 days or more depending on the destination and aren't possible to all countries. In order to cash a money transfer sent to you, you must produce an official form of identification.

Foreign currency exchange facilities (*cambiavalute*) are provided at some main post offices, although only major currencies are exchanged. There's a charge for each transaction, but it's usually less than the fee charged by banks. Certain types of travellers' cheque (*assegni turistici*), e.g. American Express, can be cashed at post offices in Italy.

You can also collect your pension and pay tax bills at a post office, and arrange for your salary to be paid into your *conto bancoposta* account.

Portoferraio, Livorno

7.
COMMUNICATIONS

The largest telecommunications provider is Telecom Italia (formerly SIP), once state owned but now a private company. Until 1997, it was the only provider of telephone lines and fixed-line (non-mobile) telephones but a number of other companies such as Tiscali and Infostrada now supply much-needed competition. A number of companies provide mobile phone services (see page 107).

INSTALLATION & REGISTRATION

Until the mid-'90s, the installation of telephones in Italy was severely restricted by the unavailability of phone numbers due to an old-fashioned system that couldn't meet demand. As a result, people in some areas had to wait literally years for a phone line to be installed! But a major modernisation of the telephone system introduced fibre optics and electronic switching and this greatly increased the availability of phone lines, although a few remote areas still have mechanical switchboards. Nowadays, tone dialling is the rule rather than the exception. A number of telephone companies can install a fixed line and supply a phone service (see page 104), although Telecom Italia remains the market leader.

To have a fixed-line phone installed – at least for the first time – you must visit your local Telecom Italia office (there's one in most large towns and cities and all provincial capitals). Staff can provide information about the equipment and services available, and help you to complete an application form. However, they usually speak only Italian, so you may need to take along an interpreter, plus your passport (with a photocopy) for identification purposes. Alternatively, you can call ☎ 187 or visit the Telecom Italia website (🖥 www.telecomitalia.it).

The fee for installing a line in a property where one wasn't previously installed is €96 for the installation and €16 for the monthly subscription. Changing the name of the user of an existing telephone line is free of charge, as is the transfer of a telephone number to another location within the same code area. Additional charges apply (depending on the distance involved) if a phone is to be installed in a remote area that isn't considered 'inhabited' (*oltre perimetro abitato*). Nowadays, it usually takes just a few working days to have a line installed.

The contract for a phone line includes the requirement to use equipment provided by Telecom Italia or approved (*omologato*) by it, although this is seldom enforced. In principle, Telecom Italia could confiscate a phone connected to its network that isn't *omologato*, but this is highly unlikely unless it's a cordless phone that uses frequencies allocated to the emergency services. Telecom Italia's shops sell phones that have been approved, although it isn't illegal to sell non-approved phones and most electronics shops stock a wide variety.

Telecom Italia usually installs sockets which take a three-prong telephone plug or an international registered jack (RJ11) connector, which you need when connecting to the internet. It's up to you to change the socket or use adapters if necessary.

EMERGENCY & USEFUL NUMBERS

The general emergency number in Italy is 113. However, people are discouraged from using this except in cases where the caller or someone else is in serious danger, or there has been a serious accident. Otherwise, the preferred emergency procedure is to call the relevant organisation directly. For example, people witnessing someone being beaten up at night and calling 113 on their mobile phones have been told to call 112 for the *carabinieri* (see below) instead. Even calling 112 may not produce the expected result. Some youngsters once called this number when they saw a car being stolen. The reply was, 'We only have two cars and they aren't for that sort of thing', from which you may conclude that car theft isn't a particularly high priority for the Italian police. The most important emergency numbers are:

Emergency Numbers

112	Paramilitary police (*carabinieri*) for crimes and traffic accidents. This is also the EU-wide general emergency number;
113	General emergency number for serious emergencies only (*soccorso pubblico di emergenza*);
115	Fire brigade (*vigili del fuoco*);
118	Ambulance or first aid (*emergenza sanitaria*).

Calling the above numbers from public phones is usually free of charge. Other useful numbers include:

Telephone operators usually speak only Italian, although a translation service (in Arabic, English, French or German) is available on 170.

There's a range of special numbers in Italy that are classified using a system of colours.

♦ **Green numbers** (*numeri verdi*): 'free' numbers (you're charged one or more units for each call!) with a prefix such as 147 or 800. Free numbers are often printed in a box with a green *numero verde* logo.

♦ **Blue numbers** (*numeri azzurri*): to report child abuse;

♦ **Pink numbers** (*numeri rosa*): to report abuse of women;

♦ **Violet numbers** (*numeri viola*): to report any other kind of abuse;

♦ **Red numbers** (*numeri rossi*): to obtain prenatal advice;

♦ **Orange numbers** (*numeri arancioni*): for general psychiatric counselling.

USING THE TELEPHONE

Telephone use in Italy is much the same as in any other country, with a few Italian eccentricities thrown in for good measure. One unusual feature of the Italian phone system is that you must include the area code (*prefissi*) when making local calls, not just when making calls outside your local code area. If you leave out the area code when making a call, you

---

Useful Numbers

12	Directory enquiries (*informazioni elenco abbonati* – see page 107);
114	Alarm call (*sveglia automatica*);
116	Vehicle breakdown assistance (*soccorso stradale*), provided by the Automobile Club d'Italia (see page 164);
161	Time signal (*ora esatta*);
172	Reverse charge (collect) calls; for international calls, 172 must be followed by the international code of the country you wish to call (an operator will answer in the language of the country you're calling);
176	International operator (*informazioni internazionali*), who can provide general information in English;
197	For urgent phone calls (*chiamate urgenti*): if the number you want is busy, the operator will interrupt the call for you.

an engaged tone, with no further explanation, which has caused a lot of confusion and upset many people who have often tried for days on end to call someone in Italy! Italy's international code is 39.

Telephone numbers in Italy are often written with a dash (as in this book) or forward slash after the area code and a space after each two or three digits, e.g. Milan 12345678 should be shown as 02-123 456 78 or 02/123 456 78. However, there may only be a space after the area code, or the code and number may be written with no spaces at all, e.g. 0212345678. Italian phone numbers vary in length; for example, Rome numbers may be between five and eight digits. When a number is recited orally, it's usually read in double digits, e.g. zero two, twelve, thirty-four, fifty six, seventy eight.

Mobile phone (see page 107) numbers start with 03 and are more expensive to call than fixed lines.

Answering the Phone

Italians usually answer their phones with 'pronto' (ready), with the exception of companies and office switchboards. Sometimes the caller asks 'Chi parla?' (Who's talking?). However, this is generally considered bad manners and the answer is usually 'Con chi vuole parlare?' (With whom do you wish to talk?). If the caller has the wrong number, you can say 'sbagliato numero' (wrong number).

hear a recorded message telling you to dial it before the number. However, this message is (naturally) given in Italian, so visiting friends or relatives who try to call you from within the country (who leave out the code) may not understand why they cannot get through. If you don't know the area code, you can obtain it from the operator (dial 12 for domestic codes). A booklet listing area codes (and postcodes) is published by Telecom Italia and available from bookshops and stationers. There is also a website which allows you to check phone prefixes and postcodes (💻 www.nonsolocap.it).

When calling Italy from abroad, you must include the initial 0 of the area code, unlike when making calls to almost every other country (Italy doesn't care much for international standards). If you omit the zero when calling from abroad you hear

Useful Everyday Phrases	
English	**Italian**
I would like to speak to ___	*Vorrei parlare con ___*
Could you connect me with ___ ?	*Mi potrebbe collegare con ___ ?*
Please wait, I will connect you.	*Un attimo, prego, faccio il collegamento.*
___ is not in	*___ è fuori* or *___ non c'è*
I will try again later	*Chiamo di nuovo più tardi*
You've reached the wrong number	*Lei ha sbagliato il numero*
I'd like to leave a message for ___	*Vorrei lasciare un messaggio per ___*
Could you ask ___ to call me back?	*Mi farebbe richiamare ___ ?*

Phonetic Alphabet

When spelling names on the telephone, you should use the following words:

A	Ancona	N	Napoli
B	Bologna	O	Otranto
C	Como	P	Palermo
D	Domodossola	Q	Quaderno
E	Empoli	R	Roma
F	Firenze	S	Savona
G	Genova	T	Torino
H	Hotel	U	Udine
I	Imola	V	Venezia
J	Jolly	W	Washington
K	Kennedy	X	Icks
L	Livorno	Y	York
M	Milano	Z	Zara

Nuisance Calls

Nuisance calls are no more frequent in Italy than elsewhere, but they happen. The best advice is to hang up as soon as you realise the nature of the call; most telephone pests soon lose interest if they fail to receive a response. If the calls continue, you could blow a piercing whistle down the line the next time they call to discourage them. You should also report the problem to the police.

Answering Machines

The standard phrase used on answering machines in Italy is 'We are momentarily out', even if you're away for three months in another country. Burglary is endemic in Italy, where burglars often monitor people's movements, sometimes by phone. A message such as, 'We have left for England for two weeks and will be back on 15th October' is an invitation no burglar is likely to resist. Most answering machines are built into a phone, but they can be purchased separately from electronics and phone shops. Prices start at under €50, rising to €100 or more for top-of-the-range models. The latter may provide a wide range of special features, including automatic ring-back, call forwarding, remote playback of messages (accessible using a code), and recording of the date and time of incoming calls.

TELEPHONE COMPANIES

In addition to Telecom Italia, there are a number of providers of telephone services, the largest of which are Infostrada (🖥 www.infostrada.it), BTItaly (🖥 www.italia.bt.com), TeléTu (🖥 www.teletu.it), Tiscali (🖥 www.tiscali.it) and Uno (🖥 www.uno.it). Some will install a telephone line for you; others just offer call packages which you can use on a Telecom Italia line. Costs vary, e.g. Infostrada charges around €100 to install a line, whereas if you're lucky, some companies will install a line free of charge as part of a promotion. The cost of calls varies widely as well, and you need to compare charges on their websites to get the latest picture. Most also provide broadband/ADSL. You can check if your home is suitable for ADSL connection by checking on the phone company's website.

CHARGES

Line rental and call charges in Italy are among the highest in Europe, although they've fallen considerably recently due to increased competition. Telephone charges from Telecom Italia include line rental, telephone and other equipment rentals, special services such as call transfer and three-way conversation, credit card calls and general call charges. If you have a line installed or reconnected, the charge appears on your first bill. The charges and tariffs listed below apply only to calls made via Telecom Italia, and you should compare these rates with those of alternative providers (see above), which are sometimes cheaper.

Charges range between €0.10 and €0.13 for a three-minute local call and between €0.17 and €0.40 for a national long-distance call of the same duration, depending on whether you call at off-peak or peak times. Peak hours vary but are usually between 8am and 6.30pm Monday to Friday and 8am-1pm Saturday. Most companies now offer a range of deals which include all calls within Italy charged at a fixed rate of about €0.13 per call for a monthly fee, or even free national calls if you sign up to their internet service. Check websites for the latest and best deals.

International calls can be expensive but telephone providers sometimes run offers which are open to all customers, albeit for a limited time. For example, Telecom Italia's 'Nuova Welcome Home' includes up to

57 minutes a month of international calls to landlines and mobiles in 106 countries for a monthly fee of €5. If you go over the allowance, calls are charged at just over €0.10 per minute (depending on the destination). Telecom Italia also offers international calls at a fixed rate, e.g. calls to the US or UK are charged at just over €0.06 a minute for a monthly cost of €0.98. Meanwhile, Infostrada offers international calls at €0.20 per call – to Europe, the US and Canada – for €5 a month. It's important to check the conditions and duration of any offer, as once it finishes you'll be charged according to the company's regular tariff, which can be €4 per minute, depending on the destination, plus a connection fee.

Telecom Italia's charges for calls from a fixed-line phone to a mobile phone depend on the type of mobile phone contract, which is indicated by the number's prefix. Cheaper rates usually apply on Saturdays and Sundays. There are call packages which discount calls to mobile phones.

If you have access to the internet, free and heavily discounted calls (including international calls) can be made using an internet telephony service such as Skype (see page 110).

PHONE BILLS

Phone bills (*bolletta*) are issued bi-monthly for standard fixed-line and mobile phones. A phone bill contains the following information:

Reading Your Phone Bill

Italian	English
Giorno entro il quale deve essere effettuato il pagamento	Deadline for payment
Periodo al quale si riferiscono i canoni	Period covered by the bill
Nome ed indirizzo dell'intestatario	Name and address of the subscriber
Codice fiscale	Fiscal code of the subscriber
Prefisso e numero di telefono	Area code and phone number
Ubicazione del telefono	Location of the phone
Numero totale dei secondi addebitati tra le date di rilevazione delle letture	Number of seconds, based on readings made at the beginning and end of the period
Costo unitario e totale dei secondi	Cost of seconds and total
Costo fisso per la linea urbana e la categoria installata	Fixed costs for urban line and category installed (rural lines may cost more; the standard user category is B)
Canone per noleggio dell' apparecchio	Cost of lease of phone
Canone per la documentazione del traffico, se richiesta	Charges for an itemised bill, if requested
Servizi telefonici supplementari	Supplementary telephone services
Costo totale delle chiamate	Total cost of phone calls
Saldo imponibile.	Total subject to VAT
IVA totale	Total VAT
Totale bolletta.	Total to pay

If a bill is unpaid 45 days after the deadline, Telecom Italia can suspend outgoing calls and a penalty must be paid for re-activating the line. Bills can be paid at any post office or bank, by automatic bank payment (direct debit) or at a Telecom Italia office using an 'autobank' (*bancobol*). Some banks have machines that accept payment of bills from their clients, including phone bills. Receipts for phone bills should be kept for five years.

Cancellation

You must provide 15 days' notice of cancellation of a phone line in writing and pay the final bill when it arrives. It's better to do this in person at a Telecom Italia office, where you can obtain a receipt, than to entrust a letter to the Italian post office (see **Chapter 6**).

PUBLIC TELEPHONES

Public telephones (*telefono pubblico* or *cabina telefonica*) are located in bus and railway stations, airports, bars, cafés and restaurants, motorway rest areas, various business premises, main post offices, and in streets in cities and towns. All public phones allow 'international direct dialling' (IDD), although international calls can also be made via the operator. Most public phones accept only phone cards (*scheda telefonica prepagata*).

Phone cards are available from bars, news kiosks, tobacconists, post offices, shops and dispensing machines, for €5, €10 and €20. To activate a phone card, you tear off the perforated tab at the corner and insert it in the slot provided. The outstanding credit on the card is displayed when it's inserted and used cards can be replaced mid-way through a call. Units are recorded on the card and subtracted automatically after each call. Don't expect to be able to use a credit or debit card in Italian public phones, although airports, railway stations and hotels may have a few phones providing this service.

You can usually make both national and international calls from public phones, provided you have sufficient credit on your phone card. Bear in mind that calling a mobile phone from a public phone involves a connection charge of around €0.50.

Throughout the country there are *posto telefonico* offices, usually in small towns, where you can obtain assistance when making calls, and automatic telecommunication centres (*centri di telecomunicazione automatici*) offering self-service automatic calls (no assistance) in major cities and resorts. In cities and many towns in Italy there are also private telephone offices from where you can make international calls.

TELEPHONE DIRECTORIES

Telecom Italia issues directories for the major cities annually, while provincial towns usually receive a new directory every three years or so. Directories provide an alphabetical list of subscribers, tariffs, international and national direct dialling codes in the white pages (*pagine bianche*), plus yellow pages (*pagine gialle*) containing business phone numbers, other useful phone numbers and a map of the city concerned. All Telecom Italia subscribers are entitled to a free copy of the white and yellow pages, which are delivered to your door (the old ones must usually be recycled), and extra copies can be purchased from local Telecom offices.

Yellow- and *White Pages* can be accessed via the internet (www.paginegialle.it and www.paginebianche.it respectively).

Telecom Italia also issues a free booklet entitled *Tutto Città* in major cities, containing maps, useful phone numbers and addresses, and postcodes for local streets, which is delivered annually with the white and yellow pages.

English-speaking residents will find the English *Yellow Pages* (EYP) useful; this is a directory of English-speaking professionals, organisations and services in Bologna, Catania, Florence, Genoa, Milan, Naples and Rome and their surrounding areas. Unlike ordinary telephone directories, the listings contain full postal addresses with postcodes, telephone and fax numbers, and email and website addresses. For more information contact EYP, Lungotevere dei Mellini, 7, 00193 Rome (☎ 06-4740 861, 💻 www. insidersabroad.com/englishyellowpages).

Directory Enquiries

To find the phone number of a subscriber in Italy, you can call directory enquiries on 12. The system is now fully automated and if you don't know much Italian it's difficult to use; however, if you stay on the line a human operator will assist you. You can request only one number per call and each call costs around €0.50. Some information is free, however, such as information about dialling codes and the numbers of new subscribers who aren't yet listed in directories.

MOBILE PHONES

Needless to say, mobile phones are everywhere in Italy (which ties with Hong Kong in 'boasting' the world's highest rate of mobile-phone use). In 2008, a study by the European Commission found that Italy has the highest number of mobile phones in the EU: 152 per 100 people.

You should be aware that in recent years there has been widespread (and conflicting) publicity regarding a possible health risk to users from the microwave radiation emitted by phones.

Networks

There are four mobile phone networks in Italy: TIM (💻 www.tim.it), Tre (💻 www.tre.it), Vodafone (💻 www.vodafone.it) and Wind (💻 www.wind.it). TIM (Telecom Italia Mobile) is a subsidiary of Telecom Italia.

Vodafone and TIM are the most popular providers, each with some 30m subscribers, followed by Wind (17.90m) and Tre (8.93m). Between them, all four operate on a range of systems and technologies including GSM, GPRS, EDGE, UMTS and HSDPA. Wind is an exclusive provider in Italy of i-mode, a mobile internet service (alternative to WAP) popular in Japan. Virtual Network providers (which operate through the above networks) include CarrefourUNO (Vodafone), CoopVoce and PosteMobile (both TIM).

The best national cover is provided by TIM, although it's reluctant to provide access to international calls on a pay-as-you-talk phone (i.e. one without a contract). Vodafone and Wind don't cover the whole of Italy, although they're more generous with international access (which they provide through the TIM network!). When you're considering which company to sign up with, you must ensure that its network covers your home area and any other areas where you travel frequently or do business.

Call Charges & Contracts

All the mobile phone companies provide a choice between a contract and pay-as-you-go option. If you choose the latter, top-up-cards (*ricariche*) can be bought in amounts of €5 to €50 (see below). With a contract, you can choose from a range of tariffs, with terms to suit light, medium and heavy users. In all cases there's a fixed monthly network charge and sometimes also a monthly minimum call charge.

The cost of calls varies considerably according to the provider, the tariff and the day of the week and/or time of day a call is made. Due to increasing competition, the terms and conditions change frequently, with extras such as 'voicemail' frequently included free of charge. Before signing up with a provider, obtain the latest information on tariffs and special offers from phone shops, which are agents for the mobile phone manufacturers and the call providers. You can then compare and calculate which is likely to be the most cost-effective, bearing in mind your anticipated usage. If you make a lot of calls, you should select a tariff with a higher monthly charge and lower call charges. Conversely, if you make few calls or need a phone mostly for incoming calls, you should choose a tariff with a low monthly payment. Ask about personalised tariffs which may include offers on calls made to countries abroad, roaming abroad and calls made to other mobiles using the same network (which may be free).

Payment terms vary according to how you plan to pay. No deposit is required if bills are charged to a credit card, but if they're paid by direct debit, phone companies usually require a deposit of up to €50. If you'll be paying on receipt of a monthly bill, the deposit may be as high as €100 and there may be a fixed charge of around €25 for the initial network connection. Connection is often made within a few hours of signing a contract, although contracts usually state that connection will be made 'within 24 hours'.

When shopping for a new pay-as-you-go mobile phone, you can take advantage of competitive offers by switching from one Italian mobile company to another. Making a switch (passaggio) can save around 40 per cent on selected mobile phone models, or you can keep your old phone and make use of cut-price text or call packages or double credit with a new company. Switching companies involves signing a contract with your new company and obtaining a new SIM card, which takes about a week to become activated, after which your old SIM becomes defunct. Most switch-overs allow you to retain your old number.

Most mobile phone companies don't include a cancellation clause in their contracts, as many foreigners have discovered, and customers are stuck with monthly payments for the full term of the contract. Mobile phone companies will continue to bill you, even if you leave Italy during your contract period, and will pursue you until the money is paid (if necessary, by engaging debt collectors in other countries).

Short-term phone rentals aren't common but are possible for visiting business people with generous expense accounts (suffice to say, they don't come cheap).

Choosing a Phone

The cost of mobile phones themselves, affectionately called 'little phones' (telefonini), is quite high in Italy. Unlike people in countries such as Germany and the UK, where mobile phones are often provided 'free' on signing a contract with a provider (although they remain the property of the provider), Italians must usually buy their phones at the market price. The cost of a phone varies according to the manufacturer and its level of sophistication, and ranges from around €50 to €800, the average being around €175. Mobile phone retailers advertise in newspapers and magazines, where a wide range of offers is promoted.

There's also an active market in second-hand mobile phones. Good places to look are the classified advertisements in newspapers such as Porta Portese (Rome – named after the city's famous flea market), La Pulce (Florence) and Secondamano (Milan) – there are equivalents in most cities. There are a number of 'bazaars' on the internet offering used mobile phones at competitive prices – search on cellulari usati or di seconda mano. Bear in mind, however, that as well as buying a phone you must negotiate a contract with a service provider, unless you choose to use it with a pay-as-you-go SIM card.

Before buying a mobile phone you should compare battery life (lithium battery packs last the longest), memory capacity, weight (now down to 100g or less for the lightest models), size (some are now so small they're difficult to use) and features. The last may include alphanumeric store, automatic call-back, unanswered call store, call timer, minute minder, lock facility, call barring, mailbox, messaging services, a digital camera, internet surfing and email. However, bear in mind that the last two items may require a special contract with a service provider and additional equipment, which may cost as much as the mobile phone. This usually isn't mentioned when a shop tries to sell you a more expensive *telefonino*.

How to 'Top Up' a Pay-As-You-Go Phone

The audio instructions for adding call units to your mobile using a top-up card (*ricarica* or *scheda telefonica Wind/Vodafone/Tim, etc.*) are in Italian. You will initially be presented with a choice of options which correspond to keying in a number. Repeatedly pressing the number 1 invariably gets you to the *ricarica* option, where you'll be asked to key in the 16 digit code on the top-up-card: *digiti ora il numero segreto di sedici cifre riportato sulla scheda*. If the number you have typed is correct, you're usually asked to confirm both the code and your telephone number by typing 1 each time when they're voiced-over, and the operation is complete.

If all that sounds too complicated, you can give your mobile number and payment to the cashier at a tobacconist's or news kiosk and they'll top your phone up for you. This service isn't available everywhere; most shops offer only one option, either top-up cards or a cashier-operated machine.

It's also possible to top up your phone at an ATM or by going to the service provider's website.

Texting in Italian

In a nation of mobile-phone addicts, it's hardly surprising that the Italian language has its own 'SMS-speak'. Its abbreviations crop up in texts (not only those written by teenagers!),

on computer screens, in scribbled notes and even as wall graffiti. Here are some of the most commonly-used abbreviations and what they mean in English:

Texting in Italian	
Abbrevation	**Meaning**
C	*ci* (there)
Cmq	*comunque* (anyway)
K	*che* (that)
Nn	*non* (not/don't)
6	*sei* (you are)
Sn	*sono* (I am)
TVB	*Ti Voglio Bene* (I love you)
Vv	*viva* (hurrah for)
X	*per* (for)
Xk	*perché* (why)
xo'	*però* (but/however)

So *Io nn c sn, tu c6?* I'm not there, are you?

INTERNET

Perhaps due to the high cost of telecommunications, Italy has been slower than many other European countries to adapt to the internet. However, this is changing and most large and medium-sized companies now quote an email address and often a website in their advertising. Private consumers are also joining up in droves, lured by the recent arrival of a number of free internet service providers (ISPs). About 60 per cent of the population has access to the internet (at school or work or elsewhere outside the home) and about 50 per cent has access at home.

All the phone-service providers offer an internet service, usually based on ADSL/broadband and often bundled in with a calls package so you pay a single monthly charge for phone and internet. Infostrada (⌨ www.infostrada.it) offers unlimited internet access at speeds of up to 8Mb, plus a phone line and free national calls for €39.95 (activation is free and the monthly cost is reduced to €23.28 for the first year). Some of the least expensive options are with Tiscali (⌨ www.tiscali.it), whose budget options include internet-only (8Mb speed) for €19.95 a month (reduced to €9.95 for a limited promotional period).

Telecom Italia's internet provider Alice (⌨ www.alice.it) offers tariffs with different levels of access and conditions. It's more expensive but there are frequent introductory offers and discounts, e.g. unlimited internet (up to 7Mb speeds), a phone line and a lower rate for national calls, reduced from €36 per month to €17 for the first eight months with free activation (which usually costs €80).

It's worth noting that all offers are conditional on your signing up with a service provider for a period of time, usually not less than a year.

You can check whether you're in a broadband-enabled zone by going to the provider's website and inputting your address. In the case of Telecom Italia, you can enter your fixed line home number into a search engine on its website (⌨ http://adsl2.csi. telecomitalia.it), which tells you if your address is viable (green) or unviable (red) and, if viable, what sort of download speed is available.

If you already have internet access (e.g. at work) and don't want to pay for an email account of your own, you can sign up with one of the free web-based email services such as Yahoo Mail (⌨ www.yahoo.com) or Hotmail (⌨ www.hotmail.com). One advantage of these services is that you can access your email from any computer with internet access, e.g. at a library or internet cafe. Note, however, that mail sent to and from such services isn't necessarily secure.

Modems

You can use any modem but should note that a modem imported from abroad may not work in Italy without modification. You must ensure that your modem accepts a four-wire cable where the two wires in the middle are active (the UK system, for example, uses the two outer wires). You may also need a telephone plug adapter, available from any hardware store (*ferramenta*).

In order to avoid problems it may be better to purchase a new modem in Italy. Modern 56k (V90) internal and external modems can be obtained for around €50 and €75 respectively although many ISPs provide them as part of the package.

An USB stick modem (*chiavetta*) allows you to go online using your mobile phone. They cost around the same price as a modem but are often discounted or even provided free when you take out a contract on a phone. This is the best option if you plan to do a lot of web-surfing as contract phones include a greater number of internet hours. You can use a USB stick modem with a pay-as-you-go phone, but your hours may be limited, e.g. 20 hours a month, and if you exceed your limit the charges for additional hours are high and will soon eat up your phone credit.

Internet Telephony

If you have a broadband internet connection, you can make long-distance and international phone 'calls' for free (or almost free) to anyone with a broadband connection using 'voice over internet protocol' (VOIP). The leading company in this field is Skype (⌨ www.skype.com) which has over 150m users worldwide (and at least 20m online at any one time). Other major players include VOIP (⌨ www.voip.com) and Vonage (⌨ www.vonage.com).

All you need is access to a local broadband provider and a headset (costing as little as €10) or a special phone. Calls to other computers anywhere in the world are free, while calls to landlines start at less than €0.01 a minute. The downside is that lines are prone to interference and sudden disconnections.

Lerici, Liguria

8.

TELEVISION & RADIO

Italy's pride in its cultural heritage is by no means evident in its television (TV) programmes; you could be excused for thinking that Italians invented junk TV. Italian radio (including expatriate stations), on the other hand, is generally excellent and the equal of that in most other European countries.

TELEVISION

Italians are avid television viewers (virtually every Italian household owns at least one TV) and according to some surveys Italians rate third in Europe (after the Portuguese and British) in average viewing time per head per day (around four hours). Some 90 per cent of Italians over the age of 14 watch TV every day and most receive their news from the TV (relatively few Italians buy newspapers). There's usually a TV in the kitchen/dining room, which seems to be permanently switched on, and conversation often has to be pitched several decibels higher than normal to be heard above the incessant din.

The choice of programmes is vast, although it's a disappointing hotchpotch of mind-numbing game shows, boring cabarets, bizarre dubbed soaps (where sound and mouth movements are rarely synchronised), trashy films and relentless repeats. Annoyingly for expatriates, foreign films and TV programmes are dubbed into Italian rather than subtitled. Some local TV stations broadcast programmes on a continuous loop that they rarely change, which can give a distinctly 'Groundhog Day' feel to channel-hopping. All this is knitted together with endless advertising, most of which is of equally poor quality.

After a campaign in 1996 by parents worried about the influence that certain programmes could have on their children, programmes with a sexual or violent content aren't shown between the hours of 7am and 10.30pm. If an image of a child in red is shown on the screen at the start of a film, it indicates that it should be viewed in the presence of an adult. Italians also pioneered the 'violence chip', which is an electronic device designed to filter out violent programmes on TV when children are watching.

There's no cable TV in Italy; some cables were installed, but it became too expensive and was abandoned in favour of satellite TV. Television reception (both terrestrial and satellite) is good in most of Italy.

Many TV magazines are available, including *TV Sorrisi & Canzoni*, *Guida TV*, *Onda TV*, *Radio Corriere* and *Film TV*, all of which are sold by newsagents and include radio programmes. There are separate magazines for satellite TV such as *Tele +*, *Tele 7*, and *TV Sat*. TV magazines are also provided free each week with the major daily newspapers.

Standards

The standards for television reception in Italy aren't the same as in some other countries. Due to the differences in transmission standards, TVs, video recorders and DVD players operating on the British (PAL-I), French (SECAM) or North American (NTSC) systems won't function in Italy, which, along with most other continental European countries, uses the PAL-BG standard. It's possible to buy a multi-standard European TV containing automatic circuitry that switches between different systems. Some multi-standard TVs also offer the NTSC standard and have a jack plug connection allowing you to play back American videos or DVDs.

A standard British, French or US TV won't work in Italy, although British TVs can be modified. The same applies to foreign video recorders/DVD players, which won't operate with an Italian TV unless they're dual-standard. Some expatriates opt for two TVs, one to receive Italian programmes and another (e.g. SECAM or NTSC) to play their favourite videos.

A portable 36cm (14in) colour TV can be purchased in Italy for around €100, a 55cm (21in) TV costs from around €150 and a 71cm (28in) model from around €350. Many TVs feature Nicam stereo sound, and digital sound is available in most of Italy. Digital wide-screen televisions are also widely available and prices, although still high in comparison with those of standard TVs, are falling. Most new TVs offer a teletext system, which apart from allowing you to display programme schedules provides a wealth of useful and interesting information.

> Teletext information is called *Televideo* on RAI stations and *Mediavideo* on Italia Uno, Rete 4 and Canale 5 stations.

Terrestrial TV

Italian TV changed dramatically after deregulation of the Television Board in 1976, up to which time it had been totally state-owned and censored by the Catholic Church. Today, Italy has seven main terrestrial stations – RAI 1, 2 and 3, Italia 1, Rete 4, La7 and Canale 5 (see below) – plus hundreds of local stations. The country has the highest density of independent broadcasting companies in the world, exceeding even Japan and the US. The number of stations had reached almost 1,000 by the early '90s and continues to grow, with more than a million hours of programming broadcast each year.

RAI

The public broadcaster RAI has three main channels, which generally offer the best quality programmes and together attract around 40 per cent of viewers. These are RAI UNO (RAI1), RAI DUE (RAI2) and RAI TRE (RAI3). RAI3 is the most 'cultural' of the three, although as most of RAI's administrative council members are elected by parliamentary committee, the broadcasting on all three channels can be somewhat less than unbiased. For further information, visit the RAI website (🖥 www.rai.it), which has an English-language version.

♦ **RAI 1** is the most popular RAI station among older viewers and shows major events, popular series (usually about the Mafia) made by RAI, quiz/game shows, film premieres and news. At the weekend, it broadcasts children's programmes in the early morning. On Sundays, it shows a popular soap called *Domenica In* (now surpassed in popularity by Italia 1's *Buona Domenica*), which accompanies Sunday lunch in many households and lasts most of the afternoon.

♦ **RAI 2** has more films and 'tele-films' (films made for TV, usually American) and soaps such as the US comedy series *Friends*. During the day, it shows its own programmes. Children's programmes are shown late on Sunday morning and at 4pm on weekdays.

♦ **RAI 3** features more sport than the other RAI stations, plus regional news programmes, and shows a film at around 8.40pm most days. Children's programmes are shown just before lunchtime on Sunday.

Independent Stations

The most important independent TV stations in Italy are Canale 5, Italia 1, Rete 4 and La7 – the first three are owned by media magnate and prime minister, Silvio Berlusconi through his Mediaset organisation. They're most famous for their mildly pornographic shows, some of which involve contestants stripping to win bonus prizes. These channels collectively attract over 50 per cent of Italian viewers.

♦ **Canale 5** shows a mixture of tele-films, soaps and sitcoms (some Italian), news and weather, with a film at 9pm each day.

♦ **Italia 1** is similar to Canale 5 and has excellent news reports and good entertainment programmes in the evening, including a film at 8.45pm. It shows a surfeit of cartoons from morning until early evening and *Buona Domenica*, a popular soap.

♦ **Rete 4** mainly broadcasts a series of tele-films interrupted by feature films at 4pm, 8.35pm and 11pm. It's supposed to be the most highbrow of the three Berlusconi stations but there isn't much difference between them.

♦ **La7** broadcasts a mix of cultural programmes and documentaries, news, sport and foreign TV shows, and mini-series including *Sex and the City* and *Midsomer Murders* (though dubbed into Italian). It's considered the third TV network in Italy and it's owned by the media branch of Telecom Italia, Telecom Italia Media.

Other significant stations include Telemontecarlo, TMC and TMC2, Italia 7/Telecity and Odeon/Quadrifoglio TV. There are many local TV stations and in northern Italy you can also receive terrestrial broadcasts from Austria, France and Switzerland. Around 1,000 local channels 'share' around 10 per cent of viewers; with little money and resources, programming is dominated by the most appalling amateurism, film repeats, abysmal locally-produced advertising and soft porn (especially late at night).

Digital Television

Like the rest of Europe, Italy is moving from analogue to digital TV, with analogue transmission due to be 'switched off' in 2012. Digital terrestrial television (DTT) broadcasts both free-to-air and pay-TV programming and is now watched by about 40 per cent of Italian households. Mediaset Premium (💻 www.mediasetpremium.mediaset.it) has the largest platform for digital pay TV and broadcasts a range of packages and options including football, films and reality programmes. Services are also offered by Sky Italia and Dahlia TV.

The benefits of digital TV include a superior picture, CD-quality sound, wide-screen cinema format and access to many more stations.

To watch digital TV you require a decoder box and smart card. Customers must sign up for a 12-month subscription and agree to have the connection via an ISDN line (to allow for future interactive services).

Satellite Television

Satellite TV has recently increased hugely in popularity in Italy, where there are both domestic and international offerings to choose from. Many satellite stations provide teletext information and most broadcast in stereo.

Domestic

Sky Italia (💻 www.sky.it) is one of the largest satellite TV providers. Owned by the News Corporation Group, it claimed to have almost 5m subscribers in 2009, around 20 per cent of Italian households. Subscribers to Sky Italia are bound to a 12-month contract that is automatically renewed each year unless cancelled at least 60 days before the termination of the contract. Subscription costs vary according to the channel package and begin at €29 per month. The decoder is free but it costs around €85 to have a satellite dish installed (which is periodically discounted).

Sky offers several options to mix packages of channels starting at €29 for three options, €47 for five options, and €69.90 for six options with Sky x2 (which allows Sky to be viewed simultaneously on two televisions). Channel packages include Entertainment (28 channels), Music (17 channels plus 25 radio channels)

and News (eight channels) and you can add on options such as Cinema (12 channels) and Calcio (football, 15 channels, although how this is possible – let alone desirable – is anyone's guess!). There are also pay-per-view options for movies and major sporting events.

Since 2006, Italian football clubs have had the right to sell their broadcast rights, unlike most European clubs. Sky Italia is a major buyer, so you can watch most matches on Sky and on the digital TV provider Mediaset Premium (see above).

However, Sky Italia has had competition since summer 2009 with the advent of Tivusat (🖳 www.tivu.tv), which is similar to the UK's Freesat package in that it offers free access (via a decoder and viewing card) to around 30 digital channels. Tivusat is owned by a combination of RAI, Mediaset and Telecom Italia.

A bonus for Sky (UK) subscribers is the availability of radio stations, including all the national BBC stations (see **Radio** on page 117).

UK Sky Television

In order to receive Sky television you need a Sky digital receiver (digibox) and a dish. There are two ways to obtain a receiver (digibox) and Sky 'smart' card. You can subscribe in the UK or Ireland (personally, if you have an address there, or via a friend) and take the Sky receiver and card to Italy. However, there may be restrictions as the digibox is supposed to be connected to a phone line and Sky can determine where the receiver is being used (and when it isn't connected to a phone line) and may terminate the service if it isn't being used in the UK or Ireland. Alternatively, you can obtain a Sky card from Store Satellite (🖳 http://storesatellite.com/sky-tv-italy.php) or Insat International (🖳 www.insatinternational.com).

In the UK, a basic Sky subscription costs around £18 per month and give you access to around 100 channels, including BBC1, BBC2, ITV1, CH4 and CH5. Various other packages are available costing up to around £60 per month, for the which you have access to all channels including the Movie

and Sports channels plus 'free' broadband internet. For further information, see 🖳 www.sky.com.

Equipment

To receive satellite TV from Sky (or any other broadcaster) you'll need a satellite receiver, commonly know as a digibox, with a built-in decoder and a viewing card (e.g. a Sky card) to receive scrambled programmes. Astra's satellite's footprint is tightly focused on the UK and Ireland, and although surrounding countries have the ability to pick up the signal, it depends upon the size of your satellite dish. In the UK and Ireland, a 60cm dish is sufficient, but in northern Italy (which is on the edge of the satellites's footprint) you require a 1-1.2m dish to receive programmes from the Sky Astra 2d satellite; the further south you go the weaker the signal becomes and you may need a 3m dish in Rome and southern Italy.

The cost of equipment varies, depending on the brand of digibox and the size of the dish, but is usually between €500-1,000. There are many satellite sales and installation companies in Italy (see 🖳 http://storesatellite.com/sky-tv-italy.php). Shop around and compare prices. Alternatively you can import your own satellite dish and digibox and install it yourself.

Location & Installation

To be able to receive channels from any satellite, there must be no obstacles between the satellite and your dish, i.e. no large obstacles such as trees, buildings or mountains must obstruct the signal, therefore check before renting an apartment or buying a home.

Before buying or erecting a satellite dish – or even before buying or renting a home – check whether it's possible to install one. If you're renting an apartment you'll need to obtain permission from your landlord, and if you wish to install a large dish you may also need a building permit.

Dishes can usually be mounted in a variety of unobtrusive positions and can be painted or patterned to blend in with the background. Apartment blocks may be fitted with a communal satellite dish or have cable TV and it may not be possible to install your own dish.

Programme Guides

Most satellite stations provide teletext and extensive programme information. Sky satellite programme listings are provided in a number of British publications such as *What Satellite and Digital TV* (💻 www.futureplc.com) which is available on subscription. Satellite TV programmes are also listed in some expatriate newspapers and magazines in Italy. If you're interested in receiving TV stations from further afield, you should obtain a copy of the *World Radio TV Handbook (WRTV)* by Nicholas Hardyman (Watson-Guptil Publications, 💻 www.wrth.com).

TV Licence

A TV tax (*canone*) is payable in Italy and costs €106 per year for a colour TV; it can be paid quarterly, half-yearly or annually (at a post office). A single licence covers any number of TV sets in a household. When you buy a TV in Italy, your name is automatically registered with the authorities, although many people avoid tax by buying a second-hand TV or making an 'arrangement' with the vendor. The tax must be paid to customs if you personally import a TV. The authorities have powerful detector vans to identify homes where people are watching TV and then check whether they've paid the tax. There are fines for non-payment, but since the **maximum** fine is just 50 per cent of the licence fee it isn't surprising that many people don't bother to pay for a licence but just pay the fine instead.

DVDs & Videos

DVDs and, to a lesser extent, videos are available to hire (*noleggiare*) or buy from shops in all main towns and cities, listed in the *Yellow Pages* under *Audiovisivi*. To rent them you usually need to join a club and pay an annual fee; you can then rent a film for between €2 per night (for an old 'classic') and €5 to €7.50 per night for the latest Hollywood blockbuster. The American company Blockbuster has stores in major towns with a wide selection of films in the original language (you can also rent a DVD player). In some places you may also be offered pirate DVDs of new films that

haven't yet been released, which should be avoided as the quality is usually terrible; they're also illegal! Market stalls often have a good selection of authentic DVDs, including classics and fairly recent releases for as little as €3. Music and video stores sell DVDs starting from around €7.

You may be able to buy or swap English-language videos and DVDs with other foreigners through expatriate clubs, and you can buy English-language videos and DVDs via the internet and through mail-order video catalogues. Choices UK, Queen Street, Burton upon Trent, Staffordshire, DE14 3LP, UK (☎ 0844-573 3836, 💻 www.choicesuk.com) will search for anything you request.

As in the rest of the developed world, DVDs have superseded videos. Most have the advantage of being playable in various languages, either dubbed or subtitled. Be careful, however, to buy DVDs for the correct 'zone' (see box).

☑ **SURVIVAL TIP**

DVD Zones

DVDs may be encoded with a region code, restricting the area of the world in which they can be played. The code for Western Europe is 2, while discs without any region coding are called all-region or region 0 discs. However, you can buy all-region DVD players and DVD players can be modified to be region-free, allowing the playback of all discs (see 💻 www.regionfreedvd.net and www.moneysavingexpert.com/shopping/dvd-unlock).

RADIO

Radio is popular in Italy with an estimated audience of some 35m people, over a third of whom listen exclusively to popular music stations. Radio was deregulated in Italy in 1976, at the same time as television, since when there has been an explosion in the number of stations available; there are now some 2,500, from large national stations to small local stations with just a 'handful' of listeners. The three main channels are Radio 1, 2 and 3 operated by the state controlled company RAI. Radios 1 and 2 are split into light (dance) music and general entertainment on one wavelength and popular music on another, while Radio 3 broadcasts serious discussion programmes and classical music.

A favourite station among young listeners is Radio DJ, which features well known club disc jockeys (mostly on Friday and Saturday nights), while Radio Italia offers a selection of Italian singers and bands, and Radio Globo plays mostly dance music.

English-language Stations

During the summer, RAI broadcasts daily news in English, and Vatican Radio broadcasts news in English at various times. There are expatriate English-language radio stations in the major cities.

The BBC World Service is popular with expats and you may be able to pick it up on medium or long wave – it has ceased its short-wave broadcasts to Europe – but the best way to tune in is via the Astra and Eutelsat satellites

(see **Satellite TV** on page 115).' For a free programme guide and frequency information, contact BBC World Service, Bush House, Strand, London WC2B 4PH, UK (☎ 020-7240 3456, 🖳 www.bbc.co.uk/worldservice).

Both digital and analogue satellite services offer a range of radio stations from around the world. BBC Radio 1, 2, 3, 4, 5, 6 and 7, BBC World Service, Absolute Radio, Classic FM, Jazz FM, Talk Sport, Voice of America and many non-English language stations are broadcast via satellite. Satellite radio stations are listed in British satellite TV magazines, and schedules can also be found on the internet. If you're interested in receiving radio stations from further afield you should obtain a copy of the *World Radio TV Handbook* (🖳 www.wrth.com). Radio is one of the most web-friendly mediums there is, provided you have a computer with an internet connection or even a state-of-the-art mobile phone, you can stream in live radio broadcasts from around the world without the need for a satellite connection.

Riomaggiore, Cinque Terre, Liguria

9.
EDUCATION

The foundations for Italy's current education system were established in 1946, when the country became a parliamentary republic. Since then, the state has provided free education for all, from nursery school to university. The state sector is the backbone of the Italian education system and most students attend state schools and universities, although there are also private schools. The education system is divided into a number of stages: pre-school, primary school, lower and upper secondary school, and higher and further education. State education is also free for the children of foreigners living in Italy, irrespective of whether they're registered residents. According to the Italian Association of Italian Municipal Councils (ANCI), in 2009 there were 690,000 foreign students from 190 different countries in enrolled Italian schools.

Compulsory education (*scuola dell'obbligo*) applies from the ages of 6 to 16. After students have reached the age of 16 tuition remains free, although an enrolment tax (*tasse d'iscrizione*) of around €20 is payable at the beginning of each school year. At university, enrolment tax increases to around €130, although the amount depends on each university faculty and after the first year it's often based on family income – this means that some families pay nothing while others may be charged as much as €1200 a year. University education is free for foreign students and there are no quotas, though students from outside the European Union (EU) require a student visa (see **Chapter 3**).

Qualifications are of great importance in Italy, where very few school-leavers go directly into employment without studying for a diploma, degree or professional qualification, and Italy boasts one of the highest proportions of university students in the world. Despite this, the percentage of students who graduate from university or even obtain secondary school qualifications is low compared with other EU countries. Two reasons for this are the traditional (and rigorous) nature of education in Italy and the number of years (seven or eight)

most students require to complete a degree, which leads to a high dropout rate: only one in three who enrol graduate. However, due to its demanding curricula, Italy considers its school and university qualifications to be of a higher standard than those of many other countries, with the consequence that educational qualifications gained abroad aren't necessarily recognised in Italy or given equal status.

Both the curricula and examinations in state schools are set by the Ministry of Education (Ministero della Pubblica Istruzione), in consultation with an advisory body, the National Education Council. The Ministry is represented at regional level by school authorities (*sovrintendenze scolastiche*). Italy is divided into scholastic districts (*scholastici*) administered by provincial local education offices. In theory, this centralised system should ensure the same standard of education throughout the country, but in practice there's a considerable disparity between the quality of education in northern and southern schools, the former being regarded as far superior. (The adult illiteracy rate is officially around 1.5 per cent, although unofficially it's much higher and almost exclusively limited to the south.) More recent years have seen a progressive devolvement of responsibility to regional education authorities and schools, one effect of which has been to give schools a (limited) degree of freedom in setting their own curricula, and state schools are responsible for managing their own finances.

As educational courses at school and university are largely determined by the Ministry of Education, they aren't tailored to the needs of individual students. At university a certain amount of choice can be exercised through a student's individual study plan, but a frequent criticism is that the structure of courses does little to encourage self-expression and personal development. Teaching methods at all levels are often criticised as old-fashioned, with over-emphasis on learning by rote. The rigid adherence to a core curriculum (with textbooks often standardised) in state schools helps to ensure uniform standards but can be hard on slow learners. The need to introduce more flexible study programmes in schools has long been a subject of debate in Italy, and recent years have seen a gradual broadening of the school curriculum, partly through the introduction of experimental classes (*classi sperimentali*) based on students' own choices and needs.

The drive to improve quality while reducing public spending has resulted in some controversial education reforms which were due to come into effect in 2010. Proposed changes include school closures, staff cuts and increased class sizes, reduced hours in some schools, a longer summer break and the reintroduction of conduct marks for bad behaviour. Other proposals include a 30 per cent cap on intake of foreign pupils in an attempt to promote integration and avoid the creation of 'ghetto' schools. In universities, there are plans to cut budgets and the number of degree subjects offered.

A child's progress is based on annual evaluations, which in turn are based on tests and continuous assessment. Written tests are held each term and oral tests (*interrogazioni*) at the discretion of the teacher. This can come as something of a shock to foreign children who aren't used to responding orally and who come from a system where greater emphasis is given to written work and exams. At university, the emphasis on oral examinations, as opposed to

written ones, is even more marked, the majority of exams being conducted orally.

The need to obtain a satisfactory level in all subjects each year, as well as passing exams at the end of each school cycle, means Italian children must study hard from an early age. From primary school onwards, children are expected to do regular homework (*compiti*), the amount increasing with the age of the child (parents often set aside a considerable amount of time to help children with their homework).

Information about Italian schools and universities can be obtained from Italian embassies and consulates abroad, from foreign embassies and from educational departments within the Ministry of Education, Ministero della Pubblica Istruzione, Viale Trastevere, 76/a, 00153 Rome (☎ 06-5849 1, 🖳 www.istruzione.it). Local school information can be obtained from town halls (*comuni*) and from local education offices (*provveditorati*), as well as from the Ministry's website, which lists the names and addresses of all state schools and many private schools by province (the direct link is 🖳 www.trampi.istruzione.it/ricscu/start.do).

The Italy Schools page of the Worldwide Classroom's online directory (🖳 www.worldwide.edu/ci/italy) lists many educational institutions accepting both Italian and foreign students, including language schools, universities, private institutes and international schools.

STATE OR PRIVATE SCHOOL?

If you're able to choose between state and private education and between Italian and foreign-language schooling, the following information will help you to decide.

Language

Choosing the language of study is one of the most important decisions to be made when selecting the best type of school for your children. How do you and your children view the thought of their studying in Italian? What language is best for them from a long-term point of view? Is schooling available in Italy in your children's mother tongue?

The only schools in Italy using English as the teaching language are a few private foreign and international schools. If your children attend any other school, they must study all subjects in Italian. For most children, studying in Italian isn't the handicap it may at first appear, particularly for young children, who usually adapt easily. The watershed age for learning a foreign language is between 10 and 12, after which children tend to learn languages more slowly. In recent years, Italian state schools have made a great effort to integrate foreign children and provide intensive Italian-language lessons, remedial classes and cultural activities. Nevertheless, some children have great difficulty learning Italian and many foreign parents arrange private Italian lessons, often with the children of other foreign parents in their area, or send their children to an international school, where lessons are taught in English and they can learn Italian at a more leisurely pace without the pressure.

English is generally the second language taught in state schools in Italy, where it's introduced as a compulsory subject in primary school and continued throughout secondary school. However, the level of instruction will do little to maintain your child's ability to read and write in English; Italian students are rarely fluent by the time they leave school.

In some areas of Italy, the languages most commonly spoken are French and German, and Italian is a second language (see **Language** on page 37). Schools in the Val d'Aosta and the Trentino-Alto Adige region teach school syllabi in French and German respectively plus Italian, and bilingualism is often a prerequisite for employment. Other minority languages, including Slovenian, Albanian and Greek, may be included in the school curriculum if there's sufficient demand from parents.

Other Considerations

There are many factors to take into account when choosing a school in Italy, including the following:

♦ State education is perceived to be of an equal or higher standard than private education, and Italian parents generally

send their children to private schools only for religious reasons or to obtain extra help that's unavailable in a state school.

♦ Due to language (see above) and other integration problems, enrolling a child in an Italian state school is recommended only if you're planning to stay for at least a year, particularly for teenage children who aren't fluent in Italian. If you're uncertain how long you'll be staying in Italy, it's probably best to assume a medium or long stay.

♦ The area where you choose to live may affect your choice of school. For example, state schools may give preference to children living locally, and international schools (where the curriculum is taught in English) tend to be situated in or near the major cities. Children usually attend local nursery and primary schools, although Italy's falling birth rate has led to many school closures in rural areas, with the result that children may need to travel some distance to the nearest large town or city to attend school, particularly at secondary level.

♦ Your children's current ages and educational level will affect how easily they'll fit into a private school or the Italian state school system. The younger they are, the easier it will be to place them in a suitable school.

♦ Consider whether your children will require your help with their studies and, more importantly, whether you'll be able to help them, particularly with their Italian. Is special or extra tutoring available in Italian and other subjects, if required?

♦ Compare the school hours and holiday periods. State schools generally have compulsory Saturday morning classes. How will the school holidays and hours affect your family's work and leisure activities?

♦ Where you plan to move to after Italy may be an important consideration with regard to your children's language of tuition and system of education in Italy. Consider how old your children will be when you plan to leave Italy and what plans you may have for their further education.

♦ If religion is an important aspect in your choice of school, you may have few options if you're seeking a non-Catholic school. However, there are very few strictly denominational schools in Italy, where most Catholic private schools accept non-Catholic students.

♦ All Italian state schools are co-educational, therefore if you want your children to attend a single-sex school, you have no alternative but to go private.

♦ Find out whether the school has a good academic record.

♦ Ask how large the classes are and what the pupil:teacher ratio is. State schools have about 30 children in a class.

Consider also the secondary and further education prospects in Italy (or another country) and whether Italian examinations are recognised in your home country or the country where you plan to live after leaving

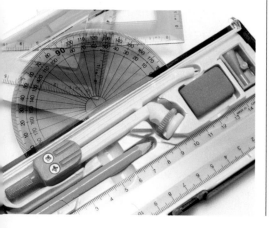

Italy. If neither state nor private schools in Italy match your criteria, consider whether to send your children to a boarding school and, if so, in which country.

Obtain the opinions and advice of others who have been faced with the same decisions and problems, and collect as much information from as many different sources as possible before making a decision. Speak to teachers and the parents of children attending the schools on your shortlist. Finally, most parents find it pays to discuss the alternatives with their children before making a decision. See also **Choosing a Private School** on page 132.

STATE SCHOOLS

State-funded schools in Italy are termed both state schools (*scuole statali*) and public schools (*scuole pubbliche*), although the term 'state' has been used in preference to 'public' in this book to prevent confusion with the British term 'public school', which refers to a private, fee-paying school. The state school system in Italy differs considerably from school systems in, for example, the UK and the US, particularly regarding secondary and university education.

Schooling is divided into four educational cycles, as follows:

♦ **Nursery** school: a three-year cycle from three to six years of age;

♦ **Primary** school: a five-year cycle from 6 to 11;

♦ **Lower secondary** school: a three-year cycle from 11 to 14;

♦ **Upper secondary** school: a three, four or five-year cycle from 14 to 17, 18 or 19.

In small towns and villages, nursery, primary and lower secondary schools often form one unified school (*istituto comprensivo*), and state nursery and primary schools are also sometimes grouped together within one teaching circle (*circolo didattico*).

Attendance at a state nursery school isn't compulsory and there are a number of other private pre-school options for children aged under six. Compulsory schooling begins with primary school and continues until the age of 16 or the first year of upper secondary school, provided a year's schooling hasn't been repeated.

A pupil is promoted (*promosso*) to the next class only after attaining a satisfactory level in all subjects at the end of the academic year. Pupils who fail (*bocciare*) to reach the required standard in a particular subject carry forward an educational debit (*debito formativo*), which must be made up either through extra tuition during the summer holidays or by attending extra classes during the following academic year. If pupils fail in a number of subjects (usually over half the total), they may be refused admission into the next year's class and must repeat the entire year (*ripetere l'anno*). All schools have regular parent-teacher meetings, where every attempt is made to prevent this happening.

Students are required to make specialist subject choices on entry into upper secondary school, and a number of options are available at this stage. Admission to Italian secondary schools isn't selective and, provided students obtain their lower secondary school-leaving certificate, they may go to the upper secondary school of their choice. At the end of the upper secondary cycle, pupils take a state examination; if they pass, they receive a leaving certificate that allows them to progress to higher education.

Each school has a principal (*dirigente scolastico* in primary schools and *preside* in secondary schools) who's responsible for day-to-day management, co-ordinating school activities and establishing disciplinary sanctions. An important role is played by the school's consultative committee (*consiglio d'istituto*), made up of the principal, teaching and non-teaching staff, and (in secondary schools only) parents and pupils, who make decisions about the school's budget as well as organising teaching and extra-curricular activities. A teaching committee (*collegio dei docenti*) prepares a school's educational plans, including timetables and the choice of textbooks. There's also a class council (*consiglio di classe*) consisting of a panel of teachers, whose main task is to assess pupils' progress at the end of each term and decide on their promotion to the following year's class.

An hour of religious studies per week is part of the curriculum of all Italian schools, although this isn't obligatory and parents may ask for their children to be exempted.

The presence of disabled children in a class, provided they aren't too seriously disabled (mentally or physically), is considered a source of general enrichment. Disabled children are entitled to up to 12 hours' tuition per week with a specially qualified teacher (*maestro di sostegno*) and, where applicable, schools must provide lifts.

A general criticism of Italian state schools often made by foreigners is the lack of extra-curricular activities such as sport, music, drama, arts and crafts. Although these subjects all form part of the school curriculum, they're limited to a small number of hours per week; inter-school sports competitions, for example, are rare. Extra-curricular activities offered by Italian schools generally take place during afternoons and operate on a much more limited scale than in the UK and the US. To play in a sports team, a child must usually join a private (and therefore fee-paying) association, which entails parents ferrying him back and forth after school hours. Similarly, for music lessons it may be necessary to find a local teacher or enrol at a private music school.

Classes (grades) in Italian schools differ considerably from those in the American and British systems. Classes at each level are numbered from one upwards. Thus, the first class in primary school is the *prima elementare*, followed by the *seconda elementare* and so on, until the fifth and final class (*quinta elementare*). In lower secondary school, the classes are *prima media*, *seconda media* and *terza media*. In both upper secondary school and university, the numbering refers to the year: *primo anno*, *secondo anno* and so on.

Enrolment

Information about schools in a particular area can be obtained from the local education office (*provveditorato*) or the town hall (*comune*), although this may simply be a list of schools with addresses and phone numbers. It's up to parents to apply to schools directly. If your child has already attended school in another country, a translation of his qualifications is required for enrolment in the Italian school system, together with a letter from the previous school's principal. You also need to contact the Italian consulate before arriving in Italy and obtain an evaluation certificate (*dichiarazione di valore*). Once this has been done, getting started in an Italian school is relatively straightforward, as schools are generally flexible about accommodating foreign students. However, it's difficult or impossible to organise state education in advance from your country of origin.

Visiting Italy before your relocation is recommended, particularly as school places may be limited, and you may end up ferrying children long distances to school if the one nearest to your home has no vacancies. Bear in mind that all schools and many public offices are closed during August.

Enrolment in an Italian state school doesn't depend on your living within its catchment area, as is the case, for example, in France and the UK. You can make an application to the school of your choice and, provided a place is available, your child should be admitted, although when places are limited, priority is given to those who live in the local area. Schools have a deadline (around 25th January of the previous school year) by which they need to know the number of students who will be attending school the following September. Most

schools have a flexible attitude to pupils who need to start school or change schools during the academic year. Provided you have a good reason, it may be possible for a child to change schools within the same area or to another part of the country; a request must be in writing and be signed and approved by the principal of your child's previous school.

To enrol a child in an Italian school, you need to complete an application form and provide the following documents:

♦ certificate of family status (*certificato di stato di famiglia*) – available from the registry office (Ufficio Anagrafe) in your *comune*;

♦ your child's birth certificate (*certificato di nascita*) and proof of immunisation against hepatitis B, polio, diphtheria and tetanus (with relevant translations, if necessary);

♦ a photograph of your child and your permit to stay (*permesso di soggiorno*) or residence certificate (*certificato di residenza*). Alternatively, written evidence of your intention to move permanently to Italy (if you haven't already done so) is acceptable.

♦ if possible, a summary of the home country's school curriculum translated into Italian to enable the school to properly place the child.

Parents can declare that they possess the necessary documents without actually producing them (a process called *autodichiarazione*). However, you can be prosecuted if details on an application form are subsequently found to be incorrect.

School Hours

School hours vary considerably according to the kind of school. Nursery school hours are usually from 8am to 4pm, with an hour's break for lunch, five or six days per week. Primary and lower secondary schools schedule classes for 24, 27 or 40 hours per week, Mondays to Saturdays. Most primary schools start at 8am and finish at 1pm, although attendance may be required for afternoon lessons on a few days per week. Some primary schools operate from Mondays to Fridays only, when lessons end at 4 or 4.30pm, with an hour's break for lunch. Lessons at most lower secondary schools start at 8.15am and end at 1.15pm. Upper secondary school classes usually finish at 1.30pm.

Lessons in both primary and secondary schools traditionally last an hour, although schools now have the option of introducing 50-minute lessons. In primary schools, there's usually a mid-morning break of 30 minutes, while in secondary schools it's typically just ten minutes. Extra-curricular activities or afternoon lessons (if scheduled) generally commence at around 2.30pm.

School Holidays

Children attend school for 200 days in the school year, which runs from mid-September to mid-June and is divided into three terms (*trimestri*). The regional school authorities set the calendar (*calendario scolastico*) for all state schools in the region. School holiday dates vary little between regions in Italy, although schools in Sicily start a few days later in September due to the hotter weather. Typical holiday periods for a school year (all dates inclusive) are shown below:

School Holidays	
Holiday	**Dates**
Christmas	23rd December to 6th January
Easter	Around six days, between mid-March and mid-April
Summer	9th June to 14th September*
* This may change to 29th September.	

State exams are held after 9th June. Schools are closed on public holidays (see page 45) when they fall within term time. In addition, schools in some regions are closed for one or two days in March. However, schools don't have half-term holidays.

Absence from school is usually permitted only for a visit to a doctor or dentist, or for reasons of illness. In primary school, a note to the child's teacher is sufficient, while in secondary school students have an official booklet (*libretto delle giustificazioni*) that must be signed by both a parent and a teacher if a child is absent for any reason. A medical certificate must be produced after five days' absence from school.

Parental Costs

State education is free until the age of 16, after which an enrolment tax (*tasse d'iscrizione*) of around €20 is payable at the beginning of each school year. However, pens, stationery and sports clothing must be provided by parents. Textbooks are free only until the end of primary school. Parents can expect to pay an average of around €500 per year for books and other supplies for a child at lower secondary school and perhaps double for a child at upper secondary school, depending on the subjects studied. Up to the end of compulsory schooling, families on low incomes receive a contribution from regional authorities to buy textbooks, and books can be purchased second-hand (but you must make sure that they're current). Italian schoolchildren usually carry their schoolbooks to and from school in a small rucksack (*zaino*).

Nursery and primary schools usually require children to wear school aprons (*grembiule*), which have a distinguishing pattern of little squares at nursery school and are a plain colour (usually blue) at primary school. These can be purchased from most clothing shops and supermarkets. Secondary schools generally don't have a uniform.

State schools don't usually provide meals during the day. Where there are canteen facilities (*mensa*), a small contribution is generally required. Otherwise, children with afternoon lessons who don't have time to go home for lunch must make their own arrangements by either bringing a packed lunch or going to a local *pizzeria* or snack bar near the school. There may be somewhere for children to buy snacks to eat during the mid-morning break.

Italian schools don't provide transport for children who live in outlying districts, although local councils are obliged to provide transport for state nursery schools, together with an adult chaperone. School buses are provided for primary and secondary schools only if there's no school within 3km (2mi), when a small contribution towards the cost of transport (usually between €15 and €30 per month) is usually payable.

Pre-school

Pre-school education isn't compulsory in Italy. However, around 95 per cent of children attend some form of nursery or pre-primary school and the country's pre-school education is internationally recognised as one of the best in the world. Pre-school comprises two levels: day nursery or kindergarten (*asilo nido*, literally 'refuge nest') and nursery school proper (*scuola materna*).

Asilo nurseries take children from as young as three months. They're primarily a facility for working parents who are unable to look after their children during the day. Costs vary according to the number of hours children attend and the particular nursery, but they're generally lower when facilities are run by the local council (*comune*). Places in such nurseries are consequently in huge demand and priority is usually given to parents who are on a low income (applicants must complete a form at the town hall stating their family income).

Materna schools are also both state and privately run (communal, religious and private establishments account for over 40 per cent of *materna* schools) and take children from the ages of three to six, before entry to primary school. Attendance at state *materna* nurseries is free, although a contribution is requested from families for transport and meals provided by the local council. Places are usually limited and you must submit an application well in advance to be sure of a place. For private *materna* schools, parents pay enrolment fees at the beginning of the year plus further monthly contributions.

☑ SURVIVAL TIP

It's worthwhile checking the fees and extra expenses likely to be incurred at different nursery schools before enrolling your child (see also Private Schools on page 132).

In the Rome area you can pay around €50 for enrolment at a private nursery school, with monthly fees starting at between €100 and €200, and increasing to around €600 and over, depending on whether your child attends for a half or full day. For extra-curricular activities, such as physical education and music, where specialist teachers may be required, an extra monthly fee may be payable.

Hours & Holidays

Asilo nursery school hours are usually from 8.30am to 12.30pm, but parents have the option of leaving their children later. At *materna* schools, activities last a minimum of seven hours per day – four hours in the morning and three in the afternoon – and may be held on five or six days per week. Parents can often leave their children under the supervision of a qualified help after school (*doposcuola*) until 5 or 5.30pm, during which time activities are less structured and non-educational. State nurseries generally have the same holiday periods as state schools, therefore working parents must find alternative provision for their children during these periods. Schools may also organise summer activity programmes for children whose parents are working, and some local councils organise educational and recreational courses during July and August.

Classes

Materna schools are organised into groups (*sezioni*) according to age, with a minimum of 14 children and a maximum of 28. In schools in less populous areas, however, a school may have only one group comprising children of different ages. Each group must have two teachers (generally female), who usually remain with the same group for three years. The minimum number of children required to establish a school is 16, and they must all live within 2km (1.3mi) of the school.

Curriculum

In *materna* schools, the emphasis is on learning through play, rather than the day-care facility provided by the *asilo nido*. Teaching at *materna* schools can take a variety of forms, although all are governed by a number of educational aims. These stipulate certain 'fields of experience' to be included in educational activity: body and movement, speech and words, space, order and measure, time and nature, messages, forms and media, and the self and others.

Music, physical activity and arts and crafts all form part of the nursery curriculum, although children don't usually begin to learn the rudiments of reading and writing until they begin state primary school at the age of six. Therefore you may wish to consider a private school if you want your children to get a head start, particularly if your mother tongue isn't Italian. Children are assessed by teachers on entry into nursery school and several times during the course of the school year, a final report on their capabilities being made before their transfer to primary school.

Primary School

Five years' attendance at primary school (*scuole elementari*) is compulsory and children must reach the age of six by 31st December of the year in which they enrol. The school timetable usually involves around 27 hours' tuition per week, increasing in the second year to accommodate learning a foreign language (usually English). Provision is made for pupils with special educational needs. Attendance is generally mornings only, with one or two afternoon classes per week. Reforms have recently resulted in one teacher for all subjects for each primary-school class.

Primary Cycle

The five-year primary cycle is divided into two parts, the first two years concentrating on basic skills and the final three years introducing pupils to broader concepts. Subjects are grouped into areas as follows:

Area A: Italian, art and a foreign language;

Area B: mathematics, sciences and physical education;

Area C: history, geography, social studies and music.

There's also usually a specialist teacher for religion.

Some primary schools are full-time schools (*scuola a tempo pieno*), where children attend both mornings and afternoons for five days per week. The timetable usually includes one and a half hours' rest in the middle of the day, during which lunch is provided in a school canteen. There are typically two teachers per class, one taking the morning session and one the afternoon session, with all subjects divided between them. This kind of school generally appeals to working parents, who find it more convenient to collect their children later in the day.

Most primary schools use a system of assessment based on teacher observation throughout the school year. Assessments are recorded on each child's report card (*scheda*), which is designed to provide a detailed profile of the pupil's academic ability and personality. The record card is passed to a pupil's next school when he leaves. In the fifth year of primary school, pupils must usually obtain a primary school leaving certificate (*diploma della licenza elementare*) to progress to lower secondary school; those who are unsuccessful may need to repeat their final year.

Lower Secondary School

Attendance at lower secondary school (*scuola media*, literally 'middle school' and equivalent to a junior high school in the US) is compulsory for all children between the ages of 11 and 14. As with primary school, there's a national curriculum that must be studied by all children. In addition, the number of hours each subject must be taught each week is stipulated by the Ministry of Education. For the first and second years, the weekly requirements include:

♦ seven hours of Italian (including lessons in literature, grammar and writing);

♦ six hours of mathematics, physics, chemistry and natural sciences;

♦ four hours of history, geography and social studies;

♦ three hours each of a foreign language (usually English) and technical drawing;

♦ two hours each of physical education, music and art/design;

♦ one hour of religion.

In the third year, pupils lose one hour of Italian in favour of an extra hour of history, geography and social studies. Each subject is taught by a different specialist teacher, with the exception of Italian, history, geography and social studies, which are generally divided between two teachers.

The timetable totals 30 hours per week, schools having the option of extending this to up to 40 hours for extra-curricular or subsidiary study activities if there's sufficient demand from parents (e.g. computer studies or learning a second foreign language). In recent years, schools have introduced a number of optional, experimental classes. These classes, which are generally financed from a school's own budget, take place in the afternoons and may include sports, music lessons (instruments must usually be purchased by parents), film, computer and chess clubs, and foreign language conversation classes.

As at primary school, a report is completed by teachers each term on all subjects, which provides an overview of the aptitude, behaviour and achievement of each pupil. A separate, shorter report is produced for a student's performance in religious instruction. Assessments include excellent (*ottimo*), very good (*distinto*), good (*buono*), satisfactory (*sufficiente*) and unsatisfactory (*non sufficiente*). At the end of the third year, pupils sit a state examination comprising written papers in Italian, a foreign language and mathematics and science, followed by an oral

exam in all subjects except religion. Successful students are awarded their lower secondary school diploma (*diploma di licenza media*) and graduate to upper secondary school.

Upper Secondary School

At the age of 14, students must choose the kind of upper secondary school (*scuola superiore*, equivalent to a senior high school in the US) they want to attend, according to which subjects they would like to specialise in and what they would like to do when they leave school.

There are essentially two categories of upper secondary school: a *liceo* (similar to a British grammar school), which provides a more academic training, and an *istituto*, where more practical and technical disciplines are taught. Within these two categories, there are several types of school. In every school district there's a classics school, a science school and a technical or a vocational school. In larger districts and provincial towns, there's also a teacher training school and an arts school, and there may be a number of vocational schools, which often reflect the needs of local industries. Details of these schools are as follows:

♦ **Arts school** (*liceo artistico* or *istituto d'arte*): Provides a four-year foundation course for students wishing to enrol at arts academies, study art or architecture at university, enter a career in the arts or teach art subjects at school.

♦ **Classics school** (*liceo classico*): Latin, Greek and Italian literature form a large part of the demanding academic curriculum. Philosophy and history of art are also studied in the last three years.

♦ **Language school** (*liceo linguistico*): Students study three foreign languages.

♦ **Science school** (*liceo scientifico*): Traditionally, this is for students planning to study science and medicine at university, with the emphasis on physics, chemistry and natural sciences. Latin and one modern language (usually English) are also studied to a high level.

◆ **Teacher training school** (*scuola magistrale* or *istituto magistrale*): Provides a four-year training course for primary school teachers (*istituto magistrale*) and a three-year training course for nursery school teachers (*scuola magistrale*). A nursery school teaching diploma doesn't qualify you to enrol at a university.

◆ **Technical school** (*istituto tecnico*): By far the greatest number of upper secondary school students enrol in technical school, which prepares students to work in a technical or administrative capacity in agriculture, industry or commerce. Technical schools have responded to Italy's fast-growing economy by offering an ever-widening range of courses tailored to the needs of employers, courses in computer skills in particular seeing tremendous growth in recent years. Technical schools follow the common curriculum for the first two years (see below), with some practical training carried out in workshops and businesses. In the last three years, the number of hours of practical training increases.

The main kinds of technical schools are agricultural, commercial (with specialisations in business administration, accountancy, commerce, foreign languages and computer programming), surveying, tourism, nautical, aeronautical and industrial (including many specialisations such as mining, electronics, engineering, industrial physics, computer science and food processing). There are also 'feminine technical schools' (*istituti tecnichi femminili*), which were originally for the study of subjects traditionally associated with women, such as home economics, but now cater for both sexes and include the study of dietetics, social work and child care.

◆ **Vocational school** (*istituto professionale*): Vocational schools are the least academic of upper secondary schools. They aim to train people in a variety of craft and industrial skills, such as cabinet-making, carpentry, mechanics and engineering, building and construction, food and catering, secretarial and office work. The timetable varies between 35 and 40 hours per week, and for the first two years it includes 14 hours per week of practical training relevant to a pupil's chosen area of specialisation. In the third year, the number of hours of specialist practical training increases to between 21 and 24 hours per week. After three years, students gain a diploma in their specialist subject (*diploma di qualifica*), after which they may take a two-year course in order to earn their upper secondary school diploma, either at the vocational school or at a technical school.

Entry to upper secondary school isn't competitive and, provided there are sufficient places available, students may attend the school of their choice.

Since 2001, all pupils have had the same core curriculum for the first two years of upper secondary school; this comprises Italian language and literature, mathematics, at least one foreign language (usually English), science, history, geography and social studies, religion and physical education. Their specialised courses (*indirizzi*) start in the third year.

In all schools a considerable amount of homework is set for each subject, which may take the form of memorising information or writing an essay. As in lower secondary school, teachers test a student's knowledge (and the extent to which he has done his homework) through regular oral and written tests (*prove scritte*), which, together with a more general evaluation of a student's performance, form the basis of a student's report (*pagella*). Marks (*voti*) for all work are given out of ten, six being the minimum score required to proceed to the next year.

All students can enter university, provided they complete a five-year course at secondary school and acquire their upper secondary school diploma (see below), and it's now common for students who have attended technical and vocational schools to go on to university. In schools where the duration of the diploma course is only four years (e.g. arts schools), students must stay on for an extra year to qualify for university entrance.

Before deciding on the right kind of school for your child, it's important to study carefully the curriculum offered by each. This is particularly important if a child is planning to attend a university outside Italy. In many countries (including the US and UK), university admission is based on competitive entry, and therefore the choice of secondary school and curriculum should reflect a specialisation in the subjects the student plans to study at university.

Diploma

At the end of the upper secondary school cycle, students study for the upper secondary school diploma (*diploma di maturità*), which automatically qualifies them for enrolment at a university. It consists of three written exams (*esame*) plus an oral test (*colloquio*). The first exam involves writing an essay or newspaper article in Italian on a historical, social, scientific or literary subject. The second is a test of one subject from a number of options relating to a student's specialisation; the subject of the exam is given to students two months in advance. The third is an inter-disciplinary exam that includes questions on cultural and social issues and tests the knowledge of a foreign language.

The oral test follows the written exams and is conducted by a board of six teachers, who question students on all the subjects they've studied in their final year. Out of a possible total of 100 marks, a maximum of 45 is awarded for the written exams, 35 for the oral and 20 for scholastic credits, which are earned from students' school reports during their last three years of study. To pass the *maturità*, a minimum of 60 marks is required.

The full title of the diploma depends on the kind of school students have attended, e.g. *diploma di maturità classica* for students who have attended a classics school and a *diploma di maturità scientifica* for students who have attended a science school. Diplomas gained at technical school are further qualified by the specialisation students have followed.

The *maturità* is recognised throughout the world as a university entrance qualification, although it isn't accepted by all institutions.

PRIVATE SCHOOLS

Private schools (*scuole private*) educate less than 10 per cent of Italian schoolchildren. They include schools run by religious organisations (the majority by the Jesuits), schools following unorthodox teaching methods such as Montessori and Rudolf Steiner, and a number of foreign and international schools, including American and British schools. The majority of private schools are co-educational, non-denominational day schools (Catholic private schools usually admit non-Catholic students), many of which operate a Monday to Friday timetable. There are very few boarding schools in Italy.

Most private schools in Italy are either authorised or given legal recognition by the state and many receive state funding and must therefore adhere strictly to central government directives on syllabi and curricula. Teachers' qualifications must also be recognised. As a result, there's little difference between the quality of education in the state and private sectors, and many people consider standards in private schools to be inferior. The majority of

private schools duplicate the curriculum offered in state schools, with perhaps the inclusion of a few extra courses.

One advantage of most private schools is that they offer a more caring and protective atmosphere, and the opportunity to take additional or intensive lessons, which some parents believe to be more conducive to learning. Some parents in wealthier areas of the major cities send their children to a private school simply for the cachet.

Private schools usually have fewer pupils than state schools, but class sizes aren't necessarily any smaller. Private schools often cater for a wide age range (from 6 to 19) and some also offer nursery facilities. At secondary level there's a bias toward classics, scientific and linguistic schools, few private schools offering technical or vocational training. There's sometimes a stricter regime in private schools, particularly as many are run by religious orders, and uniforms may be compulsory (whereas in state schools uniforms aren't usually worn, although children sometimes wear a smock over their clothes).

Private school fees vary according to the kind of school and the variety of services that are offered. Most require parents to pay an enrolment fee (e.g. between €300 and €550) followed by either annual or monthly fees (e.g. between €175 and €350 per month).

Among the private schools that aren't state supported are schools known as *scuole di ricupero* (literally 'schools of recovery'), designed to meet the needs of students who, for various reasons, must repeat one or more years' schooling in order to gain their upper secondary school diploma. Fees are generally high, particularly if you want to cover the *maturità* syllabus. These schools don't function as exam centres and pupils must usually take their examinations at a recognised centre and pay an additional fee. *Ricupero* schools usually also offer exam preparation at university level.

International & Foreign Schools

There are a number of international schools in Italy, whose main language of instruction is English. These tend to offer the best alternative for expatriates who want their children to continue their education in the American or British system. International schools are invariably situated in the major urban centres, including Florence, Genoa, Milan, Naples, Padua, Rome, Treviso, Trieste and Turin, and range from pre-schools and kindergartens to secondary schools, with pupils aged from 3 to 19 years.

Private schools teach a variety of syllabi, including the British GCSE and A-level examinations, American High School Diploma and college entrance examinations (e.g. ACT, SAT and AP exams), and the International Baccalaureate (IB), which is recognised worldwide as a university entrance qualification.

Class sizes tend to be small, with students of a wide range of nationalities, and schools pride themselves on the variety of sports and extra-curricular activities on offer, some even boasting campus sites of several acres. Many international schools offer bi-lingual programmes, enabling students to sit Italian state exams (for reintegration into the Italian state system), as well as English as a Foreign Language (EFL) exams if their first language isn't English. Fees for international schools range from around €4,250 to €15,700 per year, and only a few offer boarding facilities for which there are extra charges. Admission is usually based on previous school reports and, sometimes, a personal interview.

Among the most prestigious international schools is the United World College of the Adriatic near Trieste, Via Trieste, 29, 34011 Duino, Trieste (🖳 www.uwcad.it). Pupils are selected on academic ability and scholarships are offered annually. Students who aren't resident in Italy must apply via the UWC committee in their home country – see the United World Colleges' website (🖳 www. uwc.org/how_to_apply/find_your_national_ committee/default.aspx).

A list of American and British schools can be obtained from the cultural sections of Italian embassies abroad and from the European Council of International Schools (🖳 www.ecis. org). The Worldwide Schools directory lists many English-speaking schools on its website (🖳 http://italy.english-schools.org). There are also French *lycées* in Rome and Milan, and a number of private schools that teach in other foreign languages.

APPRENTICESHIPS

Many young people in Italy look forward to starting work and learning a trade, and the majority who don't go on to higher education enter an apprenticeship (*apprendistato*) or vocational training. Over half a million young people in Italy are involved in apprenticeship schemes each year. An apprenticeship aims to give people between the ages of 16 and 26 a combination of on-the-job training and further education, with around four hours per day spent on practical training and three-and-a-half in theoretical learning at an apprentice training centre. Apprenticeships last from 18 months to four years and cover a huge range of occupations, including waitressing, cooking, plumbing, carpentry, hairdressing, car repairs and agricultural work. Employers pay apprentices 80 per cent of the salary of a fully qualified worker, which increases with age and experience. They also pay for schooling and sometimes the cost of travel to and from school. Apprentices are entitled to the same holiday periods as fully qualified staff (see **Holidays & Leave** on page 45).

Another kind of vocational training is a combined training and work contract (*contratto di formazione lavorativa/CFL*) for those aged between 16 and 23, whereby employers provide a training programme for a specific professional qualification as part of a fixed-period employment contract. Contracts last one or two years and include an initial trial period. The state pays insurance contributions but employment isn't guaranteed at the end of the training period.

Careers advice for young people is available via the nationwide network of *informagiovani* offices.

HIGHER EDUCATION

Over a million students attend institutes of higher education in Italy, although the country produces a smaller percentage of graduates than most other developed countries. The country has around 80 universities, including state universities, state polytechnics, private universities, university institutions and two universities for foreigners. There's a university in every major city in Italy, some with branches in a number of towns throughout a region. The University of Bologna (founded in the 11th century) is the world's oldest university and highly regarded, while Rome has three universities, the oldest being La Sapienza which is also Europe's largest university, with some 147,000 students. Other higher education facilities include the University Naval Institute in Naples and the College of Education in Pisa.

Higher education is controlled by the Ministry of Education, Universities and Research (Ministero dell'Istruzione, dell'Università e della Ricerca, or MIUR). Universities are organised into faculties, for teaching, and departments, for research. Most degree subjects are offered by all universities (apart from a few specialised fields, such as music, which is taught in academies or *conservatori*) and anyone with an upper secondary school diploma can apply to study any subject provided there are places available. However, for degree courses that are heavily over-subscribed (which include architecture, dentistry, medicine and veterinary science), universities set entrance examinations (*esame di ammissione*) to select the best candidates.

> Non-EU higher education students are required to take an Italian-language exam unless they possess a *CILS* certificate (see **Learning Italian** on page 137).

Enrolment

There's no central clearing system for enrolment in Italian universities and you must apply to each university separately. There are enrolment fees (*tasse di iscrizione*), which are payable at the beginning of each year or in instalments throughout the year, plus regional taxes of around €100. Each faculty sets its own course fees, average fees for first-year students being around €700 (for the year). Students from families with medium to low incomes are entitled to grants, information about which is available from the student welfare office (Diritto allo Studio Universitario/DSU). Foreign applicants must provide a translation of their qualifications (obtainable through Italian consulates), which must usually be equivalent to a high school diploma or 12 years' education. Applications must be made to Italian consulates by May for enrolment the following September; non-EU students must apply through an Italian consulate in their home country.

Curriculum & Exams

Italian universities are frequently criticised for the rigidly academic nature of their courses. Although students have some choice over their study programme (*piano di studi*), the curriculum for each subject is fairly standardised (there's little variation between courses offered by different universities) and there's generally little room for self-expression. As in schools, students are expected to study set texts (sometimes written by the professors) and are examined on their knowledge. The emphasis is firmly on self-motivation and determination, particularly in view of the drawn-out nature of university degrees. Overcrowding in lecture halls for popular courses is common, resulting in a more distant relationship between students and professors than in some other countries, and the student drop-out rate is high. Italian universities offer little in the way of extra-curricular sports and social activities (there's no 'campus' feel as in American universities), although most have a refectory (*mensa*) where inexpensive, wholesome food is available.

The average student must pass over 20 exams to obtain a degree (some subjects, such as medicine, require students to take around 50 exams), most of which are oral. Of these, a certain number are obligatory and common to all study programmes, while the rest are in subjects chosen by students. Courses, each of which is followed by an exam, can be pursued in any order and, if you fail an exam, you're permitted to retake it any number of times. Attendance at lectures is mostly voluntary, leaving students free to pursue their studies at home if they prefer, although some professors insist on attendance at lectures. The regular

submission of essays throughout a course isn't generally required, although students must write a thesis (usually of 50 pages or about 18,000 words) at the end of their course in order to earn a degree.

The structure of the Italian university system allows students to take a longer time to complete their degrees than is usual in the UK and the US. The number of years necessary to complete a degree (*corso di laurea*) at an Italian university is laid down by law. Most degree courses last for three – or sometimes four – years and are then followed by a specialisation; some (e.g. medicine and architecture) are for six years. However, few students manage to complete their degrees in the minimum period and it's usual for students to take seven or eight years, with the result that many are in their mid to late 20s by the time they graduate.

The traditional qualifications awarded at Italian universities are a basic university degree (*laurea*), a two-year specialised degree (*laurea specialistica*), a further specialisation aimed at a particular profession such as medicine lasting another two to three years (*diploma di specializzazione*) and a research doctorate (*dottorato di ricerca*) which takes at least three more years. Universities have recently introduced a university diploma (*diploma universitario*) lasting two or three years but these lead to a vocational qualification, rather than an academic degree. These are currently in specialised fields of engineering, physical education, auxiliary medicine (e.g. nursing and physiotherapy) and languages, with admission for the limited number of places subject to competitive examination. Foreign students who wish to accumulate credits at an Italian university without completing a degree course may apply to do individual subject courses (*corsi singoli*).

Accommodation

Many students live with their parents and attend the nearest university to their home, particularly in large cities such as Rome where accommodation is prohibitively expensive. Others enrol at a university in the north or in Rome as this enables them to look for part-time work to support themselves during their study (even part-time work is difficult to find in the south) and have better employment prospects when they graduate.

> Student accommodation isn't usually provided by Italian universities, although some subsidised student housing (*casa dello studente*) may be available through the student welfare office (DSU).

The majority of students make their own accommodation arrangements and there's usually a university notice board where rooms and apartments are advertised for rent. Students should expect to pay anything between €240 (central and southern regions) and €350 (Rome and northern cities) per month for a room in a shared apartment. In addition to rent, students must usually pay utility bills plus maintenance for items such as cookers, refrigerators and washing machines.

Foreign Colleges & Students

In addition to Italian institutions of higher education, there are a number of American colleges and universities in Italy offering an American degree programme, e.g. Johns Hopkins University in Bologna (🖳 www.jhu.edu) and John Cabot University in Rome (🖳 http://johncabot.edu). John Cabot University offers four-year BA degrees on a rolling admission basis in art history, business administration, English literature, international affairs and political science, as well as associate degrees and credit transfers on a semester basis for students wishing to do part of their study in Italy.

Fees are around €10,500 per year, but there are various financial aid and scholarship packages. Students come from around 40 countries and universities offer many extra-curricular activities. A list of American institutions of higher education in Italy and information about American study programmes at Italian institutions can be obtained from the American embassy in Italy (🖳 http://italy.usembassy.gov/usa/education/universities.asp) and from the cultural sections of Italian embassies abroad.

EU nationals who wish to complete part of their studies at an Italian university may be interested in the Erasmus programme, part of the EU Socrates programme funded by the European Commission. Under this programme, students don't pay fees for attending an Italian university (although you may need to continue to pay fees at your own university) and grants are available to cover the costs of moving, language training and a higher cost of living (if applicable). For further information, contact the Erasmus Bureau, Rue Montoyer 70, B-1040 Brussels, Belgium (☎ +32-2 233 0111), your country's national Erasmus agency or your university's Erasmus representative. The Italian Ministry of Foreign Affairs also allocates a number of scholarships to foreign students attending courses at Italian universities. Information is available from Italian embassies abroad.

Further Information

For further information about universities in Italy, contact the Dipartimento per l'Autonomia Universitaria e gli Studenti, Ministero dell'Istruzione, dell'Università e della Ricerca, Piazzale J. F. Kennedy, 20, 00144 Rome (☎ 06-97721). The Ministry of Foreign Affairs also provides information about applying to universities on its website (💻 www.esteri.it), and *Campus* magazine (💻 www.campus.it) provides a wealth of information about Italian universities (in Italian).

FURTHER EDUCATION

Italy has many private schools and university-level institutions (some affiliated to American universities), including business and commercial colleges, hotel and catering schools, and language schools, which offer a range of further education courses for school leavers, university graduates, workers and the unemployed. They include post-degree courses (specialist diplomas, masters and doctorates) and a wide range of vocational training courses. Courses vary in length from a few months to two or three years and may be either full or part time.

Many further education courses are vocational (*corsi di formazione professionale*) and aim to facilitate access to employment through a mixture of practical and theoretical training. Courses are either first level (aimed at school leavers who haven't attained a secondary-school diploma) or second level (for holders of specific qualifications such as a secondary-school diploma or a university degree). Many courses are targeted at job seekers and employees wishing to specialise or re-qualify in order to obtain a new position. Applicants usually outnumber available places and you may be required to sit an admission test. Courses for secondary school diploma holders usually consist of between 400 and 1,200 hours' tuition for five hours per day and usually include placement periods in industry.

Free courses are available in some deprived regions (part-funded by the European Social Fund) for certain categories of people, including the unemployed, graduates seeking work, young people who have failed

to complete compulsory schooling and disabled people. Details can be obtained from regional education offices, vocational training centres, the information sections of trade union offices, local newspapers or by browsing through regional websites. Information about further education can also be obtained from regional Centro di Informazione e Orientamento (CIO) offices.

A number of educational institutions in Italy offer an American MBA degree, e.g. St John's University in Rome and the Bocconi University in Milan. Subjects include banking, business administration, communications, economics, information systems, management, marketing, public relations, and social and political studies. Tuition costs are high and study periods strictly organised, most courses being taught in English.

Another institution offering further education courses in English is the European University Institute in Florence. Founded in 1972, the Institute offers postgraduate courses and research opportunities in the field of human and social sciences. Admission is merit-based and courses are open to students from all EU and some other European countries with a high mark in a first degree. The British Open University (💻 www.open.ac.uk) offers distance learning degree courses (from BA to MBA – a choice of over 150 courses) to residents of the EU and Switzerland. It has a coordinator based in Milan at the British Chamber of Commerce (Via Dante 12, 20121 Milan, ☎ 02-877 7798) and there are exam centers in Milan and Rome.

LEARNING ITALIAN

If you don't speak Italian fluently, you may wish to enrol in a language course. If you want to make the most of your time, it's **essential** to learn Italian as soon as possible. For people living in Italy permanently, learning Italian isn't an option, particularly as in many areas little or no English is spoken. Although it isn't easy, even the most non-linguistic (and oldest) person can acquire a working knowledge of Italian. All that's required is a little hard work and some help and perseverance. You won't just 'pick it up' (apart from a few words), but must make an effort to learn.

> ☑ **SURVIVAL TIP**
>
> Your business, career and social enjoyment and success in Italy will be directly related to the degree to which you master Italian.

Classes are offered by language schools (see below), Italian colleges and universities (see below), private and international schools, foreign and international organisations, town councils, cultural associations, vocational training centres, clubs and private teachers. Tuition ranges from introductory courses for beginners to specialised business or cultural courses and university-level courses leading to recognised diplomas.

Many universities in Italy have language centres (*Centri Linguistici Atenei/CLA*) offering a variety of courses; these are generally held only in the summer and are cheaper than most private schools. The Universities for Foreigners (*Università per Stranieri*) in Siena and Perugia (not strictly universities but large language schools) offer year-round, Italian-language courses at various levels.

Families planning to move to Italy may be interested in Intercultura, the Italian branch of the American Field Service (🖳 www.afs. org) organisation – an international, voluntary, non-profit organisation offering worldwide educational and cultural exchanges for young people. Exchanges with Intercultura are for students of 15 or over wishing to stay with an Italian family for between two weeks and a year. For more information, contact Intercultura, Via Gracco del Secco, 100-53034 Colle Val d'Elsa (SI), ☎ 0577-900 011, 🖳 www. intercultura.it.

A number of scholarships and grants are available from the Universities for Foreigners at Siena and Perugia. For information, contact the cultural sections of Italian embassies abroad.

Language Schools

There are many language schools (*scuole di lingua*) throughout Italy offering a wide range of classes to suit your language ability, how many hours you wish to study a week, how much money you want to spend and how quickly you wish to learn. Language classes roughly fall into the following categories: standard (up to 20 hours); intensive (20 to 30 hours); total immersion (40 hours plus). The cost of a one-week (40 hour) total immersion course starts from around €185, depending on the school. Courses vary in length from four months to a year and can be attended either in small groups or individually.

Many language schools offer a variety of other courses, ranging from translation and interpreters' courses to business, cooking, literature and the history of art. Schools offer a variety of language diplomas (including their own internal qualifications) but only a few offer the *Certificato d'Italiano come Lingua Straniera* (*CILS*), which is recognised as an entry-level qualification for non-EU students wishing to study at Italian universities.

One of the longest-established language associations in Italy is Dante Alighieri (🖳 www.ladante.it), which has schools throughout the country (not to be confused with schools that use *Dante Alighieri* in their title but don't belong to the society) and promotes the Italian language and culture through a network of worldwide committees. International House (🖳 www.ihworld.com) has a number of schools in major cities, where it teaches both Italian to foreigners and English to Italians. Cactus Language offers courses in a number of cities (🖳 www. cactuslanguage.com/en), and the Italian Schools database has links to language schools (🖳 www.it-schools.com). As with all private schools, it pays to shop around and compare fees, as there's a considerable variation in standards and facilities, and famous international schools don't necessarily offer the best value or the best tuition.

Some city authorities sometimes offer free (although unaccredited) Italian courses for foreigners and details can be found at local *informagiovani* centres. A list of addresses of *informagiovani* centres is given on the Turin's city *comune* website (🖥 www.comune.torino.it/infogio/cig/icr.htm).

Private Lessons

A quicker, although more expensive, way to learn Italian is to have private lessons. Because Italian school teachers are among the worst paid in Europe, there's no shortage of people prepared to give private lessons. Rates vary widely according to where you live, from around €15 per hour in some central and southern regions to €35 or more per hour in Rome and Milan with a qualified teacher. Some good places to look for a suitable teacher or to place an advertisement include local newspapers, and university and public notice boards. Friends, neighbours and work colleagues may be able to recommend a good teacher. In some areas, the local youth advisory service (*informagiovani*) provides free conversation classes for foreign students.

A guide to many language schools, institutions and organisations offering Italian-language tuition is provided by the Associazione Scuole di Italiano come Lingua Seconda/ASILS (🖥 www.asils.it) and from the Italian Cultural Institute, 39 Belgrave Square, London SW1X 8NX, UK (☎ 020-7235 1461, 🖥 www.icilondon.esteri.it). The Institute's website has a useful directory of Italian-language schools in most regions of the country, with links to a number of schools' websites.

Colosseum, Rome

Frecciarossa high-speed train

10.
PUBLIC TRANSPORT

The standard of public transport (*mezzi pubblici*) services in Italy can best be described as mixed; at its best it can be excellent, but sometimes it's simply dire. Like many other aspects of Italian life, it's marked by excessive complication and a lack of co-operation and co-ordination – between companies, regions and modes of transport. The railway system in particular reflects two other aspects of the Italian character: on the one hand the zest for speed, manifested in the super-fast *ETR* trains (the equivalent of France's *TGV*), and on the other hand the easy-going, unhurried approach to life, as depicted by local trains.

There's a huge difference between services in (and connecting) the major cities and those in rural areas. Most cities have an efficient, inexpensive and reliable transport system, consisting of underground trains or trams in some cities, buses and suburban trains. However, in rural areas you're dependent on a few, generally very slow buses, and services vary from infrequent to non-existent on Sundays and holidays. If you're going to be living in a rural area, you'll almost certainly need your own transport. On the positive side, most forms of public transport in Italy are good value.

All modes of public transport are susceptible to strikes, although they've been less frequent in recent years. Strikes are usually short, lasting 12 or 24 hours only, but they can be extremely disruptive as it takes a long time for services to return to normal. The problem for foreigners is knowing when strikes are about to take place. If you don't have Italian friends, who complain vociferously about the latest *sciopero* (strike), or watch the television news avidly, they can easily catch you unawares.

Long journeys often require planning, particularly in the high season. As far as holidays are concerned, Italians are creatures of habit, and most inhabitants of the major cities take their holidays in August.

Consequently, long-distance public transport is in great demand, and booking months in advance is recommended.

A wealth of information about travelling to and within Italy is available on the internet from a multitude of websites, including 🖥 www.initaly.com and www.informare.it, a website devoted to transportation but only in Italian.

Most cities and regions have websites dedicated to them with have sections on transport, e.g. Rome (🖥 www.romeguide.it), Florence (🖥 www.florence.ala.it), Milan (🖥 www.aboutmilan.com) and Venice (🖥 www.ciaovenezia.com).

DISABLED TRAVELLERS

Few Italian public transport companies make concessions for disabled people, although things are slowly improving. Italian railways offer a blue card (*carta blu*), which allows a disabled person and an accompanying person to travel for the price of one ticket. It costs €5 and is valid for five years. The railways also offer assistance for disabled passengers and some trains allow wheelchair access. A number of seats are reserved on high-speed (*ETR*) rail services for disabled travellers and their travelling companions (where applicable). Enquire in advance if you require assistance when travelling.

RAIL

Trains are operated by Trenitalia, a division of the national railway company, Ferrovie dello Stato (⌨ www.ferroviedellostato.it) which is usually referred to by the initials FS. Italy's rail network is one of the most extensive in Europe, running to around 16,000km (circa 10,000mi) of track, some two-thirds of which is electrified, and over 3,000 stations. There are also a number of private lines. FS was the first railway in Europe to be nationalised (or re-nationalised, as it was originally government-owned), in 1908, but is now officially privatised, although the majority of shares remain in the hands of the government. After years of mismanagement and neglect, all aspects of Italian railways are currently being modernised, with huge investment in infrastructure and rolling stock, particularly in new high-speed trains, although the system still has a way to go to compete with Europe's best.

It's possible to travel between virtually any two points in the country by train, with the exception of some of Italy's more isolated mountainous regions, although incredible feats of engineering in the form of tunnels and viaducts have made inroads even into these seemingly inaccessible areas. However, there's a significant difference between services in the northern and southern parts of the country, the north enjoying more frequent and faster trains, and more electrified and double-track lines than the south. In an effort to reduce state subsidies, fares have been increased in the last few years, although rail travel is still good value and cheaper than in most other European countries.

Italy has direct rail connections with many other European countries, including Austria, France, Germany, the Netherlands, Spain and Switzerland. Italy's railways are connected with those in neighbouring countries by a number of mountain routes, linking Milan with Switzerland via the Milan-Simplon Tunnel, Turin with Fréjus in France, Venice to Eastern Europe via Tarvisio, and Verona to Austria and Germany via the Brenner Pass.

Trains can be crowded, particularly at weekends and in high summer, when southern Italians working in the north return home to their families. On the faster trains, seats should usually be reserved – look for the sign 'Prenotazioni' (Bookings) at stations. Bookings can be made between two months and three or four hours before a train's departure – except for Eurostar Italia trains (see page 143), for which bookings can be made right up to departure time. If you have a booking, it's wise to locate your carriage while you're on the platform, rather than struggling up and down the corridors with your luggage. Most locomotives and rolling stock are fairly modern and well maintained, although some of the slower, local services use old equipment. A surprisingly large number of carriages are covered in graffiti, often very artistically, but unless you're into Italian youth culture the message is unfortunately (or maybe fortunately) impossible to interpret.

It's possible to take your bicycle with you on all classes of train. Cycles are transported at a charge of €3.50 on local trains and €12 on international trains, and even free of charge on some national trains, but your bike must be carried in an appropriate bag.

> ### ☑ SURVIVAL TIP
>
> When travelling at night, take good care of your belongings (particularly your money and credit cards) and be wary of thieves.

If you have a sleeping compartment, always lock the door and open it only for railway staff. Be careful about accepting food or drink from strangers, as there have been cases of thieves giving drugged food and drinks to travellers and stealing their belongings.

A map of Italy's rail network is in **Appendix E**.

Stations

In the broad river plains and coastal towns, the main railway station is usually in the city centre; for example, in Rome and Florence you can walk from the station to the historic centres in just a few minutes. However, in hilly regions, such as Tuscany and Umbria, many towns

Pendolino train

baggage delivered to their home or to the main station. Left-luggage lockers and offices are available at major city stations such as Rome, Naples, Florence, Trieste, Padua, Bologna and Milan.

Types of Train

Italian railways operate a variety of trains (painted in attractive red and white designs) from slow electric and diesel commuter trains to the high-speed *ETR* 450, 460 and 480 and 600 *Pendolino*, and *ETR* 500 trains on major routes. *Pendolino* trains are so-called because they lean to the centre of their path on bends to compensate for centrifugal force, which allows them to travel up to 35 per cent faster than standard Intercity (IC) trains. Like France's *TGV* trains, *ETR* trains were designed to compete with air services and travel at speeds of up to 360kph (225mph). They're air-conditioned and offer a hostess service, video screens, hi-fi system with earphones, card-operated telephones, meals at your seat, a dining car and minibar, a free welcome drink and newspaper (in first class) and other perks. Business lounges are provided on *ETR* 500 trains, in which seats can be reserved for a fee of around €10.

The types of Italian train, from the fastest to the slowest, are as follows:

♦ **Eurostar Italia (ETR):** Italy's high-speed *ETR* trains which can whisk you from Rome to Milan in around three hours, although journey times vary considerably according to the number of stops made. Bookings (free to make) are obligatory on Fridays and Sundays, and on certain other days plus the Easter and Christmas periods (contact FS for exact dates).

Most *ETR* high-speed trains come under the following three categories:

♦ **Frecciarossa** (Red Arrow) trains which connect the cities of Turin, Milan, Florence, Rome, Naples and Salerno on the high-

and cities were built on hilltops for defensive reasons and stations are situated on the plain. Fortunately, there are (usually) regular bus services, co-ordinated with train arrivals and departures, to whisk you to and from town centres. It's as well to check on the situation in advance, particularly if you're going to arrive loaded with luggage. A service is provided for transporting disabled passengers to and from main stations in Bologna, Florence, Milan, Naples, Padua, Rome and Venice (a fee is payable).

If a station isn't equipped with airport-style arrival (*arrivo*) and departure (*partenza*) boards, look for an indicator board on each platform listing (fairly well in advance) the trains arriving or departing there. Printed timetables also tell you the platform number where your train will arrive, but timetables are usually changed twice per year (around the 30th May and the 26th September), so make sure you're consulting the current one.

Main stations, including Rome and Milan, still have a uniquely Italian institution, a 'daytime hotel' (*albergo diurno*), open daily between 6am and midnight, where travellers can freshen up before or after a journey. It has no beds but provides services such as showers, hairdressers, cleaning and laundry facilities, and a place to relax and read the newspapers.

There are official porters at main stations, who charge a fee of around €4 per bag. In the same cities, passengers can also have their speed line, travelling at speeds of up to 360kph (225mph).

♦ **Frecciargento** (Silver Arrow) trains which connect Rome with Venice, Verona, Bari/Lecce, Lamezia Terme and Reggio di Calabria, travelling on both high-speed and standard lines, at speeds of up to 250kph (155mph).

♦ **Frecciabianca** (White Arrow) trains which connect Milan with Venice, Udine and Trieste, Genoa and Rome, and the Adriatic Riviera to Bari/Lecce, using the standard lines at speeds of up to 200 kph (125mph).

Other Eurostar trains connect Rome to Ancona, Genoa, Lamezia Terme, Reggio di Calabria, Perugia, Ravenna, Rimini and Taranto.

♦ **Eurocity International Trains:** Fast, limited-stop international expresses operating between major cities in Italy and Europe. Sometimes only first-class seats are available and bookings may be obligatory.

♦ **Intercity (IC):** These trains connect large and medium-size cities. They use a combination of high-speed and standard track and, while the journey may take longer than on an ETR train, tickets are often good value.

♦ **Local** (*locale/regionale*): The 'snails' of the system, which stop absolutely everywhere, often with no station in sight! These trains serve rural areas and small towns, so if you're touring rather than on business, they can be a relaxing way to see the countryside, and the rolling stock is often quite ancient and interesting, particularly for train buffs.

Car Trains

Car trains (*auto al seguito*) operate on a number of international routes, including connections to Spain (Figueras, Girona, Barcelona), France (Paris), Austria (Vienna), and cities in Germany, Switzerland and Eastern Europe.

Long-distance and international night trains often have sleeping accommodation in the form of first- and second-class cabins (one to three berths), and couchettes or 'sleeperettes' (reclining seats – first class only). It's recommended to avoid couchettes in the school holiday season (roughly June to September) if you wish to sleep!

There are diagrams in stations showing the layout of carriages for the different types of train, i.e. the position of first- and second-class carriages, buffet/restaurant cars and sleeping cars, etc. Most long-distance trains have a trolley service for drinks and snacks, and some fast trains have a restaurant car or buffet, although these are rare; when on a long journey, it's wise to follow the Italians' example and take your own snacks and packed lunch/dinner.

To further complicate matters, Ferrovie dello Stato operates many categories of train – some have only first class carriages, some just second class, while for others you must book a seat – and it's important to check which type you're travelling on. If you board a first-class-only train with a second-class ticket, the ticket inspector may just charge you the difference, or you may need to pay a fine.

Fares

Rail fares are good value compared with those of most other European countries, although ticket (*biglietto*) prices are rising along with the investment in improved services and the reduction in state subsidies. There is, however, a wide range of concessionary fares, season tickets and special offers, many of which are listed below. All children under four automatically travel free (but shouldn't occupy a seat) and those aged from 4 to 12 can travel for half fare. First-class tickets cost almost double the price of a second-class ticket.

Fares on local trains on journeys of up to 100km (62mi) are calculated on the distance travelled. For all other trains, including Eurostar, International and Intercity trains, fares are set by FS based on 'market values'. However, if you wish to upgrade to a train in a superior category or from second to first class, you must pay a 'change of service' fee, or, in the case of a downgrade, you can claim a refund. If a ticket is unused (through no fault of FS), a refund will be made within two months of the date of issue and is subject to a fee of 20 per cent of the fare or a minimum of €5.

If an Intercity train arrives over 30 minutes late, you receive a 'bonus' equal to 30 per cent of the fare and booking charge. For Eurostar trains the bonus is increased to 50 per cent. Take note of the train's number, point of departure/arrival and its scheduled and actual arrival times, and complete a bonus request (*richiesta di bonus*) form available at stations. You can do this at any station up to 15 days after the journey, and aren't required to make a claim on arrival at your destination. Your bonus is sent by post in the form of a discount coupon that you can use to buy future train tickets. If you buy tickets online, you can obtain a refund direct to the card you used to buy them.

As an example of current fares, the cost of a single (one-way) journey by Eurostar's Frecciarossa from Rome's Termini Station to Florence's Santa Maria Novella, a distance of around 240km (145mi), is around €62 (first class) or €46 (second class).

Concessions & Discounts

Ferrovie dello Stato offers a range of reduced and concessionary fares, which, if you're planning to do a lot of travelling, are worth looking into. These include the following (although they change frequently):

♦ **season card** (*tessera d'abbonamento*): a monthly season ticket for Eurostar or Intercity trains that provides unlimited return journeys on the same route up to 1,000km (620mi). You can order and pay online at 💻 www.trenitalia.com, although you must order the ticket at least four working days (weekdays) prior to the starting date and pay by credit card. The ticket is posted to you.

♦ **families** (*famiglie*): Children under four travel free and children under 12 accompanied by two paying adults travel free. The offer is valid for first- and second-class travel on most domestic journeys.

♦ **group ticket** (*biglietto di gruppo*): Groups of at least six people receive a discount of 20 per cent (first and second class) on Intercity trains or 10 per cent on Eurostar trains and couchettes; you must book and the fee is

€1.50. Groups of 50 or more people receive larger discounts; details (which vary) are available at main stations. Certain periods are excluded.

♦ **Cartaviaggio cards:** *Cartaviaggio, Cartaviaggio Smart, Cartaviaggio Relax* and *Cartaviaggio Executive* cards offer various benefits and discounts, geared towards different types of traveller (e.g. regular/irregular commuter at peak/off-peak times). The first three cards are free, the fourth costs €89 per year. For further details and to keep abreast of changes, see the website 💻 www.trenitalia.com.

♦ **Cartafreccia cards:** The *Cartafreccia* card is available free of charge and allows frequent Frecciarossa and Frecciargento passengers to accumulate points, and upgrade to the *Cartafreccia Oro* (gold) and *Cartafreccia Platino* (platinum) cards. These entitle holders to discounts and privileges including the use of a members-only waiting lounge at stations in the main cities and an on-board recreation area.

Other Frecciarossa and Frecciargento offers include Meno 15 and Meno 30 – these offer 15 per cent and 30 per cent discounts respectively on travel when a booking is made 7 or 15 days before travel.

If you find all the different tickets, offers and discounts bewildering, it's hardly surprising. With such an abundance of season and special tickets available, the only thing you can be sure of is that unless you qualify to travel for free, you're probably paying too much. The solution may be simply to tell a ticket office clerk where you want to go, when and how often you want to travel, and whether first or second class. However, you may not be able to rely on him to provide you with the cheapest ticket available, as he may be just as confused as you are!

You can check the Trenitalia website (💻 www.trenitalia.com) for the latest fare offers.

Buying Tickets

You need to buy a single/one-way ticket (*solo andata*) or return/round trip (*andata e ritorno*) ticket before commencing your journey. Tickets can be purchased at ticket offices at most railway stations, although it's recommended to buy your ticket in advance at a travel agency or online via the 💻 www.trenitalia.com website, which saves you (often a lot of) time queuing. If you plan to buy a ticket at a main station, you should allow plenty of time (at least 30 minutes). There's usually a dedicated ticket window for Eurostar tickets. Boarding a train without a ticket is punishable by a fine (usually around €50, although this isn't enforced if passengers board at a station without a ticket office or with non-operational ticket offices.

Many stations are equipped with ticket machines on which instructions can be displayed in English. They're similar in operation to the timetable on the FS website, except that you can pay for a ticket using a credit card or by inserting banknotes into the machine and receive it immediately. In the cities of Bologna, Florence, Milan, Naples, Padua, Rome and Venice, you can telephone the Welcome Centre and arrange for tickets to be delivered to your home. Most tickets are valid for two months and passengers can make unlimited stops within the period of validity.

Before boarding a train you must validate your ticket by inserting it in a small yellow validation (*convalida*) machine (*macchine obliteratici*), where it's punched to indicate that it has been used. If there's no machine, you should write the date and time by hand on the back of the ticket and find the ticket inspector after you've boarded a train; otherwise you can be fined for travelling without a ticket. Once punched, a ticket is valid for six hours on journeys of up to 200km (124mi) and 24 hours for journeys over 200km.

Rail Information

Information about rail services is available from an FS central line (☎ 89-2021). There are also numbers for other enquiries, ☎ 199 892 021 and for disabled passengers, ☎ 199 30 30

tram, Milan

60, although it can be difficult to get through and you need to speak Italian. Timetables can also be displayed on a television via the *Televideo* service (see page 114) and other 'teletext' services. If you have access to the internet, FS has an excellent website (💻 www.ferroviedellostato.it) that includes the following information, most of which can be displayed in English (plus Italian, French, German and Spanish):

◆ a do-it-yourself timetable. This is in English but you must enter the town or city names in Italian, e.g. Firenze not Florence, Venezia not Venice. You enter your departure station, arrival station, date of journey and earliest starting time, and all scheduled trains are displayed for that day (for long journeys it may also include trains departing on the following day), including journey times, connecting stations, on-board facilities, whether booking is necessary and wheelchair access.

◆ information about the main Italian railway stations, such as the facilities available (restaurant, news kiosk, change office, etc.), telephone numbers, and opening hours for information and reservation services;

◆ a list of FS agencies (the best place to buy tickets) for all major towns in Italy;

♦ offers such as reductions, monthly tickets and excursion tickets (many of which are listed above under **Concessions & Discounts**). Bear in mind, however, that these change frequently, so it's recommended to check with an FS agent or main railway station information office.

♦ detailed information about Eurostar services;

♦ telephone numbers for tourist hotels and car hire companies.

BUSES, TRAMS & UNDERGROUND RAILWAYS

The are two main types of buses in Italy, long-distance and rural buses, and city buses.

Long-distance & Rural Services

Italy has no national bus (*autobus*) or coach (*pullman*, or sometimes *pulman*) companies, but has more local and regional buses and operators than any other European country. Buses are more expensive than trains, although they're often quicker for short journeys. Companies usually operate at a fairly local level and although some of the larger companies provide long-distance, intercity services, these are limited. Because of the lack of national services, it's difficult to obtain detailed information on fares and there's little published on the internet. Timetables, route maps and fares are available from local bus and railway stations, tourist information offices, bookshops and newsagents.

☑ SURVIVAL TIP

As with rail travel, there's a bewildering range of concessionary fares for frequent travellers; obtain the latest information direct from bus companies.

To give just one example, Florence has several bus companies, most with their headquarters at or near S. Maria Novella railway station in the centre. The most important companies are Lazzi (🖥 www.lazzi. it) and Sita, either of which will get you to most of Tuscany's major destinations, albeit in their own good time. Lazzi also operates long-distance coaches to Rome and other major cities. Timetables for all routes can be obtained from an information booth outside the railway station.

A single ticket (*biglietto*) from Florence to Pisa (100km/62mi) should cost no more than €10 and takes around an hour. Sienna is particularly well geared to bus travellers and has a huge complex to the west of the city at Piazza San Domenico (from where a shuttle service operates to the city centre), equipped with tourist and hotel information offices, destination boards and ticket offices. In addition to serving the local area, long-distance coaches also go to Rome, Pisa and other destinations.

Major bus companies usually offer a variety of tickets, including single/one-way (valid for the day of issue only), return/round trip (valid for a number of days and usually cheaper than two single tickets), weekly (valid for five or six return trips) and monthly, which may be valid for a limited number of return journeys. Tickets for both long-distance and local services must usually be purchased from tobacconists', bars, news kiosks or bus company offices – you cannot buy them on buses! You may be given a number of tickets when a journey involves using a number of bus companies. If you live in a rural area, arm yourself with a sheaf of tickets of different values and, as you get to know the fares, use them as necessary.

Many bus companies in rural areas operate on the request stop (*fermata a richiesta*) system, whereby they stop to pick you up or let you off only if you request it by signalling to the driver (from a stop) or ringing a bell (on board). A bus's route and destination is shown by a sign in the front window.

A final word of caution: because of the large number of bus companies operating in most areas, all with their own rules and schedules, journeys in rural areas need careful planning and a good deal of local knowledge. Services can be infrequent or even non-existent on Sundays and public holidays.

City Services

This is where Italy often excels in the field of public transport, with bus and other city transport generally comprehensive, frequent, inexpensive and fairly rapid. This is particularly true as more cities are closing streets around historic centres to private cars and introducing more bus lanes. However, Italians have an enduring love affair with their cars and sometimes drive into city centres when it's forbidden and often treat bus lanes with total contempt. Although there are a few variations, most cities use the same system for buses. There's a flat fare, usually around €1, that entitles you to make as many journeys as you like within an hour. Single tickets and blocks of five or ten can be purchased from tobacconists', bars, news kiosks and sometimes ticket machines near bus stops. Local information offices provide route maps and timetables. Some cities (e.g. Rome) have introduced buses adapted for disabled passengers on certain routes. Many modern buses and trams, mercifully, are now air-conditioned. If possible, it's wise to avoid the 'school run' between around 1 and 2.30pm, when schoolchildren crowd buses.

City buses and trams usually have three doors; you board through a door at either end of the bus and exit via the central door. If you're changing buses/trams and have a stamped ticket or hold a pass, you should enter via the front door. If you have a standard ticket, you usually enter the bus or tram at the back and insert it in the orange or yellow validation (convalida) machine, which is usually on the right (driver's side) near the central doors. The ticket is stamped (the machine may also cut the corner off) and is then valid for 60 or 75 minutes, including changing buses or trams. Failure to validate your ticket can result in a fine of around €50. Bus stops are called fermata or fermata a richiesta, the latter being request stops where you must hold out your arm to signal the driver to stop. If you wish to get off at a request stop, you must push an orange or red button before your stop.

Many cities in Italy's lower-lying regions, including Genoa, Milan, Naples, Rome, Trieste and Turin, operate tram or light rail networks. Turin has several enclosed tram routes, completely separated from other traffic, which transport you quickly around the outskirts of the city or from one side to the other. The ticket system is essentially the same as for buses, but trams tend to be a bit quicker because they have right of way over all other traffic. (In some of Turin's streets, there are tram lines on either side of the road, and cars park in a line in the middle!)

Naples, Milan and Rome also have underground railways, known as 'metros', but don't expect anything like London, New York or Paris. Rome has only two lines, in the form of a cross, with Termini Station in the centre. Several stations on line B near the centre have been upgraded to be more user-friendly for disabled travellers. Line A hasn't been upgraded but the route is also served by bus route 590, which operates buses adapted for disabled passengers.

Most city transport operates from around 5.30 or 6am until 11.30pm or midnight, although you should check the times of the last service if you're out for the evening.

Trams and buses in Rome continue until around midnight and there are night buses (servizio notturno) on some routes. Transport services are less frequent on Sundays and public holidays.

In cities where there are two or more modes of public transport, it's usually possible to buy a ticket that can be used on all services. In Rome, for example, these tickets are known as metrobus and can be used on buses, trams, underground and main line (FS) trains, except the shuttle service to Fiumicino Airport. There are the usual concessions in nearly all cities. Both Rome and Milan issue an unlimited-travel, 24-hour ticket for €3-4, Milan offers a 48-hour ticket for €5.50, and Rome provides monthly city transport passes, costing €30 for a personal pass (this contains personal details of the holder and can only be used by him) or €46 for a pass which can be used by more than one person. Some cities provide discounts of up to 50 per cent for pensioners and students.

There are river buses in many cities, e.g. Rome, although most of these are strictly for tourists and aren't useful for residents.

TAXIS

Taxis in Italian cities are usually yellow, sometimes white, while in smaller towns white is the most common colour with a small number in other colours. They're usually found at official taxi ranks, for example at railway stations or near town centres, and aren't usually hailed in the street, although they may stop if they're empty. Taxis should have a meter, which you should ensure is switched on! If the driver claims that it's broken, you must agree the fare before starting a journey. If you're familiar with a town, it may be worthwhile mentioning that you wish to go via a particular landmark on the direct route to your destination, so that you aren't taken via the 'scenic route'. Taxi journeys in Italian cities aren't for the faint-hearted and can be hair-raising for the uninitiated, with drivers ignoring speed limits and any semblance of road rules, while roundly cursing other motorists.

Fares are set by the local authorities, starting at around €3 in large cities and then charged on a time and distance basis. There are also supplements for such sins as having luggage, wishing to travel at night and for journeys to local airports, although these have been fixed by some local authorities, e.g. Rome, where a journey from the city centre to the city's Ciampino and Fiumicino airports is fixed at €30/40 for up to four people with luggage. It isn't necessary to tip taxi drivers, although most Italians round up the fare to the nearest euro or leave some small change. In rural areas, drivers will usually take you to small villages or isolated houses, and the fare is invariably reasonable; for example, from Chiusi Station to a farmhouse in deepest Umbria costs around €25 for an 8km (5mi) journey, including a few kilometres on dirt roads.

FERRIES

Italy has a well-developed network of ferry services. Large ferries (*navi*) service the islands of Sardinia and Sicily, while smaller islands are served by small ferries (*traghetti*) and hydrofoils (*aliscafi*). Regular services connect the mainland with Italy's many islands, and ferries and hydrofoils also operate between towns on the lakes of Como, Garda, Maggiore and a number of smaller lakes. The most important domestic ferry routes include:

♦ Piombino to Elba;

♦ Civitavecchia, Genoa, Livorno (Leghorn) and Naples to Sardinia;

♦ Genoa, Naples, Reggio di Calabria and Villa San Giovanni to Sicily;

♦ Naples to the Lipari Islands (Stromboli, etc.);

♦ Naples to the Pontine islands (Ponza, Ischia, Procida);

♦ Naples to Capri.

There are also connections from Sicily to Sardinia and international car and passenger ferry services between Italy and various countries, including Albania, Croatia, Egypt, France (Corsica), Greece, Israel, Malta, Spain (the Balearics), Tunisia, Turkey and parts of the former Yugoslavia. Ticket prices are usually reasonable but vary according to the time of year and are (naturally) most expensive during summer.

Some ferry services operate during the summer only and services are severely curtailed during the winter on most routes or may be suspended altogether.

Some journeys are very long. For example, the Genoa-Palermo boat takes 23 hours and the Naples-Palermo ferry departs at 8pm and arrives at 7am the next day, although there's also a hydrofoil service taking just over five hours but operating only once per day, three days per week. On the other hand, boats leave from Villa San Giovanni for Messina (Sicily) every 15 minutes during peak hours; the trip takes half an hour and the service operates 24 hours per day.

Ships range from quite small, no-frills, no-services vessels on the shortest routes, to leviathans carrying 1,800 passengers and 500 vehicles, with restaurants, bars, shops, discos and cinemas on the longer routes. Long-haul ferries also provide sleeping facilities in the form of reclining seats (*poltrona*), couchettes and deluxe cabins with showers and toilets. Demand for these facilities is high at most times of year, so early booking is essential. You also need to book well in advance when travelling during peak holiday periods, particularly if you're taking a car. Bear in mind when planning a trip that services are infrequent on the longer routes, some of which have only one departure on three or four days per week.

The major companies serving the main destinations are as follows:

♦ **Adriatic Coast:** the Adriatic Company serves Ancona, Bari, Brindisi, Trieste and Venice (plus a number of international destinations);

♦ **Bay of Naples** (Naples, Capri, Ischia and Procida): Caremar, Alilauro and SNAV;

♦ **Elba:** Nav.Ar.Mar and Toremar;

♦ **Lipari Islands** (Vulcano, Lipari, Stromboli, etc.): Siremar and SNAV;

♦ **Sardinia:** Tirrenia, Sardinia Ferries, I Grandi Traghetti and FS (Italian railways);

♦ **Sicily:** Tirrenia, I Grandi Traghetti, Aliscafi SNAV (Hydrofoil) and FS.

Information about times and fares is available on the internet at 🖥 www.traghetti.com, which has a link to the sites of several ferry companies, most with an English version. To give an idea of fares, the average prices (mid-season, medium-sized car, etc.) on the Naples-Palermo route are around €26 for a deck passenger and €57 for a car; the short Villa San Giovanni-Messina trip costs around €25 for a medium-size car and €5 for a foot passenger.

A map showing Italy's main ports is shown in **Appendix E**.

AIR TRAVEL

There are direct international scheduled and charter flights to all major cities in Italy (e.g. direct flights from the UK to around 20 Italian cities) and many towns are served by domestic flights. International airlines serving Italy (apart from the national carrier Alitalia) include Aer Lingus, Air Canada, Air France, American Airlines, BMIbaby, British Airways, Continental Airlines, Delta Airlines, Easyjet, Emirates, Flybe, Iberia, Icelandair, KLM, Lufthansa, Meridiana, Qantas, Ryanair, SAS, Swissair, US Airways and Wizz Air. The major international gateways are Rome, Milan, Pisa, Venice and Naples, although more cities are becoming accessible by direct international flights, including Florence, Bologna and Perugia.

The Italian national airline, Alitalia, has its hub at Rome's Fiumicino airport and flies to over 100 cities in six continents, while its subsidiary

Air One offers budget short-haul flights within Italy and to Mediterranean destinations. Not surprisingly, Alitalia dominates the busy and lucrative Milan-Rome route.

For years, Alitalia had a reputation for being one of Europe's least efficient national carriers, plagued by strikes, over-manning and restrictive practices, and in 2006 the then Italian Prime Minister Romano Prodi described Alitalia's finances as 'completely out of control'. In 2008, entrepreneurs and the Intesa Sanpaolo bank took over the airline's assets to form the Compagnia Aerea Italiana (CAI), while keeping the Alitalia brand name. By 2010, losses had decreased by 95 per cent, and the airline is estimated to break even in 2011.

International Services

There are usually several direct flights per day to/from London Heathrow to Bologna, Florence, Genoa, Milan, Naples, Pisa, Rome, Turin and Venice, and there are also scheduled and charter flights from London Gatwick and other UK airports to various Italian cities (including Palermo). Normal scheduled fares to Rome are can be as low as £60 one way and £120 return with budget airlines (or even less!).

☑ **SURVIVAL TIP**

Fares vary considerably according to the time of the year, when you book and the airline, so shop around.

The vast majority of flights go to Milan or Rome, although there's usually at least one per day to Bologna, Naples, Pisa and Turin. There are also flights from Manchester (UK) to Milan and Rome, and Meridiana fly from London to Olbia and Cagliari (Sardinia) via Florence. Most European airlines fly via their European base to Italy, rather than direct.

Several airlines fly direct to Italy from the US, including Alitalia, Delta and American Airlines, although scheduled fares are expensive. Alitalia offers the widest choice of direct flights from the US, including daily flights from Boston, Chicago, Los Angeles, Newark, New York and Miami to Rome and Milan. Delta flies daily from Chicago, Los Angeles and New York to Rome and American Airlines daily from Chicago and Los Angeles via New York to Milan and Rome. The cheapest return fares from the US are around US$500 from New York to Rome, rising to US$700 during the shoulder season and to US$900 during the peak season; add around US$100 for flights from Chicago and Miami, and US$200 from Los Angeles.

Charter flights are available from the US to Italy but aren't such good value as from European countries, as scheduled airlines can often beat the prices, and offer more convenience and fewer restrictions. Flights take around nine hours from New York to Milan or Rome. From Canada, both Alitalia and Air Canada have direct flights to Rome and Milan from Toronto and Montreal.

Domestic Services

A number of airlines provide domestic services within Italy, including Air Dolomiti, Air Italy, Air One/Air One CityLiner (a subsidiary of Alitalia), Alitalia, Blue Panorama and its low-cost brand Blu-express, Efly, ItAli Airlines, Livingston, Meridiana fly, Mistral Air, Neos and Wind Jet. Some 40 Italian airports are served from Rome and most domestic flights take under an hour. However, travelling by air within Italy is expensive, although discounts are available, notably for evening and night flights. You can also buy Apex tickets (these must be booked and paid for at least seven days before departure and include at least one Saturday and Sunday night between the outward and return journeys). 'Juniors' (those aged under 22), students (up to 26) and families (consisting of a minimum of three people) can purchase one-way tickets for half the price of reduced tariffs. You should allow at least 20 minutes to check in for internal flights. Private air taxi services also operate from many airports.

Airports

Italy has international airports in Rome (Leonardo da Vinci, better known as Fiumicino, and Ciampino, which handles mainly charter flights), Milan (Linate for domestic and European flights, and Malpensa for intercontinental flights), Bari, Bologna, Brindisi, Catania (Sicily), Genoa, Olbia (Sardinia), Naples, Pisa, Palermo (Sicily), Perugia, Rimini, Trapani, Trieste, Turin, Verona and Venice.

Milan's Malpensa airport, which opened in 1998, suffers the disadvantage of being 53km (33mi) from Milan, compared with Linate which is just 10km (6mi) from the city centre; many Alitalia flights still operate out of Linate. However, express trains operating every 30 minutes connect Malpensa with Milan's Cadorna railway station, taking around 40 minutes (which will eventually be reduced to 30 minutes). The service operates from 6am to 1.30am and costs €11 single (one-way).

There are over 100 small airports in Italy, only some of which cater for international flights (particularly during summer), including Alghero, Ancona, Bari, Bergamo, Bologna, Brindisi, Cagliari, Catania, Florence, Genoa, Lamezia Terme, Lampedusa, Olbia, Palermo, Pantelleria, Parma, Perugia, Pescara, Reggio di Calabria, Rimini, Sassari, Trapani, Trieste, Treviso, Turin and Verona.

A map showing Italy's main airports is shown in **Appendix E**.

Information

Alitalia has a website (🖳 www.alitalia.com) detailing offers on international and domestic flights (some information is in Italian, but fairly comprehensible). Airport information telephone numbers are listed below.

Airport Information

Airport	Telephone Number
Alghero	079-935 282
Ancona	071-28271
Bari	080-5800 200
Bergamo	035-326 323
Bologna	051-6479 615
Brindisi	0831-416511
Genoa	010-60151
Milan (Malpensa)	02-232323
Milan (Linate)	02-232323
Perugia	075-592 141
Pescara	895-898 9512
Pisa	050-500 707
Rimini	0541-715755
Rome (Ciampino)	06-65951
Rome (Fiumicino)	06-65951
Trapani	0923-842502
Turin	011-567 6361
Venice	041 2609260

autumn in Tuscany

bellissima Ferraris!

11.
MOTORING

The love affair between Italians and their cars is well documented (most would rather lend you their wife for a weekend than their car), so it comes as no surprise to find that Italy has the sixth-highest number of cars per head of population in the world – around 547 for every 1,000 inhabitants (according to Forbes, 💻 www.forbes.com). The problems caused by this high rate of car ownership have been exacerbated by many Italians' refusal to dispose of their pride and joy for a newer and safer model.

As long ago as 1997, the Italian government introduced a 'scrappage' scheme, offering incentives to get old cars off the road by offering to pay an inflated price for the old car if it was sold (for scrap) in exchange for a new one. Until then you would still see large numbers of old Fiat 500s (*cinquecenti*) rattling around Italian towns, some with their bodies held together by little more than innumerable layers of paint. The subsidies for scrapping old cars coupled with more frequent technical inspections have significantly reduced the number of such 'death-traps' on the roads in the last decade. Nevertheless, the accident rate remains one of the highest in Europe and every day in Italy there are some 600 road accidents, resulting in the deaths of around 15 people and the injury of over 850.

Italian roads are generally good, with an excellent motorway (*autostrada*) network covering some 6,400km (3,977mi), though most of them are toll (*pedaggio*) roads. However, many town centres are based on medieval street plans and are unable to cope with today's levels of traffic, to say nothing of the pollution it generates. This has led several cities, including Rome and Milan, to introduce measures to reduce the number of cars entering the city centre during peak hours. Hundreds of cities and towns throughout Italy have also introduced 'car-free' days once a month, on which motor vehicles are banned from city and town centres – though these are invariably on Sundays.

Cycling as a means of transport has also received welcome publicity in recent years as a result of these car-free Sundays. With cars banned from town centres, the strangely quiet streets are full of bicycles and a few horses. However, dedicated cycle tracks (*pista ciclabile*) are something of a rarity, although there are some in national parks and a few in towns around the country and cycling groups are pressing for more. A recent initiative in Florence is bicycle taxis, which operate in the city centre and carry two passengers.

As a glance at any major city in Italy will confirm, cities aren't ideal places for cycling due to the volume of traffic and the level of pollution. Most Italians don't use bicycles in town centres, but rely instead on scooters or motorbikes. If you do cycle in traffic it's wise to wear a face-mask, although, according to medical experts, they offer little or no protection against carbon monoxide. It's important not to underestimate the dangers of cycling (particularly for children) in Italy's cities and towns, where many cyclists are killed and injured each year. Helmets are essential attire, particularly for children, as are reflective clothing and bright (preferably flashing) lights at night. Head injuries are the main cause of death in cycle accidents and you should buy a quality helmet that has been tested and approved.

There's a general emergency number (113) for reporting accidents and breakdowns, but for a quicker response in an emergency you can call the EU-wide emergency number 112 and ask for the *carabinieri* or call 118 for an ambulance. In the event of a breakdown, call 116 and the nearest Automobile Club d'Italia (ACI) office will be advised to come to your assistance, although they may charge you for this service if you aren't a member. Road conditions can be checked 24 hours per day by calling the CCISS (Road Safety Information Coordination Centre) on 1518. Their call centre is operational 24 hours a day, 365 days a year, and the call is free of charge from any telephone in Italy (landline or mobile) irrespective of duration.

> A journey planner with road traffic news for Italy in English can be found on the Autostrade per L'Italia website (🖥 www.autostrade.it/en/autostrade/home.do).

IMPORTING A VEHICLE

It's usually cheaper to buy a vehicle abroad and import it into Italy, where cars are **very** expensive owing to high taxes. If you intend to bring a vehicle, either temporarily or permanently, ensure that you know the latest regulations. If you have a new private vehicle purchased in another EU country with an EU type-approval certificate, no formalities or checks on the technical specifications of the vehicle are necessary. However, if you plan to import a vehicle permanently from outside the EU, it may need expensive modifications. For information about type-approval (*omologazione*), contact the Ministry of Infrastructure and Transport (Ministero delle Infrastrutture e dei Trasporti, Direzione Generale Motorizzazione Civile, IV Direzione Centrale, Via Caraci, 36, 00157 Rome (☎ 06-4158 2143 or 06-4158 2144, 🖥 www.mit.gov.it).

The problem of finding spare parts and service facilities for foreign-made vehicles should also be taken into account. With the increase in the number of foreign-made cars in Italy in the last dozen years, service facilities now exist for all European-manufactured cars and even most Japanese and Korean models. Facilities for American-made cars, however, remain rare.

Foreigners staying temporarily in Italy are permitted to drive vehicles with foreign registrations for up to 12 months, provided the vehicle registration remains valid while in Italy. A registration document with an Italian translation may be required. The use of the vehicle is duty and tax-free for six months only, unless you're a diplomat. If you become resident in Italy, your car must be imported within your first six months of residence.

If you'll be in Italy for less than six months and won't be a resident, it may pay you to buy a car in another European country and re-sell it when you no longer need it (it's illegal for non-residents to buy a car in Italy unless it's for export). If you buy a car privately and strike a good deal, you could even make a profit! Some dealers will sell you a car and buy it back for an agreed price after six months.

Duty & Tax

A vehicle can be imported from another European Union (EU) country without any taxes (e.g. VAT or import duty) being payable, provided tax was paid in the former EU country and the vehicle has been owned and used for at least six months in that country before importation. Note that this is a one-time concession.

Temporary residents may import a vehicle registered outside the EU for private use for a maximum of six months in any 12-month period without being liable for duty or tax provided they don't lend, hire out or give the vehicle to an EU citizen. Vehicles (which are classed as household goods) can be imported duty and tax free when moving to Italy from a non-EU country and establishing residence, provided that:

◆ the vehicle has been in your possession, was registered abroad at least six months before your arrival in Italy **and** has covered over 6,000km (3,728mi).

- you can supply proof of residence outside the EU for 12 months.

- the vehicle is for personal use only.

- you register as a resident in Italy.

- the vehicle is immediately registered in the *Pubblico Registro Automobilistico* (*PRA*) at the local motor vehicle office (Motorizzazione Civile) – see **Vehicle Registration** on page 158.

- the vehicle isn't sold, lent or hired out for one year after its importation.

After payment of any duty and tax due, you receive a customs receipt or clearance certificate. If no duties are to be paid, a permit of customs exemption is issued. These documents are required when registering the vehicle.

For those who don't qualify for exemption under the above criteria, the following tariffs are levied:

- **import duty** at 11 per cent of the purchase price, plus freight costs to the place of destination in Italy, plus freight insurance;

- **VAT** at 20 per cent of the purchase price, freight costs and import duty.

These rates apply irrespective of the type of vehicle being imported. The importer must present a dealer's invoice as evidence of the purchase price of the vehicle. If, however, customs officials don't consider this a fair and accurate representation of the vehicle's market value, they may calculate their own figure by reference to a dealer's car buying guide or obtain a certified appraisal. The Italian authorities recommend that private importers without a recent invoice or who ship an unusual model should have their vehicle appraised before declaring the value. Some shipping agencies will complete

clearance and customs formalities on your behalf for a fee.

SAFETY INSPECTION & EMISSIONS TEST

Until the '80s, technical inspections were made only when a car was imported or new, therefore Italian roads were filled with cars that were a danger to both the occupants and other road-users. Then regulations were introduced that required cars to be inspected 'regularly'. With the limited capacity of the motoring authority to achieve this, however, this usually meant once every ten years. With the recent delegation of the work to authorised garages, capacity has increased, and inspections are now due (and carried out) when a car is three years old and every two years thereafter.

Safety inspections are controlled by the motor vehicle authority (Motorizzazione Civile), which licenses garages to carry out inspections. Vehicles can also be inspected at any office of the Motorizzazione. The process is usually straightforward. You don't require an appointment and can simply take your car to an inspection centre and ask for the inspection to be carried out; you hand over your car and the keys, and return the next day to collect it and – hopefully – the certificate. A mechanic checks your car for any operational defects (brakes, lights, exhaust, etc.) and repairs these if necessary. The basic fee is around €125 (excluding repairs).

If your vehicle doesn't pass the inspection, you're told what repairs or alterations are required. You're then obliged to have the repairs carried out and return it to the test centre for another inspection.

In addition to the safety inspection, an exhaust emissions test is required annually for both petrol- and diesel-engine cars. This is also performed by authorised garages, who issue a *bollino blu* on satisfactory completion of the test. The cost of the emissions test and certificate is around €10-15.

If you're unsure when your car is due for an inspection, check the sticker on the windscreen for the emissions inspection deadline and the sticker in your registration book for the date of the safety inspection. If the two dates coincide, they can be performed at the same time (which is recommended in any case).

If you're stopped by the police with out-dated stickers for either inspection, you're fined on the spot and are given a short period in which to take your car to a test centre – you aren't permitted to drive it until it passes.

VEHICLE REGISTRATION

If you import a vehicle temporarily, you're given a customs receipt (*bolletta doganale*) and can drive it on foreign registration plates for up to a year if you're a non-resident. However, if you become a resident, the vehicle must be imported permanently and registered (*immatricolata*) in Italy. Registration must be applied for within ten days of taking up residence. In order to register a vehicle, you must produce your residence permit. If you have provisional residence and are waiting to receive your residence permit, you'll be given 'tourist' registration plates with the letters 'EE' (*Escursionisti Esteri*) on them; these are only valid for six months and must be exchanged for regular Italian number plates as soon as your residence permit is granted.

If you buy a car directly from the previous owner, you must pay a fee to transfer ownership (*passaggio di proprietà*), which is usually between around €375 and €450. The registration plates remain with the car, but the car must be registered in the name of the new owner. To do this, you and the buyer must go to an Automobile Club d'Italia (ACI) office or an agent (*agenzie pratiche auto*), who takes care of the paperwork. It isn't recommended to try to do it yourself. You may need to wait months for your car registration papers to arrive, although you can obtain interim documents (*foglio sostitutivo*), which must be renewed every three months.

If you buy a new or second-hand car from a dealer, he'll take care of the registration for you.

Foreign Vehicles

Vehicles can usually be registered only if there's a general operating licence for that model issued by the motor vehicle authority (Motorizzazione Civile). Each new model made in or imported into Italy is subject to a general inspection, including safety and emissions tests. This inspection is usually instigated by the manufacturer or importer when a new model is released and guarantees that the performance of the vehicle meets Italian technical, environmental and safety standards. After successful completion, an operating licence is granted. The vehicle authority issues a 'title' for each different model, listing its main technical features, a copy of which is issued to car buyers by the manufacturer or dealer. You're therefore recommended not to make any substantial modifications to an already licensed vehicle without obtaining expert advice, or you may lose the general operating licence and your insurance cover.

Foreign vehicles imported privately won't usually have the necessary Italian title among their papers. If the model in question has already been granted a general operating licence in Italy, a copy should be obtained at the beginning of the registration procedure from the local car registration office. If a licence hasn't previously been issued, it's the responsibility of the applicant to supply the necessary technical data. This applies particularly to American cars, as these aren't common in Italy. To avoid the time-consuming and expensive procedure of establishing the technical specifications of a

car through a general inspection, you should contact the manufacturer of your vehicle before importing it for information on the vehicle identification number (VIN), year of manufacture, vehicle type and other technical data, including:

♦ engine type/displacement;

♦ power (DIN hp/kW);

♦ maximum speed;

♦ emissions data;

♦ admissible wheel and tyre sizes;

♦ admissible gross front/rear axle weight.

If the vehicle doesn't have valid registration plates, temporary plates (*targa di prova*) must be obtained to drive it to an inspection station. You must request these from the local motor registry (Motorizzazione Civile).

> You must provide the date of an imported vehicle's first registration, which determines the legal standard that applies. However, even when an overseas model has been granted a general operating licence, modifications may be necessary to meet Italian safety and environmental standards.

In order to ascertain whether modifications are necessary, all imported vehicles must pass an inspection (*collaudo*). The regulations surrounding this are complex and change constantly, so unless you enjoy getting to grips with Italian bureaucracy at its worst you're recommended to have the inspection and paperwork done by an agent (*agenzie pratiche auto*). Most agents charge around €175 for this service, but you should make sure that you receive a written quotation beforehand. Most authorised garages can carry out any required modifications.

Registration Procedure

To register a motor vehicle you must apply at the local motor registry in the town where you live and present:

♦ proof of your identity and residence, i.e. your passport and residence permit. Only residents and resident companies may register a car – either themselves or through an authorised representative, who must have power of attorney.

♦ a customs clearance certificate stating payment of (or exemption from) import duty and VAT (see **Importing a Vehicle** on page 156);

♦ proof of ownership, e.g. a bill of sale or commercial invoice;

♦ vehicle documents, including the operating licence or title if one has been issued. If no title has been issued, you'll be given a blank title to be completed by a certified expert.

♦ safety inspection and emissions test certificates (see above).

You must pay a fee of around €70 (in cash), plus an additional amount of around €45 for registration plates (front and rear). After you've paid the fee and been given a receipt, your vehicle registration certificate (*libretto*) is issued. Be prepared to fit your plates before driving away.

Italian registration plates no longer carry provincial letters, which means that it's no longer necessary to change the number of a car to that of a new owner's province, although you must still register a change of ownership and/or address. Plates are valid for as long as you own a car and they belong to the car not the owner, i.e. you cannot transfer them to another vehicle.

ROAD TAX

Road or 'circulation' tax (*tassa di circolazione*) is calculated according to the power of your vehicle and whether it runs on petrol or diesel. For petrol-engine cars, you currently pay €2.60 per kW. Therefore, if your car has a power of 80kW (which is average), you pay around €208 per year. You can find out the cost of road tax from ACI offices, from charts posted in post offices and from the January edition of *Quattroruote* magazine.

The first payment must be made within a month of registering a car. The local office of the ACI or a car dealer can advise you where it can be paid the first time (the location varies with the region). Subsequent annual payments are made at a post office. On payment, you receive a *bollo di circolazione* (commonly called a *bollo auto*), which no longer needs to be displayed behind your windscreen but should be carried by the driver.

Road tax is required even when a car isn't being used or parked on a public road. You can make your initial application for road tax at any time during the year, but for most drivers it expires on 31st December, after which you have one month (until 31st January) to renew it for the following year. Before buying a second-hand car in Italy, you should check that the road tax payments are up-to-date; otherwise you'll be liable for any back payments when you renew it.

BUYING A CAR

You need a residence permit (*certificato di residenza*) and a fiscal code (see page 213) to buy a car in Italy. Non-residents can purchase a vehicle only from a manufacturer and must export it within a year. Before you can drive a car, you must have valid insurance cover (see **Car Insurance** on page 162).

Car manufacturers often want to sell the current year's 'stock' before the end of the calendar year and consequently may offer special deals from October to December. The choice may be limited in terms of colour and options, but you can often get a new car for 20 per cent or more below the normal price.

Before buying a second-hand car, it's wise to consult the magazine *Quattroruote* (🖥 www.quattroruote.it) which lists the average prices for all new and second-hand cars in Italy. Prices vary according to how many kilometres a car has done, its general condition and where it's sold, but the prices quoted are usually a good guide.

SELLING A CAR

You can advertise a car for sale in local newspapers, on free local notice boards, in major newspapers (the Saturday editions are best) and in many motoring newspapers and magazines. A check of your local news kiosk

will reveal a range of publications listing used cars (and possibly other items) for sale. There are also a growing number of internet-based advertising sites. If you belong to any clubs or organisations that publish a newsletter, they usually have a classified advertising section (even if you aren't a member, many accept advertisements for a small fee).

The best place to advertise a car depends on its make and value. Inexpensive cars are best sold in local newspapers, while expensive and collectors' cars are often advertised in the national motoring press. Buyers usually travel a long way to view a car that appears good value – if nobody phones, you know why! You can also put a 'for sale' (*vendesi*) sign (traditionally yellow or orange) in a car and park it in a prominent place, but make sure there are no parking restrictions.

☑ **SURVIVAL TIP**

Selling a Car

Be aware of the following when selling a car:

To find its approximate market value, consult the magazine *Quattroruote*.

Insist on a cash deposit and full payment of the balance in cash on delivery.

Inform your insurance company that the car has been sold.

Although the registration plates remain with the car when you sell it, the car must be registered in the name of the new owner (see Vehicle Registration on page 158).

DRIVING LICENCE

The minimum age for driving in Italy is 18 for a motor car or for a motorcycle over 125cc, 16 for a motorcycle of between 50 and 125cc, and 14 for a moped (motorcycle up to 50cc). In Italy young drivers (14 or over) can drive small cars, called mini-cars without a licence; this is possible because the cars, which have a maximum speed of 48kph (30mph), are classified as mopeds. Young drivers without a full Class B license aren't allowed to carry passengers – in mini-cars or on mopeds – although this rule is often flouted. To ride a motorcycle over 50cc, you must have a motorcycle licence (Class A); you cannot ride a motorcycle over 50cc on a car (Class B) licence. Moped riders require a Certificate of Aptitude (see page 171). You must carry your licence (and other car papers) with you at all times when driving in Italy. If you wear spectacles or contact lenses, you're required always to wear them and carry a spare pair.

EU Licences

Since 1st July 1996, EU residents have enjoyed full recognition of standard driving licences in other EU member countries for an unlimited period (though, officially, an old green UK driving licence is valid only with a translation). You aren't obliged to apply for a new licence, even when you transfer your permanent residence to Italy. However, an EU licence must be 'validated' at your local motor registry or an ACI office. A voluntary exchange for an Italian licence is also possible; in which case you must apply to an ACI office and pay a small fee.

From 2013 drivers will be issued with the new, micro-chipped credit-card style licence which is planned to replace the 110 different driving licences currently used in the EU. The new-style licence must be renewed every 10-15 years; if you're an EU national, you may wish to update your licence in your home country before travelling to Italy.

If you have a driving licence of a class that allows you to drive professionally or in a larger vehicle than those allowed under Class B, you must reapply for such a licence in Italy. For example, if you were a bus driver and wish to drive a bus in Italy, you must obtain the appropriate Italian licence.

Non-EU Licences

Non-EU nationals resident in Italy can drive there for a year with a valid foreign licence but generally require a translation (or an international driving permit issued in their home country), which can be obtained from offices of the ACI. During this period, and before obtaining a residence permit, non-EU nationals must swap their foreign licence for an Italian licence (*patente*) – this applies to selected countries only (see below) – or take an Italian driving test. If you live in Italy for a year without obtaining an Italian licence, you **must** take an Italian driving test (see below).

An Italian licence is valid for ten years if you're under 50, five years if you're between 50 and 70 and three years if you're over 70. At the end of the licence validity period you must pass a medical examination and, if you're over 70, a certificate from your doctor may be required stating that you don't suffer from a medical condition that could affect your driving. If you're over 80, it can be difficult to obtain (or retain) a driving licence. The standard licence was changed in 1999 to a pink plastic credit card (*tessera*) format, which contains the EU logo in the top left-hand corner with an 'I' (for Italy) in the middle and the holder's photograph.

If you lose (i.e. mislay) an Italian licence, you must make a report (*denuncia*) to the police, where you complete a form and provide a photograph, and they'll request a duplicate on your behalf. The police will issue you with a provisional licence, which is valid until you receive your new driving licence (by post), which should be within 90 days. The cost is around €100!

With Reciprocity

The following countries have reciprocity agreements with Italy, which means that driving licences from these countries can be converted to an Italian licence: all EU countries, Albania*, Algeria, Argentina, Croatia, El Salvador*, Iceland, Japan, Lebanon, Liechtenstein, Macedonia, Moldova, Monaco, Morocco, Norway, Philippines,

San Marino, South Korea, Switzerland, Taiwan, Tunisia, Turkey and Uruguay* (*reciprocity being phased out in 2014).

☑ SURVIVAL TIP

Drivers must first qualify for a residence permit as without one they aren't permitted to hold an Italian driving licence.

If your licence was issued in any of the above countries, you aren't required to take an Italian theory or driving test, but you must apply to have your licence converted. To begin this process, you require:

♦ a valid passport or identity card and your residence permit;

♦ two passport photographs;

♦ a translation of your driving licence by an official translator with approval from the Italian courts or by one of the recognised automobile clubs in Italy;

♦ the original and a copy of your foreign driving licence;

♦ a medical certificate (*certificato medico*) confirming that you're fit to drive;

♦ an eye test certificate, not more than two years old, stating that your eyesight is acceptable. *Agenzie pratiche auto* can give you the names of doctors who perform this test.

If your driving licence has been renewed since your arrival in Italy and the date it was first issued isn't noted, you need to prove that your driving history pre-dates your arrival in Italy – an expired licence or a letter from the licence issuing authority will suffice.

The process can cost up to €200 and, as with anything to do with officialdom in Italy, the procedure is highly complicated; don't attempt to handle it yourself unless you speak fluent Italian and have lots of spare time, but take the above documents to an *agenzia pratiche auto* and let them handle the application.

Without Reciprocity

If your driving licence was issued in any country other than those listed above, e.g. in Australia, Canada, New Zealand or the US (unless you're a Canadian or US diplomat), commiserations! After obtaining an Italian residence permit, you must take Italian written and road tests (see below). Once you have an Italian licence, your original licence is no longer valid and the Italian authorities may insist that you surrender it and, if you have one, your international driving permit (IDP). It's wise to take a photocopy of your licence or even obtain a duplicate before handing it over. Your original licence is usually returned to the authority that issued it with a note stating that you now have an Italian licence, although it may simply be stamped to that effect and returned to you. As your original licence is no longer deemed valid, neither is an IDP which is based on it. If you return to your home country, you may need to apply for an international licence based on your Italian licence, unless you can trace your old licence and have it returned in exchange for your Italian one!

CAR INSURANCE

All motor vehicles plus trailers and semi-trailers must be insured for third party liability when entering Italy. It isn't mandatory for cars insured in most European countries to have an international insurance 'green' card, but British drivers are recommended to obtain one. Vehicles insured in an EU country, or in Liechtenstein, Norway or Switzerland, are usually automatically covered for third party liability in Italy when visiting the country.

If you have comprehensive insurance in Italy and plan to drive abroad, however, you should obtain a green card (*carta verde*) from your insurance company, which is usually provided free of charge. A green card is compulsory for driving in Andorra, Bulgaria, Poland and Romania and strongly recommended for Greece, Portugal, Spain and Turkey. Many insurers offer breakdown assistance (*assistenza e soccorso stradale*) as a supplement, which is useful if you aren't already covered, e.g. by a motoring organisation.

Insurance premiums are high in Italy, reflecting the high accident rate, the large number of stolen cars and the lack of competition; they can be as high as €1,000 per

you must have additional cover called *infortunio del conducente*.

♦ **third party, fire & theft** (*assicurazione contro terzi furto e incendio*): called part-comprehensive in some countries; can be added to your third party insurance for an additional fee;

♦ **collision cover:** pays for damage to your car in the event of an accident for which you're responsible;

♦ **comprehensive cover** (*casco*): includes collision damage and non-collision damage (e.g. from falling rocks or vandalism). Non-collision damage may also be included in third party, fire and theft cover, so check when you take out your policy. Comprehensive insurance doesn't provide the same level of cover as in many other countries and doesn't include injuries to passengers, although family members travelling as passengers can be included for an additional fee. Note that comprehensive cover is a separate policy from third party or collision insurance and doesn't need to be taken out with the same insurance company.

year or even more, even with the maximum no-claims bonus. In theory, you aren't required to insure your car with an Italian insurance company or an insurance company in Italy and can insure it with any company in any EU member state, provided the company is licensed to do business in Italy. In practice, however, it may be difficult or impossible to persuade a foreign insurer to insure your car in Italy.

There are several levels of car insurance in Italy, including the following:

♦ third party (*responsabilità civile*, commonly referred to as RC auto) – the basic category of car insurance and the minimum required by law for all motor vehicles. This covers you for the cost of damage to other vehicles or property and injury to other people in accidents for which you're to blame. The compulsory minimum cover for private cars in Italy is €775,000 per accident, irrespective of the number of victims or the nature of the injury or damage. However, it's wise to take out a policy with a much higher level of cover than this – at least €2.5m. Most insurance companies offer cover up to ten times the legal minimum, and there may be no maximum limit.

Note that it's the car and not the driver which is insured in Italy. Therefore, if you wish to be covered when driving any vehicle in an accident for which you're responsible,

Insurance is available from many sources, including direct insurance companies and brokers. Shop around (you can do this via the internet at 🖥 www.assicurazione.it – see also **Insurance Agents & Companies** on page 195), as rates vary considerably; however, if you find a particularly low premium, it's wise to check that important benefits haven't been excluded. Premiums vary considerably according to a range of factors, including the type of insurance, a vehicle's horsepower, your age and driving (and accident) record, the province where you live, whether your car is garaged overnight and the maximum compensation to be paid out to a third party in the event of a claim. Premiums are based on a points system whereby points are allocated for the above factors. Premiums are subject to VAT at 20 per cent.

Italian insurance companies maintain tables showing the value of different makes of car of various ages. Except for new cars, their values are around 20 per cent lower than the market value and they pay compensation only according to those values. It's therefore important to check that a vehicle isn't over-insured.

Car insurance policies are valid for a year and must usually be cancelled two months before the renewal date (in writing by registered post), or the policy is automatically extended for a further year. If you haven't paid your renewal premium within ten days of the expiry date, you're deemed to be driving without insurance. If you're changing insurance companies, the new company will be happy to cancel your old policy for you and will usually give you a standard letter to sign. It's important to shop around for the best deal each time your insurance comes up for renewal.

No-claims discounts apply only to third party and comprehensive cover. You're placed in a no-claims 'class' according to your number of years' insurance without a claim. For each claim-free year you're automatically moved into a higher class, although the maximum premium reduction is just 30 per cent. If you're involved in an accident for which you're deemed wholly or partly at fault, you may lose some, or all, of your no-claims bonus. If you're a young (e.g. under 25) or inexperienced driver or have a poor accident record, you may be required to pay a higher than normal penalty (*malus*) or an excess (deductible), e.g. €250, on each claim.

Your insurance certificate must be displayed behind your vehicle's windscreen; while you're waiting for your official insurance documentation, you can display your receipt as proof of insurance.

There used to be a number of dubious companies providing car insurance in Italy; they charged low premiums but used delaying tactics to avoid paying claims – ever! Although these companies have mostly been weeded out, Italian insurers can still be **very** slow to pay in the event of accidents (especially serious ones) and a delay of six months or longer isn't uncommon.

If a car is repaired after a fire, vandalism or an accident, the insurer pays the labour cost in full (less any excess specified in the policy) but doesn't pay the full cost of any new parts because the parts replaced weren't new. Therefore it would be beneficial from an owner's point of view, for example, to have a dent in a door repaired rather than replace the door with a new one, even if the latter would actually cost less in labour! The catch is that the insurance company's assessor (*perito*) may make his estimate according to the cheaper solution and he may not accept in full the bill or estimate you present. The difference between what he accepts and the cost of repairing a car may be as high as 20 per cent, even in a straightforward case. For this reason, most Italians don't claim for minor accidents (which would also affect their no-claims discount) or even bother to have the damage repaired.

If an accident is caused by an uninsured or unidentifiable car, under EU law you're entitled to compensation from the motor vehicle guarantee fund of the member state in which the accident occurred, in accordance with the rules in that country. The fund also covers motorists whose insurance company was being compulsorily wound up at the time of an accident or is put into compulsory liquidation some time thereafter.

Breakdown Insurance

Insurance against breakdowns in Italy and other European countries is provided by Italian car insurance companies and motoring organisations (see page 178). If you're motoring abroad or you live abroad and are motoring in Italy, it's important to have car breakdown insurance, which may be combined

with holiday and travel insurance (see page 207), including repatriation for your family and your car in the event of an accident or breakdown. Most foreign breakdown companies provide multilingual, 24-hour centres where assistance is available for motoring, medical, legal or travel problems.

SPEED LIMITS

Speed limits in Italy change frequently. The general motorway (*autostrada*) speed limit is currently 130kph (81mph) for vehicles with an engine capacity of over 1,100cc. Vehicles with smaller engines and motorcycles with engines below 150cc are restricted to 110kph (68mph). Cars towing caravans or trailers are limited to 100kph (62mph) on motorways.

On regional highways the general speed limit is 110kph (68mph), although cars towing caravans or trailers are limited to 80kph (50mph); on secondary local roads it's 90kph (56mph), but it may be lower for certain stretches of road. In urban and populated areas the general speed limit is 50kph (31mph), which is sometimes reduced to 30kph (20mph), e.g. near schools or hospitals. If you see a sign indicating 'end of speed limit', it doesn't mean that there's no longer a speed limit, but that the general speed limit for the type of road now applies.

Speed limits are widely ignored in Italy, where people often drive at 150kph (93mph) or faster when the speed limit is just 90kph. However, the road police (*polizia stradale*) use electronic speed-testing (radar) equipment and are cracking down on offenders; fines are high (up to €3,100) and you can face a stiff fine and/or lose your licence if you're caught speeding three times or exceed the limit by over 40kph (25mph). Recent revisions to the country's Highway Code could also put an end to the Italian motorist's habit of not stopping for pedestrians, with eight penalty points applied for those caught not heeding crossings.

ROAD SIGNS

Italy generally adheres to the international standard road signs and most signs conform to the following shapes and colours:

Road Signs	
Colour/Shape	**Function**
Red triangle	Warning
Red circle	Restriction
Blue circle	Requirement
Square/rectangle	Guidance
Diamond	Priority
Octagon	Stop

See ⌨ www.alltravelitaly.com/italy/car_rental/road_signs.htm for information about Italy's most common road signs. You can test your knowledge of Italian road signs at Hidden Italy (⌨ www.hidden-italy.com/car/italianroadsigns.html).

GENERAL ROAD RULES

The following general road rules may help you adjust to driving in Italy:

♦ Your vehicle registration certificate (and driving licence, receipt for your road tax payment, insurance certificate, and safety inspection and emissions test certificates) must be carried at all times when driving a vehicle (the last three must be displayed on the inside of your windscreen). If you're stopped by the police without one of these documents, you can be fined on the spot. It's wise to make copies of all your car papers (in case your car or documents are stolen) and keep them in a safe place.

♦ When motoring outside the country where your car is registered, your vehicle must display either the new EU-style number plates, which incorporate a letter or letters showing the country of registration and 12 yellow stars in a circle, or a separate nationality sticker alongside the rear number plate. You can be fined on the spot for not displaying this, although judging by the number of cars that fail to do so, this law is seldom enforced. Cars must show only the correct nationality sticker and not an assortment. Foreigners living in Italy often like to emphasise their nationality by displaying their nationality sticker (or maybe it's an attempt at self-protection), which is illegal but seems to be tolerated.

♦ All motorists must carry a red breakdown triangle (*triangolo*), which must be placed 50 to 200m (164 to 656ft) behind a stationary vehicle, depending on the type of road (see **Accidents** on page 174). It's recommended also to carry a spare set of bulbs/fuses, a fire extinguisher and a first-aid kit.

♦ If you need to wear spectacles or contact lenses when motoring, it will be noted on your Italian driving licence and you must always wear them **and** carry a spare pair.

♦ The wearing of seatbelts is compulsory in Italy and includes passengers in both front and rear seats – this law also applies to passengers in taxis. Children up to the age of 12 and less than 1.5m (4ft 11in) tall must use an approved safety seat or a safety belt suitable for their age. You can be fined between €74 and €299 on the spot if you or one of your passengers isn't wearing a seatbelt. Pregnant women are permitted not to wear seatbelts but only if they have a written statement from their doctor. If you have an accident and aren't wearing a seatbelt, your insurance company can refuse to pay a claim for personal injury.

♦ You may already have noticed that the Italians drive on the right (when not driving in the middle!). It saves confusion if you do likewise. If you aren't used to driving on the right, take it easy until you're accustomed to it. Be particularly alert when leaving lay-bys, T-junctions, one-way streets, petrol stations and car parks, as it's easy to lapse into driving on the left. It's helpful to display a reminder (e.g. 'Think Right!') on your car's dashboard.

♦ Most main roads are priority roads, indicated by a sign. The most common priority sign is a yellow diamond on a white background, in use in most of continental Europe. The end of priority is shown by the same sign with a black diagonal line through it. On secondary roads without priority signs and in built-up areas, you must give way to vehicles coming from your RIGHT. **Failure to observe this rule is the cause of many accidents.** The priority rule was fine when there was little traffic, but nowadays most countries (Italy included) realise the

necessity of having 'stop' or 'give way' (*dare la precedenza*) signs at junctions.

♦ Most motorists no longer treat priority as a God-given right, although some still pull out without looking. The priority to the right rule usually also applies in car parks, but not when exiting from car parks or dirt tracks. If you're ever in doubt about who has priority, give way to trams, buses and all traffic coming from your right. Emergency (ambulance, fire, police) and public utility (electricity, gas and water) vehicles attending an emergency have priority on all roads.

♦ Roundabouts (traffic circles or rotaries) conform with other EU countries, where vehicles on roundabouts have priority and traffic entering is faced with a give way or stop sign. Traffic flows anti-clockwise around roundabouts and not clockwise as in the UK and other countries where driving is on the left.

♦ The sequence of Italian traffic lights (*semafori*) is red, green, yellow (amber) and back to red. There's no red-and-amber phase after red. Yellow means stop at the stop line; you may proceed only if the yellow light appears when you're no longer able to stop behind the line. You can be fined around €138 for jumping (running) a red light (or get a ticket to the next life!), which nevertheless is a national sport in Italy. (It has been said that traffic lights in Italy are merely decorative.)

♦ At traffic lights, a yellow or green filter light – usually flashing and with a direction arrow – may be shown in addition to the main signal. This means that you may drive in the direction shown by the arrow but must give priority to pedestrians or other traffic. Flashing yellow lights are a warning to proceed with caution and are often used at crossroads during periods when traffic is light (e.g. after midnight); you must give priority to traffic coming from your right.

For left turns off a main road with traffic lights, there's often a marked filter lane or circle to the **right**, taking you to a junction where you cross the main road at right angles (indicated by a stop sign or traffic lights).

◆ Always come to a complete stop when required at junctions and ensure that you stop behind the white line – junctions are a favourite spot for police patrols waiting for motorists to put a wheel a few centimetres over the line.

◆ Don't drive in bus, taxi or cycle lanes, as you can be fined for doing so, although it's permitted when necessary to avoid a stationary vehicle or an obstruction. Be sure to keep clear of tram lines (i.e. outside the area shown by lines on the road). Trams **always** have priority over other vehicles.

◆ The use of horns is forbidden in cities and areas indicated by a 'silent zone' (*zona di silenzio*) sign. However, it's tolerated by wedding parties, New Year's Eve revellers, football fans (e.g. when AC Milan have won the European Champions League), cars trapped by large vehicles or double/ treble parked cars, drivers attempting to wake drowsy drivers at traffic lights, etc. A car travelling at high speed with the horn permanently blaring and a white handkerchief or cloth waving from the window usually indicates that someone in the car is in need of urgent medical attention and drivers should clear the way as they would for an ambulance.

◆ Dipped (low beam) headlights must be used from half an hour after sunset to half an hour before sunrise. They're also required in tunnels and when visibility is less than 200m (656ft), e.g. in fog, snowstorms and heavy rain. It's illegal to drive with only side (parking) lights at any time. Front fog or spotlights must be fitted in pairs and rear fog lights singly, and should be used only when visibility is less than 50m (164ft). Full beam can be used only outside cities and towns, and when no vehicles are approaching. When a stationary vehicle isn't clearly visible, side lights must be switched on.

◆ Headlight flashing, although strictly for warning purposes only, has different meanings in Italy according to the situation. It may mean 'After you, my friend', 'Get out of the ****** way!', 'Idiot!', 'I want to overtake you (but you're driving in the left-hand lane)', 'Your headlights are on in daylight', 'Your headlights aren't on at night', 'Hi babe!', 'There's a police checkpoint ahead', or any combination of these – you must decide.

◆ White or yellow lines mark the separation of traffic lanes. A solid single line or two solid lines means no overtaking in either direction. A solid line to the right of the centre line, i.e. on your side of the road, means that overtaking is prohibited in your direction. You may overtake only when there's a single broken line in the middle of the road or double lines with a broken line on your side of the road. No overtaking may also be shown by the international road sign of two cars side by side (one red and one black). Always check your rear view and wing mirrors carefully before overtaking, as Italian motorists often appear from nowhere and zoom past at a 'zillion' miles an hour, particularly on country roads. If you drive a right-hand drive car, take extra care when overtaking. It's wise to have an 'overtaking mirror' fitted to a right-hand drive car.

◆ Mopeds (*ciclomotore* or *motorini*) and scooters (*scooter*) are extremely popular in Italy and are excellent for getting around cities but a menace if you're a motorist. You should be particularly wary of moped riders and cyclists, as it isn't always easy to see them, particularly when they're hidden by the blind spots of a car or are riding at night without lights. Many young moped riders seem to have a death wish and tragically hundreds lose their lives annually. They're constantly pulling out into traffic or turning without looking or signalling. **Follow the example set by Italian motorists, who when overtaking mopeds and cyclists, always give them a WIDE berth.** If you knock them off their bikes, you may have a difficult time convincing the police that it wasn't your fault; far better to avoid them (and the police).

♦ On roads where passing is difficult or isn't allowed, slower traffic is required to pull over when possible to allow faster traffic to pass. When two vehicles meet on a narrow mountain road, the ascending vehicle has priority and the other must give way or reverse as necessary.

♦ On-the-spot fines can be imposed for minor traffic offences such as slight speeding, not being in possession of the required documents (see above), not removing your ignition key when leaving a vehicle unattended, driving at night on side lights and parking infringements. If you wish to contest a fine, you must still deposit half the amount of a fine in cash.

♦ Anything hanging off the end of a vehicle (e.g. a bicycle) must be tagged with a reflective red-and-white-striped plate, 50cm (20in) square, which are available from motoring shops in Italy. You can be fined if you fail to observe this law.

♦ It's illegal to use a mobile phone when driving except with a hands-free system.

♦ The following rules apply to motorways (*autostrade*):

– Vehicles with a maximum speed of less than 60kph (35mph) are prohibited from using motorways, as are bicycles, mopeds and pedestrians.

– Overtaking on the right is prohibited. Slower vehicles must move to the right to allow faster traffic to overtake (unless travelling at the speed limit). The left-hand lane is only for overtaking and, as soon as you have completed your manoeuvre, you must return to the right-hand lane. Unfortunately, overtaking (or undertaking) on the right is common, so you should always ensure that nobody is overtaking you on the right before changing lanes.

– During traffic jams, motorists must leave the hard shoulder free for emergency vehicles.

♦ Take particular care when crossing the road, even when using a pedestrian crossing, as drivers aren't required to stop, only to slow down – being hit by a 'slow' truck or bus can still kill you! Cross quickly when and where there's plenty of space for drivers to see you, and reduce speed or stop as necessary.

> All motorists in Italy must be familiar with the Italian Highway Code, which is published as a guide for each category of licence. The information is available, in Italian, on the ACI website (🖥 www.aci.it/index.php?id=61).

ITALIAN ROADS

The Italian road network is divided into four categories: motorways (*autostrade*), national highways (*strade statali*), provincial roads (*strade provinciali*) and municipal roads (*strade comunali*).

Motorways

Italy has an excellent motorway (*autostrada*) network, covering around 6,400km (3,977mi). Most motorways are toll (*pedaggio*) roads, although there are some 1,000km (620mi) of free 'superways' (*superstrade*) around cities. Italy lays claim to having Europe's first motorway, which was built between Milan and Venice in the '30s. Today, the main north-south route is the *Autostrada del Sole* from Milan to Reggio di Calabria (via Bologna, Florence, Rome and Naples), designated the A1 from Milan to Naples and the A3 from Naples to Reggio di Calabria (the latter stretch being toll-free). Given Italy's mountainous terrain, the country's motorways include many spectacular bridges and tunnels, especially through the Alps in the north of the country.

Motorway tolls depend on the official horsepower rating (*cavalli fiscali*) of your car

(not necessarily its actual horsepower) or the wheelbase and number of axles and on the company operating the toll. For a standard car the charge is usually around 5 or 6 cents per km. On most motorways you collect a ticket when you join a motorway and pay when you leave it. On some stretches, however, there are fixed charges that are payable on joining. Tolls can be paid in euros and most major currencies, including pounds sterling, Swiss francs and US dollars. However, you usually receive a poor rate of exchange, so you're better off paying in euros. Credit cards are usually accepted, but don't take it for granted. When paying by credit card, look for a lane with a large sign showing a depiction of credit cards. Insert the toll ticket first (with the arrow pointing forward) followed by your credit card with the hologram outward. To obtain a receipt, push the red button after removing your credit card.

Some companies offer season tickets at reduced rates and you can also buy a Viacard (like a telephone smartcard) at some motorway tolls, bars, restaurants and certain banks (costing €25/50/70). This makes paying tolls easier and faster, as you can use reserved lanes. Alternatively you can obtain a Telepass that requires a sensor to be installed in your car, which records the distance you travel on toll roads when you pass through the Telepass gates. You're billed by direct debit from a bank account. Note that Viacards and Telepasses aren't available on all motorways.

Emergency phones are set on yellow posts every 2km (1.25mi), some of which have separate buttons for breakdowns (depicted by a spanner) and injuries (shown by a red cross). Simply press the appropriate button and wait for help to arrive. There are service stations at around 25km (15mi) intervals, where you can have minor repairs carried out.

If you plan to travel long distances on the motorway network, the Autostrade website (🖥 www.autostrade.it/en) will prove invaluable. It provides information in English about routes, tolls and service stations, traffic forecasts and interactive maps.

A map showing Italy's motorways and major roads is in **Appendix E**.

Other Roads

State roads (*strade statali*) (or national routes) are major roads indicated by blue signs and shown on maps with the prefix 'SS' followed by a number. They're often multi-lane, dual-carriageway roads and although slower than motorways, have no tolls. Many *strade statali* follow the routes planned by the ancient Romans, including the famous consular routes, which have illustrious names such as the Via Appia, Via Pontina and Via Flaminia. Provincial roads (*strade provinciali*), also with blue signs, are shown on maps as 'SP' and vary considerably in quality; they may be little more than rough tracks in some areas. Community roads (*strade comunali*), with white signs, are maintained by the local communes they serve. Unlike motorways and state roads, and most provincial and community roads aren't numbered.

Most cities have a ring road (*circonvallazione* or *tangenziale*), but access to the centre is often restricted to certain vehicles and there may also be a limited number of access routes and one-way systems in which you can get lost for weeks. Road navigation in cities can be chaotic and traffic moves at a crawl – if it moves at all; you're recommended to park on the outskirts and use public transport to reach and get around city centres. In some cities, e.g. Milan, car parks on the edge of the city are near major metro stations.

Driving in Italian cities, especially Naples, can be a nightmare and is best avoided. Traffic congestion and pollution in Italian cities are among the worst in Europe and consequently a pass is now required to enter many historic city centres (*centri storici*), and which is available only to residents and local businesspeople. Restricted areas are known as ZTL (*Zona traffico limitato*) zones, and if you enter one without a pass you're almost guaranteed to receive a fine. This is a particular problem for unwary tourists. Technically, Italian hotels are obliged to pass information on clients' cars to the police, so if you're registered at a hotel you shouldn't receive a fine, but the system is by no means foolproof and doesn't apply if you're staying in a bed and breakfast or a rented apartment.

Italian cities are handling the problem of pollution in different ways. Rome hasn't allowed vehicles without a catalytic converter to enter the city centre since 2000, and recently passed a 'blue band' (*fascia blu*) law banning most vehicles from the city centre, which has allowed local residents to breathe something resembling air once again. Meanwhile several cities, such as Bolzano, have introduced restrictions on high-emissions vehicles during winter months. Milan has introduced a year-round emissions-dependent congestion charge, called an Ecopass, which exempts vehicles compliant with the Euro3 and Euro4 emission standards or higher, plus vehicles using some alternative fuels, e.g. electric-powered cars. To access an Ecopass zone from Monday through Friday between 7.30am and 7.30pm, motorists driving non-exempt vehicles must pay between €2 and €10 or face a fine of around €70.

Italy has a number of toll tunnels, including Mont Blanc and Fréjus between Italy and France, both around 11km (7mi) in length, and the Gran San Bernardino linking Italy and Switzerland. It costs about €35 for an average car to make a one-way trip through the Mont Blanc tunnel; camper vans pay around €46.

☑ **SURVIVAL TIP**

Road conditions can be checked 24-hours per day by dialling 1518.

WINTER DRIVING

If you drive in winter in northern Italy, when snow, ice and fog are commonplace, take it easy! Fog is a common problem in northern Italy and is the cause of many multiple car accidents. In poor conditions, most Italian drivers slow down considerably and even the habitual tailgaters leave a larger gap than usual (at least a metre!). A light snowfall can be treacherous, particularly on an icy road. When road conditions are bad, you should allow two to three times longer than usual to reach your destination (if you're wise, you'll stay at home). Many mountain passes are closed in winter (check with the ACI).

You may need to use snow chains (*catene da neve*) in winter in mountain areas – or in any area where there's heavy snow. (When it last snowed heavily in Rome, back in 1985, shops sold out of snow chains and chaos reigned for around three days – but at least the Romans drove carefully for a while!) For the uninitiated, putting on snow chains can be an unpleasant task. Usually you lay the chains on the road (or snow or ice) and drive onto them. Then you kneel down and try to link the ends above the wheel. Your knees become cold and wet unless you have some sort of plastic sheet to kneel on, and feeling around for the bit of chain in ice and snow makes your fingers go numb, thus adding to the difficulty. Once you leave the area where snow chains are required, you can look forward to performing the process in reverse. Bear in mind that snow chains must be fitted on the wheels that are driven, depending on whether the vehicle is front- or rear-wheel drive (on a four-wheel drive vehicle you can choose front or rear).

If you live in an area of Italy where snow is common in winter, e.g. in the mountains or in the north, you need to purchase snow tyres, which have tiny metal studs embedded in the rubber. With these you can drive all winter and you don't even need to fit them yourself, as any tyre supplier (*gommista*) will do it for you. The regulations regarding the use of snow tyres vary with the province, so check with a local garage or ACI office.

ITALIAN DRIVERS

Driving in Italy is a matter of the survival of the fittest and it isn't a place for the faint-hearted.

Many newcomers to Italy, even those used to driving on the right, find Italian driving undisciplined and frightening. (Incredibly, Italians are often alarmed at the way some foreigners drive!) If you've ever seen a demolition derby, you'll have some idea of Italian driving, the main difference being that demo drivers are much more skilled and there are far fewer fatalities. The foreigner's first impression is that Italian drivers pay no attention to speed limits, have little or no concept of lane discipline, and stop at red lights or pedestrian crossings only when necessary to avoid a collision. In Italy a red light is generally viewed as a sign to take care rather than stop, and some (colour blind?) drivers simply drive through them (particularly in Naples, the motoring anarchists' spiritual home).

Not surprisingly, Italy has one of the highest road accident rates in the European Union, although the death rate (around 5,000 per year) is relatively low considering the number of accidents. Poor discipline, lack of enforcement, inadequate road laws and the Italians' frenetic lifestyle all combine to create havoc. In this chaos, the only thing that saves the day is Italian flexibility. Everyone tries to keep the traffic moving and accommodate other drivers and their intentions, however stupid. To show clearly what you want to do and then do it is the basic principle of city driving in Italy – even if it means driving the wrong way down a one-way street!

What makes driving in Italy even more of a lottery is that for many months of the year the roads are liberally sprinkled with foreigners whose driving habits vary from exemplary to suicidal and include many (such as the British) who don't even know which side of the road to drive on. The best way to introduce yourself to driving in major cities in Italy is to buy a second-hand car with a number of dents that show it has 'lived'; Italians will then give way more readily, as they respect veterans.

One quality most Italian drivers have is an inability to know when to slow down, and they're notorious for their impatience. The shortest unit of time in Italy is said to be the period between traffic lights changing to green and the driver behind you honking his horn.

When not overtaking you, Italian drivers may sit a few centimetres from your rear bumper while trying to push you along, irrespective of traffic density, road and weather conditions, or the prevailing speed limit. Italians are among Europe's worst tailgaters and there's no solution, short of moving out of their way or stopping, which is often impossible.

Always try to leave a large gap between your vehicle and the one in front. This isn't just to give you more time to stop should the vehicles in front decide to brake suddenly, but also to give the inevitable tailgater behind you more time to stop as well. The closer the car is behind you, the further you should be from the vehicle in front. On motorways and main roads, you must (by law) keep a safe distance from the vehicle in front and can be fined for not doing so. You should avoid the outside lane on motorways, unless you're prepared to drive at least 150kph (93mph).

Nevertheless, although many Italian drivers are reckless (or worse), in general they aren't as bad as their reputation may suggest, and many are careful and patient.

MOTORCYCLES

To ride a motorcycle or moped (*motorino*) with an engine size of up to 50cc, you must be at least 14 years old, pass an exam (called *il patentino*) and carry the Certificate of Aptitude (*Certificado di Idoneità*) but no licence is required. You must be a resident to take the exam. A bicycle must be registered before it's permitted on public roads. The registration procedure is different from that for cars in that moped registrations are personal, so when selling a moped you must keep the registration plate. The rider must also carry proof of his age and the bicycle must be insured against third party claims.

Since January 2000, all riders of mopeds have had to wear a helmet (*casco*), and moped riders are prohibited from carrying passengers, although these are among many Italian laws which are flouted, and it's common to see youths riding with a friend on board and no helmets, to which the police often turn a blind eye. Many teenage moped riders are killed each year in Italy, where moped accidents are the number one cause of death for people under 24.

To ride a motorcycle over 50cc, you must have a motorcycle licence (Class A), for which the minimum age is 16. Up to the age of 18, you're limited to motorcycles with an engine capacity of under 125cc, after which there's no restriction. As in other European countries, a standard car driving licence (Class B) no longer qualifies you to drive motorcycles as well.

If you're considering buying a motorcycle, bear in mind that bikes without a catalytic converter may be restricted from some city centres. Like a car, a motorcycle must pass a technical inspection every two years. Motorcyclists and passengers must wear helmets and are required to use dipped (low beam) headlights at all times. You must also have at least third party insurance when driving a motorcycle, and carry proof with you.

PARKING

Parking in Italy can be a challenge, particularly in large cities, where it's often so difficult to find a parking space that near anarchy rules (in cities, a car is a device used to create parking spaces). Cars are frequently parked in 'no parking' areas, half or completely on the pavement and even alongside other parked cars (double-parked). The only place where a 'no parking' sign is usually respected is in front of busy exits and entrances, although even here someone may leave a car briefly while popping into a shop or withdrawing money from an ATM. Parking on pedestrian crossings or on corners, although prohibited, is common in most Italian cities, although not in smaller towns. In most European countries you

must park at least 5m (16ft) from a pedestrian crossing, but if such a regulation ever existed in Italy it has long since been forgotten and isn't enforced.

In many cities, entry to the city centre is restricted and parking (even for residents) can be prohibitively expensive. Parking in Naples and some other cities in southern Italy isn't recommended if you ever hope to see your car again, and it's better to park some distance from the city and use public transport. (Driving in Naples is, in any case, an experience most motorists will want to live without!)

Some cities have introduced green zones (*zona verde*), where parking is prohibited between 8 and 9.30am and from 2.30 to 4pm on weekdays. Others impose an all-day ban: the sign '*zona tutelata*' indicates that parking is prohibited from 7.30am until 6.30pm on weekdays. You must usually park on the right-hand side of the road in a two-way street, but parking may be limited to odd and even-numbered days on one side of a street, or it may be restricted to local residents. In some cities, parking restrictions are indicated by coloured kerb stones, e.g. blue means parking is permitted (but you must pay), while yellow may mean parking is permitted for residents only or is prohibited. There are strict penalties for illegal parking.

In many cities there are blue zones (*zona a disco*) where you must display a parking disk behind your windscreen between 9am and 2.30pm and from 4 to 8pm from Mondays to Saturdays (except public holidays). Parking

disks resemble a cardboard clock and are available free or for a nominal cost from petrol stations, motor accessory shops, tourist offices and motoring organisations. You must turn the dial to your time of arrival and are permitted to stay for up to an hour free of charge.

All cities have paid parking zones, usually marked with blue lines. To park in one you must find a ticket machine, buy a ticket (e.g. €1.50 per hour) and display it behind the dashboard. You must return and move your car before the period you've paid for has expired, and aren't permitted to buy another ticket without moving your car. Note that ticket machines accept only coins, so you should carry a supply. During the summer, some resorts provide parking areas close to the beach, usually marked with blue lines, where a youth on a moped drives around and collects the fixed parking fee. This varies but is usually a maximum of around €5 per day.

In cities and towns there are also multi-storey car parks and underground garages, although parking can be expensive. Some shopping arcades have free parking spaces for customers, as do certain shops, hotels and restaurants. There are reserved parking spaces for disabled motorists in major towns and cities, although they aren't common or always respected by other drivers. Parking permits for the disabled are issued by the local office for invalid permits (Ufficio Permessi Invalidi).

DRINKING & DRIVING

Although it may sometimes appear as if there are no laws against drinking and driving in Italy, this is definitely not the case! In recent years there has been a marked increase in serious accidents with drunken drivers late at night. These are often caused by youths who race each other after a night at a disco. As a result, the police have become more serious in their attitude towards drinking and driving. You're considered unfit to drive if you have over 50mg of alcohol per 100ml of blood, with higher alcohol levels attracting steeper penalties. The blood-alcohol limit for new drivers with less than three years' experience is zero.

If you're found to be over the limit, you'll be heavily fined (you may even face a jail sentence of up to five years) and your driving licence will be suspended for a period. Driving under the influence of drugs is also taken seriously and, if you're found driving with traces of marijuana, hashish or cocaine in your system, you'll lose your licence for at least a year. Penalty points are also allocated to your licence, and you're fined and required to undergo a psychological examination before you receive your licence back.

The police can stop and breathalyse drivers at random and, if you're involved in an accident and they suspect that you're under the influence of alcohol or drugs, they're authorised to carry out tests.

Having an accident while under the influence of drink or drugs can also be expensive. Your insurance company isn't obliged to pay for damage to your car or any other vehicle that you damage, and you can be held personally liable for all medical expenses and property damage resulting from the accident.

If you want to enjoy a few drinks, it's wise to have a driver who remains sober – or to take a taxi.

Fines & Penalty Points

Each new Italian licence is assigned 20 points, and points are deducted for motoring offences with the number depending on the severity of the offence. The maximum number of points that can be lost at any one time is 15; however, double points are deducted for offences by novice drivers, i.e. those with less than three years' driving experience. Lose all 20 points and you must re-take a driving test. If you lose 20 points within three years of passing your test, for the first or a subsequent time, you can expect to be banned from driving for up to two years. Lost points can be regained by taking special courses authorised by the Ministry of Infrastructure and Transport and held at driving schools. A clean licence is rewarded every two years with the addition of two bonus points, to a maximum accumulation of 30 points. You can check the points-status of your licence by calling ☎ 848782782. A full list of offences and penalty points is given on the State Police website (💻 http://poliziadistato.it/articolo/544-La_tabella_delle_penalita).

Drivers of foreign-registered cars and hire cars, and those driving on their home country's licence, may avoid penalty points but cannot avoid fines, which may be sent to your home address up to a year after you commit the offence.

ACCIDENTS

Knowing the correct procedure in case of an accident (*incidente*) is important in Italy, where motorists who see an accident are required by law to stop and render assistance:

1. Stop and secure the scene of the accident.
2. Attend to the injured.
3. Call for help.

If your car is damaged or you're involved in an accident, stop immediately and pull over to the side of the road if possible. Place your red warning triangle (*triangolo*) at the edge of the road at least 50m (164ft) behind your car if on a secondary road, 100m (328ft) on a major road and 200m (656ft) on a motorway. If necessary, e.g. when the road is partly or totally blocked, switch on your car's hazard warning lights and dipped (low beam) headlights, and direct traffic around the hazard.

If anyone is injured, call immediately for emergency help. The general number for the emergency services is 113, but for a quicker response dial 112 for the police (*carabinieri*) or 118 for an ambulance. If someone is trapped, or oil or chemicals have been spilt, dial 115 for the fire brigade.

If someone has been injured more than superficially, the police **must** be notified. Don't move an injured person unless absolutely necessary and don't leave him alone except to call for help. Cover him with a blanket or coat to keep warm.

If there are no injuries, and damage to vehicles or property is minor, it isn't essential to summon the police to an accident

scene. (If you're involved in an accident with an Italian – a likely occurrence in Italy – you should wait ten minutes for him to calm down and stop berating you for denting his pride and joy, even if he was to blame.) However, it's usually recommended to call them and obtain an official report unless all parties have signed an accident declaration form (*constatazione amichevole di incidente/CID*) for your respective insurance companies. If this cannot be done (e.g. because you don't agree on what happened), you should play safe and call the police.

When the police arrive, under no circumstances should you admit guilt, even if you know you were in the wrong. Stick to telling what happened and let the police and insurance companies decide who was at fault. If you admit responsibility, either orally or in writing, it can absolve your insurance company from responsibility for paying a claim under your policy. In any case, an Italian driver never admits that he is to blame – at least not straight away; even if he has driven into the back of your car while you're waiting in a queue, it's obviously your fault – you shouldn't have been there!

If the other driver has obviously been drinking or appears incapable of driving, call the police immediately! Don't sign any police statements unless you understand and agree with every word. The *carabinieri*'s report is usually available within a few days. They may fine one or all parties in varying proportions according to their deemed culpability. The insurance company then pays

compensation according to the proportion of blame assigned to their client.

If either you or the other driver(s) involved decide to call the police, avoid moving the vehicles unless they present a traffic hazard. If they must be moved, record their positions before moving them by taking photographs, making drawings or marking their positions on the road. The accident form from your insurance company requires drawings of the positions of all vehicles involved, therefore it's recommended to have the situation clear on paper rather than just in your memory (which can go blank after an accident).

Check whether there are any witnesses to the accident and try to obtain their names and addresses, making a particular note of those who support your version of events. Note the registration numbers of all vehicles involved and their drivers' names, registration numbers, addresses and insurers. In return, you're expected to give the same information to any other drivers involved.

Use your insurance company form to report an accident involving your car, even if the other party is clearly at fault and agrees to pay the damages. If you don't report it and the other party later withdraws his admission or offer to pay damages, your insurance company can refuse your claim if you haven't previously filed a report with them. Don't forget to sign it and to obtain a new accident report form.

Minor scratches and dents are a way of life in Italy, where they aren't considered as 'accidents' but normal wear and tear. Inevitably you'll accumulate them simply by parking your car in a street or a car park. Most Italians don't make a fuss over these and have them repaired when they've accumulated a reasonable number of them or need a major repair – or even ignore them altogether and wear them proudly as the scars of their daily battle on Italy's streets.

If you're the victim of a hit-and-run accident, report it to the local police immediately. If possible, summon them to the accident scene before moving your car. They will inspect your vehicle and take photographs and paint samples, which will assist with an insurance claim as well as help to find the culprit.

☑ **SURVIVAL TIP**

If you're involved in an accident involving an injured animal, you're obliged to stop and immediately notify the authorities; if you fail to stop you can receive a large fine.

CAR CRIME

Most European countries have a problem with car crime, i.e. thefts of and from cars, and Italy is no exception. If you drive anything other than a worthless heap, you should have third party, fire & theft insurance (*assicurazione contro terzi furto e incendio*), which includes your car stereo and belongings. New vehicles should be fitted with an alarm, an engine immobiliser of the rolling code variety (the best system) or another anti-theft device, plus a visible deterrent, such as a steering or gear stick lock. It's particularly important to protect your car if you own a model that's desirable to professional car thieves, e.g. most new sports and executive models, which are often stolen by crooks to order.

Few cars are fitted with deadlocks and most can be broken into in seconds by a competent thief; even the best security system won't usually prevent someone from breaking into your car and may not stop your car from being stolen, but it at least makes it more difficult and may persuade a thief to look for an easier target.

Windows are often broken to steal a car's contents and it happens so often that they can be replaced while you wait in major cities. When leaving your car unattended, store any valuables in the boot (trunk) or under a seat, or preferably take them with you; a thief may be tempted to force open the boot with a crowbar. It isn't recommended to leave your original car papers in your car (which may help a thief to dispose of it).

Vehicles should also be garaged whenever possible. When parking at night, it's wise to use a secure car park or garage, or at least park in a well-lit area. If possible, you should avoid parking in long-term car parks (*parcheggi a lungo termine*), as they're favourite hunting grounds for car thieves, as are motorway service stations; when stopping in a service station, you should park your car where you can keep an eye on it.

Some criminals specialise in robbing motorists at motorway toll booths or traffic lights. When driving in cities and large towns, it's wise to keep your doors locked and your windows partly or fully closed, and to store valuables and bags on the floor (not on seats).

Thieves in Italy operate various scams, including pretending that you have a flat tyre (they may even puncture your tyre in slow moving or stationary traffic) or that fuel is leaking from beneath your car. While one is pretending to help fix your car, another is stealing your belongings (women are popular targets). View any strangers offering to help you with suspicion. There has also been an increasing incidence of highway piracy, where gangs deliberately bump or ram cars to force drivers to stop (usually late at night when there's little traffic). Thieves may even pose as policemen and try to get you to stop by flashing a 'badge' or setting up a bogus road block. In the worst cases, thieves take not just the car and its contents but even the clothes their victims are wearing. Travelling at night in some areas (particularly in the far south of Italy) is hazardous due to armed highwaymen and should be avoided if possible. **Be on your guard!**

FUEL

Since January 2002, leaded petrol has been unavailable in Italy. Unleaded petrol (*benzina senza piombo*) is available in 95 octane (*Euro Super*) and 98 octane (*super senza*). The price of petrol can vary from week to week according to the value of the US dollar and the world market price of crude oil (not to mention taxation). In February 2010, *EuroSuper* cost around €1.35 per litre. Prices on motorways are a few cents higher per litre and there's also a surcharge of a couple of cents per litre for night service (unless a pump is automatic and accepts cash or credit cards). Diesel (*gasolio*) is widely available and costs around €1.20 per litre. LPG (known in Italy as *GPL* or *gas liquido*) is widely available in major cities in northern and central Italy – in petrol stations displaying a

GPL or *Autogas* sign – and costs about €0.65 per litre.

Petrol station opening hours in towns are usually from 7 or 8am until between noon and 1pm, when they close for lunch, and from around 3 or 3.30 until 7 or 7.30pm. On Sundays, most petrol stations are closed, but there's usually one in each area open on Sunday mornings (which is then usually closed on Mondays). When a petrol station is closed, there's usually a sign showing its opening hours and directing you to the next station. There are also 24-hour self-service filling stations in towns and on main roads, including all motorways.

Credit cards are increasingly accepted by petrol stations, although it's wise to carry sufficient cash to fill your tank, particularly in rural areas and at weekends. Some petrol stations have automatic pumps that accept euro banknotes when the station is closed.

 Caution

It's illegal to carry a can of petrol in a car in Italy.

SERVICING & REPAIRS

Italian garages (service stations) are often highly specialised and, although the range has diminished somewhat in recent years, you're likely to find the following specialists:

♦ *autofficina*: handles most general jobs except bodywork and tyre changes;

♦ *carrozziere*: repairs dents and scratches (a good business to be in, in Italy!);

♦ *gommista*: sells and repairs tyres, and also does wheel-balancing;

♦ *elettrauto*: fixes all electrical problems and installs car sound systems and alarms.

Two specialists that are slowly disappearing are the *carburatorista*, who tunes engines, and the *radiatorista*, who repairs and makes radiators.

The quality of work carried out by garages is usually good and they're generally well equipped to deal with any kind of problem.

A garage will also check your car before the bi-annual safety inspection and, if required, take it for its inspection. Once a problem has been identified, always ask for an estimate, even an oral one (*preventivo*), which will save embarrassment and arguments later.

Garages are usually open from 8.30am to 1pm and from 3.30 to 8pm on weekdays, but are usually closed on Saturdays and always on Sundays and public holidays. If your car breaks down at a weekend, you can call 116 to get the ACI to

tow you to a garage, where you can leave your car until it can be repaired. Some Italian insurance companies provide you with a card containing the phone number of a free towing service. If you use ACI, the service is free up to 50km (30mi) for members, while non-members may be charged a fee (members of the UK's Automobile Association can make use of some of the ACI's services for free). There may also be a storage charge for keeping the car in a garage's storage enclosure, unless it's repaired as soon as they open. Some manufacturers provide an emergency number in case of breakdown – check with a dealer whether this service applies to your car.

CAR HIRE

To hire (rent) a car in Italy you must usually be at least 21, although the minimum age can be up to 25 or even as high as 30 for some vehicles. Drivers must have held a full licence for a minimum of a year and most companies have an upper age limit of 60 or 65. Each hire (rental) is for specifically named drivers only and nobody else is permitted to drive the car – the licences of the drivers concerned must be shown to the hire company. If payment isn't with a credit card, a cash deposit is usually required (the whole hire period may have to be paid in advance).

Car hire in Italy is expensive compared with most other European countries, particularly for short periods, and includes VAT at 20 per cent. There's also a 14 per cent government tax if you pick up a car from a major airport. If you're a visitor, it's wiser and generally cheaper

to reserve a hire car before your arrival (you may be able to save money booking online). Fly-drive deals are available through most airlines and travel agents, and frequent flyer programmes also offer discounted car hire from some agencies. Bookings can also be made at some main railway stations in Italy. You may find it cheaper to hire a car in the US (irrespective of whether you live there) through the office of a multinational rental company such as Avis or Hertz.

Major car hire (*autonoleggio*) companies such as Avis, Europcar, Hertz and Maggiore have offices in most large towns and at major airports. Hertz, which has offices in many Italian cities, charges around €60 (including optional insurances and taxes) for a one-day hire of its cheapest models, e.g. a Fiat Panda, with unlimited mileage. Rates reduce considerably over long periods, e.g. a week or a month. The weekly rate for a Ford Fiesta is around €265, including unlimited mileage, although extras such as a satellite navigation system can push the bill up by another €80. Lower rates are available for weekends, usually from noon on Fridays until 9am on Mondays, and there are also special offers outside periods of peak demand. Local rental companies are often cheaper than the multi-nationals, although cars must be returned to the pick-up point. Older cars can be rented from many garages at lower rates than those charged by the multi-national companies, although they aren't always in good condition and can even be unsafe.

Rates usually include collision damage waiver (CDW), although you may need to pay extra for personal accident insurance (PAI) and others insurance (e.g. against theft). When paying with a credit or charge card issued in the US, your card company may cover damage to a vehicle. Always ensure that you know what's included in (and excluded from) the price and what your liabilities are.

☑ **SURVIVAL TIP**

If required, check in advance that you're permitted to take a car out of Italy, as it may be prohibited or you may be allowed to visit certain countries only.

Hire cars can be ordered with a luggage rack, and child seats can be fitted for an extra charge. You can usually request snow chains and ski racks if you're heading for a winter sports destination. You can also hire a four-wheel-drive vehicle, estate car (station wagon), minibus, luxury saloon, armoured limousine or convertible, possibly with a choice of manual or automatic gearbox (although automatics are scarce, so you may need to book well in advance). There are also moped and motorcycle hire companies in the major cities. Minibuses accessible to wheelchairs can be hired, e.g. from Hertz, and vans and pick-ups are available from some major hire companies by the hour, half-day or day, and from smaller local companies (which, once again, are cheaper).

Finally, if you want to hire a car but don't want to drive it yourself, some companies offer a chauffeur service and a 'welcome' service for visitors arriving at an airport or railway station. Private sightseeing tours are also available in chauffeured cars, which are a pleasant (although expensive) way to take in a city's highlights.

MOTORING ORGANISATIONS

The main motoring organisations in Italy are the Automobile Club d'Italia (ACI), Via Marsala, 8, 00185 Rome (☎ 06-49981, 🖥 www.aci. it) and the smaller Touring Club Italiano (TCI), Corso Italia, 10, 20122 Milan (☎ 02-85261, 🖥 www.touringclub.it). There are a number of local clubs, such as Automobile Club di Roma

(ACR), which are affiliated to the ACO or TCI. Members benefit from:

♦ emergency assistance;

♦ legal advice for motoring-related problems;

♦ car and travel insurance;

♦ translation of foreign licences;

♦ advice on local servicing facilities and spares suppliers;

♦ a wide range of driving and travel accessories.

Emergency assistance (☎ 116 or 800 11 68 00 from a mobile phone) includes towing to a garage, hotel and travel expenses, and a courtesy car for a period. The ACI offers various levels of cover, costing from €35 a year for the most basic package.

Isle of Capri

Vitruvian man, Leonardo da Vinci

12.
HEALTH

Italy's spending on health is around 8.7 per cent of GDP, just below the average of 8.9 per cent in the Organisation for Economic Co-operation & Development (OECD) countries. The quality of healthcare and of healthcare facilities varies from poor to excellent according to the region you live in and whether you use private facilities. Italian doctors and other medical staff are dedicated and well trained, the best Italian doctors being among the finest in the world (many pioneering operations are performed in Italy).

The best private hospitals in Italy are also the equal of those in any country. However, state hospitals, particularly in the south of the country, are notoriously bad, a situation made worse by Mafia corruption and doctors fleeing to find work in better equipped (and run) hospitals in the north. Throughout Italy, nursing care and post-hospital assistance are also well below the standards that most northern Europeans and Americans take for granted.

Italy has a national health service, which provides free or low-cost healthcare to all residents who contribute to social security and their families, plus university students and retirees, including those from other EU countries. It also provides emergency care to all visitors, irrespective of nationality. In addition to those provided by the state health service, Italy has many private doctors, specialists and clinics. Many Italians use these in addition to the national health service, e.g. to avoid long delays for operations, to obtain better hospital accommodation or simply to obtain treatment from a preferred specialist. Many Italians and most foreigners have private health insurance, which ensures that you receive the medical treatment you need, when you need it. Non-EU citizens taking up residence in Italy should note that immigration officials may ask you for proof of health cover before issuing a permit to stay (see page 60).

Despite the shortcomings of the health service, Italians are generally healthy and have one of the highest life expectancies in Europe – around 83 for women and 77 for men – which is attributed in large part to their Mediterranean diet of fresh fruit, vegetables, olive oil and red wine (in moderation). Infant mortality is around average for Europe, at just under six deaths per 1,000 live births. The generally mild Italian climate (at least in central and southern Italy) is therapeutic, particularly for sufferers from rheumatism and arthritis, and those who are susceptible to bronchitis, colds and pneumonia. The slower pace of life – outside the major cities, at least – is also beneficial to those susceptible to stress. However, the country has a high incidence of diseases of the circulatory system, as well as of cancer (often smoking-related) and liver-related illnesses (due to excess alcohol consumption). Common health problems among expatriates include sunburn and sunstroke, stomach and bowel problems (due to a change of diet and, more often, water), and alcoholism. Italians' love of the car also gives rise to excessive air pollution in Italy's major cities, which is blamed for the increasing number of asthma and hay fever sufferers.

Consumption of alcohol per head is high (many Italian adults drink alcohol with every meal, although overall consumption is decreasing) and alcohol is responsible for a number of alcohol-related illnesses, e.g. cirrhosis of the liver and some forms of cancer. There's no official age for the legal consumption of alcohol (children tend to drink moderate amounts of wine from a young age), although children under the age of 16 aren't permitted to buy alcohol. In common with other European countries, Italy has an increasing illegal drugs problem, particularly among young people (ecstasy and amphetamines have flourished in recent years). Drugs are comparatively cheap in Italy, but the law is strict on prohibition and the penalty for drug dealers can be life imprisonment.

Otherwise, there are no special health risks in Italy and no vaccinations are required before visiting. Pollution levels in the sea are tested regularly (particularly during the tourist season) and swimming is generally safe unless there's a sign to the contrary, e.g. *divieto di balneazione* (bathing prohibited). On trains and other places where water isn't fit for drinking, you often see the sign *acqua non potabile*. You can safely drink most tap water in Italy, although many people prefer bottled water, and the wine tastes much better.

If you're planning to take up residence in Italy, even for part of the year, it's wise to have a health check before your arrival, particularly if you have a record of poor health or are elderly. If applicable, you should bring a spare pair of spectacles and contact lenses, and spare dentures and a hearing aid with you.

☑ SURVIVAL TIP

Whether you opt for state or private healthcare, it's important to have some form of health insurance, without which healthcare in Italy can be prohibitively expensive (see page 203).

EMERGENCIES

The action to take in a medical emergency depends on the degree of urgency, as follows:

◆ In a life-threatening emergency, such as a heart attack or serious accident, call the free public ambulance number 118. State clearly where you're calling from and the nature of the emergency, and give your name and the telephone number from where you're calling. Don't hang up until the operator asks you to. The appropriate emergency service is sent to you. Provided you call in response to a genuine emergency, you won't be charged for the use of the emergency services.

◆ If you need an ambulance (*ambulanza*), call the local ambulance service (*pronto soccorso ambulanza*). Most ambulances are equipped with cardiac equipment.

◆ If you're able, go to a hospital emergency or casualty department (*pronto soccorso*). All foreigners in Italy have the right to be treated in an emergency, irrespective of whether they have insurance.

◆ If you need medical treatment outside surgery hours and cannot get to your nearest casualty department, call the local duty doctor service (*guardia medica*), which should be listed in the phone book. This service is usually available from 8pm to 8am on weekdays and from 2pm on Saturdays (and the day before a public holiday) until 8am on the Monday (or the day after a public holiday).

◆ If you need to see a doctor but are unable to visit a surgery, a doctor will visit you at home provided you call him during surgery hours. If he is away, his office will give you the name and number of a substitute doctor.

Keep a record of the telephone numbers of your doctor, local hospital and clinic, ambulance service, dentist and other emergency services (e.g. fire and police) next to your telephone. Emergency numbers are also displayed prominently at the front of all telephone directories. If you're unsure whom to call, dial the free national emergency number 113, or 112, which is the universal, multilingual emergency number across the European Union (EU), and you'll be put in touch with the relevant service.

In Italy it's an offence to offer medical assistance in an emergency if you aren't a doctor or qualified in first aid, although it's also an offence **not** to assist someone in an emergency, e.g. by calling the appropriate emergency service or offering first aid when qualified to do so.

NATIONAL HEALTH SERVICE

Italy's national health service (Servizio Sanitaria Nazionale/SSN) was established in 1978 and replaced the previous system of state insurance founded after the Second World War. The aim of the SSN was to create an efficient and uniform health system covering the entire population, irrespective of income or contributions, employment or level of health. The SSN provides free or low-cost healthcare to all residents and their families, plus visitors from EU countries, and emergency care to visitors from non-EU countries.

Since 1998, the SSN has been funded directly by central government via the *IRAP* (*Imposta Regionale Sulle Attività Produttive*) tax, which is paid by employers on behalf of employees; the self-employed pay for themselves through their taxes. You don't pay direct contributions and need only be a resident in Italy or a citizen of the EU to receive the same health benefits as an Italian. If you qualify for healthcare under the SSN, your dependants receive the same benefits and are listed on your card. Dependants can include your spouse, children under 16 (or 26 if they're students or unable to work through illness or invalidity), and ascendants, descendants and relatives by marriage living in the same household.

If you aren't entitled to public health benefits through payment of Italian taxes or by receiving a state pension from another EU country, you must usually have private health insurance and must present proof of this when applying for a residence permit. If you're a retired EU national planning to live permanently in Italy, you need form E121. EU citizens who retire before qualifying for a state pension can receive free health cover for two years by obtaining form E106 from their country's social security department. If the temporary cover expires before you reach retirement age, you need to make voluntary social security contributions or take out private health insurance (see page 203).

The SSN is largely under the control of regional governments and is administered by local health authorities (Azienda di Sanità Locale/ASL – often referred to by their former name Unità Sanitaria Locale/USL). Those who are registered with the SSN are entitled to free or subsidised medicines (see page 186), a 75 per cent reduction on the cost of outpatient and after-care treatment, and some subsidised dental treatment (see page 190). All inpatient treatment, i.e. treatment requiring hospitalisation, is free under the national health service.

Many medical expenses can be totally or partially deducted for tax purposes, including the cost of spectacles, hearing aids and visits to medical specialists, therefore you should retain all medical receipts.

The Italian health service places the emphasis on cure rather than prevention and treats sickness rather than promoting good health. There's little preventative medicine in Italy, such as regular health checks. The public health service has limited resources for outpatient treatment, nursing and post-operative care, geriatric assistance, or terminal illnesses and psychiatric treatment. Inadequate treatment due to staff shortages and long waiting lists as a result of a lack of hospital facilities are frequent complaints made against Italy's health service. Many problems are related to crippling bureaucracy, mismanagement, general disorganisation and spiralling costs. Despite the huge advances in medicine and the progress in

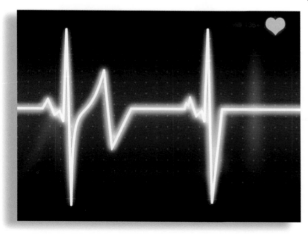

healthcare in Italy in the last few decades, the public health service is facing enormous problems. Health service reform is a matter of intense public debate in Italy and it's likely that there will be major changes in the coming years.

Registration

You must register for membership of the SSN at your nearest local health authority (Azienda Sanità Locale/ASL), whose address you'll find under ASL or USL (pronounced 'ahsle' and 'oosle') in your local telephone directory. You need to take the following documents with you, as applicable:

♦ your permit to stay or residence permit (see pages 60 and 63);

♦ your passport or other official identity document, such as an Italian driving licence;

♦ a family status certificate (certificato di stato di famiglia) if you want to claim benefits for your spouse or children (see **Applications** on page 62);

♦ your fiscal code card (see page 213);

♦ a letter from your employer stating your employment start date (dichiarazione de datore di lavoro) and a statement from the INPS confirming that you're regularly employed, or a registration card (attestato di iscrizione) from the unemployment office (Ufficio di Collocamento) or proof of admission from an approved educational establishment.

Once you've completed the registration formalities, you're asked to choose a family doctor (see below) with a social security agreement (medico convenzionato or con la mutua) and, if you have children under six, a paediatrician (pediatra). You and each member of your family are issued with a national health number and receive a health card (tessera sanitaria) in which all medical occurrences, e.g. illnesses, general medical care and surgery, are recorded. Health cards are valid for a year and must be renewed (stamped) annually; if you lose your card or change your address, you must apply for a replacement.

There are certain health requirements for employees and schoolchildren in Italy. Employees who work in the food industry (bars, restaurants, food shops, factories producing food products, etc.) must obtain a health record book (libretto sanitario) from the public hygiene office at the town hall and undergo an annual medical examination. Schoolchildren at lower and upper secondary school are required to produce a medical certificate (certificato di sana e robusta costituzione fisica) from their school before participating in any sports. Participation in a competitive sport (sport agonistico) outside school also requires a medical examination, which must be conducted by a specialist in sports medicine, usually at a local sports centre or your local health authority. Medical examinations for participation in sports are free under the national health scheme.

DOCTORS

Italy has one of the highest numbers of doctors (medici) per head of any country in the world (one for every 160 or 180 inhabitants, depending on which survey you believe), and they're generally well trained and professional. Not surprisingly, however, it's difficult to find English-speaking doctors in some areas of Italy, although most cities and resorts have a medical service for tourists

(*guardia medica turistica*) with English-speaking staff. Embassies and consulates in Italy keep lists of doctors and specialists in their area who speak English and other languages, and your employer, colleagues or neighbours may also be able to recommend someone. If you live in Milan, the International Health Center (☎ 02-7634 0720, 🖳 www.ihc.it) has a number of English-speaking medical specialists.

General practitioners or family doctors (*medici generici*) are listed in *Yellow Pages* under *Medici Generici,* and specialists under *Specialisti*, followed by their speciality e.g. *Ostetricia e Ginecologia* (obstetricians and gynaecologists). Note that the word *dottore* is a courtesy title used to address university graduates.

If you wish to have free consultations with a doctor, you must register with the Servizio Sanitario Nazionale (see **Registration** above). When registering, you're required to choose a family doctor with a social security agreement (*medico convenzionato*) and, if you have children aged under six, a paediatrician (*pediatra*) also. Local health authorities provide you with a list of doctors with whom you can register and you can choose any doctor who's willing to accept you (there's no requirement to register with a doctor within a certain distance of your home). Each member of your family is issued with a national health number and a health card (*tessera sanitaria*), which you must take with you when visiting a doctor or other health practitioner.

As well as single private practices there are group surgeries, known as *poliambulatori*. Group practices can be either state, operating within an Azienda Sanità Locale (ASL) building, or private, and they offer a range of specialities usually unavailable at doctors' surgeries. These may include allergology, cardiology, dentistry, dermatology, gynaecology, ophthalmology, orthopaedic treatment, physiotherapy, psychotherapy, radiology, sports medicine, surgery and urology.

You can make an appointment to see a private doctor, specialist or consultant at any time, provided you don't mind paying for their services. This means that you have total freedom of choice and can obtain a second opinion, should you so wish. In Italy, many family doctors who work for the national health service also work privately as specialists, and it's quite common for family doctors to suggest that you see them privately for specialist treatment; in this case, you'll usually visit them at their private surgery (*studio medico*), which may be separate from their state practice. Unless you know exactly what the problem is, however, it's wise to see your family doctor first. To see a private doctor or specialist, you may need to pay an initial registration fee (around €15) plus a fee for each visit, which may be anything from €50 to €200. Note that you're usually expected to settle the bill in cash immediately after treatment, even if you have health insurance. (It's important to keep all medical receipts, as some can be offset against your income tax bill.)

For a list of group surgeries and hospitals in your area, contact your local health authority.

Doctors' surgery hours vary: usually surgeries are open Mondays to Fridays only, from 8 to 10am and from 3 to 5pm or from 8am to 1pm. Appointments aren't usually required and most surgeries operate on a first-come, first-served basis, therefore it's recommended to arrive early to avoid a long wait. Your family doctor will diagnose your problem and may write out a prescription (*ricetta*) for you to take to a chemist. He will arrange for you to have any necessary laboratory tests or X-rays at an authorised medical centre. If he thinks that you need to see a specialist, he'll refer you to one who's registered with social security. He then writes a referral (*impegnativa*), which you must take with you if you wish to claim the cost from social security. If you want a doctor to visit you at home, you must telephone during surgery hours. House calls made by family doctors are free during normal working hours.

Your family doctor may suggest a specialist, but you can also choose your own. Specialists registered with the SSN have their consulting rooms (*ambulatorio*) in state hospitals, local health authority buildings or other centres with an agreement with the SSN. Some private specialists, known as *privati accreditati*, also treat social security patients at their private surgeries. If you're registered with social security, you must pay the subsidised charge *(ticket sanitario)* to a cashier *(cassa)*, so don't forget to take enough cash with you; you're then given a receipt, which you must hand to the specialist.

Certain categories of people pay nothing for specialist treatment, including families with an income under €11,362 (the threshold increases €516 with every child), children under the age of six provided their family's annual income is less than €36,000, unemployed people and those aged over 65, and anyone who suffers from a disability or a long-term, chronic illness such as rheumatoid arthritis, diabetes or epilepsy. Everyone else pays the *ticket sanitario* price which is up to €36.15. This covers the entire referral and your doctor can request a maximum of six treatments for each referral so you pay the same ticket price even if X-rays and blood tests are included. If you have X-rays or laboratory tests done, it's your responsibility to collect the results and take them to your family doctor or specialist, so you must find out when they'll be ready.

If you need the services of a medical auxiliary, e.g. a nurse, physiotherapist or chiropodist, you also need a referral from your family doctor in order to pay the reduced amount. If you don't, you must pay the full cost. Depending on where you live, home visits by nurses (for example, to administer injections) may not be covered by social security and you may need to pay the full cost.

If you're away from home and need the services of a doctor, provided you visit a doctor who's registered with the health service, you won't need to pay for his services. He will write a request *(richiesta)* on headed notepaper, which you can take to your own doctor and exchange for a referral if medical treatment is required.

MEDICINES

Medicines *(medicine)* prescribed by a doctor are obtained from a chemist's or pharmacy *(farmacia)*, denoted by the sign of a red or green cross on a white background. Most chemists' are open from 8.30am until 12.30pm and from 3.30pm to 7.30pm. Outside these hours, at least one chemist's in all areas or towns is open until late (or 24 hours in major cities); a duty roster is posted on the door and published in local newspapers. After midnight you may need to ring a bell to summon the chemist. Chemists' are privately owned in Italy, often passed from one generation to another within the same family, and the number is strictly controlled. There are no chain chemists' as in the UK and the US.

Many medicines are available without a prescription in Italy that would require one in some other countries. Pills *(pillole)* are the most common prescriptions given by doctors, although you may also be prescribed a series of injections *(iniezioni)*, suppositories *(supposta)* or, less commonly, powders *(polveri)*. If you need a small quantity of medicine, your doctor may provide it free from his own supplies. Some common medicines, e.g. vitamins and cough linctus, can be surprisingly expensive. Prices of medicines aren't controlled by the government and vary considerably according to the brand.

If you're eligible for care under Italy's national health service, you pay the 'ticket' price for each medicine – currently set at €3.50 for most drugs, although you must produce a doctor's prescription. Exemptions are the same as for specialist treatment. For certain medicines you may be able to obtain one or more repeat doses (e.g. within a three-month period) without the need for another prescription. Non-prescription medicines, such as cold cures, vitamins and aspirin, must be paid for at the full cost.

Italian doctors commonly prescribe homeopathic medicines, which are popular in Italy and stocked by all chemists, some of which specialise in homeopathic medicine (look for the green *Omeopatia* sign). Note that the word *droga* means illegal drugs (narcotics).

Italian chemists stock a narrower range of goods than is the case in, for example, the US or the UK. Products are generally medicinal, although some cosmetics (usually skin creams) and toiletries are sold, plus health and diabetic foods, and some orthopaedic items. Chemists also sell prescription spectacles and some can perform simple tests such as those for measuring blood pressure. They are often consulted for minor ailments and many Italians use them as their local clinic (often in order to avoid a long queue at a doctor's surgery).

Herbalist shops (*erboristerie*) selling 'alternative' medicines are found in many towns and cities. There are also shops known as *negozi sanitari*, which specialise in orthopaedic medical equipment and stock a wide range of products for disabled people, including wheelchairs and bath aids, plus items such as prostheses, knee and arm supports, and orthopaedic shoes. Provided you have a clinical need, part of the cost of each item (up to around €50) is paid by the state.

☑ SURVIVAL TIP

If you're visiting Italy for a short period, you should bring sufficient medicines to cover your stay. You may also wish to bring your favourite non-prescription medicines (e.g. aspirin, cold and flu remedies, lotions, etc.), as they may be difficult or impossible to obtain in Italy or be much more expensive.

If you're visiting Italy and take a medicine regularly, you should ask your doctor for the generic name, as the brand names of medicines vary from country to country. If you wish to match a medicine prescribed abroad, you need a prescription with the medicine's trade name, the manufacturer's name, the chemical name and the dosage. Most medicines have an equivalent in Italy, although particular brands may be difficult or impossible to obtain. It's also possible to have medicines sent from abroad, for which no import duty or VAT should be payable.

HOSPITALS & CLINICS

All Italian cities and large towns have at least one clinic (*clinica*) or hospital (*ospedale*), indicated by the international signs of a white 'H' on a blue background or a red 'H' on a white background. Public hospitals are listed in the *Yellow Pages* under *Ospedali* and private hospitals under *Case di cura private*. If your Italian is poor or you prefer to be treated by English-speaking practitioners, the Salvator Mundi International Hospital, Viale Mura Gianicolensi, 67, 00152 Rome (☎ 06-588 961, 🖳 www.salvatormundi.it), the Rome American Hospital, Via E. Longoni, 69, 00155 Rome (☎ 06-22 551, 🖳 www.rah.it) and the Milan Clinic, Via Cerva, 25, Milan (☎ 02-7601 6047, 🖳 www.milanclinic.com) have English-speaking doctors and staff.

There's a wide discrepancy between public and private hospital facilities in Italy, although it's generally considered that there's little difference in the quality of medical treatment (e.g. surgery). The best hospitals are usually found in northern and central Italy, some of which, e.g. the Cancer Hospital (*Centro Tumori*) in Rome, have excellent reputations for specialist treatment. There are also a number of highly-regarded university hospitals. Private hospitals (*cliniche*), many run by the Roman Catholic Church, offer a pleasant alternative to the sometimes grim facilities of public hospitals, although they don't necessarily have the most sophisticated equipment. Some specialise in particular fields of medicine, such as obstetrics and surgery, rather than being full service hospitals. A number of private clinics have agreements with regional health authorities and provide beds that can be used by national health patients, although there may be long waiting lists. Most public hospitals have a 24-hour accident and emergency (casualty) department (*pronto soccorso*), where you'll wait a long time (sometimes hours), depending on how your level of urgency is coded – white

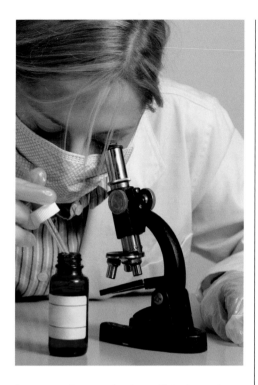

(non-urgent), green (no immediate danger), yellow (serious injury) or red (urgent/ life threatening).

Except in emergencies, you may be admitted or referred to a hospital or clinic for treatment only after consultation with a doctor. Normally you're admitted to a hospital in your own province, unless specialist surgery or treatment is unavailable there. In some regions, if a hospital cannot offer treatment within a reasonable period, patients may be referred to a private clinic without having to pay extra fees. Under Italy's national health service, you can request that an operation be performed in a hospital in another city, although the best-equipped hospitals in the north of Italy often have long waiting lists. In an emergency outside your own city or province, you'll obviously be treated in a local hospital.

A recent law banned private specialists from performing operations in state hospitals. If you're treated in a public hospital under the national health service, you must be operated on by the medical specialist on duty. If you request the services of a particular specialist or want to avoid a long waiting list

for an operation, you must pay the full cost of treatment.

If you need to visit a hospital, don't expect to be able to find your way easily to the right ward or consulting room, as few Italian hospitals have reception facilities and signs can be confusing or out of date. All patients have the right to an information booklet (*carta dei servizi*) containing details such as meal schedules, visiting hours, floor plans, doctors' names, hospital rules and the location of telephones and toilets. However, the information may not be up to date or patient-friendly, and it may be quicker simply to ask the nearest person in a white coat.

Basic accommodation in public hospitals usually consists of wards with between three and six beds, although single bedrooms are usually available with an en suite bathroom for a supplement of around €60 to €75 per day. You can usually rent a television for a small daily fee if it isn't included. Patients must usually bring everything they need with them, including towels, toiletries, pyjamas or nightdresses and dressing gowns, although meals are provided free of charge. Note, however, that the food may be inedible and you may need a regular supply of 'food parcels' if you're to survive a stay in a public hospital! In contrast, in private clinics and hospitals, accommodation is generally of luxury hotel standard, with air-conditioned single rooms, TV and telephone, and an extra bed for a relative if required. Public hospitals usually have restricted visiting hours of around two or three hours per day, while private clinics generally have no restrictions.

In public hospitals, all inpatient treatment under the national health service is free. For outpatient treatment, e.g. consultations, tests and operations that don't require you to be hospitalised, you pay the ticket cost, which is a maximum of €36.15 for each referral. As with other medical treatment, you must produce a doctor's referral.

The cost of hospitalisation in a private clinic can be extremely high, e.g. from €500 to €3,000 per day for hospital accommodation (including meals and medicines), plus the costs of medical treatment, e.g. over €5,000 for major surgery. The Ministry of Health sets minimum charges for all private operations, and costs vary enormously according to the reputation of the specialists involved. It can be much cheaper to have an operation abroad, particularly in France. If you have health insurance, be sure to check beforehand whether this covers you for the treatment planned.

If you aren't covered by the national health service, you must pay before you receive any treatment, irrespective of whether you have private health insurance, although some foreign insurance companies have arrangements with certain hospitals to pay bills directly.

If you're discharged from hospital and don't have transport home, you can usually pay for an ambulance to take you. Volunteer ambulance services such as the Red Cross (*Croce Rossa*) provide non-urgent ambulance transport services, for which a list of fees is usually available in hospitals.

CHILDBIRTH

Childbirth in Italy usually takes place in a hospital, where a stay of three days is normal, although it can be longer if complications arise. Maternity wards usually have two or three beds; mothers must provide clothing and accessories for their babies, although medical supplies are provided. Childbirth is supervised by a gynaecologist, an obstetrician, a nurse and a medical specialist who looks after babies during the first four weeks (*neonatologo*). Husbands usually attend the birth, although mothers can ask for any relative to do so. Italian women don't generally give birth at home, and if you want to do so, you must arrange (and pay) for a private obstetrician to attend the delivery.

A number of services relating to childbirth are provided by family planning centres (*consultori familiari*). These are staffed by medical professionals and provide free advice and testing at all phases of childbirth, including ante-natal classes, gynaecological examinations and post-natal assistance by an obstetrician (including home visits). All services at family planning centres are free under the national health service, although preference may be given to low-income families and it may be quicker to pay for a private consultation.

Family planning centres also provide free information and counselling on a range of other health issues, including contraception, abortion, parenting, and sexual and marital problems.

If you contribute to social security, the national health service pays for all treatment relating to pregnancy. To qualify, however, mothers must undergo a number of pre-natal examinations, including ultrasonography (*ecografia*) within the first, fourth, seventh and (if applicable) tenth months of pregnancy, where sound waves are used to check foetal growth, detect abnormalities and test for hepatitis B and HIV. Where there's a risk of miscarriage, a baby is monitored throughout a pregnancy and women over the age of 35 undergo testing for Down's syndrome. The public health service also pays for a number of pre-conception health tests, for both men and women, to determine whether any genetic malformations are present.

Giving birth in a private clinic in Italy can be very expensive; typical costs start from between €3,000 and €5,000 and can be considerably higher. You must also bear in mind that, although the surroundings are likely to be considerably more pleasant and less crowded than in a public hospital, private clinics may lack vital equipment in the event of an emergency. It's therefore important to check the level of equipment and facilities available, and obtain a complete list of fees in advance.

After you've given birth and left hospital, there's no specific post-natal provision, although a number of services relating to childbirth are provided by family planning centres (see above).

Abortion (*interregional volontaria di gravidanza*) is legal in Italy and must usually be performed within 12 weeks of conception in a public hospital or private clinic (there are no specialist abortion clinics). The consent of the father isn't required, but the woman must sign a consent form. Girls under the age of 18 require the consent of both parents or guardians, or the decision is referred to a judge. 'Therapeutic' abortions, i.e. when there's a likelihood of a child being seriously malformed or the mother's life is at risk, can be performed up to 20 weeks after conception. Authorisation by a medical specialist is required for all abortions performed more than 12 weeks after conception. The cost of an abortion is paid by the health service, although you can choose to pay for an abortion in a private clinic. The word *aborto* means both miscarriage and abortion.

CHILDREN'S HEALTH

If you're registered with the national health service, you can choose a paediatrician (*pediatra*) from a list at your local ASL. Paediatricians generally treat children up to the age of 14 (although some parents prefer to use their family doctor). Children are given a vaccination record booklet (*libretto delle vaccinazioni*) and are required to have vaccinations against diphtheria and tetanus (*antidifterico-tetanica* or *DT*), polio (*antipolio*) and hepatitis B (*antiepatite B*) at three months, with boosters at 5 and 11 months. A polio booster is required at three years, and diphtheria and tetanus just before entry into primary school. A booster for hepatitis B is necessary at the age of 12. Vaccinations are provided free of charge and are compulsory.

Although not compulsory, vaccinations against whooping cough, measles, mumps, German measles and HIB (which can cause serious illnesses such as meningitis) are also recommended. A whooping-cough vaccination (*anitpertosse*) can be administered in combination with the diphtheria and tetanus vaccinations (called *DTP*). Some doctors recommend a multiple vaccination (called *MPR*) against measles (*morbillo*), mumps (*parotite*) and German measles (*rosolia*), between the age of 12 and 15 months.

Italian hospitals have paediatric units where children aged up to 17 are treated. Wards are usually well stocked with games, toys, books and other children, and facilities are provided for one parent (usually the mother) to stay overnight. Mothers with children under one year must usually provide milk, bottled drinking water (if required), nappies and changes of clothes, although food is provided. Children requiring long-term hospitalisation are usually given school lessons in hospital by volunteer teachers.

When travelling in Italy, you should take proof of your children's immunisations with you, with official translations obtainable from Italian consulates.

DENTISTS

Italy has few dentists (*dentisti*) per head of population in comparison with doctors, and treatment can be astronomically expensive, which means that many Italians wait until they have serious problems before making an appointment. Few dentists speak English; you can contact your country's embassy or local consulate for a list of English-speaking dentists in your area. Your employer, colleagues or neighbours may also be able to recommend a dentist. Dentists are listed in *Yellow Pages* under *Dentisti*. However, only names and addresses are listed and information such as specialities and surgery hours isn't provided.

Dentists' surgery hours vary considerably but are typically from 8.30am until 1pm, and from 4.00 to 7.30pm, Mondays to Fridays. Dentists come under the category of specialists in Italy and if you wish to pay the national health service ticket (i.e. a maximum of €36.15), you must obtain a referral from your family doctor and choose a dentist who's registered with the SSN. Private dentists generally have a better reputation than those working for the state and many Italians pay for private treatment, particularly for cosmetic work (public-health dentists don't tend to have the most modern dental equipment).

> ### ☑ SURVIVAL TIP
>
> If your family requires expensive dental treatment, e.g. crowns, bridges, braces or false teeth, it's worthwhile checking whether treatment is cheaper abroad, e.g. in your home country.

Always check exactly what treatment has been recommended and how much it will cost before committing yourself – you must be wary of unnecessary treatment, which is a common practice in all countries. Private dentists generally charge between €80 and €200 per visit – they can be up to 50 per cent cheaper than British private dentists – which may include a number of treatments, e.g. a scale and polish, and a filling. But for more extensive work, such as the removal of teeth or root canal treatment, bills can be astronomical. As with private doctors, it's usual to pay a dentist before a course of treatment begins.

OPTICIANS

It isn't necessary to register with an optician or optometrist (*ottico*). You simply make an appointment with the practitioner of your choice, although it's wise to ask friends, colleagues or neighbours if they can recommend someone. Opticians are listed in the *Yellow Pages* under *Ottici* and eye specialists under *Oculisti*. Prices for spectacles (*occhiali*) and contact lenses (*lenti a contatto*) aren't controlled, therefore it's wise to shop around and compare costs, although the eye care business is competitive. A pair of spectacles typically costs between €100 and €190, which may include €80 or more for the frame. Italy lacks large optical chains where spectacles can be made on the spot or within 24 hours, although if you have a prescription you can sometimes buy ready-made reading spectacles from chemists'. Always obtain an estimate for lenses and ask about extra charges for fittings, adjustments, lens-care kits and follow-up visits.

To receive free treatment under the national health service, you must have your eyes examined by an eye specialist or ophthalmologist (*oculista*). You must first obtain a referral from your family doctor, which you take to an oculist, who usually works in a state hospital or ASL building. An ophthalmologist can make a more thorough

test of your eyesight than an optician, and is able to test for certain diseases that can be diagnosed from eye abnormalities, e.g. diabetes and some types of cancer. If glasses are necessary, he'll write a prescription for you to take to an optician.

It's recommended to have your eyes tested before arriving in Italy and to bring a spare pair of spectacles and/or contact lenses with you. You should also bring a copy of your prescription in case you need to obtain replacement spectacles or contact lenses urgently.

SEXUALLY TRANSMITTED DISEASES

As in most developed countries, AIDS (*AIDS* or *SIDA*) is on the increase: Italy reported a total of 62,000 AIDS cases between 1982 and 2009, 27 per cent of them female. HIV prevalence is 0.4 per cent – 82 per cent below the worldwide average but higher than the EU average – and official figures show that in 2010, 150,000 people were living with HIV. Condoms (*preservativi*) can be purchased in packets from chemists' and supermarkets; there are few vending machines, and neither family planning centres nor family doctors generally issue them free.

Free and anonymous testing for HIV (pronounced *akka-ee-vee*), which is conducted at least one month after patients have been at risk, is available at departments of infectious diseases (*malattie infettive*) in public hospitals and other public health centres. A doctor's referral isn't usually required, although if you're a visitor to Italy and aren't in possession of a national health card, you may need to obtain a *straniero temporaneamente presente* (STP) card from your local health authority declaring that you're temporarily resident.

For the testing and treatment of other sexually transmitted diseases (*malattie a trasmissione sessuale*), e.g. hepatitis B and C, syphilis and gonorrhoea, you must be referred by your family doctor and pay the ticket price. AIED centres (see above) offer information and testing for all STDs, as well as advice on a range of other health issues.

SMOKING

Italy has just over 11m smokers (around 22 per cent of the population) and, not surprisingly, this results in a high incidence of smoking-related diseases, including at least 85,000 deaths a year. Many Italians start smoking at an early age, cigarettes are still inexpensive (although their price has increased to between €3.80 and €5 for 20) and, in keeping with the Italians' sense of individual liberty, the government has, until recently, made little effort to persuade people to stop smoking. Another reason for this may be that the cheapest cigarettes (known as *nazionali*) are manufactured by the state!

However, in a radical move designed to protect the health of passive smokers, in 2005 the government introduced a draconian anti-smoking law, and smoking is now banned in all enclosed spaces, including schools, offices, banks, shops, hospitals, airports, railway stations and work places. Smoking is also banned on public transport, other than in train carriages reserved for smokers, and on all Italian domestic flights and Alitalia international flights. Employers must provide separate areas equipped with extractor fans for employees who smoke, and bars and restaurants must provide separate areas for smoking customers (*fumatori*) and non-smoking customers (*non fumatori*).

☑ SURVIVAL TIP

If you smoke where it isn't permitted you can be fined up to €275 (first-time offenders are likely only to be asked to extinguish their cigarettes) and landlords who disregard the law can be fined up to €2,200.

SPAS

When you've had a surfeit of *la dolce vita*, a variety of cures is available at Italy's many spas (*terme*). Italy has over 100 spas, attracting millions of visitors each year. Many offer not only treatment for ailments such as rheumatism, arthritis, respiratory complaints, skin diseases and obesity, but also 'healthcare tourism' packages, which include beauty treatments, hydro-massage, heliotherapy (sun treatment), respiratory treatments or just relaxation. Many spas stress the scientific aspect of the treatments they offer, listing the mineral composition of their waters and sometimes the scientific research conducted there. All spas have qualified doctors.

Your family doctor can prescribe treatment at a spa centre and, if you're registered with the national health service, you pay only the cost of the ticket. However, the SSN doesn't pay for board and lodging. Spas can usually be visited on a daily basis, with fees ranging from around €6 for a dip in a natural thermal bath to around €200 for a day of self-indulgence in a city centre spa.

BIRTHS & DEATHS

Births and deaths in Italy must be registered within seven days at the registry office (Ufficio di Stato Civile) of the town (*comune*) where they take place. Registration is obligatory for everyone, irrespective of their nationality and whether they're residents or visitors. In the case of hospital births, registration is done by the hospital or clinic where a child is born. If you give birth at home, you must complete the registration yourself. An Italian birth certificate (*certificato di nascita*) is issued automatically.

In the event of a death, all interested parties must be notified. If a death takes place in a hospital, the attending doctor completes a certificate stating the cause of death (*constatazione della morte*); you should make several copies of this, as they're required by banks and other institutions. If a death occurs at home, you should call your family doctor or the local *guardia medica*. If there are suspicious circumstances, you should call the *polizia mortuaria* by ringing 113 and they'll arrange for a post mortem examination (autopsy). As with births, deaths must be registered in the town where the death occurred, although undertakers (see below) usually do this for you.

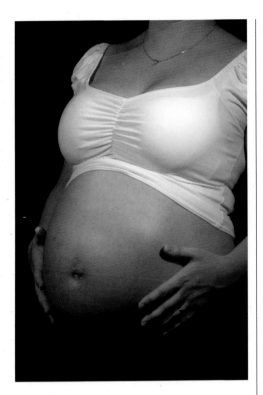

When a death occurs, it's important to find a reliable undertaker as soon as possible, particularly as they handle most of the documentation. Funerals in Italy are among the most expensive in Europe, frequently costing around €3,000, and it's important to obtain personal recommendations and check that an undertaker abides by the Italian Code of Conduct for Undertakers (*Codice Italiano di Comportamento per le Imprese Funebri*). You're recommended to ignore recommendations given by hospital staff (who may be getting a commission) or people hanging around hospital mortuaries offering their services.

Bodies can be buried in three ways in Italy – in a family tomb, in an individual tomb (*loculo*) or in a communal burial ground (*campo comune*) – or they can be cremated. Plots for individual or family tombs are expensive (between €2,750 and €5,750), whereas *loculi*, which are layered blocks of marble tombs, can be bought for between €500 and €1,500 (usually for an initial period of around 30 years, after which the 'lease' is renewable). Interment in a communal burial ground is free but considered demeaning by many Italians, as the remains can be exhumed after just ten years (there's an acute shortage of cemeteries in Italy). Embalming isn't usually available.

Cremation is becoming increasingly popular, not least because it's paid for by the local municipality, although crematoria are few and far between. If the deceased hasn't requested cremation, a family member must make a formal request via a notary to the registry office. Families usually keep the ashes in the family tomb or *loculo*, lease an urn from the *comune* or dispose of the ashes in the local *campo comune*, which is free of charge. It's illegal to keep ashes at home or dispose of them in any other way.

When a death occurs at home, the body is prepared for shipment or burial in the home, as Italian law forbids undertakers to store them.

The body or ashes of a deceased person may be sent to another country for burial or cremation. You'll need to provide the funeral agent with the documents relating to the death and the identity of the deceased, so that he can obtain the necessary permits.

13.

INSURANCE

In all matters concerning insurance, you're responsible for making sure that you and your family are legally insured in Italy. Italian law provides for various obligatory state and employer insurance schemes, including health insurance and family allowances (see Social Security on page 197). Insurance (*assicurazione*) that must be taken out by individuals includes third party car insurance (see page 162), although if you lease a car or buy one on credit, a lender will insist that you have comprehensive car insurance; third party liability insurance (for tenants and homeowners); and mortgage life insurance if you have a mortgage (depending on the amount borrowed).

Voluntary insurance includes supplementary pensions, disability, health, household, dental, travel, car breakdown and life insurance. Insurance is generally more expensive in Italy than in many other European countries; policies also attract various taxes and 20 per cent VAT, and the average Italian is more prone to taking risks than many other nationalities and carries less insurance than, for example, northern Europeans (although the market has grown considerably in the last decade, particularly in private health insurance and pensions).

Most Italians and other EU residents and their families qualify to receive medical treatment under the Italian social security system (see **Chapter 12** and **Health Insurance** on page 203). You should, however, ensure that your family has full health insurance during the interval between leaving your last country of residence and obtaining health insurance in Italy. One way is to take out a travel insurance policy (see page 207). If you're opting for private health insurance, it's better to extend your present health insurance policy than to take out a new policy (most policies can be extended to provide international cover). This is particularly important if you have an existing health problem that won't be covered by a new policy.

If you wish to make a claim against an insurance policy, you may be required by your insurer to report the incident to the police within 24 hours (this may also be a legal requirement). If you're unsure of your rights, it's wise to obtain legal advice for anything other than a minor claim. Italian law is likely to differ from that in your home country or your previous country of residence, so never assume that it's the same.

It's unnecessary to spend half your income insuring yourself against every eventuality from the common cold to being sued for Italian mispronunciation, but it's important to insure against any event that could precipitate a major financial disaster, such as a serious accident or your house being demolished by a storm.

As with anything connected with finance, it's important to shop around when buying insurance. Just collecting a few brochures from insurance agents or making a few telephone calls could save you a lot of money.

Regrettably, you cannot insure yourself against being uninsured or sue your insurance agent for giving you bad advice.

INSURANCE AGENTS & COMPANIES

Italy had a relatively undeveloped insurance market until the '80s, when many foreign companies stepped in to fill the vacuum and now control a large slice of the market. There are numerous Italian and foreign insurance companies to choose from, either providing a range of insurance services or specialising in certain fields only (some foreign insurance companies operating in Italy cater particularly for the needs of expatriates), major insurance companies having offices or agents in all main cities. Insurance agents, brokers (*agenti*) and companies are listed in the *Yellow Pages* under *Assicurazioni* and many advertise in the expatriate press in Italy.

Most insurance companies or brokers will provide a free appraisal of your family's insurance needs and there are many independent brokers, who can offer you a choice of policies and save you money. However, as in many countries, it's often difficult to obtain completely independent, unbiased insurance advice, as brokers may be influenced by the commission offered for selling a particular policy. As with all financial matters in Italy, be careful who you choose as your broker and the company you insure with, as a number of companies have gone bust in recent years and insurance fraud isn't unknown.

When buying insurance, particularly car insurance, it's important to shop until you drop! Obtain recommendations from friends, colleagues and neighbours (but don't believe everything they tell you!). Compare the costs, terms and benefits provided by a number of companies before making a decision. Note that premiums (*premi*) are sometimes negotiable. However, the most important point is whether an insurance company pays claims fully and promptly, or, as many do, delays paying for as long as possible and fights every euro of a claim. Major Italian insurance companies include Genertel (☎ 800-202 020, 🖥 www.genertel.it), Genialloyd (☎ 02-2805 2854, 🖥 www.genialloyd.it) and Generali (🖥 www.generali.it).

The entire insurance industry has been going through a crisis in recent years and (at long last) is becoming more consumer-driven. One major change has been the advent of telephone and internet insurers, which allow you to obtain and

compare estimates in minutes. Some internet brokers allow you to compare rates online (e.g. 🖥 www.assicurazione.it).

While buying insurance over the phone or on the internet is a great convenience, you need to exercise some caution, particularly if you're buying a policy from an insurance company you aren't familiar with. Not all insurance companies are equally reliable or have the same financial stability, and it may be better to insure with a large international company with a good reputation than with a small Italian company, even if this means paying a higher premium. You can check whether a company is registered in Italy with the Istituto per la Vigilanza sulle Assicurazioni Private e di Interesse Collettivo (ISVAP), the Italian insurance industry trade association (🖥 www.isvap.it).

INSURANCE CONTRACTS

Read insurance contracts carefully before signing them. If you don't understand Italian, ask someone to check a policy and don't sign it until you fully understand the terms and the cover provided. Policies often contain traps and legal loopholes in the small print, particularly exclusion clauses, therefore it's recommended to obtain professional advice before signing on the dotted line.

Always check the notice period required to cancel (*annullare*) a policy. Policies are usually automatically extended for a further period if they aren't cancelled in writing by registered letter two months before their expiry date. Most Italian insurance policies are valid for

ten years, with the exception of car insurance policies, which run for one year. If possible, you should insure with a company whose contracts are valid for one year and renewable annually.

If you haven't paid your renewal premium within ten days of the expiry date, your insurance may become invalid. You may cancel an insurance policy before the term has expired if the premium is increased, the terms are altered (e.g. the risk is diminished), or an insured object is lost or stolen. This must, however, still be done in writing and by registered post. Cancellation is also permitted at short notice under certain circumstances beyond your control. If you're changing insurance companies, the new company will be happy to cancel your old policy for you and simply give you a standard letter to sign.

If you wish to make a claim, you must usually inform your insurance company in writing by registered letter within two to five days of the incident (e.g. accidents) or 24 hours in the case of theft. Thefts must be reported to the local police within 24 hours, as the police report (*denuncia*) usually constitutes irrefutable evidence of your claim.

> If you have a problem with a claim or other problems with an Italian insurance company that you cannot resolve, contact ISVAP, Via del Quirinale, 21, 00187 Rome (☎ 06-421 331, 🖥 www.isvap.it).

Like insurance companies everywhere, some Italian companies do almost anything to avoid paying in the event of a claim and use any available loophole. In fact, Italian insurance companies have taken the art of delaying payments or not paying claims at all to unimaginable heights, which is why it's essential to deal with only reputable companies (not that this provides a guarantee). It isn't unusual for legitimate insurance claims to take years to be resolved – and even then for the outcome to be unsatisfactory.

SOCIAL SECURITY

Italy has an extensive social security (*previdenza sociale*) system covering the vast majority of the population and providing benefits to cover unemployment, sickness and maternity, accidents at work and occupational diseases, as well as old age, invalidity and survivors' pensions, and family allowances. It **doesn't** include the national heath service (Servizio Sanitario Nazionale/SSN – see page 183), which is funded from general taxation. The system is run by a number of state agencies, which have been brought together under the umbrella of the National Institute for Social Security (Istituto Nazionale della Previdenza Sociale/INPS).

If you disagree with a decision taken and notified in writing by a social security body, you may lodge an appeal within certain time limits; it must be lodged by registered letter (with advice of delivery). If the appeal is dismissed or no decision is taken within 90 days, you may then appeal to the ordinary courts, which in the first instance means the magistrate's court for employment matters (*pretore del lavoro*). The time limit is three years in the case of pensions and one year in the case of temporary benefits.

Eligibility & Exemptions

Italy has reciprocal social security agreements with some 40 countries (including all EU countries, Canada and the US) whereby expatriates may remain under their home country's social security scheme for a limited period. Agreements usually apply for a maximum of two years and may usually be extended for up to five years. For example, under an agreement between the US and Italy, an American employee of a US company who's transferred to Italy for up to five years can continue to pay US social security contributions. Similarly, EU nationals transferred to Italy by an employer in their home country can continue to pay social security abroad for one year, which can be extended for another year in unforeseen circumstances. This also applies to the self-employed. However, after working in Italy for two years, EU nationals **must** contribute to Italian social security (see below).

If you or your spouse work in Italy but remain insured under the social security legislation of another EU country, you're able to claim social security benefits from that country and your foreign contributions are taken into account when calculating your qualification for benefits. This is particularly important with regard to state pensions (see page 201). Contact your country's social security administration for information. In the UK, information is provided by the international department of the Department for Work and Pensions (🖥 www.dwp.gov.uk/international) and by the International Pension Centre (☎ 0191-218 7777).

Contributions

With a few exceptions (see **Eligibility & Exemptions**, above), resident employees and self-employed workers pay social security contributions (*contributi previdenziali*).

If you're an employee (*lavoratore dipendente*), your employer completes all the formalities necessary for you to register with social security. Your contributions are deducted from your gross salary by your employer, who pays around two-thirds of your pension contributions; you pay around a third of these, plus a small contribution towards other types of social insurance. The standard total social security contribution made by employees is around 10 per cent of their gross salary, while the employer's contribution is around 35 per cent (making a total of some 45 per cent). There are different contribution rates for employees in industry, commerce and agriculture, and for workers (*operai*), office staff (*impiegati*) and managers (*dirigenti*), who also receive different benefits. For managers in industry, an income ceiling applies for certain types of social security contributions, such as disability, old age pension and survivor's benefits.

The self-employed (*lavoratori autonomi*) must register and make contributions either to a separate organisation (called a *cassa*), which is a social security fund allied to their profession, or directly to the INPS. Self-employed people who make contributions to their own *cassa* include architects, accountants, lawyers, engineers, surveyors, medical specialists and other freelance professionals, who each have different rates of contributions varying between 17 and 25.7 per cent of their income. The self-employed who make contributions to INPS include part-time employees (*collaboratori*) – including university

students – freelance workers (*indipendenti*), small businessmen, shopkeepers, traders, tenant farmers, sharecroppers and smallholders, plus employees of relatively new industries (e.g. some high-tech sectors) which don't yet have their own *cassa*.

In certain circumstances where contributions aren't made, they're credited by the state. These are known as accredited contributions (*contributi accreditati*). For example, contributions are automatically credited for periods of unemployment where an employee has paid contributions for unemployment benefit (*indennità di disoccupazione*), for periods of military service, maternity leave, and illness of not less than a week and no longer than 12 months, after making the relevant application to INPS. Applications for notional contributions during periods of illness must be accompanied by a statement from your employer.

☑ SURVIVAL TIP

For information about your particular situation, you can contact the INPS (☎ 803164, 🖥 www.inps.it), although you'll need to get an Italian-speaker to contact them for you if your Italian isn't up to it.

Contributions in Other EU Countries

If you've paid regular social security contributions in another EU country for two full years before coming to Italy (e.g. to look for a job), you're entitled to social security cover for a limited period from the date of the last contribution made in your home country. You're also entitled to be covered by the national health service (see page 183). Form E106 must be obtained from the social security authorities in your home (or previous) country and given to your local social security office in Italy. If you're receiving an invalidity pension or other social security benefits on the grounds of ill-health, you should establish exactly how living in Italy affects those benefits. In some countries there are reciprocal agreements regarding invalidity rights, but you must confirm that they apply in your case.

Benefits

Benefits are detailed below. In many cases there are different regulations and payments for blue-collar workers (*operai*), white-collar staff (*impiegati*) and managers (*dirigenti*).

Sickness Benefit

Sickness benefit (*indennità di malattia*) is payable for an illness or accident that results in an absence from work of at least seven days and is paid for a maximum of 180 days. The amount payable is calculated from your average daily earnings during the month preceding your illness and is equal to around 50 per cent of your earnings for the first 20 days and two-thirds of earnings for the remaining days. However, if you're hospitalised and don't have any dependants, the benefit is equal to 40 per cent of your average earnings. If you have an accident at work, you receive full pay during the recovery period; if an injury prevents you from working permanently, you receive an invalidity pension. Sickness benefit is generally paid by the employer, who recovers the payment from the INPS, but in certain cases is paid directly by INPS. Sickness benefit doesn't apply to the self-employed. See also **Sick Leave** on page 46.

Maternity Benefit

Italian maternity benefit (*per maternità*) is among the most generous in the world and is equal to 80 per cent of your salary and paid for a total of five months before and immediately following a birth. Mothers are also entitled to receive a reduced benefit of 30 per cent of their salary for six months (called *congedo facoltativo*) during the year following the birth. An application for maternity benefit must be made at your local INPS office; you require a medical certificate (*certificato medico*) confirming your pregnancy and a statement from your employer certifying that you've stopped work due to pregnancy. After the birth you must provide the INPS with a copy of the birth certificate (*certificato di nascita*) and a certificate of family status (*certificato di stato di famiglia*), available from the registry office (Ufficio Anagrafe) in your *comune*. See also **Parental Leave** on page 47.

Disability Benefits

All workers and many other employees are covered against work-related illnesses (e.g. occupational diseases) and accidents. Disability benefits (*indennità di inabilità*) include salary for temporary disability and pensions for permanent disability. Temporary disability benefit is 60 per cent of your average daily wage during the two weeks preceding the accident or onset of illness. Permanent disability benefits vary according to the seriousness of the disability and may take the form of a lump sum payment (for minor disability) or an annuity (for major disability) – see **State Pensions** on page 201. Those who are totally disabled also qualify for a 'constant attendance supplement' of €465.09 per month. Disability benefits don't apply to the self-employed.

Family Allowance

If you're an employee and the only wage earner in your family, you can apply for family allowance (*assegno familiare*) if your salary falls below a certain level, which varies according to the number of people in the family. Levels change regularly and up-to-date figures can be found on the website of the Istituto Nazionale della Previdenza Sociale (🖳 www. inps.it). Family allowance is dependent on family size, income and other circumstances, but in 2010 a family with a collective income of under €13,211 received between €137 and €1,368 per month. An application form is available from your employer or an INPS office and must be accompanied by a certificate of family status (*certificato di stato di famiglia* – see **Maternity Benefit** on page 199). The form is given to your employer, who pays the allowance with your salary.

Unemployment Benefits

There are various kinds of unemployment benefit (*indennità di disoccupazione*), as detailed below.

◆ **Ordinary benefit:** To qualify for ordinary benefit (*indennità ordinaria*), you must have worked for at least a year and contributed for at least the previous two years. Benefit is available for a maximum of 180 days (six months) or for up to nine months if you're aged over 50, and is paid from the eighth day after termination of work, provided that an application is made within seven days. However, applications can be made up to 90 days after ceasing work. Benefit is calculated at 40 per cent of your average earnings during the previous seven months, but cannot exceed a certain maximum, which was €1,065.26 per month in 2009.

◆ **Reduced benefit:** If you've worked for at least 78 days in the previous year (including public holidays) but less than a year in total, or have made two years' voluntary contributions, you qualify for reduced benefit (*indennità ridotta*). Benefit is calculated at 30 per cent of your average net earnings during the previous three months, but the entire amount received, which is paid as a lump sum, cannot exceed €830.77. This rises to €998.50 for workers whose average gross monthly earnings are over €1,826.07.

☑ SURVIVAL TIP

The self-employed and those who have never worked in Italy or resign from their job don't qualify for unemployment benefit.

◆ **Special allowance:** A 'special' allowance (*trattamento speciale*) is awarded to employees who have been made redundant in the agriculture and construction industries. Contributions paid in other EU member states are taken into account when making an application for benefit.

An application for unemployment benefit must be made at your local INPS office or the employment office (Ufficio di Collocamento) with your notice of dismissal and a certificate of family status (*certificato di stato di famiglia* – see **Maternity Benefit** on page 199). You're issued with an unemployment registration card (*attestato di iscrizione*).

If you're unemployed in another EU country, you retain the right to your unemployment benefit (under certain conditions) for up to three months while looking for work in Italy. The country paying your employment benefit issues you with form E303, which you must take to an INPS office in Italy. If you return home before the end of the three months, you continue to receive your unemployment benefit in your home country.

In addition to unemployment benefits, Italy has a state fund for employees in industry whose companies put them on temporary redundancy through no fault of their own (e.g. market crisis, natural disaster, etc.), called *Cassa Integrazione Guadagni* (*CIG*), which is designed to 'integrate' employees' earnings until work is resumed. There are two types of *CIG*:

◆ **Ordinary CIG:** This comprises 80 per cent of your salary for hours not worked, e.g. if an employer agrees to provide five hours' work in a 35-hour week, 80 per cent of the salary for the remaining 30 hours is remunerated. This cannot exceed a monthly maximum, which in 2010 was €1,073.25 per month if monthly income exceeded €1,931.86 or €892.96 per month for those on lower incomes.

◆ **Extraordinary CIG:** Designed to cover special situations, e.g. when a production line is being reorganised or converted and work must temporarily cease, and lasts for 36 months in cases of reorganisation or conversion or 12 months in cases of company crisis. Benefit is the same as for ordinary *CIG* above.

In both cases, if the market hasn't changed, companies aren't obliged to take back employees, so *CIG* often becomes the start of unemployment benefit. See also **Dismissal & Redundancy** on page 50.

State Pensions

State pensions comprise old age, invalidity and survivors' pensions (*pensione di vecchiaia, di invalidità* and *superstiti*). All employees and certain categories of self-employed people (who pay obligatory contributions to INPS) are entitled to a state pension, which is paid by the INPS. For employees, total state pension contributions are around 30 per cent of gross salary; the employee contributes approximately 7 per cent and the employer pays the remainder. There are various state or semi-state entities that collect contributions and pay pensions on behalf of particular groups. Certain employees and the self-employed receive a pension through a semi-private (*para-statale*) organisation responsible for their profession. These include the INPDAI for industrial managers, the INPADAC for commercial managers, the INPGI for journalists and the ENPALS for those employed in the

entertainment industry. The National Fund for the Liberal Professions provides pensions for a wide range of professionals, including doctors, chemists, veterinary surgeons, engineers, architects, surveyors, lawyers, tax advisers, employment consultants, notaries, customs agents and accountants.

As in all EU countries, state pensions are under pressure from governments that can no longer afford to pay them, due to the fact that a dwindling number of workers are supporting a growing number of retirees. Italy has particular problems, as state pensions are too generous (for the government – pensions are **never** too high for pensioners!), despite reforms in recent years, and more people receive their income from the state than from the private sector. Italy (along with Japan) has the highest number of retired people as a percentage of population and in 25 years' time some 30 per cent of Italians will be over 65, which will put public finances under intolerable strain because the ratio of workers to pensioners will be almost equal (currently it's around two to one). Since 1st January 2001, the government has offered greater incentives for people to invest in private pension funds (*fondi privati* or *fondi integrativi pensioni*), in the hope of shifting some of the burden to private insurance companies (see **Private Pensions** on page 202).

When you reach state pension age, each EU country where you've paid social security for at least a year pays you an old-age pension. For example, if you've worked in three EU countries, you receive three separate old-age pensions. Each pension is calculated according to your insurance record in that country. If you move to Italy after working in another EU country (or move to another EU country after working in Italy), your state pension contributions can be exported to (or from) Italy. Italian state pensions are payable abroad and most countries pay state pensions directly to their nationals who are resident in Italy. Non-EU nationals who haven't reached pension age can request reimbursement of their pension contributions (plus their employer's contributions) on leaving Italy permanently.

Further information about pensions can be obtained from the Ministero del Lavoro e delle Politiche Sociali, Direzione della Previdenza, Via Venato, 56, 00187 Rome (☎ 800-196 196)

and the Istituto Nazionale della Previdenza Sociale, INPS (💻 www.inps.it).

Old age pensions: There are three kinds of old age pension:

♦ **Full earnings-related pension** (*pensione di anzianità*): paid to those who have contributed for a minimum of 40 years and are at least 60 years old.

♦ **Standard old age pension** (*pensione di vecchiaia*): paid to employees who have reached retirement age. This is 60 for women and 65 for men in the private sector and 65 for both men and women in the public sector. You must have contributed for at least 20 years to earn a pension, which is calculated from your last ten years' income.

♦ **Social pension** (*pensione sociale*): people who have never made any social security contributions may claim a pension of up to €409.05 per month, providing their annual income and assets are no higher than €5,317 or €10,635 for couples.

Except for a social pension, the amount you receive depends on your number of years' contributions. To qualify for a standard pension, you must have made at least 156 weekly contributions or 36 monthly contributions in the previous five years, or 260 weekly contributions or 60 monthly contributions in total. Insurance contributions made in other EU member states can be taken into account when calculating this total. You can choose to make a one-off contribution (*riscatto*) to 'redeem' periods when insurance contributions haven't been made. Such periods may include time spent at university or working abroad in countries without a social security agreement with Italy.

If you've paid five years' contributions, you can make voluntary contributions (*contributi volontari*) for periods spent raising a family or looking after a disabled person. If you aren't employed, you can also make voluntary contributions.

The maximum old age pension is 80 per cent of your highest average annual income received in the previous ten years of employment. In the event of the death of a pensioner, a pension is transferred to a surviving spouse or children. Pensions are indexed to the cost of living and increase annually in line with inflation (currently around 1.4 per cent per year). Pensions are paid on the first day of the month following an application to your local INPS office. State pensions aren't taxable.

Invalidity pension: An invalidity pension is paid if you're totally and permanently unable to work. You become eligible after five years of contributions, including at least three years in the five years preceding a claim; you must have no other form of income. The payment is dependent on contributions.

Survivor's pension: A survivor's pension is paid to the spouse of a deceased pensioner; if he has two or more children, the survivor is entitled to 100 per cent of the pension, if one child 80 per cent and if no children 60 per cent. A survivor's pension is also payable to dependent children and grandchildren who lose both (pensioner) parents/grandparents, students younger than 26 and disabled children of any age: rates are 100 per cent for three or more children or grandchildren, 80 per cent for two children/grandchildren and 70 per cent for one child/grandchild. Other qualifying dependents such as siblings may be entitled to 15 per cent.

PRIVATE PENSIONS

Italy's pension system used to be dominated by state provision, with the few private pension plans concentrated at industry level. This is changing, and reforms have set out to promote participation in private pension plans by encouraging workers to transfer their statutory severance pay (*trattamento di fine rapporto/ TFR or liquidazione*) – due to all employees at the end of their service – to either a privately-managed 'open-ended' pension fund, or an industry-wide 'closed-end' pension fund. Pension funds are authorised to pay a lump sum of up to 50 per cent on maturity; the other 50 per cent must be taken as an annuity. There may be tax advantages to taking out a private pension, most of which are linked to life insurance policies.

Private 'open-ended' pensions (*forme pensionistiche individuali*) are regulated by ISVAP (L'Istituto per la Vigilanza sulle Assicurazioni Private e di Interesse Collettivo), whereas 'closed-ended' industry-wide pensions are regulated by INPS (L' Istituto Nazionale per la Previdenza Sociale).

There are a number of rules and regulations governing private pensions. These include the following stipulations:

♦ The insured reaches pensionable age no earlier than five years after signing a life insurance contract.

♦ 15 years after signing for an individual pension, the insured must not be more than ten years below pensionable age

♦ Three years after the conclusion of a privately managed pension contract, you're free to choose an alternative form of life insurance.

For further information, see the websites for ISVAP (🖳 www.isvap.it) and INPS (🖳 www. inps.it), both of which are in Italian.

Note that you should obtain professional advice before investing in a pension fund or insurance policy, particularly as the legislation regarding private pensions is liable to change.

HEALTH INSURANCE

Most Italians and other EU residents and their families qualify to receive medical treatment under the Italian social security system (see Chapter 12). If you don't qualify, it's essential to take out private health insurance, which may be obligatory for some people. If you aren't covered by Italian social security and need comprehensive private health insurance to obtain a residence permit, you must ensure that your health policy will be accepted by the authorities. Even if you do qualify for social security benefits, you should bear in mind that these are fewer and less generous than in many other EU countries, and in most cases you'd be unwise to rely solely on state benefits to meet your needs.

In particular, you should ensure that your family has full health insurance during the interval between leaving your last country of residence and obtaining health insurance in Italy. One way is to take out a travel insurance policy (see page 207). However, it's better to extend your present health insurance policy than to take out a new policy (most policies can be extended to provide international cover). This is particularly important if you have an existing health problem that won't be covered by a new policy.

Even if you qualify for state health treatment, you may wish to take out a private health insurance policy (*assicurazione sulla salute*) which pays the portion of medical bills that isn't paid by social security. When choosing an insurer, you should avoid a company that reserves the right to cancel (*recesso* or *facoltà di rescessione*) a policy unilaterally when you have a serious illness or when you reach a certain age (shown as *età massima assicurabile* in policies), as it will prove difficult or impossible to find alternative cover. You should also steer clear of a one-year contract, which a company can refuse to renew. Nowadays, policies often have a period (e.g. five years) during which the insurance company cannot exclude you from cover (*rinuncia al diritto di recessione*), even if you have a serious illness costing the insurance company a lot of money.

When taking out a policy, you must usually choose a maximum limit (*massimale*) on claims, unless it's already fixed. Ensure that it isn't too low and that it includes all members of your family. Obviously, the higher your cover the higher your premiums. Companies usually have a 'nuclear' family policy (*polizza per nucleo familiare*) offering substantial discounts.

> Most policies include optional cover for loss of earnings (*polizza di indennità giornaliera*) if you're unable to work for a period after an illness or accident, which is worth considering, particularly if you're self-employed.

When comparing policies, check the extent of cover and exactly what's included and excluded from a policy (this is often indicated only in the **very** small print), in addition to premiums and excess charges. In some countries, premium increases are limited by law, although this may apply only to residents of the country where the company is registered and not to overseas policyholders. Although there may be significant differences in premiums, generally you get what you pay for and can tailor your premiums to your requirements. If you're in good health and able to pay for your own out-patient treatment, such as visits to your family doctor and prescriptions, the best value policy may be one covering only specialist and hospital treatment. To compare policies, it's best to visit an insurance broker offering policies from a number of companies.

If your stay in Italy is to be short, you may be covered by a reciprocal agreement between your home country and Italy. If you already have private health insurance in another country, you may be able to extend it to include Italy or save a substantial amount by switching to another company without losing any benefits (you may even gain some). If you're planning to change your health insurance company, you should ensure that important benefits aren't lost, e.g. existing medical conditions won't usually be covered by a new insurer.

When changing employers or leaving Italy, you should ensure that you have continuous health insurance. If your family is covered by a company health scheme, your insurance probably ceases after your last official day of employment. When changing health insurance companies, it's wise to inform your old company if you have any outstanding bills for which they're liable.

Italian Companies

Most health policies offered by Italian insurance companies are supplementary policies for Italians who are covered by the national health service, and aren't intended for foreigners who aren't covered and are seeking a comprehensive health policy. Most Italian health insurance policies either don't pay family doctors' fees or pay for medicines other than those provided in a hospital, or have an excess (deductible), e.g. around €100 for each 'illness', which may exceed the cost of treatment. Most, however, pay for 100 per cent of specialists' fees and hospital treatment in the best Italian hospitals. Private policies vary considerably in price but generally cost from €1,250 to €2,500 per year for a family of four, although they're higher for the elderly. Many companies, retirement groups and other organisations offer lower group rates.

The largest insurers in Italy include the National Insurance Institute (Istituto Nazionale delle Assicurazioni/INA), formerly state owned but now privatised, Europa Assistance, Filo Diretto, Pronto Assistance and Sanicard. Shop around and compare policies, which vary considerably. Also bear in mind that (as in many countries) Italian insurance companies are reluctant to pay claims. (One of the reasons they don't insist on a medical examination is so that they can refuse to pay a claim because you omitted to tell them you had a heavy cold three years previously.) When completing the questionnaire (*questionario sanitario*), be sure to list **all** previous illnesses, hospitalisation, current ailments and treatment.

Foreign Companies

You can also take out health insurance with a foreign company such as AXAPPP (🖳 www.axappphealthcare.co.uk) *and* Bupa International (🖳 www.bupa-intl.com) in the UK and BlueCross BlueShield in the US (🖳 www.bcbs.com). Most companies offer international policies for different regions – not just Italy – for example Europe, worldwide excluding North America, and worldwide including North America. A policy may offer full cover anywhere within Europe and limited cover in North America and certain other high-cost countries (e.g. Japan). An international policy allows you to choose to have non-urgent medical treatment in another country. Most companies offer different levels of cover; for example, AXAPPP International offers Basic, Standard, Comprehensive and Prestige cover.

The cost of international health insurance varies considerably, according to your age and the extent of cover. Premiums can sometimes be paid monthly, quarterly or annually (credit card payment is usually accepted), although some companies insist on payment annually in advance. Annual premiums vary from around €3,000 to well over €20,000 for the most comprehensive cover.

Shop around and compare premiums – which can vary considerably for the same level of cover – before buying international health insurance,

HOUSEHOLD INSURANCE

There's no requirement in Italy to have insurance for your home or belongings and many Italians don't bother to insure either, although if you have a mortgage (*ipoteca*), your lender will require you to have building (*edificio*) insurance. Nevertheless, it's highly recommended to take out insurance covering damage to the building due to fire, water, explosion, storm, freezing, snow, theft, vandalism and natural catastrophes. Household insurance (*assicurazione sulla casa*) generally constitutes a multi-risk policy for building and contents, although some companies issue separate policies for fire and theft (*assicurazione contro furto e fuoco*) and for liability (*assicurazione contro terzi*) and others offer fire and damage (*incendio ed altri danni ai beni*) with an extra premium for theft and liability. Special conditions apply to holiday homes.

It's possible (and legal) to take out building and contents insurance in another country for a property in Italy, although the policy may still be written under Italian law (so always check). The advantage is that you have a policy you can understand and you're able

to handle claims in your own language (you may also be more likely to be paid or be paid earlier). This may seem like a good option for a holiday home in Italy, although it may be more expensive than insuring with an Italian company and can lead to conflicts if the building is insured with an Italian company and the contents with a foreign company.

Buildings Insurance

It's particularly important to have insurance against storm damage in Italy, which can be severe in some areas. Read the small print and check that you're covered for natural disasters such as floods. However, if you live in an area that's hit by a succession of natural disasters, your insurance may be cancelled. Note also the following:

♦ Water damage caused by burst pipes due to old age or freezing may be excluded; under Italian law you're required to turn off the water at the mains if a property is left empty for more than 24 hours (although almost nobody does).

♦ If you use bottled gas, you must inform your insurance company, as there's an extra premium to pay.

♦ You must also specifically insure electrical systems and major apparatus against risk such as lightning strikes, or an insurance company won't pay.

- Italian policies usually exclude trees in your garden damaging your house and garden walls falling down.

- You cannot insure against earthquakes on an Italian policy, although a foreign insurance provider (e.g. Lloyd's of London) may offer cover for an exorbitant premium. If there's an earthquake, the Italian government assumes responsibility, which is limited to the value stated in the land registry (usually well below a property's actual value), although the insured value of your home is also taken into consideration.

In the event of total loss, building insurance is based on the cost of rebuilding your home. Make sure that you insure your property for the true cost of rebuilding. If you have a property restored or modernised, you must obtain a professional valuation on completion for insurance purposes.

Apartments

If you own an apartment or a property that shares elements with other properties (e.g. entrance hall, stairs, lift), building insurance is included in your service charges, although you should check exactly what's covered. You must, however, still be insured for third party risks in the event that you cause damage to neighbouring apartments, e.g. through flood or fire. Having insurance also helps you claim against a neighbour if they cause damage to your apartment.

Rented Property

Your landlord usually insists that you have third party liability insurance, as detailed in the rental contract. A lease requires you to insure against 'tenant's risks', including damage you may make to the rental property and to other properties if you live in an apartment, e.g. due to flood, fire or explosion. You can choose your own insurance company.

Contents Insurance

Contents (*contenuto*) are usually insured for the same risks as a building (see above) and are insured for their replacement value. Contents policies are restrictive with regard to security, including locks, window shutters or grilles (all windows less than 3m/10ft from the ground must be barred), armoured doors, etc. All security requirements must be adhered to or claims are reduced or won't be paid. Note that Italian

policies usually exclude loss of frozen food (after a power cut). There's invariably an excess of between €125 and €350 for each claim.

You cannot usually insure valuables (e.g. antiques, jewellery and other precious objects) unless they've been valued by an approved Italian expert, and they generally need to be stored in a safe, which must be approved by your insurance company. You should insist on a safe being approved by your insurer and a certificate being issued to verify this (otherwise your insurance company is liable to use the argument that your safe was insecure to avoid paying a claim). Valuables are usually covered only when you're present, rather than abroad or on holiday. Due to the many loopholes, you may be better off keeping your valuables in a bank safety deposit box.

> ### ☑ SURVIVAL TIP
>
> When making a claim for contents, you should produce the original bills (keep bills for expensive items) and bear in mind that imported items may be much more expensive in Italy.

Holiday Homes

Premiums are generally higher for holiday homes due to their high vulnerability (particularly to burglaries) and are usually based on the number of days per year a property is inhabited and the interval between periods of occupancy. Cover for theft, storm, flood and malicious damage may be suspended when a property is left empty for more than three weeks at a time. It's possible to negotiate cover for periods of absence for a hefty surcharge, although valuable items are usually excluded. If you're absent from your property for long periods, e.g. more than 60 days per year, you may also be required to pay an excess on a claim arising from an occurrence that takes place during your absence (and theft may be excluded). You should read all small print in policies. Where applicable, it's important to ensure that a policy specifies a holiday home and not a principal home. There are companies which specialise in offering insurance for holiday homes in the UK and abroad, including Italy, such as Schofields (💻 www.schofields.ltd.uk).

In areas with a high risk of theft (e.g. most major cities and resort areas), you may be required to fit extra locks and other security measures. Some companies may not insure holiday homes in high-risk areas. It's unwise to leave valuable or irreplaceable items in a holiday home or a home that's vacant for long periods. Some insurance companies do their utmost to find a loophole which makes you negligent and relieves them of their liability. Always check carefully that the details listed in a policy are correct, or your policy could be void.

Premiums

Premiums are usually calculated according to the size of a property (either the habitable area in square metres or the number of rooms) rather than its value. Usually the sum insured (house and contents) is unlimited, provided the property doesn't exceed a certain size and is under a certain age. Premiums depend on the area, although you should expect the premium for a policy that includes theft to be around double what you'd expect to pay in most other Western European countries. The cost of multi-risk property insurance in a low-risk area is around €100 per year for a property with one or two bedrooms, €175 for three or four bedrooms and around €375 per year for five or six bedrooms. Premiums can be much higher in high-risk areas. If you have an index-linked policy, cover is increased each year in line with inflation.

Claims

If you wish to make a claim, you must usually inform your insurance company in writing (by registered letter) within two to five days of an incident or 24 hours in the case of theft. Thefts should also be reported to the local police within 24 hours, as the police statement (*denuncia*), of which you receive a copy for your insurance company, usually constitutes irrefutable evidence of your claim. Check whether you're covered for damage or thefts that occur while you're away from the property and are therefore unable to inform your insurance company immediately.

THIRD-PARTY LIABILITY INSURANCE

Many people have third party liability insurance (*assicurazione contro terzi*) in Italy. This covers all members of a family and includes damage done or caused by your children and pets – for example, if your dog or child bites someone – although where damage is due to severe negligence, benefits may be reduced. Check whether insurance covers you against accidental damage to your home's fixtures and fittings. Third-party liability insurance can be combined with household insurance (see above).

HOLIDAY & TRAVEL INSURANCE

Holiday and travel insurance (*assicurazione sul viaggio*) is recommended for all who don't wish

Verona, Veneto

to risk having a holiday or business trip ruined by unforeseen problems. As you probably know, anything can and often does go wrong with a holiday, sometimes before you even get started (particularly when you **don't** have insurance). The following information applies equally to residents and non-residents, whether you're travelling to or from Italy or within Italy.

Travel insurance is available from many sources, including travel agents, insurance companies and brokers, banks, motoring organisations and transport companies (airline, rail and bus). Package holiday companies and tour operators also offer insurance policies, some of which are compulsory, but these are often overpriced and don't provide adequate cover. You can also buy 24-hour accident and flight insurance at major airports, although it's expensive and doesn't offer the best cover.

Before taking out travel insurance, you should carefully consider the range and level of cover you require and compare policies. Policies may include cover for holiday cancellation or interruption, missed flights, departure delay at both the start and end of a holiday (a common occurrence), delayed, lost or damaged baggage, lost belongings and money, medical expenses and accidents (including evacuation home), personal liability and legal expenses, and default or bankruptcy, e.g. a tour operator or airline going bust.

Always check any exclusion clauses in contracts by obtaining a copy of the full policy document, as all relevant information won't be included in an insurance leaflet. High-risk sports and pursuits should be specifically covered, i.e. listed, in a policy (there's usually an additional premium). Winter sports policies are available and more expensive than normal holiday insurance ('dangerous' sports are excluded from most standard policies, as is riding rented scooters and mopeds). Third-party liability cover should be at least €3m in North America and €1.5m in the rest of the world.

Health Cover

Medical expenses are an important aspect of travel insurance and you shouldn't rely on insurance provided by reciprocal health arrangements, charge and credit card companies, household policies or private medical insurance (unless it's an international policy), none of which usually provides adequate cover, although you should take advantage of what they offer. The minimum medical insurance recommended by experts is €500,000 for Italy and the rest of Europe and €1.5m for the rest of the world (many policies have limits of between €2.25m and €7.5m).

> If applicable, check whether pregnancy-related claims are covered and whether there are any restrictions for those over a certain age, e.g. 70, as travel insurance is becoming increasingly expensive for those aged over 65, although they don't usually need to worry about pregnancy – particularly the men!

European Health Insurance Card (EHIC)

The EHIC allows European Economic Area (see page 13) residents to access state-funded healthcare in Italy and all EEA countries at a reduced cost or sometimes even free of charge. Applications for an EHIC are free and it's valid for up to five years. If you're resident in an EEA country, you can apply for an EHIC and should carry it with you when travelling in Europe – but don't forget to check that it remains valid. Britons planning to visit Italy can obtain information about reciprocal health treatment abroad from the EHIC Information Service (☎ 0845-606 2030, 🖳 www.ehic.org.uk).

Note, however, that not every hospital or practitioner recognises the EHIC (either deliberately or due to ignorance) – even when they're obliged to – and you may need to pay for treatment and try to obtain a refund later. To be on the safe side, it's advisable to purchase private health or travel insurance.

Portofino, Liguria

14.
FINANCE

The Beatles might have had Italy in mind when they wrote their song *Taxman*. It's one of the most highly taxed countries in the EU (it's also estimated to have the highest number of tax dodgers, including many of Italy's most famous names) and there seems to be a tax stamp (*bollo*) for everything. To make matters worse, Italian tax law is inordinately complicated (it has been simplified in recent years, although you wouldn't believe it) and the taxes, regulations and procedures are constantly changing; just when you think you understand them, they change everything and hit you with new taxes. It's important to check all tax information, including the information contained in this book, with an accountant or tax office (get it in writing) in order to establish that it's correct.

If you plan to live permanently in Italy, you must ensure that your income is and will remain sufficient to live on, bearing in mind exchange rate fluctuations (if your income isn't paid in euros), rises in the cost of living and unforeseen expenses, such as medical bills or anything else that may reduce your income (such as stock market crashes and recessions!). Foreigners, particularly retirees, often underestimate the cost of living in Italy (see page 211) and some are forced to return to their home countries after a few years. However, the cost of living in Italy is still lower than in many other European Union (EU) countries, inflation was only around 1.4 per cent in early 2010, and for many the quality of life/cost of living ratio is unsurpassed.

If you're planning to invest in property or a business in Italy that's financed with money earned or held in a currency other than euros, it's important to consider both present and possible future exchange rates (don't be too optimistic!). If you wish to borrow money to buy property or for a business venture in Italy, you should carefully consider where and in what currency it should be raised. It's difficult for foreigners to obtain business loans in Italy, particularly for new ventures, and you shouldn't rely on it. On the other hand, if you earn your income in euros, this may affect your financial commitments abroad, particularly if the currency is devalued. List all your probable and possible expenses, and do your homework thoroughly **before** moving to Italy – afterwards, it may be too late!

When you arrive in Italy to take up residence or employment, ensure that you have sufficient cash, travellers' cheques, credit cards, luncheon vouchers, coffee machine tokens, gold coins, diamonds, etc. to last at least until your first pay day, which may be some time after your arrival. During this period you'll also find an international credit card (or two) useful.

Italy hasn't traditionally been a credit economy and Italians have preferred to use cash rather than credit cards or even cheques. However, the use of plastic money (credit, charge, debit and cash cards) has become increasingly popular in recent years, although it's still less common than in many other EU countries.

COST OF LIVING

No doubt you would like to estimate how far your euros will stretch and how much money (if any) you'll have left after paying your bills. Inflation in Italy in August 2010 was around

1.4 per cent and the country has enjoyed a relatively stable and strong economy in recent years. Salaries are generally reasonable and Italy has a high standard of living, although the combined burden of social security, income tax and indirect taxes make Italian taxes among the highest in the EU.

Anyone planning to live in Italy, particularly retirees, should take care not to underestimate the cost of living, which has increased considerably in the last decade. Italy is one of the most expensive countries in the EU and very expensive by US standards, although there's a huge difference between the cost and standard of living in the prosperous north and central regions of Italy and the relatively poor south (and between major cities and rural areas). Luxury and quality products are expensive, as are cars, but wine and spirits are inexpensive. Food costs almost twice as much in Italy as it does in the US, but is similar overall to most other western European countries, although you may need to modify your diet. However, you should be wary of cost of living comparisons with other countries, as these are often wildly inaccurate and usually include irrelevant items that distort the results.

In the Mercer 2010 Cost of Living Survey (🖳 www.mercer.com/costofliving) of 214 cities worldwide, Milan was ranked 15th and Rome 26th. Luanda (Angola), Tokyo, Ndjamena (Chad) had the dubious honour of holding the top three places. The most expensive European cities were Moscow (4th), Geneva (5th), Zurich (8th), Copenhagen (10th), Oslo (11th), London and Paris (both 17th). Other expensive European cities included Berne (22nd), Vienna (28th), St Petersburg (30th) Helsinki (31st), Amsterdam (35th), Athens (40th), Dublin (42nd), Istanbul (44th), Barcelona (49th), Frankfurt (50th), Madrid (52nd) and Lisbon (72nd). Selected other rankings included Hong Kong (8th), Sydney (24th), Shanghai (25th), New York (27th – the only US city in the top 50), Melbourne (33rd), Brisbane and Los Angeles (55th), Perth (60th), White Plains (83rd), Chicago (91st), San Francisco (93rd), Miami (100th), Auckland (149th) and Wellington (163rd).

The fundamental flaw with most cost of living surveys is that they convert local prices into $US, which means that any ranking changes are as much (or more) the result of currency fluctuations as of price inflation. Therefore in the last few years, the Eurozone, Australia, Switzerland and Japan, with their harder currencies, have become more expensive in dollar terms, while the UK (e.g. London) and the USA have become cheaper.

It's also possible to compare the cost of living between various cities, using websites such as the Economist Intelligence Unit (🖳 http://eiu.enumerate.com/asp/wcol_wcolhome.asp), for which a fee is payable. There are numerous websites which give you an idea of costs in Italy (e.g. 🖳 www.expatarrivals.com/italy/cost-of-living-in-italy and www.numbeo.com/cost-of-living/country_result.jsp?country=Italy), however, you need to take the information with a pinch of salt as it may not be up to date.

It's difficult to estimate an average cost of living in Italy as it depends very much on where you live and your lifestyle. If you live in Milan, drive a BMW and dine in expensive restaurants, your cost of living will be much higher than if you live in a rural area, drive a small Italian car and eat mostly at home. You can live relatively inexpensively by buying local produce whenever possible and avoiding expensive imported goods, which are more expensive, not only because of the distance they have to travel, but also because they're considered fashionable.

However, even in the most expensive cities, the cost of living needn't be astronomical. If you shop wisely, compare prices and services before buying, and don't live too extravagantly, you may be pleasantly surprised at how little you can live on.

FISCAL CODE

All residents of Italy need a fiscal code (*codice fiscale*), which Italians receive at birth. This is required to apply for a job, open a bank account, register a car, buy or rent a home, and even to pay utility bills. Italians obtain a fiscal code from their local tax office (*intendenza di finanza*), whereas foreigners go to a Sportelli Unici per l'Immigrazione/SUI (immigration desk, which can be found in every city administration) or to a police station (*questura*), where you must present your passport and a copy of the pages containing your particulars.

Codes for individuals comprise letters and figures (figures only for companies). The code is made up of the first, third and fourth consonants of your surname (or fewer if there aren't four), the year and month of your birth (the months being represented by the letters A to L), and your day of birth (1 to 31 for men, 41 to 71 for women). So, for example, if your name is Joe Bloggs and you were born on 1st January 1950, your fiscal code would be BGGS1950A1. Husbands and wives have separate codes, as a wife in Italy retains and uses her maiden name after she is married. But if you do change your name, you must let the tax authorities know.

You will be given a card showing your code and your country of birth (or a *comune* number if you were born in Italy). Your fiscal code must be used on all official correspondence with the tax authorities and on tax declarations. It's useful to keep a note of your code with you at all times, as you never know when you may be required to provide it. If you lose your fiscal code card, you need to contact you local tax office to obtain a replacement, and should also inform them when you move home (you retain the same fiscal code).

ITALIAN CURRENCY

On 1st January 1999 the euro (€) was introduced in Italy (along with Austria, Belgium, Finland, France, Germany, Ireland, Luxembourg, the Netherlands, Portugal and Spain) and is now the official currency. Euro notes and coins were introduced on 1st January 2002, although the lira continued to circulate until 1st July 2002, when it was withdrawn. Although prices are no longer discussed in lire (€1 = 1,936.27lire), you'll hear the idiomatic expression *non c'ho una lira* (I don't have a penny).

The euro is divided into 100 cents (*centesimi*) and coins are minted in 1, 2, 5, 10, 20 and 50 cents, and 1 and 2 euro denominations. Coins all have a common European face with a map of the European Union (EU) and the stars of the European flag, while the obverse is different for each member country. Italian coins have the following designs: the Castel del Monte (1 cent), Turin's Mole Antonelliana tower (2 cents), the Colloseum (5 cents), Botticelli's 'Birth of Venus' (10 cents), a Boccioni sculpture (20 cents), the statue of Marcus Aurelius (50 cents), Leonardo da Vinci's Vitruvian Man (€1) and Dante by Raphael (€2). Coins are minted by individual countries, although they can be used throughout the euro zone irrespective of where they were made.

Euro banknotes are printed in 5, 10, 20, 50, 100, 200 and 500 denominations and are identical in all countries. The design of the notes was subject to considerable debate and contention, and the winning design depicts 'symbolic' representations of Europe's architectural heritage. None of the 'representations' on any of the notes are supposed to show actual buildings, bridges or arches, although there have been numerous claims in the press and elsewhere that the structures shown are actually landmarks in certain countries.

☑ **SURVIVAL TIP**

If you plan to send a large amount of money to Italy or abroad for a business transaction or to buy property, you should ensure that you receive the commercial rate of exchange rather than the tourist rate.

IMPORTING & EXPORTING MONEY

There are no exchange controls in Italy and no restrictions on the import or export of funds. An Italian resident is permitted to open a bank account in any country and to export unlimited funds. You may import or export up to €12,500 in any combination of foreign currency, Italian currency, travellers' cheques and securities without formality. Amounts over €12,500 (e.g. to buy a home) must be declared to the Exchange Controls Office (Ufficio Italiano dei Cambi) in order to prevent money laundering (and provide statistical data for the Banca d'Italia).

When transferring or sending money to (or from) Italy you should be aware of the alternatives and shop around for the best deal. One of the safest and quickest methods of transferring money is to make a direct transfer or a telex or electronic transfer (e.g. via the SWIFT system in Europe) between banks. A SWIFT telex transfer **should** be completed in a few hours, funds being available within 24 hours. The cost of transfers varies considerably, not only in commission and exchange rates, but also in transfer charges (such as the telex charge for a SWIFT transfer).

Always check charges and exchange rates in advance and agree them with your bank (you may be able to negotiate a lower charge or a better exchange rate). Shop around a number of banks and compare fees. Some foreign banks levy a flat fee for electronic transfers, irrespective of the amount. British banks charge between £10 and £45 (though somewhat less via online banking) for 'express' electronic transfers taking from one to five days. When you have money transferred to a bank in Italy, make sure that you give the IBAN number in full (you'll find it on your bank statement), otherwise, money can be 'lost' while being transferred to or from an Italian bank account and it can take weeks to locate it.

If you're transferring large sums of sterling, dollars or another non-euro currency to Italy, e.g. to buy a house, it may be cheaper to use a specialist foreign exchange (FX) currency dealer to make the transfer. Dealers such as Moneycorp (🖥 www.moneycorp.com) and Currencies Direct (🖥 www.currenciesdirect.com) buy euros on your behalf and arrange the transfer. They claim to save you money by buying currency at the best rate and not charging for transfers, but you must open an account with them to use their services (which delays the process). **You should also compare their rates with your bank, as in some cases the bank may be cheaper.**

Most banks in major cities have foreign exchange windows and there are banks or exchange bureaux (ufficio di cambio) with extended opening hours at airports, major railway stations and in all main cities. Here you can buy or sell foreign currencies, buy and cash travellers' cheques, and obtain a cash advance on credit and charge cards. There are many private exchange bureaux in major cities and resorts with longer business hours than banks, particularly at weekends. Most offer competitive exchange rates and low or no commission (but always check). They're easier to deal with than banks and, if you're changing a lot of money, you can usually negotiate a better exchange rate.

The exchange rate (tasso di cambio) against the euro for most major international currencies is listed in banks and daily newspapers. Exchange rates are usually better when obtaining cash with a credit or debit card, as you're given the wholesale rate, although there's a 1.5 to 3 per cent charge on cash advances and ATM transactions in foreign currencies.

☑ **SURVIVAL TIP**

One thing to bear in mind when travelling anywhere is not to rely on only one source of funds.

BANKS

There are three kinds of bank in Italy: commercial or credit banks (banchi commerciale), co-operative banks (banchi popolari cooperative) and co-operative credit banks (banche di credito cooperativo). As in other countries, co-operative banks were established to provide loans (particularly home loans) to their customers. Co-operative credit banks are savings banks funded and owned by farmers and craftsmen. They comprise the largest number of banks (over 500) in Italy, but because their average size is very small they account for just a tiny percentage of total deposits. The Banca d'Italia is owned by the public sector banks and is the only bank permitted to issue notes in Italy.

There are some 900 banks (*banche*), around 200 of which are large (*grandi*), including around 50 branches of foreign banks (mostly in Rome and Milan). The remaining 700 or so are primarily local banks with few branches. The number of banks in Italy is continually decreasing as banks merge with or are taken over by others. For example, in early 2007, two of Italy's medium-size banks – Banca Intesa and Sanpaolo – merged to become Intesa Sanpaolo, which is now the largest bank in Italy.

The Banca Nazionale del Lavoro, Cassa di Risparmio, Banca Commerciale Italiana, Banca di Roma, Banco di Napoli and Banco di Sicilia are among the best-know Italian banks (all have nationwide branch networks). The post office also has a nationwide network and serves as a savings bank for many Italians and foreign residents, although non-residents may find it difficult to open a post office account.

Italy has traditionally had one of the least efficient and most ponderous banking services in Europe, where even the simplest operation was inordinately complicated and time-consuming. However, banking has become highly automated in recent years, although Italian banks still lag behind those in many other European countries in terms of efficiency, customer service and the range and quality of services provided.

On the other hand, Italians banks are quite safe and most deposits are covered by a Bank Deposit Insurance Fund (*Fondo Interbancario di Tutela dei Depositi*). Branches of EU banks operating in Italy can join the fund and increase the amount of financial protection they offer clients above the protection provided by their home country's guarantee plan. If a bank from a non-EU country is licensed to operate in Italy, the Italian branch must be part of the deposit insurance system unless they're members of an equivalent foreign plan. The maximum amount reimbursed to each depositor is limited to the very precise figure of €103,291.38.

Opening Hours

Bank opening hours vary according to the bank and town but are generally from 8 or 8.30am until 1 or 1.30pm and for one to one and a half hours in the afternoon, e.g. from 2.30 or 3pm until 4 or 4.30pm, Mondays to Fridays. Some branches in major cities also open from 9am to noon on Saturdays. On the day before a public holiday, banks usually open only in the morning. Offices at major airports and railway stations have longer opening hours for changing money and cashing travellers' cheques, and there are also exchange bureaux in major cities and resorts with extended opening hours.

Charges

Italian banks have traditionally levied some of the highest charges in the world, although they've been reduced in recent years. The interest rates charged by many Italian banks are still exorbitant, particularly for business and consumer loans. The interest rates levied

on credit cards are also excessive. However, lenders are now required to publish the highest rates they charge and the market average, so that borrowers can make comparisons. Shop around and compare rates before signing any contracts or taking out a loan (banks must also publish their conditions).

Opening an Account

You can open a bank account in Italy whether you're a resident or non-resident, although some banks may not be keen to allow non-residents to open a current account. Foreigners have the option of opening a non-resident account (*conto estero*) for imported euros and foreign currency only.

Non-residents

Only foreign currency or imported euros can be paid into a non-resident account, which pays higher interest than resident accounts. There's no withholding tax on interest earned on deposits in non-resident accounts, as there is for resident euro accounts (when withholding tax is deducted at source). If you're a non-resident, it's possible to survive without an Italian account by using cash, travellers' cheques and credit cards, although this isn't wise and is an expensive option. If you have a second home in Italy, you can have all documentation (e.g. cheque books and statements) sent to an address abroad. Some Italian banks also provide written communications in English.

Residents

You're considered to be a resident of Italy (*residenti valutari*) if you have your main centre of interest there, i.e. you live or work there more or less permanently. To open a resident's account you must usually have a residence permit (*certificato di residenza*) or evidence that you have a job in Italy.

Withholding tax is deducted at source on interest earned on deposits in resident accounts.

Procedure

It's best to open an Italian bank account in person, rather than from abroad. Ask friends, neighbours or colleagues for their recommendations and go to the bank of your choice and introduce yourself. You must be at least 18 and provide proof of identity, e.g. a passport, and your address in Italy (a utility bill usually suffices). Before choosing a bank, it's wise to compare the fees charged for international money transfers and other services, which can be high.

If you wish to open an account with an Italian bank while abroad, you must obtain an application form from a branch of an Italian bank (either in Italy or your home country). You need to select a branch from the list provided, which should be close to your home or place of business in Italy. If you open an account by correspondence, you must provide a reference from your bank, including a certificate of signature or a signature witnessed by a solicitor or lawyer. You also need a photocopy of the relevant pages of your passport and a euro draft to open the account.

It isn't recommended to close your bank accounts abroad even when you're living permanently in Italy, unless you're absolutely certain that you won't need them in the future. It's cheaper to keep some money in local currency in an account in a country that you visit regularly than to pay commission to convert euros. Many foreigners living in Italy maintain at least two accounts: a foreign account (possibly offshore) for international transactions and a local account with an Italian bank for day-to-day business.

Current Accounts

The normal bank account for day-to-day transactions in Italy is a cheque or current account (*conto corrente/interno*). Non-EU residents usually need Italian residence and a fiscal code (see page 213) to open a current account. Couples can open a joint account (*conto corrente cointestato*) and some banks have accounts for children, pensioners, students and women. Always shop around and compare fees and benefits before opening an account. When opening a cheque account, you should request a debit card, which can be used to pay for goods and pay bills and withdraw money at ATMs throughout Italy. You must usually collect your cheque book (*libretto di assegni*) and debit card from your branch, around two to three weeks after opening an account.

Interest is paid on cheque accounts quarterly, although it may be as little as 0.5 per cent. Many banks offer accounts where the balance above a sum of your choice (e.g. €2,500) is automatically invested in mutual funds. Most banks issue cheque books free of charge, but there's a fee for each cheque you write. Bank charges vary according to factors such as the number of cheques you write, the average balance maintained and whether you're a resident (charges are usually higher for non-residents) and may be negotiable, but each entry on your bank statement usually costs you about €1.50, although most banks allow you 100 free operations per year (and withdrawals by debit card from one of your bank's ATMs are generally free).

Writing Cheques

Cheques (*assegni*) may be crossed (*sbarrato*) or open (*non-sbarrato*). Cheques require endorsement on the back before they can be paid into an account. Note that open cheques are freely negotiable and even crossed cheques can be endorsed to a third party (up to €10,350), although you can write 'not transferable' (*non trasferibile*) on the back of a cheque to prevent it from being endorsed by anyone other than the payee. Cheque guarantee cards (*carte di garanzia*) are available in Italy, but few people accept personal cheques even with a guarantee card and you're unlikely to be able to use your cheque book with businesses outside your local area unless you deal with them regularly.

To obtain cash at a bank counter, you must complete a form or write a cheque made out to yourself (*me medesimo*, usually written as *m.m.*, or *me stesso*), which can usually be done only at your own branch. All cheques must be written in Italian and in blue or black ink. When writing the amount in words, don't use capitals and or leave spaces between words. When writing figures in Italy (or anywhere in continental Europe), you should cross the down stroke of the number 7 in order to avoid confusion with the number 1, which is often written with a leading upstroke and resembles a seven to many non-Europeans (and Britons). Like other Europeans, Italians write the date with the day first followed by the month and year; for example, 1.9.10 is 1st September 2010 and not 9th January 2010. The conventional US form 1/9/10, with the month first and slashes

between the digits, is unknown and must never be used!

Most banks now have tellers who can cash cheques, thus eliminating the previous two-step operation where you presented the cheque/form at one counter and were given a receipt to take to a cash desk (*cassa*) to obtain your money.

It's illegal to bounce cheques (*assegno a vuoto*) in Italy, for which you can be banned from holding a bank account and prosecuted. You should also take care not to become overdrawn, which can be expensive (overdrafts may be possible for a hefty interest rate). Post-dating cheques is also against the law, and all cheques can be presented for payment on the day they're written, irrespective of their date. The time taken to 'clear' cheques (after which the funds are credited to your account and start earning interest) varies from two days for a cheque drawn on the same bank to a week or longer for a cheque drawn on a different bank. You can stop payment of a cheque only when it has been lost or stolen (not simply because you've changed your mind), when a report must be made to the local police.

Statements & Bill-paying

Bank statements (*estratto conto*) are issued monthly or quarterly (you can usually choose) and contain your account details such as your bank, branch and account number at the top. This information is required when payments are to be made directly to or from your account, e.g. by standing order (*ordine di pagamento*) or direct debit (*domiciliazione*). Regular bills (such as utility bills) can be paid by direct debit and most banks make these payments without charge. Bills can also be paid in cash at banks by completing a payment slip (*richiesta di bonifico*).

If you're a non-resident, it's advisable to keep an emergency amount on deposit for unexpected (or unexpectedly high) bills.

MORTGAGES

Mortgages or home loans (*mutuo ipotecario* or simply *mutuo*) are available from all major Italian banks and many foreign banks. Mortgages from Italian banks can take some time to be approved (although approval is now much quicker than it used to be) and you may be able to obtain better terms and a larger loan from a foreign lender. Italian mortgages are repaid using the capital and interest method (repayment); endowment and pension-linked mortgages aren't offered.

Interest Rates

Italian loans can have a fixed or variable interest rate (*tasso*). The fixed rate (*tasso fisso*) is higher than the variable rate (*tasso variabile*)

to reflect the increased risk to the lender, but the advantage of a fixed rate is that you know exactly how much you must pay over the whole term.

Interest rates in Italy are similar to those throughout the Eurozone, where the interest rate was 1 per cent in June 2010 (for the thirteenth consecutive month), with most mortgage rates around 1 to 2 per cent higher. However, Italian lenders' margins and fees are among the highest in Europe (mortgages may also contain restrictive clauses). Among the first banks to offer low-rate home loans in Italy was the UK's Barclays, followed by the Banco Popolare di Milano (BPM) and Rolo. Loans are also now available from telephone mortgage lenders such as Banca Manager, who offer a fast response and lower fees than most traditional banks. When looking for a mortgage, shop around for the best deal. It may be worth asking a bank in your home country, or if you're resident in Italy, using a mortgage search engine such as Mutui Online (💻 www.mutuionline.it)

Those seeking a first mortgage are usually offered the best deals. Many lenders offer low-start mortgages (*tasso/rata d'ingresso*), which are at a fixed rate for two or three years, after which they may change to a variable rate. Some banks offer lower interest rates to attract buyers in certain areas. You can have a clause in your mortgage whereby you aren't required to accept an increase of over 10 per cent in your payments or more than the cost of living index (i.e. inflation). Any additional amount owed is added to your loan or the loan period is extended. It's possible to assume the mortgage (*accollo del mutuo*) of a vendor.

Limits & Conditions

Until the mid-'90s, Italian banks rarely lent more than 50 per cent of the value of a property, but the maximum loan has now risen to 80 per cent for buyers of a principal home (*mutuo prima casa*). It may be possible to obtain an even larger (e.g. 90 per cent) mortgage for a property requiring restoration (*mutuo per ristrutturazione*) The maximum loan for a second home is generally around 50 or 60 per cent (see **Second Homes** below).

Most banks don't have a maximum limit for mortgages, though mortgage repayments are generally limited to a maximum of around 30 per cent of your net income, but some have minimum limits of between €50,000 and €100,000. Some foreign lenders apply stricter rules than Italian lenders regarding income, employment and the type of property on which they lend, although some are willing to lend more than an Italian lender. Shop around for the best deal but bear in mind that it isn't wise to over-stretch your finances when taking out a mortgage. If you default on your mortgage repayments, your property can be repossessed and sold at auction, although most lenders are willing to negotiate and arrange lower repayments if borrowers get into financial difficulties.

Loans are usually repaid over a shorter period (*durata*) in Italy (e.g. 10 or 15 years) than in countries such as the UK and US, but some Italian banks now offer mortgages for up to 30 years.

If you're buying a new property off plan and therefore making payments in stages, a bank will provide a 'staggered' mortgage, where the loan is advanced in instalments as required by the contract. During the period before completion, interest is payable on a monthly basis on the amount advanced by the bank (plus life insurance). When the final payment has been made and the loan is fully drawn, the mortgage enters its normal amortisation period (*periodo di ammortamento/durata del mutuo*). Some lenders impose a similar arrangement on payments for restoration mortgages, so check the situation before taking out finance on an attractive old wreck.

It's possible to obtain a mortgage guarantee from most lenders, valid for two to four months, during which period you're guaranteed a mortgage for a specified sum, subject to an acceptable property valuation. The deposit paid when signing the preliminary contract (*compromesso di vendita*) is automatically protected under Italian law should you fail to obtain a mortgage.

It isn't usual to have a survey in Italy, where an Italian lender may value a property or simply accept the fiscal value, although foreign lenders usually insist on a valuation before they grant a loan – expect to pay between €200 and €450 for this. It's customary in Italy for a property to be held as security for a loan taken out on it, i.e. the lender takes a first charge on the property.

Mortgage Fees

There are various fees (*spese istruttoria*) associated with mortgages. All lenders charge an arrangement fee for establishing a loan, usually around 1 per cent of the loan amount. There's also a registration tax of 2 per cent of the mortgage value, and most lenders also impose an 'administration' fee of around 1 per cent. A fee is payable to the notary (*notaio*) for registering the charge (mortgage) against a property.

Applications

To obtain a mortgage from an Italian bank, you must provide proof of your monthly income and all outgoings, such as existing mortgage payments, rent and other loans or commitments. Proof of income usually includes three months' pay slips for employees, confirmation of income from your employer, and tax returns. If you're self-employed, you require an audited copy of your balance sheets and trading accounts for the past three years, plus your last tax return. If you want an Italian mortgage to buy a property for commercial purposes, you must provide a detailed business plan (in Italian).

Foreign-currency Mortgages

It's possible to obtain a foreign currency mortgage (i.e. not in euros). However, you should be wary of taking out a foreign currency mortgage, as interest rate gains can be wiped out overnight by exchange rate swings and devaluations. If you have a foreign currency mortgage, you must usually pay commission charges each time you make a transfer to pay your mortgage or remit money to Italy. However, some lenders transfer mortgage payments to Italy each month free of charge or for a nominal fee.

It's generally recognised that you should take out a loan in the currency in which you're paid or in the currency of the country where a home is situated. In this case, if the foreign currency is devalued, you have the consolation of knowing that the value of your Italian property will have increased by the same percentage, when converted back into the foreign currency. When choosing between a euro loan and a foreign-currency loan, be sure to take into account all charges, fees, interest rates and possible currency fluctuations.

However you finance the purchase of a home in Italy, you should obtain professional advice from your bank manager and accountant.

VALUE ADDED TAX

Value added tax (VAT or the 'voracious administration tax') is called *imposta sul valore aggiunto* (*IVA*) in Italy. Most prices of goods and services are quoted inclusive of VAT, but sometimes they're given exclusive of tax, e.g. for office supplies and business equipment. There are a number of exempt goods and services, including exported goods, services supplied outside the country, ships and aircraft, interest, shares and bonds, postal and medical services, and businesses. Non-profit organisations are also exempt from VAT. The following rates of VAT apply to other goods and services:

If you're in business or self-employed, you usually need a VAT number (*partita IVA*) and must charge VAT on all your services and goods. You must maintain accounts in officially stamped books (*registri*), which are used to calculate the tax payable. Where applicable, you must apply for a VAT number from your local VAT office (*ufficio IVA*) within 30 days of starting business. The VAT number of companies is also used as their fiscal code (see page 213).

Businesses with a turnover of over €309,874 (services) or €516,457 (goods) must pay their VAT monthly, while others can choose to pay quarterly. VAT due on a monthly basis must be paid by the 18th of each month. If you pay quarterly, VAT is payable by the fifth day of the second month after the end of the fiscal quarter, e.g. VAT for the first quarter, ending 31st March, is due by 5th May. You must pay interest at 0.5 per cent on the amount payable in the fourth quarter. An annual VAT declaration must be completed by 15th March of the following year. Even if you have no income, you should file an annual return in order to prevent suspicion of fraud and to keep your VAT number active (if you don't file, it could be cancelled).

There are huge fines and even prison sentences for avoiding VAT.

VAT Rates		
Rate	**Percentage**	**Applicable To**
Reduced	4%	Consumer goods; basic foodstuffs; newspapers, magazines and books; property (excluding luxury homes); meals in company restaurants, schools and canteens; home care assistants for the sick; equipment for the disabled
Intermediate	10%	Non-basic and non-luxury foodstuffs and drinks; hotel bills; cinema tickets; ornamental plants; tickets for urban public transport (except air, rail and boat travel); satellite and cable TV
Standard	20%	Luxury food and drink; clothing, fabric and textiles; raw materials and semi-finished building products; recorded music and films; petrol and other fuels; telephones and telephone bills; electrical appliances; cars, motorcycles and boats; cigarettes; leather and fur; gold jewellery; perfume, cosmetics and soaps

INCOME TAX

Italy has a pay-as-you-earn (PAYE) system of income tax (*imposta sul reddito delle persone fisiche/IRPEF*), whereby employees' tax is withheld at source by employers. The tax year is the same as the calendar year and income is taxed in the year in which the payment or advantage is received. Each person is taxed individually and, although a married couple may file a joint tax return, they're taxed separately.

Italian income tax has traditionally been among the highest in the EU and, although the rates have been reduced in recent years, it's still above the EU average. On the other hand, tax allowances are more generous than in some other countries (see **Allowances** on page 223). If you're able to choose the country where you're taxed, you should obtain advice from an international tax expert. Moving to Italy (or another country) often offers opportunities for 'favourable tax planning'.

To make the most of your situation, it's recommended to obtain professional income tax advice before moving to Italy, as there are usually a number of things you can do in advance to reduce your tax liability, both in Italy and abroad. For example, you may be able to avoid paying tax on a business abroad if you establish both residence and domicile in Italy before you sell. On the other hand, if you sell a foreign home after establishing your principal residence in Italy, it becomes a second home and you may then be liable for capital gains tax abroad. Be sure to consult a tax adviser who's familiar with both the Italian tax system and that of your present country of residence. You should inform the tax authorities in your former country of residence that you're going to live permanently in Italy.

Tax evasion (*l'evasione fiscale*) is rife in Italy, where avoiding taxes is a more popular 'sport' than soccer. The worst offenders are businesses and the self-employed, and it's common knowledge that tax inspectors accept bribes to 'turn a blind eye' to tax evasion. The tax authorities may estimate your taxable income based on your perceived wealth. All taxpayers must list (on a one-page *riccometro* form) their possessions and liabilities, such as homes, cars, boats and motorbikes, whether they employ household help, whether their spouse works, and whether they have dependent family members. This information is used to determine your financial situation and whether you're entitled to certain social services. Therefore, if you're a millionaire and declare the income of a shop assistant, it would be wise not to live in a *palazzo* and drive a Ferrari!

In recent years, Italy has intensified the fight against tax evasion. In 2008, it posted details of every citizen's income and tax details online for a brief period in a bid to improve transparency. It has also introduced a tax amnesty that allows Italians to return goods and capital with no questions asked. Tax dodgers must, however, pay a fine of 5 per cent of the total value. In 2009, goods and capital brought back to Italy amounted to €95bn, which added €5bn to the state coffers.

Further information about Italian income tax is available from local tax offices in Italy.

Liability

Your liability for Italian income tax depends on where you're domiciled. Your domicile is usually the country you regard as your permanent home and where you live most of the year. A foreigner working in Italy for an Italian company who has taken up residence in Italy and has no income tax liability abroad is considered to have his tax domicile (*domicilio fiscale*) in Italy. A person can be resident in more than one country at any time, but can be domiciled only in one country. Generally, you're considered to be an Italian resident and liable to Italian tax if **any** of the following applies:

- your permanent home (i.e. family or principal residence) is in Italy;

- you spend more than 183 days in Italy during any calendar year. Many countries, e.g. the UK, limit visits by non-residents to 183 days in any one year or an average of 91 days per tax year over a four-year period);

- you carry out paid professional activities or employment in Italy, except when secondary to business activities conducted in another country;

- your centre of vital economic interest, e.g. investments or business, is in Italy;

- If you're registered as a resident (*residenza anagrafica*) in your *comune*, you're automatically liable to income tax in Italy.

The domicile of a married woman isn't necessarily the same as her husband's but is determined using the same criteria as anyone capable of having an independent domicile. Double-taxation treaties (see below) contain rules that determine in which country an individual is domiciled.

If you intend to live permanently in Italy, you should notify the tax authorities in your present country (you'll be asked to complete a form, e.g. a form P85 in the UK). You may be entitled to a tax refund if you depart during the tax year, which usually necessitates the completion of a tax return. The authorities may require proof that you're leaving the country, e.g. evidence of a job in Italy or of having purchased or rented a property there.

If you're in doubt about your tax liability in your home country, contact your nearest embassy or consulate in Italy.

If you move to Italy to take up a job or start a business, you must register with the local tax authorities soon after your arrival. This is done at your local tax office (*intendenza di finanza*).

Double-taxation Treaties

Italian residents are taxed on their worldwide income, subject to certain treaty exceptions. Non-residents are usually taxed only on income arising in Italy. The US is the only country that taxes its non-resident citizens on income earned abroad (American citizens can obtain a copy of a brochure, *Tax Guide for Americans Abroad*, from American consulates). Citizens of most other countries are exempt from paying taxes in their home country when they spend a short period, e.g. a year, abroad. Double-taxation treaties are designed to ensure that income that has already been taxed in one treaty country isn't taxed again in another by establishing a tax credit or exemption on certain kinds of income, either in the country of residence or the country where the income was earned.

Where applicable, a double-taxation treaty prevails over domestic law. Italy has double-taxation treaties with over 60 countries, including all members of the EU, Australia, Canada, China, Cyprus, Iceland, India, Israel, Japan, Malaysia, Malta, Mexico, New Zealand, Norway, Pakistan, the Philippines, RSA, Russia, Singapore, Sri Lanka, Switzerland, Turkey, and the US.

Taxable Income

Taxable income in Italy is officially divided into the following six categories, each of which is defined by law: employment, self-employment, business, property (land and buildings), capital (principally dividends and interest), and 'miscellaneous' income. Residents are taxed on their worldwide income and non-residents on income earned in Italy only.

Income from employment includes bonuses (annual, performance, etc.), stock options, interest-free loans, overseas adjustments, cost of living allowances, a housing, car or education allowance, tax reimbursements, contributions to profit-sharing plans, storage and relocation allowances, language lessons provided for a spouse, personal company car, payments in kind (such as free accommodation or meals), home leave or holidays paid by your employer, children's education, investment income (dividends and interest), unemployment benefit, redundancy pay, pensions, and benefits for cessation of employment (e.g. severance pay) above the minimum required by law. Benefits in kind are valued for tax purposes at their fair market value. Certain social security benefits aren't subject to income tax.

Although the tax rates in Italy are high, your net income tax can be considerably reduced by allowances and credits, as explained below.

Allowances

The following allowances can be made against taxable income.

♦ mandatory social security contributions (see page 198);

♦ contributions of up to €5,164.57 to Italian-qualified pension funds;

♦ reimbursement for travel and accommodation expenses incurred on business trips up to a maximum of €46.48 within Italy and €77.47 abroad per instance;

♦ reimbursement for laundry, parking and telephone costs for work away from home;

♦ reimbursement for food provided by an employer;

♦ reimbursement for remuneration in kind (e.g. transport to and from the workplace provided by an employer);

♦ share purchase plans (under certain conditions);

♦ maintenance payments to a spouse from whom you're legally separated or divorced;

♦ expenses related to property income.

Tax Rates

Italian income tax is levied at the following rates (2010) on taxable income:

Tax Rates	
Taxable Income	**Tax Rate**
Up to €15,000	23%
€15,001 to €28,000	27%
€28,001 to €55,000	38%
€55,001 to €75,000	41%
Over €75,000	43%

In addition to the above state tax, regional tax is payable at between 0.9 and 1.4 per cent, depending on the region, and municipal tax at up to 0.8 per cent.

Credits

A tax credit of up to 19 per cent of the expenses mentioned below can be claimed:

♦ interest on a mortgage on a principal residence (*prima casa*) or land in Italy, provided that the loan is taken out in an EU country, up to a maximum of €4,000;

♦ medical expenses in excess of €129.11 for general medical expenses and €129.11 for specialist medical treatment, for both you and your dependants;

♦ funeral expenses up to a maximum of €1,549.37;

♦ tuition expenses at private universities up to the equivalent cost of attendance at a state establishment;

♦ premiums for life insurance and health insurance, up to a total of €1,291.14;

♦ veterinary expenses exceeding €129.11 up to €387.34;

♦ contributions to non-profit entities up to €2,065.83.

Tax Returns

The tax year in Italy is the same as the calendar year. If you're a resident, you must file an income tax return (*dichiarazione dei redditi*) unless **any** of the following applies:

♦ you have no income;

♦ your income is exempt from tax, e.g. a war, old age or invalidity pension;

♦ you've already paid tax at source on income, e.g. dividends, bank interest, mortgage interest;

♦ you're an employee and are taxed on a PAYE basis and have no other income.

Non-residents with income arising in Italy must also file a tax return. The tax system is based on self-assessment and the tax office won't send you a tax return or chase you to complete one. Tax returns are available free of charge from local councils (*municipio*), can be purchased from a tobacconist or stationer, or can be downloaded from the Inland Revenue's website (🖥 www.agenziaentrate. it). Declarations can be made from abroad by registered post. Many people can obtain free income tax assistance at a Centro Assistenza Fiscale (CAF), including pensioners, part-time workers, and certain categories of self-employed people, the disabled and people in receipt of unemployment benefit. See also **Using a Commercialista** on page 225.

You must file a different tax return depending on whether you're employed or self-employed.

Employees

The tax return for most taxpayers is the *modello 730*, which covers the following categories of people: employees, pensioners, members of co-operatives, anyone with a fixed-term contract (*tempo determinato*) which extends through the months of March to June, and members of the clergy and elected government officials who have received compensation payments. Those with additional income from land and property, dividends earned from corporations and income derived

from on-going work also use the 730. Income subject to taxes other than income tax, such as capital income, income from occasional autonomous work, inherited income received on a long-term basis, life insurance and accident policy pay-outs if policies are redeemed before five years, non-taxable *TFR* (redundancy payments), and taxes and fees that have been used as deductions (and reimbursed) in the previous year, can also be declared on form 730.

A married couple may file a joint tax return (both must sign) but are taxed separately, although payment is joint. The disadvantage of filing a joint return is that although the assessment may be raised against only one of a couple, there's a common responsibility for payment. A couple can use form 730 if their income is earned solely from land and/or property and the total amount is less than €2,840.51. Otherwise, they must use the *Unico* form (see **Self-employed** below).

Self-employed

If you're self-employed (e.g. an artisan, merchant or artist) or a professional with a VAT number, you must file a *Unico* form. This is a multifunctional, colour-coded (light blue, orange, green and dark blue) form, the various coloured sections denoting the type of tax. The basic *Unico* form has four pages, but there are 14 other pages comprising a total of 44 sections. No additional documentation such as expense receipts or medical expenses need be attached.

Filing

Modello 730 returns for the previous year must be filed between 1st May and 30th June. If you've completed your own form, you may hand it in at a bank or post office and no longer need to file it at the local *comune* or send it to a service centre (*intendenza di finanza*). However, forms completed by accountants using computer systems must be handed in or sent to a service centre – these are listed in the *Yellow Pages*. *Unico* forms should be presented between 1st June and 31st July at a bank, post office or Centro Assistenza Fiscale (CAF) office (a kind of citizens' advice bureau for tax matters, listed in telephone books and on the CAF website (🖥 www.

caaf-cia.it); it shouldn't be taken or sent to a service centre office. Late filing within 30 days of the due date is subject to a penalty of 15 per cent of the tax due; after 30 days penalties range from 120 to 245 per cent of the tax due! You should keep copies of tax returns and receipts for six years.

Payments

Advance tax payments must be made equal to 98 per cent of the tax paid for the previous year or the amount due for the current year (whichever is less). Some 40 per cent of advance tax payments (called an *acconto*) must be made by 31st May and the remaining 60 per cent by 30th November. If you've earned less than your advance payment, you can claim a refund, although tax rebates can take years to be paid. Income tax can be paid in two six-monthly instalments, or in seven instalments (provided you don't pay VAT), in which case annual interest of 6 per cent is payable. Payment is due on the last day of each instalment period or (for those who pay VAT) on the 15th of the month. A portion of the total interest due (where applicable) must accompany each instalment. If you choose to pay in instalments, it must be noted on your income tax return.

Late payments attract surcharges which increase considerably the later you pay; if you're two months late this could add as much as 30 per cent to your tax bill.

Using a Commercialista

Because of the complexity of the Italian tax system, it's wise to use a *commercialista* (a combination of accountant and lawyer) to prepare your tax return, particularly if you're self-employed (obligatory unless you have a doctorate in Italian bureaucracy!). A *commercialista*'s fees are fairly low, although you should obtain a quotation, and he can also advise you on what allowances you can and cannot claim.

PROPERTY TAXES

Property tax (*imposta comunale sugli immobili/ICI* – pronounced, not inappropriately, 'itchy') is paid by everyone who owns property or land in Italy, whether resident or non-resident. It's levied at between 0.4 and 0.7 per cent of a property's fiscal value (*valore catastale*), the rate being decided by the local municipality according to a property's size, location, age, condition and official category (*categoria*), as shown in the property deeds (*rogito*). Categories are decided by the land registry (*catasto*) according to the type of property (*abitazione di tipo*) as follows:

Property Taxes	
Category	Property Type
A/1	*Signorile* (refined)
A/2	*Civile* (civilian)
A/3	*Economico* (economical)
A/4	*Popolare* (working class)
A/5	*Ultrapopolare* ('ultra-working class')
A/6	*Rurale* (rural)
A/7	*Villini* (small detached)
A/8	*Ville* (detached)
A/9	*Castelli, palazzi di eminenti pregi artistici o storici* (castle or building of eminent historic or artistic importance)
A/10	*Uffici e studi privati* (private offices and studios)
A/11	*Alloggi tipici dei luoghi* (typical housing of the region)

In fact, a property's category has a relatively small influence on the amount of tax payable. If a property is unfit for habitation, the tax is reduced by 50 per cent.

Property tax is usually paid in two instalments: 90 per cent by 30th June and the remaining 10 per cent between 1st and 20th December (for uninhabitable properties, the figures are 45 per cent and 5 per cent respectively). If it isn't paid on time, you can be fined in the form of a surcharge or additional tax (*sopratassa*) of up to 200 per cent of the amount due. The form for paying tax is complicated and many people (particularly foreigners) employ a *commercialista* (see above) or agent to do it for them. You can also pay property tax from abroad using registered post, addressing payment to the tax office of your *comune*. Payments must be up-to-date when a property is sold and you should check this before buying.

Other property-related taxes include communal services (*servizio riscossione tributi ruoli*) for owners of condominiums and other community properties, refuse tax (*tassa comunale dei rifiuti*) and water charges (see page 86). Property owners also pay income tax on their property, which is based on its cadastral value.

CAPITAL GAINS TAX

Capital gains tax (*imposta comunale sull'incremento di valore degli immobili/ INVIM*) was technically abolished in 2002, but if you sell a property within five years of purchase and make a gain as a result, that gain may be subject to income tax. The capital gain is the difference between the purchase and sale prices declared in the deeds of sale (*rogito*), less expenses for renovation, improvements, repairs, etc., and is based on the increase in the cadastral value (*rendita catastale*) of a property, not the increase in its market value. It isn't wise to under-declare the value (too much), or the authorities may arbitrarily assess a new sale price (although you can appeal against this).

The main points to be aware of regarding capital gains tax (CGT) are as follows:

♦ No CGT is due on gains from the sale of property provided you've owned it for more than five years.

♦ If you sell within five years you pay CGT at 20 per cent, unless you can prove it was your primary residence (*prima casa*) for more than half that time in which case there's no tax to pay.

♦ CGT on gains from stocks and shares is levied at 12.5 per cent for individuals and 27.5 per cent for companies.

♦ Individuals pay 11 per cent on gains from a pension fund.

Calculating CGT is complicated and it's recommended to employ a *commercialista* (see page 225) to assess the sum payable. Where applicable, CGT is deducted from the amount payable to the vendor by the notary (*notaio*) handling the sale.

INHERITANCE & GIFT TAX

Inheritance and Gift Tax (*Imposta sulle Successioni e Donazioni*) is one of Italy's more perplexing taxes and has undergone frequent changes in the last ten years. In 2007, it was re-introduced, following a tax break in 2001 which aimed to halt the export of capital from Italy. The new tax rates are much lower than those applied before 2001, and compare favourably with the rates applied in other western countries. The main points are as follows:

♦ The deceased or donor's spouse, children or parents each have a tax-free allowance of €1m. Any legacy or gift they receive in excess of this is taxed at a rate of 4 per cent.

♦ The allowance for siblings is €100,000 and the tax rate is 6 per cent.

♦ Other relatives and receive no allowance pay 6 per cent on the full amount.

♦ Unrelated beneficiaries pay 8 per cent on the full amount.

Where the estate includes immovable property, e.g. land or buildings, additional taxes (*Imposte Ipotecarie e Catastali*) are also payable on the transfer of title, usually at the rate of 3 per cent. These percentages are based on the official land registry value (*rendita catastale rivalutata*) which

is usually much lower than the current market value, and if the person inheriting the property then uses it as his primary residence, the taxes are reduced to a flat fee of €336.

The current rates and allowances mean that the average property is exempt from Italian inheritance tax on the owner's death. For example, if a husband and wife jointly own a property valued at less than €2m, and inherit each other's share on the death of either party, no inheritance tax is payable. If the surviving spouse then leaves the same property to two children in equal shares, again no inheritance tax would be due.

The same rules apply to both Italians and foreigners. If the deceased was resident in Italy at the time of his death, it applies to his worldwide estate, including property in other countries. If he was not resident in Italy at the time of his death, it only applies to his Italian assets.

> An Italian inheritance tax return should be lodged with the tax authorities within one year of the death of the deceased, in order to avoid incurring interest and penalties.

WILLS

It's an unfortunate fact of life that you're unable to take your hard-earned assets with you when you take your final bow (or come back and reclaim them in a later life!). All adults should make a will (*testamento*) irrespective of how large or small their assets. The disposal of your estate depends on your country of domicile (see **Liability** on page 221). As a general rule, Italian law permits a foreigner who **isn't** domiciled in Italy to make a will in any language and under the law of any country, provided it's valid under the law of that country. However, if there's any conflict of law, the law of the country where the testator was a citizen at the time of his death applies.

Note, however, that 'immovable' property in Italy, i.e. land and buildings, **must** be disposed of in accordance with Italian law. Italian law gives the immediate family, i.e. spouse, children and parents (called the *legittima*) an absolute right to inherit a share of immovable property and it isn't possible to disinherit them. Therefore, it's important to establish where you're domiciled under Italian law. All other belongings in Italy or elsewhere (defined as 'movables') may be disposed of in accordance with the law of your home country or domicile, although this must be stipulated in your will. One solution for a non-resident wishing to avoid Italian inheritance laws may be to buy a home through a company, in which case the shares of the company are 'movable' assets and are therefore governed by the succession laws of the owner's country of domicile.

A will must be in writing (but not necessarily in the hand of the testator). There are three types of Italian will.

Holographic Will

The only requirements of a holographic will (*testamento olografo*) are that it must be written entirely in your own handwriting and signed and dated by you. This is a popular and common type of will in Italy because of its simplicity (no witnesses are required) and the fact that it's free. For anyone with a modest Italian estate, e.g. a small property in Italy, a holographic will is sufficient. However, legally it's the worst type of will you can have, as it can easily 'disappear' or be forged.

Public Will

A public will (*testamento pubblico*) is the safest type of will. It's prepared and recorded by a notary (*notaio*) and becomes part of his public records. It must be witnessed by two people (of any nationality), who must sign it in the presence of the notary, who also signs. Two copies are made, one for the testator and one for the notary. The notary may also write or oversee the writing of a public will.

Secret Will

A secret will (*testamento segreto*) is written by the testator or a third person and handed to a notary in a sealed envelope. The testator declares the authenticity of the sealed will in the presence of the notary and two witnesses, none of whom actually sees the will. Secret wills are rare in Italy.

Italian inheritance law is a complicated subject and it's important to obtain professional legal advice when writing or altering your will(s).

Venice carnival

15.
LEISURE

Italy is one of the most beautiful countries in Europe, possibly the most attractive of all, with more than its fair share of ravishing landscapes and stunning historic towns. It's a country of huge variety, offering something for everyone: magnificent beaches for sun-worshippers, beautiful unspoiled countryside for nature lovers, a wealth of magnificent ancient cities and towns for history enthusiasts (virtually every town is a history book of battles and religious milestones), an abundance of mountains and seas for outdoor sportspeople, vibrant nightlife for the jet set, fine wines for oenophiles and superb cuisine for gourmets, a profusion of culture, art and serious music for art lovers, fabulous designer goods for shopaholics, and tranquillity for the stressed.

Italy is a fascinating mix of modernity and deep-rooted traditions. Few other countries in the world offer such an exhilarating mixture of culture, history, tradition, sophistication and style – all of which can be enjoyed in fine weather for much of the year, particularly in the south. Italians live *la dolce vita* to the full and love to celebrate and throw elaborate parties. Wherever you go in Italy, you'll be attracted by the Italian lifestyle – the very essence of relaxation – as well as by some of the world's finest food and wine.

Not surprisingly, tourism is big business in Italy, which was ranked fourth (in 2009) in the world in revenue from foreign tourism, with receipts of US\$40.2bn (compared with US\$94.2bn in the US, US\$53.2bn in Spain and US\$48.7bn in France). People from all walks of life have been drawn to Italy for centuries, ever since the Romans founded one of the world's greatest civilisations, and the country has been part of the essential 'grand tour' for generations. Rome (the 'eternal city'), Florence and Venice are among the world's most visited cities. However, although tourism contributes much to the country's economy, it's also responsible (along with pollution and poor management) for the decline of some of Italy's most priceless treasures. Draconian measures

to combat excessive tourism and to save Italy's attractions are continually being proposed, particularly since the year 2000, when the capital was close to collapse. (One Italian politician even proposed that a 'No Vacancies' sign be posted at Italy's border!)

However, out of the high season even the most popular destinations aren't crowded and there's plenty to explore elsewhere. The scenery is constantly varying, with charming villages and towns set in magnificent landscapes dotted with olives and vines, hundreds of tiny coves glistening in pristine waters or sheltering picturesque fishing ports, sandy beaches, and ancient hill towns where time appears to have stood still for centuries. Italy is a treasure trove of art, which is displayed in monasteries, churches, palaces (works of art themselves) and countless museums, whose collections have been bequeathed by the region's richly varied inhabitants, from the Etruscans and Romans to the great Renaissance artists. Tuscany alone has more classified cultural monuments than most countries and each region retains relics of an artistic tradition widely acknowledged as the world's richest. There are spectacular cathedrals and churches throughout the country, including St Peter's in the Vatican and

Il Duomo in Milan, a lasting testimony to Italy's rich architectural heritage.

Rome, known for centuries as the 'capital of the world' (*caput mundi*), is one of Europe's most visited cities and its inhabitants maintain a frantic, modern pace of life amid ancient monuments. Tuscany and its gently rolling hills are home to Florence, the birthplace of the Renaissance and a mecca for culture- and art-lovers for centuries. In Veneto is Venice, floating on water and flooded by tourists keen to explore its romantic waterways and sumptuous palaces. Verona, of *Romeo and Juliet* fame, and Padua with its unique frescos are also found in the north, along with Milan, Italy's industrial and design centre, an intensely modern city that provides a fascinating contrast with more traditional cities further south.

Turin, home to the Fiat empire, is another industrial, cosmopolitan city in the north, while nearby Piedmont and the Valle D'Aosta are a winter wonderland with a number of fashionable ski resorts. The Italian Riviera is lined with chic resorts, every bit as glamorous as their French counterparts, while Capri in the south has a unique charm and beauty, and is one of Italy's most romantic spots. Sicily, the largest island in the Mediterranean, is a land of timeless beauty and world-famous monuments that are testimony to the many races who conquered and inhabited the island through the ages.

This chapter provides an overview of the various leisure activities available in Italy. General tourist information is available in numerous Italian and foreign guidebooks.

The Michelin *Green Guide to Italy* contains a wealth of information about each region, its history, architecture and art, while the *Michelin Escapade Pocket Guides* concentrate on individual cities, including itineraries, maps and colour photos. The annually updated *Michelin Red Guide* is the most comprehensive hotel and restaurant guide available, and is priceless for both residents and visitors. It contains all the latest information, including prices, opening times, facilities (including those for children and the handicapped) and town plans.

Good general English-language guides include the *Baedeker Guide to Italy*, *Fodor's Italy*, *Frommer's Italy*, *Lonely Planet's Italy* and *The Rough Guide to Italy* (see **Appendix B** for a comprehensive list).

There are also numerous local publications that provide information about local and national events such as *RomaC'è*, *Time Out*, *Wanted in Rome* and *Where Rome* in Rome, and *Firenze Spettacolo* and *Vista* in Florence and Tuscany. In Rome and Milan, the newspaper *La Repubblica* publishes the *TrovaRoma* and *TrovaMilano* weekly entertainment supplements, and all newspapers provide cinema, theatre and concert listings.

TOURIST OFFICES

The Italian National Tourist Board, Ente Nazionale Italiano di Turismo/ENIT, Via Marghera, 2-6, 00185 Rome (☎ 06-49711, 🖥 www.enit.it), is responsible for planning and promoting tourism. ENIT maintains 23 offices in 11 European countries and ten more in eight countries outside Europe, as well as offices at Italy's major border posts and airports. The national travel agency, Sestante-Compagnia Italiana di Turismo, known as CIT or Citalia outside Italy, has offices throughout the world and provides extensive information on travelling in Italy, including hotel and train bookings.

Regional Tourist Offices (Ente Provinciale per il Turismo/EPT or Azienda di Promozione Turistica/APT) are located in around 20 provincial capitals and provide information about

the local region and towns. In most large towns and cities there are the useful and approachable Informazioni e Assistenza ai Turisti (IAT) or Azienda Autonoma di Soggiorno e Turismo (AAST), which provide information about the local area, including maps, public transport and the opening times of local attractions. In smaller towns look for Ufficio Turistico or Pro Loco offices. In major tourist cities there's also a useful tourist office for students, Centro Turistico Studentesco (CTS), which provides a free accommodation-finding service and information about student discounts. Airports and main railway stations usually have a tourist information office and some main cities have street tourist guides during high season. Most tourist offices answer telephone or written requests for information.

The quality and quantity of tourist information dispensed by tourist offices varies considerably, as do office opening hours. Offices in main towns are usually open from around 8.30am to 7pm, while smaller offices close for lunch from about 12.30 or 1pm to 3pm. Most offices open from Mondays to Fridays and in major cities and resorts offices also open at weekends during summer. Many offices provide an accommodation-finding service, for which there may be a small fee.

National, regional and local tourist authorities publish free brochures and pamphlets in many languages. However, it's recommended to collect information before visiting Italy, as local offices often run out, and local and regional offices don't provide information about places outside their area. Staff at tourist offices in larger towns and main tourist areas speak English.

A wealth of information about Italy is available on the internet; some of the best websites include ⌨ www.italiantourism.com, www.travel.it, www. italianweb.org, http://goitaly.about.com, www. initaly.com and www.travel.org/italy.html. Most cities and regions also have websites dedicated to them such as Rome (⌨ www.inromenow.com and www.romeguide.it), Florence (⌨ www.florence.ala. it and http://en.comune.fi.it) and Venice (⌨ www. doge.it and www.comune.venezia.it).

ACCOMMODATION

There are some 40,000 hotels in Italy, catering for all tastes and budgets, ranging from humble hostels to villas and converted medieval palaces. If you want to rub shoulders with real Italians, start at the bottom end of the accommodation chain rather than the top. The 20 regional boards in the country classify hotels and other accommodation in Italy using stars (one to five) or classes, as described below

Hotels

Hotels are classed according to their facilities rather than their quality, therefore accommodation within the same category can vary considerably; there are also differences in criteria from one region to another. Sometimes a hotel may have a lower rating than it deserves simply because the local tourist office hasn't upgraded it yet or it has chosen to remain in a lower category to avoid paying higher taxes (a popular Italian tactic). Hotels can legally increase their charges twice per year, although many don't, and room rates must be displayed on the inside of the door in each room. Before you accept a room, it's wise to view it so that you know exactly what you get for your money.

There are various Italian chain hotels, with prices usually at the upper end of the scale, as well as the usual large international hotels such as Intercontinental and Hilton. Chains include

Hotel Classifications	
Class	**Description**
1*/4th class (*pensione*)	Basic facilities; no ensuite bathroom or toilet
2*/3rd class (*pensione*)	Slightly better facilities; usually ensuite bathroom or toilet
3*/2nd class (*pensione*)	As above but with more facilities, such as a telephone and TV
4*/1st class (*albergo*)	Excellent facilities, e.g. room service and laundry
5*/deluxe (*albergo*)	Top-quality facilities

Ciga, among the oldest in Italy with a turn-of-the-century opulence; Relais et Châteaux, which operates historic hotels usually situated in castles, villas or monasteries with excellent but expensive facilities; Agip, a Forte group partner that operates a chain of mid-range hotels and motels throughout the country; Jolly; and Best Western.

There are also useful 'day hotels' (*albergo diurno*) at railway stations in major cities, open daily between 6am and midnight, where showers, hairdressing, cleaning and laundry facilities are provided.

Rates

A rough guide to room rates is given below:

Hotel Ratings	
Star Rating	**Price Range**
1	€25 to 40
2	€40 to 50
3	€50 to 75
4	€65 to 100
5	€100+

The prices quoted (see box) are for a double room for one night (prices in Italy are usually quoted per room and not per person), inclusive of tax and service charges. As in most countries, single rooms are rare and only marginally cheaper than doubles. A double room (*camera doppia*) usually contains two single beds rather than a double bed; if you want a double bed, ask for a *camera matrimoniale*. Many hotels have 'family' rooms for three or four guests at greatly reduced rates, or provide extra beds for children in a double room at no extra charge. An extra bed for an adult usually costs a minimum of 15 per cent of the double room rate. Some room rates include breakfast (*colazione*), so if you don't want to have breakfast in the hotel you should make this clear when booking. (Breakfast is usually far better value at a local bar or café.)

Rates are fixed in agreement with the provincial tourist board and vary according to the class, season, services available and the locality, hotels in large towns, cities and coastal resorts obviously being the most expensive. Prices in Florence and Venice are particularly high, and you receive worse value there than in most other cities. However, these two cities apart, 'budget' accommodation can usually be found (see below), mostly in the old quarters, close to the main square or churches, although older hotels may not have heating and frequently have problems with electricity and plumbing.

Under Italian law, it's compulsory for a hotel to provide you with a receipt (*ricevuta fiscale*) for final payment when you leave and you should keep this receipt until you return home or leave the country.

Facilities

Room sizes vary considerably. In city centres, even top class hotels may have small rooms. Some hotels provide a small safe for your valuables, although there may be a modest charge for this service. Hotels don't usually have private garages, although some do provide parking – check whether this is covered or not and that a hotel has insurance for parking facilities. Few hotels in Italy, apart from the most expensive, provide air-conditioning, even in the summer.

Booking

April to October is high season in the most popular Italian cities and resorts (December to March in ski resorts), and hotel bookings should be made well in advance, particularly in Florence, Milan, Rome and Venice. Some hotels require a booking deposit (*caparra*) – a booking isn't considered valid until the deposit is received – which should be refunded if a booking is cancelled at least 14 days in advance or 30 days in advance during the high season. In major cities, you may be obliged to book for a minimum of three nights, particularly in July and August.

It's illegal to have unregistered guests in hotels and you're required to produce identification when you register, usually in the form of a passport. While not all hotel proprietors speak English, most are used to dealing with English-speaking clients.

There are numerous online hotel booking services for Italy, including a Hotel in Italy (⌨ www.ahotelinitaly.com) and Italy Traveller (⌨ www.italytraveller.com).

Positano, Amalfi Coast

Further Information

Most guidebooks include a selection of hotels and there are a number of Italian hotel guides. The most comprehensive hotel (and restaurant) guide is the *Michelin Red Guide Italy*. Good alternatives include *Italia Annual Guide: Hotels and Restaurants* (Michelin Guide),and *Rick Steves' Italy* by Rick Steves (Avalon Travel). The *Guida Touring Alberghi e Ristoranti d'Italia* published by the Touring Club Italiano is a much respected guide, as is the Gambero guide, *Tuttiitalia* (Arcigola Editore), which includes restaurants – but you may have to search second-hand bookshops for a copy.

Hotel guides in English include *Alistair Sawday's Special Places to Stay in Italy* by Susan Pennington (Alistair Sawdays), *Karen Brown's Italy Bed & Breakfast* by Clare Brown (Karen Brown's) and *Charming Hotels and Resorts of Italy: The Directory 2011* (Charming Hotels & Resorts). Local councils publish lists of hotels and other accommodation, and most provincial and regional tourist organisations publish hotel guides.

Budget Accommodation

There's a wide variety of budget accommodation in Italy, including hostels (*locande* or *alberghi*), guesthouses (*alloggi* or *affittacamere*), and rooms and lodgings. Most tourist guides include budget accommodation and there are a number of books written especially for those on a tight budget, including *Let's Go Italy: The Student Travel Guide* by Harvard Student Agencies (Avalon Travel). There is budget accommodation included in the *Rough Guide to Italy*.

Hostels & Guesthouses

Hostels and guesthouses aren't included in the accommodation classification system and usually provide basic facilities, although in some areas, such as Isole Eolie and the Alps, the standard of this type of accommodation can be excellent. You can expect to pay between €15 and €30 for shared facilities and dormitory beds in hostels. Food is sometimes provided, although you should be aware that in major resorts, such as Rimini on the Adriatic coast and anywhere on the Italian Riviera, you may be obliged to pay for half or full board.

Youth Hostels: There are some 50 youth hostels in Italy, providing cheap and 'cheerful' accommodation, usually in dormitories, although some more modern hostels also offer private rooms for two to four people. You must usually provide a sleeping bag or sheet, although these can sometimes be hired at hostels, and there are usually kitchen and sometimes even laundry facilities. Most hostels have curfews and daytime lockouts. If children are allowed, they must be accompanied by an adult and the minimum age is usually eight. Security in hostels is often lax, so you should keep your valuables with you at all times.

To stay at a hostel belonging to Hostelling International (HI, 💻 www.hihostels.com) you must be a member. Annual membership is available from HI affiliates abroad or from the Associazione Italiana Alberghi per la Gioventù/ AIG, Via Cavour, 44, 00184 Rome (☎ 06-487 1152), which provides a free fax booking service at its major hostels and food and transport discounts. If you book accommodation at a youth hostel, you should expect to pay a deposit of around 30 per cent of the total price.

Bed & Breakfast

Bed and breakfast (B&B) accommodation in private houses, inns and apartments is also available in Italy, although it isn't as common as in many northern European countries. The *Dolce Casa* website provides a comprehensive list of B&B accommodation with a description of each establishment; room rates range from €15 to €60 per person per night (www.dolcecasa.it). There are many other B&B websites, including www.bed-and-breakfast-in-italy.com, www.bedandbreakfast.com/italy.html and www.bed-breakfast-world.com/italy.html.

Monasteries & Convents

For a more historic experience, you can stay in many Italian monasteries and convents, where, in return for inexpensive accommodation, you're expected to make your own bed and clean up after meals. There's usually a curfew, rooms are single sex and cost between €20 and €30 per night, or slightly less than a one-star hotel. To facilitate entry, a letter of introduction from a priest, vicar or rabbi is recommended, although many institutions accept Catholic guests only. For further information, contact the local tourist office or the provincial archdiocese (*arcivescovado*) or obtain a copy of *Bed & Blessings Italy: A Guide to Convents and Monasteries Available for Overnight Lodging* by Anne and June Walsh (Paulist Press).

Farm Accommodation

'Farm holidays' (*agriturismo*) are also popular, particularly in Adige, Apulia, Trentino-Alto Veneto and Tuscany, where there are over 1,600 farms to choose from. 'Accredited' farmers let converted barns and cottages for a minimum of a week for around €300. Alternatively, and often on a nightly basis, you can rent a room in the farmhouse with full board (usually four-course meals of wholesome farm food) from around €20 to €45 per night. Note, however, that one-night stays may be unavailable in high season, when you may need to book for at least a week.

Some farms also offer facilities such as swimming pools, tennis courts and horse riding.

For more information and a list of properties contact Agriturist, Corso Vittorio Emanuele, 101, 00186 Rome (06-6852 342, www.agriturist.it), which publishes an annual guide, *Guida dell'Ospitalità Rurale, Agriturismo e Vacanze Verdi*, listing farm holiday accommodation facilities by region. Another useful guide is *Guida alle Vacanza in Campagna* published by the Touring Club Italiano. Regional and provincial tourist offices can also provide information about local facilities.

Self-catering

Most areas in Italy, particularly Sicily, Tuscany, Umbria and Veneto, have a wide range of self-catering properties, including apartments, farmhouses and villas. Standards of self-catering accommodation vary considerably, from dilapidated, ill-equipped apartments to luxury villas with every modern convenience. If you fancy somewhere with a touch of historic *ambience*, you can choose a Renaissance villa, a Venetian palace or a medieval castle apartment – just a few of the many historic buildings available for rent. You don't always get what you pay for, however, and some properties bear little resemblance to their descriptions.

Lets are usually on a weekly basis from Saturday to Saturday and you must usually arrive by 5pm on your first day and vacate the property by noon on your day of departure.

Prices vary according to the time of year – in high season, self-catering can be an expensive option. However, a villa can sometimes sleep up to 15 people, which reduces costs for a large party or a number of families. Rates usually include linen, gas and electricity, although heating in winter is usually charged extra. Beware of gas heaters with faulty ventilation ducts, as they're responsible for a number of deaths in self-catering accommodation. Extra beds, cots and high chairs may be provided on request, and televisions can sometimes be rented for a small cost per week.

Most holiday apartments are fairly basic, often with tiny kitchens and bathrooms (perhaps with a shower only), and have a combined lounge/dining room and minimal equipment. If you need special items such as a cot or high chair, you should mention it when booking. Properties are, however, generally well stocked with cooking utensils, crockery and cutlery, although you should check, as you may need to buy a good kitchen knife, a teapot, egg cups, a pepper mill or a filter coffee machine. Most people take a few essential foods and supplies with them and buy fresh food on arrival.

Properties in resort areas usually have a swimming pool, although apartments and townhouses may have a shared pool. Some properties have an indoor heated swimming pool and other facilities such as tennis courts.

Unless a company or property has been highly recommended, it's best to book through a reputable organisation such as a tourist agency. Local and national newspapers advertise properties for rent in their small ads section (*piccola pubblicità – affittasi appartamento*) and tourist offices may be able to provide a list. The Italian Federation of Real Estate Agents, Via Monte Zebio, 30, 00195 Rome (☎ 06-3619 798, 🖳 www.fiaip.it) can provide information, as can the specialist company Cuendet & Cie Spa, Strada di Strove, 17, 53035 Monteriggioni (☎ 05-7757 6330, 🖳 www.cuendet.com). Most companies send catalogues on request. It's essential to book if you want accommodation during July or August or over a holiday weekend, e.g. at Easter. There's usually a 25 per cent deposit, with the balance payable on arrival. Outside the high season, self-catering accommodation can usually be found on the spot by asking in bars and restaurants or by obtaining a list from the local tourist office.

There's also an accommodation option in Italy called a *residence*, half-way between a hotel and a self-catering flat, where kitchen facilities are provided but there's also a restaurant. Information about these can be found in the ENIT annual accommodation lists for each region, available from ENIT offices abroad or from their head office in Rome (see page 230).

Among the numerous self-catering rental agencies in Italy are The Best in Italy (🖳 www. thebestinitaly.com), Best of Sabina (🖳 www. bestofsabina.it), Milligan & Milligan Rentals (🖳 www.italy-rentals.com) and Tuscany Net (🖳 www.tuscany.net).

CAMPING & CARAVANNING

Camping is popular in Italy, where there are over 2,000 campsites throughout the country, although most are only open from April to September. Campsites are graded from one to four stars according to their facilities and comfort, and range from small sites with basic facilities to huge complexes with supermarkets, swimming pools and tennis courts. Sites are usually in scenic locations near mountains or lakes and tend to be quite a distance from major cities. They can be expensive, as rates are calculated per person, per pitch and per vehicle. Average prices range from €6 to €9 per adult, €4 to €6.50 per child under 12 (children under three are admitted free) and around €7 for a pitch. Many campsites accommodate caravans and motor caravans as well as tents.

Some campsites require campers to have an international camping carnet, which can usually be purchased on site or obtained from the Italian Camping and Caravanning Federation, Federazione del Campeggio e del Caravanning/Federcampeggio, PO Box 23, 50041 Calenzano (FI), ☎ 055-882 391, 🖳 www.federcampeggio.it. In summer, when campsites are at their busiest, you should arrive at the site before 11am to ensure a place.

Camping outside campsites is usually prohibited unless you have permission from the landowner. When camping 'wild', you shouldn't light fires or leave litter.

Federcampeggio publishes the *Guida Camping d'Italia* and a free map of campsites offering discounts to holders of an international camping carnet, plus the annual *Guida Touring Campeggi e Villagi Turistici* in association with the Touring Club Italiano (TCI, 🖥 www.touringclub.it).

FESTIVALS

Like all southern Europeans, Italians use any excuse to take a holiday and all cities, towns and villages stage an annual festival (*festa*), often lasting several days. It's well worth planning your visit to a region of Italy to coincide with the vivid and colourful local celebrations, which are usually of religious or historical origin.

Italy's colourful history provides a variety of backdrops for celebrations, of which medieval and Renaissance re-enactions are among the most popular events. You can expect to see pageants, tournaments, crossbow and jousting events, historic battles and legendary family feuds acted out by local townsfolk richly dressed in period costume.

Numerous events date back to medieval and Renaissance times, including the Palio bareback horse races in Sienna (held on 2nd July and 16th August), the 'firing of the cart' in Florence, the Feast of the Redeemer and the historical regatta in Venice, the Sardinian Cavalcade in Sassari, the feast of the almond blossom in Agrigento (Sicily), the Race of the Candles and Palio of the Crossbow in Gubbio (Umbria), and the Regatta of the Four Ancient Maritime Republics (which rotates between Pisa, Venice, Amalfi and Genoa). Other unmissable events include carnival (*carnevale*) in Venice and Verona, Corpus Christi in Spello (Umbria) with its *Le Infiorate* flower festival in June, the football match and magnificent 16th-century costume parade (*Calcio Storico Fiorentino*) in Florence on 24th June, and the Epiphany toy and sweet fair in Rome at Piazza Navona (from Christmas to 5th January).

For a full list of celebrations, contact ENIT (see page 230). Local and regional tourist offices also provide information.

Religious Festivals

Religious festivals are often more serious affairs, especially at Easter, when solemn processions of white-robed, hooded figures and flagellants parade through the streets behind a statue of the local patron saint. There are many flamboyant Easter celebrations, including those at Chieti, Florence and Taranto and in many towns in Sicily. Passion plays – medieval dramas on the themes of the suffering, death and resurrection of Christ – are also popular. One of the most spectacular religious festivals is held at Cocullo (Abruzzo) in May, when a statue of the local patron saint, San Domenico, is carried around the streets draped in live snakes. Festivals honouring patron saints are particularly colourful events and include the Feast of San Nicola in Bari, the Feast of San Gennaro in Naples and the Feast of St Antonio in Padua.

At Christmas, most churches are decorated with cribs or nativity scenes (*presepi*) and Epiphany (*Epifania*), celebrated on 6th January, is an important event, particularly for children, who are 'visited at night by an old woman (*La Befana*) on a broomstick' and left presents or coal – made of sugar and sold in sweet shops – according to whether they've been good or bad.

Pilgrimages are popular, the Vatican being, of course, the most popular

Palio, Siena, Tuscany

destination, particularly during Catholic Jubilee years; while another place of homage, the shrine of the Madonna di Polsi in Aspromonte (Calabria), attracts around a million pilgrims annually.

Arts & Food Festivals

Many towns and cities stage festivals of the performing arts, the most famous being the Spoleto two-week summer festival – a combination of film, theatre, classical music and ballet performed within the walled streets of the town.

Italy stages literally hundreds of food and wine festivals (*sagre*) – local newspapers and tourist offices are good sources of information.

MUSEUMS, GALLERIES & CHURCHES

Bellini, Botticelli, Canaletto, da Vinci, Donatello, Giacometti, Giotto, Michelangelo, Palladio, Raphael, Tintoretto, Titian ... of all the European nations, Italy has made the greatest contribution to painting and sculpture, and the country's fragmented political history has led to a rich regional diversity in the arts. The Italian Renaissance left a magnificent legacy of painting and sculpture that decorates Italian museums, buildings and churches throughout the country (it's said that Italy is home to half the world's great art).

There are some 70 state-owned museums and art galleries in Italy, in addition to countless private collections. Among the many highlights are the Accademia and Collezione Peggy Guggenheim in Venice, the Galleria degli Uffizi and Galleria dell'Accademia (home to Michelangelo's *David*) in Florence, and the Musei Vaticani (the world's largest museum complex, housing one of Italy's most important art collections and incorporating the Sistine Chapel with its unique frescoes by Michelangelo), the Borghese Gallery and the Museo Nazionale di Villa Giulia in Rome. The Borghese Gallery can be visited by just 400 or so people at a time and you must make an appointment.

State-run museums are usually open from Tuesdays to Saturdays from 9am to 1 or 2pm and on Sundays from 9am to 1pm. They usually close on Mondays. Privately owned museums operate much the same hours, but may open briefly in the afternoons as well. Entrance fees usually range from €2 to €5, although costs are considerably higher (e.g. €10 or more) for major exhibitions. Those under 18 and over 60 are allowed free entry, although proof of age (e.g. a passport) must be provided. Information regarding opening times, entrance fees, special events and the location of museums is provided by tourist offices. You can also book tickets to a number of state-run museums and archaeological sites via the internet. Rome's municipality has a useful information service (☎ 06-0608, 🖳 www.060608.it).

Churches

Because so many of Italy's Renaissance artists relied heavily on the Catholic Church for patronage, most Italian churches are 'art galleries' in their own right and you may be amazed to discover the treasures inside even the smallest and most insignificant-looking of churches. Churches are usually open to visitors from around 7 or 8am to noon and reopen from 4 to 7 or 8pm, although in remote rural areas they open only for services and possibly just on Sundays. However, visits are possible at other times by asking at the local tourist or information office. You won't usually need to pay an entrance fee but may be expected to pay your guide if you have one or leave a donation.

When visiting places of worship, you should dress conservatively, i.e. no shorts or bare shoulders, and you shouldn't walk around during services. As most of Italy's churches are hundreds of years old, many are closed for restoration (*chiuso per restauro*) from time to time. If you're making a special trip to a church or historical site, check in advance whether it will be open.

OPERA

Opera is the quintessential Italian art form – it was invented in Italy – and Italy has the world's most demanding fans, who have even been known to boo Pavarotti when he had an off-day! The country provides a rich selection of operas throughout the year and some of the world's best and most famous theatres. These include the Teatro alla Scala (known as La Scala) in Milan, the Teatro San Carlo in Naples and the Teatro dell'Opera in Rome, which are renowned for the technical perfection of their performances and the magnificent detail of their scenery and costumes. Other major opera houses include the Teatro Petruzzelli (Bari), Teatro Comunale (Bologna), Teatro Massimo Bellini (Catania), Teatro Comunale (Florence), Teatro Comunale (Genoa), Teatro Massimo (Palermo), Teatro Regio (Parma), Teatro Comunale Giuseppe Verdi (Trieste), Teatro Regio (Turin) and the Gran Teatro la Fenice in Venice (destroyed by fire in 1996 but since reopened).

> The opera season runs from December to June, but summer performances are held in magnificent open-air locations, which include the Verona Arena (July/August), the Terme di Caracalla in Rome (July/August), the Arena Sferisterio in Macerata (July), and the ancient Greek theatres of Taormina and Syracuse (July/August).

Seats for La Scala cost from €10 to €170 but are difficult to obtain, unless you book months in advance (☎ 02-88791, 💻 www.teatroallascala.org), although for most performances up to 200 standing tickets are sold for €5 about 30 minutes before the performance – people queue for hours in advance of them going on sale.

MUSIC & BALLET

Italians are great lovers of classical and popular music (as well as opera – see above). The country has produced many great classical composers, including Donizetti, Monteverdi (the father of modern opera), Puccini, Rossini, Scarlatti, Verdi and Vivaldi. There are orchestras and chamber music groups in all the major cities, the most famous being Rome's Academy of Saint Cecilia, I Musici, the Scala

Philharmonic Orchestra, the Venice Orchestra and I Solisti Veneti. These orchestras perform regular concerts in their home cities and on tour. Most concerts are held on Saturdays, Sundays and Mondays, tickets costing in the region of €30 to €75.

The Associazione Musicale Romana provides a year-long schedule of festivals and concerts, among the most important of which are the *Maggio Musicale Fiorentino* (May to June) in Florence and the Festival of Two Worlds (*Festival dei Due Mondi*) in Spoleto (mid-June to mid-July). The Gods of Metal (Milan, June), Evolution (Florence, July) and Arezzo Wave (Arezzo, July) are leading rock festivals, while Roccella Jonica Jazz Festival (Calabria, August) is a leading jazz event. For details of these and other musical events, consult the local tourist office; you can buy tickets through the Ticket One website (💻 www.ticketone.it).

Few modern Italian pop singers or groups have made much of an impact outside Italy and the country's biggest claim to pop music fame is probably Mina, who made her mark in the '60s. Nevertheless, the pop music scene is lively and whether your taste be jazz or acid funk, rock or folk, there's sure to be a bar or club playing your sort of music in most cities, often live. Ask at local tourist offices and see local newspapers for details of concerts and venues. The Festival of Italian Song (*Festival della Canzone Italiana*) held in San Remo in January/February is as popular and prestigious in Italy as the Grammy Awards in the US or the Brit Awards for pop music in the UK.

Ballet is also popular in Italy and most major opera houses have ballet seasons, including Italy's main company, the Rome Opera Ballet, which performs at the Teatro dell'Opera. Italy stages a world-renowned International Ballet Festival at Nervi (near Genoa) in July. Prestigious companies and troupes from throughout the world regularly perform in Rome, where there are also open-air performances in summer.

THEATRE

There's a strong tradition of theatre in Italy dating back thousands of years, and theatres offer a wide variety of plays and musicals,

Calcio storico, Florence

film directors, including Bernardo Bertolucci, Federico Fellini, Vittorio Gassman, Sergio Leone and Luchino Visconti, as well as actors and actresses such as Sophia Loren, Gina Lollobrigida and Marcello Mastroianni. For many years, Rome's Cinecittà was the leading film production centre in Europe, producing Italian classics such as Fellini's *La Dolce Vita* along with many international productions. Today, the film studios and Italian cinema in general are facing difficult times, in common with those in most other European countries. However, Italy retains a small film industry that's widely respected throughout the world, with many young and promising directors, such as Roberto Benigni and Leonardo Pieraccioni.

Italians are keen filmgoers and almost every large town and city has several cinemas, many with multi screens. Most foreign-language films are dubbed into Italian and it's difficult to find screenings of foreign films in their original language; in the major cities there's usually at least one cinema showing foreign-language films without subtitles, although the film may be shown on one day per week only (exceptions include the Nuovo Olimpia cinema in Rome and the Astro in Florence, which show English-language films daily). There are regular film shows at foreign cultural centres, where films are shown in their original language. Cinema tickets usually cost around €7, although prices are reduced on Wednesdays.

There's no formal film classification system, but the words *vietato ai minori di 14 anni* ('children under 14 not admitted') indicate that a film has violent or sexually-explicit content.

The Venice Film Festival in August/ September is the world's oldest film festival (established in 1932) and its prestigious prizes are highly rated in the international film world, particularly the Venetian Golden Lion award for best film, which is one of the industry's highest accolades. Tickets, however, are difficult or impossible to come by.

which are performed in Italian unless there's a visiting company from abroad. Italy boasts a vast number of theatres throughout the country, among the most famous of which are the Ponchielli in Cremona, the Carlo Felice in Genoa, La Scala in Milan, Politeama in Palermo, the Teatro dell'Opera in Rome, the Regio Lingotto in Turin and the Fenice in Venice. In summer, the amphitheatre in Verona and the Terme di Caracalla and Coliseum in Rome offer a series of spectacular plays. Local tourist offices and newspapers provide information on theatrical events, as do billboards and town hall notice boards.

CINEMA

Italy has one of the healthiest film industries in Europe and has produced many great

SOCIAL CLUBS

There are several expatriate clubs and organisations in most major cities, catering for all nationalities. In addition to a multitude of social, sports and special interest clubs, there are branches of international clubs in most

towns, including American Women's and Men's Clubs, Anglo-Italian Clubs, Business Clubs, International Men's and Women's Clubs, Lion Clubs and Rotary Clubs. Club listings and announcements are made in English-language and other expatriate publications, and most embassies and consulates in Italy maintain lists.

Most clubs organise a variety of activities such as bridge and whist, sports, appreciation of the arts, outings, dinner dances and other social events. Membership fees vary tremendously and some clubs offer short-term membership. Many clubs provide important information for new arrivals, organise free or inexpensive Italian-language classes and provide foreign newspapers to keep in touch with home.

Joining a club is one of the best ways to meet people and make friends in Italy. Ask at the local tourist office, town hall or library for information.

GAMBLING

Like most people, Italians aren't averse to placing the odd wager, and there are plenty of opportunities (but, alas, little chance) to win millions of euros on the weekly state lottery, which also offers many smaller prizes. The two Italian state lotteries are the Superenalotto (🖳 www.sisal.it/online/superenalotto) and Il Gioco del Lotto (🖳 www.lottomaticaitalia.it/lotto/gioco/gioco_lotto.html). There are also regional lotteries, and you can also check your numbers online at the lottery results website (🖳 www.giornaledellotto.it). Other lotteries and prize draws include *Gratta e Vinci* (scratch and win – or more often lose!) cards, *Totocalcio* and *Totogol* (similar to the British football pools).

Prize money varies from game to game and can sometimes be overwhelming – a huge Superenalotto jackpot in August 2009 attracted 'lottery tourists' from Italy's neighbouring countries, with the €147,807,299.08 prize scooped by one lucky ticket holder in Bagnone, Tuscany – but your chances of winning big money are generally about the same as your chance of being struck by lightning. Don't forget to check your tickets, as each year millions of euros are unclaimed by prize winners. Should you be one of the lucky few, you'll be even happier to know that all winnings are tax-free!

There are also numerous TV shows offering large cash prizes; needless to say, the Italian equivalent of *Who Wants to be a Millionaire?* is among the most popular. There's even a national association of game players (Associazione Nazionale Concorsisti Italiani) with some 200 members, which publishes a newsletter with tips on how to win radio and TV games.

If the lottery and game shows aren't glamorous enough for you, you may wish to visit a casino (*casinò*, which also means 'brothel'!). There are a number in Italy, situated in Campione d'Italia on Lake Lugano, San Remo in Imperia (Liguria), St Vincent in Aosta (Val d'Aosta) and Venice, where the glamorous Palazzo Vendramin Calergi is open all year round, while the Lido Casino provides opportunities to lose your money from June to September only. Both establishments are convenient stops on the Vaporetto ferry, the 'Casino Express'. The San Remo Casino is reminiscent of many turn-of-the-century establishments, with decor to match, while the Casinò de la Vallée in St Vincent is one of the largest in Europe.

Black ties and evening wear are usually obligatory for entry to casinos, as are passports, as Italian nationals are barred unless they're employed there (others must visit France or Switzerland for a flutter). Opening hours tend to be from around 2pm or 3pm to 2am or as late as 4.30am and the entrance fee is around €15.

Although for most people gambling is a bit of harmless fun, Italy has a huge problem with gambling addiction, particularly slot machines, and there are a number of organisations that work tirelessly to repair the damage caused by unbridled speculation.

NIGHTLIFE

Italians are gregarious by nature and their lifestyle revolves almost exclusively around socialising. All towns and cities are constructed around squares (*piazze*), where people meet and congregate, particularly in the evenings. Bars and cafés remain open long into the evening, often into the small hours (see below). Many bars in major cities have live music in the evenings and in recent years many 'pubs' have opened. These are more sophisticated than a typical British or Irish pub – more like a nightclub without the music – and drinks are usually expensive. British and Irish bars have also recently appeared on the scene, particularly in Rome and northern cities.

Discos (*discoteche*) in Italy tend to be enormous establishments on several floors with different kinds of music in different areas. Unfortunately, the prices are usually equally gargantuan. In towns and cities you can expect to pay around €15 for entry, although on special nights in large cities or on the Italian Riviera you can pay up to €100! As a small recompense, your first drink is usually included in the entrance fee, although subsequent drinks may cost between €5 and €20. Most discos are open from around 10.30pm until the small hours, although there are also discos on Saturday and Sunday afternoons for the under 16s.

Nightclubs (*locali notturni*) are generally smaller and less expensive than discos, with entrance occasionally free although you can pay up to €15. The choice of music is more limited in nightclubs and the clientele tends to be older. In the major cities there's also a wide variety of gay and lesbian bars and clubs.

Local newspapers and entertainment magazines are the best source of information on nightlife, particularly in the major cities where the most 'in' places change constantly. Local government departments also publish information about local entertainment.

BARS & CAFES

The foreign custom of 'going out for a drink' isn't particularly popular in Italy, where most people consume alcohol only with meals, although many Italians have a *grappa* or brandy with their morning coffee. Nevertheless, bars and cafés are plentiful in Italy and are an essential part of daily life. In fact, there's an ever-increasing range of bars and 'pubs' springing up throughout the country; in Rome alone, there are many hundreds of watering holes. Most bars are similar in appearance – a pristine chrome bar, bright lights and a photograph (or two) of the local football team on the wall – and serve snacks and ice cream as well as drinks all day (they also admit children).

When you enter a bar, your first decision is whether to stand or sit; once you've chosen, there's no going back! Table (*tavola*) or terrace (*terrazzo*) service is usually twice as expensive as standing – a tariff list (*listino prezzi*) must, by law, be posted behind the bar. If you choose to stand, you must usually order from the cashier (*cassa*), who gives you a receipt (*scontrino*) that you present to the bartender, although in smaller bars you may be able to order first and pay when you leave. If you decide to sit, you must wait to be served. It isn't done to order from the cashier and then sit down; if you do, the waiter will have his suspicions about your nationality confirmed instantly!

Hot Drinks

Coffee (*caffè*) is an institution in Italy and is served in many ways. Among the most common are:

Coffee Culture

- **espresso (*caffè*)**: a small, **very** strong black coffee. Note that this is known as '*un caffè*' and never '*un espresso*'.
- **caffè lungo**: also small and black, but weaker;
- **corretto**: black mixed with a liqueur, usually grappa;
- **macchiato**: black with a spoonful of milk 'foam' on top;
- **caffè latte**: large with lots of milk;
- **cappuccino/ cappuccio**: with cream and chocolate on top, often served lukewarm and drunk only for breakfast or between meals in Italy (only foreigners insist on it being served after dinner!).

A *decaffeinato* or *Hag* usually consists of a sachet of decaffeinated coffee and a cup of warm milk (decaf isn't popular in Italy). Some names for coffee vary from region to region, although none have much in common with the pale imitations dished up in many other countries. An *espresso/caffè* costs around €0.80 and a *cappuccino* around €1.25.

Italians aren't great tea drinkers and, if you ask for tea, you should be prepared to receive a glass of lukewarm water with a teabag beside it. If you want proper tea, ask for boiling water (*molto caldo* or *bollente*) and bring your own teabag! Other hot drinks include chocolate (*cioccolata*), which is thick enough to eat with a spoon.

Beer & Wine

Beer is a popular drink with Italians, particularly among the younger generation, and British- and Irish-style pubs have mushroomed in recent years. Italian beers include Moretti, Frost and Peroni, which are served in bottles containing one-third or two-thirds of a litre and on draught (*alla spina*). Prices average around €2 for a small (*piccola*, 20cl) beer, €3 for a medium (*media*, 40cl) beer and around €3.75 for a large (*grande*, 66cl) beer – although prices depend very much on the establishment and whether you sit or stand, and you can pay up to around €5. Beers from a wide range of other countries are also widely available.

Wine (*vino*) is served by the glass, costing from €2 to €3, although you can pay up to €12 for a glass of vintage wine in a wine bar. For information about Italian wine, see page 269.

Other Drinks

Non-alcoholic drinks include *granita*, an ideal summer drink made with fresh lemon or other fruit juice and crushed ice. Carbonised drinks are also popular throughout Italy, where bars and cafés are obliged (by law) to provide a free glass of tap water for anyone who wants it, irrespective of whether you buy anything else.

Food

Bars usually serve a wide range of snacks, from sandwiches to basic hot meals. Snack bars (*paninoteche*) specialise in made-to-order sandwiches with a vast choice of fillings, which are usually displayed behind the counter. The different types of sandwich available include:

Italian Sandwiches

- **tramezzino**: thin white sandwich bread cut into triangles;
- **panino**: a crusty, French bread stick;
- **schiacciata**: a large, round salted cracker which, when filled, is cut into portions;
- **tost or toast**: a toasted sandwich, which in bars is usually limited to cheese and/or ham.

RESTAURANTS

There are countless restaurants (*ristoranti*) and other eating places in Italy, including the following:

- **tavola calda**: literally 'hot table – a cheap, self-service establishment;
- **osteria**: essentially a wine bar offering a small selection of dishes;
- **rosticceri**: serving mainly cooked meats and a selection of take-away foods;
- **trattoria**: traditionally a family-run establishment, simpler in cuisine and less expensive than a *ristorante* proper, although the two have become interchangeable terms and there's usually little difference between them, except perhaps in price (a *trattoria* usually being cheaper).

Small grocery shops (*alimentari*) also sell sandwiches to take away, while ice-cream (*gelato*) is sold in a *gelateria*, although good home-made (*produzione artigianale*) ice-cream isn't as easy to find as it used to be – a tell-tale sign is a *gelateria* with a queue of Italians outside.

Restaurants rarely open for lunch before 12.30pm and for dinner before 7.30pm (up to an hour later in the south), and they usually close on one day per week, generally a Sunday or Monday.

Many restaurants offer a choice of cheaper set meals. The tourist menu (*menù turistico*) or meal of the day (*menù del giorno*), sometimes called simply the 'fixed price menu' (*menù a presso fisso*), often includes two courses (e.g. pasta and a meat dish), but not drinks, and costs about €15 to €25. The à la carte menu is divided into starters (*antipasto*), usually salads or cold meats; first courses (*primo piatto*) of pasta or rice; main courses (*secondo*), a fish or meat dish accompanied by vegetables (*contorno*); cheese (*formaggio*); and desserts (*dolci* or *frutta* – as one of the options is usually fruit). You aren't obliged to partake of all the courses on offer but you should order at least two, as few restaurants look kindly on diners who limit themselves to a plate of pasta or salad.

If you want water with your meal, tap water (*acqua semplice*) is safe to drink just about everywhere and free. However, you must be sure to specify this, or the waiter may bring you mineral water (*acqua minerale*), which Italians usually drink alongside their wine. Mineral water is available fizzy (*frizzante*) or still (*naturale*).

Italians usually drink wine with a meal. Most drink house wine (*vino della casa*) or a local wine (*vino locale*), which can be ordered by the carafe (*caraffa/vino sfuso*) or in quarter-litre (*quartino*) and half-litre (*mezzo litro*) measures, although even good quality wines are fairly inexpensive in all but the most upmarket restaurants. You should expect to pay around €10 for an average bottle in a restaurant or around double the supermarket price. Note, however, that many restaurants, including most *trattorie*, stock only a limited selection of wines and mostly cheaper varieties.

Before a meal, many Italians like to have a Campari with soda and ice or a home-made fruit cocktail, usually non-alcoholic (*analcolico*). After a meal, as a *digestivo*, liqueurs are popular and include *limoncello*, which is pure alcohol infused with lemons; the herb-based *amaro*, *strega* and *galliano*; the widely popular *grappa*, a strong, clear liqueur made from grape skins (whose bitter taste is certainly an acquired one!); *amaretto* (almond based); *sambuca*

(a sweet liqueur made from aniseed); and *maraschino*, made from the cherries after which it's named.

The bill (*conto*) usually includes a cover charge (*coperto*) of between €1 and €3 per person, which may include bread (*pane e coperto*). There may be an added service (*servizio*) charge of around 10 to 15 per cent. Tipping is often a casual affair, with bills rounded up to the nearest banknote rather than a specific percentage added.

It's unusual for Italians to share restaurant bills, so beware if you suggest going out for a meal with a large group of friends!

Restaurant guides are plentiful in Italy and most bookshops have a section on gastronomy, including excellent guides such the Touring Club Italiano's *Guida Touring Alberghi e Ristoranti d'Italia*, *La Guida d'Italia* (l'Espresso) and Gambero Rosso's *Ristoranti d'Italia*. For English-speakers, the *Michelin Red Guide* to Italy is invaluable, while those on a tight budget may be interested in *Osterie & Locande D'Italia: A Guide to Traditional Places to Eat and Stay in Italy* (Turtleback) (see also **Appendix B**).

Italian Cuisine & Eating Habits

Cooking (and eating) is an art form in Italy – one that stretches back thousands of years. Painted tombs show Etruscans enjoying huge banquets and the Romans were notorious for dining on delicacies such as flamingo tongues, peacock and crane. The modern Italian is no less interested in food, and eating is one of the nation's greatest pleasures. Italian cuisine

(*cucina*) is one of the finest in the world: light and healthy, yet full of flavour. The fact that Italy's status as a unified nation is somewhat recent explains the huge regional differences in cuisine. In the north, many dishes are reminiscent of France – rich and creamy and, surprisingly, often butter-based – while as you move south the dishes become hotter and spicier, and are cooked in olive oil rather than butter. However, most Italian cuisine is based on a few essential ingredients, notably pasta (see page 268).

When most people think of Italian food, they think of pasta dishes such as spaghetti Bolognese, lasagne and tortellini, which originated in Emilia-Romagna. Each region and many towns in Italy have their own pasta specialities, using a multitude of different shapes, sizes and colours. Short, tubular pasta, such as penne or macaroni (*maccheroni* in Italian), is best with rich, thick, meaty sauces, whereas long pasta, such as spaghetti and tagliatelle, is ideal with creamy or light sauces.

In the north of the country, pasta is often replaced by other staples such as *polenta* – a mixture of maize flour and water, which is slowly boiled and then sometimes fried – or rice, which is widely used in dishes such as risotto. Another Italian dish popular throughout the world is pizza, which originated in Naples. The 'basic' pizza, the margherita, which contains tomatoes, mozzarella and basil, is named after a former queen of Italy.

As well as these world-famous dishes, Italy boasts a vast range of regional and local culinary delights, such as cured ham (*prosciutto*) from Parma, Liguria's pesto served with sun-dried tomatoes and *focaccia* bread, Venetian risotto, a rice dish served with seafood or meat, Sienna's famous *panforte*, a rich fruity Christmas cake, Sardinia's spit-roasted piglet, Sicily's delicious desserts such as *cannoli*, *zabaglione*, *granita*, marzipan and *cassata* – a rich sponge-based dessert with ricotta cheese, liqueur and fruit – and, of course, Italian ice-cream (*gelato*), which is reputed to be the best in the world.

Italians are particularly fond of salad, especially green salads, which may include chicory, celery, cress, artichokes, radicchio, rocket and tomatoes. Italy also produces an amazing variety of cheeses, including mozzarella (used in pizzas), parmesan, *gorgonzola*, *pecorino*, *ricotta* and *provolone*. Salami and other pork products are another speciality, including the famous hams of Parma, *mortadella* from Bologna, San Daniele (*prosciutto*) from Friuli and *speck* from Trentino-Alto Adige.

Italian eating habits are similar to those of other southern European countries. Breakfast (*prima colazione*) is continental style: a coffee (maybe a cappuccino) and a pastry, often taken standing in a bar or café. Lunch (*pranzo*), served between 1 and 3pm, is traditionally the main meal of the day and a social occasion, when the world's affairs are discussed and put to rights (Italy's affairs usually take a little longer to fix); as many as four courses may be served. However, as modern living (and the outside world) encroaches ever deeper into the Italian culture, the long lunch tradition is gradually being eroded as more and more businesses work continuous days. Dinner (*cena*) is served from 7 or 8pm onwards and is traditionally a simpler meal than lunch, although it's hardly a snack and usually consists of a cooked meal.

16.
SPORTS

On arrival in Italy it won't take you long to realise the importance of sport in a country where *La Gazzetta dello Sport* (🖳 www.gazzetta.it) is by far the largest-selling daily newspaper. However, when it comes to working up a sweat, you won't see as much evidence of this as you do in many other countries. The Italians' passion for sport is usually confined to watching rather than participating, although Italy has a proud record in international competition in many sports, notably football, basketball, cycling, motor racing, skiing and boxing. For example, you see few joggers on the streets and the general fitness craze that has swept many countries in the last decade or so has, to a large extent, passed Italy by.

Italian schools aren't required to offer sport as part of their curriculum and although some have excellent sports facilities, most don't. However, appearances can be deceptive and there are plenty of opportunities to take part in amateur sport around the country; you may just need to look a bit harder to find them.

Italians tend to be serious about their sport, as they are about anything that involves dressing up and looking their best. If you want to blend in with the crowd, it isn't the 'done' thing to turn up in a pair of old shorts and an ill-fitting T-shirt advertising your favourite beer (or a university you never attended). Whatever their chosen sport, Italians invariably look the part and have the latest and best equipment, plus the most fashionable attire, even if they're beginners or incompetent. Sports equipment is generally reasonably priced in Italy, although fashionable 'designer' sportswear can be expensive. However, if you time your purchases for the low season and during sales, or buy last season's gear, a considerable amount can be saved.

Tourist and information offices can put you in touch with local sports clubs and facilities, but they cannot usually provide comprehensive information. Sports shops (*articoli sportivi*) are usually a good source of information about local sports facilities, and clubs (*associazioni*

e federazioni sportive) may be listed in the *Yellow Pages* (*pagine gialle*) or the English *Yellow Pages* (🖳 www.englishyellowpages. it). Alternatively you can contact the national federation for your chosen sport (some federations are listed in this chapter) or the Italian Olympic Committee, Comitato Olimpico Nazionale Italiano/CONI, Foro Italico, 00194 Rome (☎ 06-36851). If you have access to the internet, you'll find a wealth of information about Italian sports. For sports news, try Datasport (🖳 www.datasport.it) or the English-language version of *La Gazzetta* (🖳 http://english.gazzetta. it). If you're looking for people to play sport with, the Meet Up website (🖳 www.meetup.com) or Facebook are good places to start.

Sports such as football (especially), motor racing and cycling attract vast numbers of ardent supporters, and if you have the opportunity to attend a major event in one of these sports it will certainly be an experience to remember. This chapter includes details of the country's most popular spectator and participant sports (in alphabetical order).

AERIAL SPORTS

There are clubs and schools throughout the country offering flying and gliding opportunities and training, although flying is an expensive sport in Italy. Those arriving from North America in particular will notice that costs are much higher than they're used to, partly because of the much higher cost of aviation fuel and higher landing fees. You must be licensed before you can fly solo and all craft must be registered with the Aeroclub Italiano, Cesare Beccaria, 35/A, 00196 Rome (☎ 06-3608 461, 🖥 www.aeci.it).

Other aerial sports such as hang-gliding (*deltaplano*), paragliding (*parapendio*), parachuting and hot-air ballooning are all popular in Italy, particularly in the Alps and Dolomites, where the main season runs from June to October. For obvious reasons, all such activities require beginners to undergo an extensive training programme leading to internationally recognised qualifications. However, it's usually possible to try these sports by taking a tandem flight with a qualified instructor for a reasonable fee to see whether the freedom of the skies appeals as much in reality as it does in theory!

For further information about free flying, especially hang-gliding and paragliding, contact the Federazione Italiana Volo Libero, Via Salbertrand, 50, 10146 Turin (☎ 011-744 991, 🖥 www.fivl.it).

CYCLING

Cycling (*ciclismo*) is a hugely popular sport, despite the fact that some two-thirds of the country is mountainous and temperatures in summer are often too high for anyone but the most dedicated riders. Cycle racing has a huge following, and Italy has a long record of producing world-class riders. The 'Tour of Italy' (*Giro d'Italia*), Italy's answer to the *Tour de France* and one of the world's most prestigious cycling races, has been held annually since 1909, interrupted only by the two World Wars. The race is held in May and attracts large crowds along the route.

At local level, cycling clubs can frequently be seen touring and racing throughout the country, especially at the weekends, the brightly-clad riders seemingly oblivious to the gradients and the baking sun. However, it's noticeable that groups are almost exclusively male, despite the fact that cycling is popular among women and there's also a women's *Giro d'Italia*, which follows a route in the north of over 1,200km (745mi) in June to July each year.

For those with lesser ambitions, the largest area of flat land in Italy is the Po delta in the north, which provides an ideal area for cycling and is noted for its stunning scenery. Most towns have specialist cycling shops that sell or hire out bicycles and provide spares, assistance and advice about routes and local cycling clubs. In mountainous regions mountain-bikers often use a cable car to get to the top of a mountain, from where they take a 'leisurely' ride back down.

The price of a basic bicycle starts at about €120 and a mountain bike about €250, although prices are much higher for racing models, which can run to €1,500 or more (top Italian makes include Bianchi and Campagnolo). Shop around and compare prices and features. If you're after a standard bicycle, you could try large supermarkets and hypermarkets, where prices are generally lower than in specialist shops. Bikes should be fitted with an anti-theft device such as a steel cable or chain with a lock, as bicycle theft is rife in Italy. Bicycle hire (rental) is available in many towns and resorts, although it isn't always obvious where to go (ask at the local tourist or information office). Hire costs vary according to the model, a basic cycle starting at around €15 per day and a good mountain bike costing €35 or more per day.

For further information about cycling contact the Italian Cycling Federation, Federazione Ciclistica Italiana (🖥 www.federciclismo.it).

FISHING

Italy offers abundant fishing opportunities, both fresh and salt water, and over 2m people take part in the sport annually. The many lakes, rivers and mountain streams provide the opportunity to fish for trout, carp, perch, pike and other species. For freshwater fishing, you require an annual licence and must be a member of the Federazione Italiana della Pesca Sportiva e Attività Subacquee, Viale

Tiziano, 70, 00196 Rome (🖳 www.fipsas. it), which manages over 90 per cent of Italy's inland waters. There's also a fee to fish in most waters (e.g. €10 per day) or only when you actually catch something (sometimes according to the size and weight of your catch), payable to the local park ranger.

No licence is required for sea fishing and you can join a deep-sea fishing excursion or hire your own boat at many ports. Spear fishing is legal and popular in many places, but regulations forbid the use of scuba tanks and nets for underwater fishing. Underwater fishing is permitted only in daylight, when (by law) no more than 5kg (11lb) of fish and shellfish may be caught per day.

FOOTBALL

Football or soccer (*calcio*) is Italy's national sport and by far the most important, occupying almost the entire first half of each issue of *La Gazzetta dello Sport*. Italian football fans (*tifosi*) are among the most dedicated and fervent in Europe, matched in their fanaticism only by the English, Scottish and Spanish. No football fan should pass up the opportunity to experience the passions aroused by a first-class match (*partita*). Matches are often packed with incident, both on and off the field. Despite the chanting and passion though, there's little threat of physical violence as there is in some other countries. The concept of having several beers (or a dozen) before a match is foreign to Italian supporters, who are more likely to have a coffee, and drunkenness at matches is practically unknown, despite the sale of alcohol inside many grounds. Italian regional pride is much in evidence on the terraces and is only briefly forgotten when watching the national team (*azzurri*). Italy has a proud tradition in international football and has won the World Cup on four occasions – in 1934, 1938, 1982 and 2006; only Brazil has won more often.

Italy claims to have one of the best leagues in the world (although Spain's *La Liga* and the English Premier League have overtaken it in the 21st century), with some of the world's most famous clubs (Inter Milan and Juventus are household names) and biggest stars. Major matches can attract huge attendances – in the 2009/2010 season, the average attendance in Italy's premier league was 24,957 – and Italy's top clubs have been among the most successful in Europe.

The Italian league originally consisted of four divisions: *Serie A, B, C1* and *C2*. In 2009, however, *Serie A* announced a split from *Serie B* in an argument over finances and television rights. *Lega Calcio Serie A* was formed to create an independent tier, similar to England's Premier League; below this is the *Lega Serie B*, followed by the *Lega Pro Prima Divisione* and the *Lega Pro Seconda Divisione*. *Serie A* has 20 teams, and ticket prices cost from around €20 to €120. The season runs from around the end of August to June, with a break in December-January. At the end of the season, the top team in *Serie A* wins the championship (*campionato*) and 'Lo Scudetto', while the bottom three teams are relegated to *Serie B*. Matches are played on Sundays, usually in the afternoon, although they sometimes take place in the evening. A common sight on a Sunday is Italian families out for an afternoon stroll, the men with radios pressed to their ears so as not to miss any

of the action! The season culminates with the Italian Cup (*Coppa Italia*) final in June.

For those more interested in playing than watching, even small towns usually have several clubs and there are leagues and competitions at every level. Five-a-side football is also popular, as is eight-player football (*calciotto*), and pitches can be hired at most sports centres. Many companies have five-a-side teams and arrange matches on an informal basis or enter competitions held at a local sports centre.

Gran Paradiso National Park, Piedmont

There are a number of websites where you can obtain football results and information, such as 🖳 www.dossier.net and www.football-italia. net, and most clubs have their own websites, e.g. Inter Milan (🖳 www.inter.it) and Juventus (🖳 www. juventus.it).

GOLF

Although you may not automatically think of golf when you think of Italy, there are many 9- and 18-hole courses around the country, particularly in the north, where there's more flat land available. As in most European countries, golf is generally a sport for the wealthy and it hasn't caught on with the masses despite the best efforts of Constantino Rocco and a number of other Italian professional players to popularise the sport. It's usually necessary to join a club, many of which have long waiting lists, although there are a number of public courses where anyone can play a round for a fee and some private clubs allow visitors (with a handicap card) to pay a 'green fee' for a round. Further information can be obtained from the Italian Golf Federation, Federazione Italiana Golf (🖳 www.federgolf.it).

HIKING

Hiking (*escursionismo*), which includes anything from a gentle ramble through the countryside to serious hill walking, is popular in Italy, where there are numerous opportunities for walkers of all standards. The most popular areas include the Alps, the Apennines (particularly in the Parco Nazionale d'Abruzzo and the Sila Massif in Calabria) and Tuscany (e.g. the Alpi Apuane), along with the coastlines of Liguria and Amalfi, and the Italian lakes in the north. Those seeking challenges can find plenty on some of the alpine routes, although there are also alpine paths suitable for beginners and families with young children. Those who enjoy more remote hiking may wish to try the interior of Sardinia (e.g. Gennargentu) or Sicily, where you need to be well prepared as rescue services are rare. Alternatively, you could follow the volcanoes' route, which includes walks to the summits of two of Europe's most active volcanoes, Etna and Stromboli. Many resorts in the Alps advertise 'green weeks' (*settimane verdi*), when there are activities for summer visitors.

The main organisation for hiking (along with sports such as mountaineering and climbing) is the Italian Alpine Club, Club Alpino Italiano/ CAI, Via E. Petrella, 19, 20124 Milan (☎ 02-2057 231, 🖳 www.cai.it). It has a membership of around 400,000, making it by far the largest alpine club in the world, and oversees a network of some 450 local hiking clubs throughout Italy. The CAI is responsible for trail marking, which is generally of a high standard, particularly in northern and central Italy. It also operates around 600 mountain huts (*rifugi*), providing accommodation and meals to walkers, a highly regarded mountain rescue service, and produces maps and a range of other publications. Weekend and week-long treks in many regions of Italy and abroad are run by the Associazione Amici del Trekking e della Natura, Via Santa Croce, 2, 20122 Milan (☎ 02-8372 838, 🖳 www.trekkingitalia.com).

The main hiking season is from May to October, although there are opportunities to walk all year round in many areas. In the northern mountains, walking is often hampered by snow from November to April or later, and the official 'season' may last only from June to September. In contrast, winter and spring are ideal times for walking in much of the central and southern parts of the country, although even in the south there can be snow on higher land in winter and early spring. Alpine routes are at their busiest in August, and anywhere south of Tuscany is likely to be too hot for comfortable walking in summer. If you're hiking for more than a day, you need to arrange overnight accommodation, as camping in the wild is forbidden in most areas. In remote areas of Sicily and Sardinia, however, camping is the only alternative.

If you're hiking in a mountain area between mid-June and September you can stay at one of the network of *rifugi*, which are numerous in the northern mountains but much less common in central and southern areas. *Rifugi* may be run by the CAI (see above) or privately operated. They vary from bare, minimal huts to hostel-like accommodation, or even half-board lodgings. Rates vary accordingly, but should be around €16-€19 for dormitory accommodation, with breakfast free or for a small extra charge. Half board should cost around an extra €20, while unstaffed huts sometimes ask only a donation or are even free. *Rifugi* can be fully booked at peak times, which means that they may either send you on to the next hut (which could be several hours' walk away) or you may end up sleeping on the floor. If possible, it's therefore wise to book in advance. Details of the locations and phone numbers of *rifugi* are available from local tourist offices or search the CAI's website database (🖳 http://rifugi.cai.it) or enquire at regional CAI groups (🖳 www.cai.it).

Bookshops in major towns and cities and shops in hiking areas stock a wide range of maps and hiking books. The largest-scale maps are usually 1:25,000, which show paths and *rifugi* as well as topographical features and buildings. These include the *Tabacco* series for the northeast and the Dolomites, the *Instituto Geografico Centrale* series covering northwest Italy and the Alps, the *Edizioni Multigraphic Firenze* series for central and southern Italy, and the *Kompass* range, which covers most of the country.

> Tourist offices are also a good source of information about hiking routes, including places of interest and the local flora and fauna.

The Touring Club Italiano (TCI) and Club Alpino Italiano jointly publish a series of comprehensive walking guides, *Guide dei Monti d'Italia*, containing maps. A number of English-language hiking guides are available, including *Walking and Eating in Tuscany & Umbria* by James Ladsun & others (Penguin), *Walking in the Dolomites* by Gillian Price (Cicerone Press), *Walking in Italy: Exploring Italy's Great Cities and Finest Landscapes on Foot* by Gillian & John Souter (Chastleton Travel) and the recently published *Hiking in Italy (Lonely Planet Walking Guide)* by Brendan Sainsbury. If you wish to join a local hiking club or require further information about hiking in Italy, contact the Club Alpino Italiano, Via E. Petrella, 19, 20124 Milan (☎ 02-2057 231, 🖳 www.cai.it).

HUNTING

The hunting (*la caccia*) season in Italy extends from September until February for most animals and until March for migratory birds. Game is public property and you can hunt in most places provided you're at least 100m (328ft) from a house and don't damage crops. There are an estimated 800,000 regular hunters, mainly in Tuscany and Sardinia. Most use shotguns, and popular prey includes wild boar, rabbit, hare and many species of bird, including songbirds, many of which are protected in other countries. Hunters are a powerful group, although hunting is controversial and many protests take place on the opening day of the season; however, to date the pro-hunting lobby has managed to overcome all efforts to have it banned.

If you take part in hunting, you must ensure that you're aware of the regulations governing which species can be shot. Enthusiasm for hunting has resulted in many animals becoming rare, endangered or extinct, and new laws have been introduced to provide greater protection for many birds and animals. In recent years, further measures have been taken to protect animals in regions hit by fires and drought. Campaigns against illegal hunting are led by the World Wildlife Fund (WWF) and the Animal Rights League.

For further information about hunting in Italy, contact the Federazione Italiana della Caccia (🖳 www.federcaccia.org).

MOTOR SPORTS

Italy is synonymous with cars, being the home of such famous names as Alfa Romeo, Ferrari, Fiat, Lamborghini, Lancia and Maserati, and a love of (fast) cars is almost mandatory among Italian males. Italians (both male and female) are passionate supporters (*tifosi*) of Formula One motor racing, especially the Ferrari team. Italy has a proud history in motor racing and has produced many world champions. Two Formula One Grand Prix races are staged annually in Italy. In April the San Marino race, although not technically an Italian event, is held on Italian soil at Imola, southeast of Bologna (not far from the home of Ferrari at Modena) – this is where Ayrton Senna was killed in 1994, although not in a Ferrari. There are many links between Ferrari and the Imola track, where the stadium, Autodromo Enzo e Dino Ferrari, is named after the founder of Ferrari and his son.

The Italian Grand Prix is held in September at Monza (🖳 www.monzanet.it), where there has been motor racing since 1922. The Formula One *Autodromo* lies within a vast, attractive park on the edge of Monza, although it's little more than a northern suburb of Milan these days. Tickets for Grand Prix meetings can be obtained from the venue, although they don't come particularly cheap, varying from around €67 to well over €350.

Rallying

There are many opportunities to get involved with rallying in Italy, where you can take part in one of the many events organised by local motor clubs, or just watch the experts in the major national races such as the famous San Remo Rally held in October each year. Contact local automobile clubs for information about what's available in your area.

Motorcycle Racing

This is another hugely popular sport, which has had a long love affair with Italian superbikes such as Ducati, Moto Guzzi and MV Agusta. Mopeds and motor bikes are such a common means of everyday transport for millions of Italians that it would be strange if this didn't spill over into a love of motorcycle racing. If you wish to take part in something a little more organised than the daily race to work, contact the Federazione Motociclistica Italiana, Viale Tiziano, 70, 00196 Rome (☎ 06-324 881, 🖳 www.federmoto.it).

ROCK-CLIMBING & CAVING

Italy provides many opportunities for mountaineering (*alpinismo*), rock climbing (*roccia*) and caving (*speleologia*), particularly in the Alps, where there are challenges for those at all levels of experience. If you're new to these sports it's recommended you join a club to 'learn the ropes' before heading for the mountains. Although not for beginners, rock-climbing-made-easy is provided in several mountain ranges by the *vie ferrate* (literally 'iron ways'), which consist of permanently fixed iron ladders, pegs and cables onto which climbers can attach their karabiners. These were established as far back as the late 19th century and provide access to routes that would otherwise be too difficult for all but the most advanced climbers; for further information go to the Via Ferrata website (🖳 www. viaferrata.org).

There are climbing clubs in most towns, many of which are affiliated to the mountaineering section of the Club Alpino Italiano (CAI), Via E. Petrella, 19, 20124 Milan (☎ 02-2057 231, 🖳 www.cai.it), which has some 800 official mountaineering and climbing instructors. The Federazione Arrampicata Sportiva Italiana, Via del Terrapieno, 27, 40127 Bologna (☎ 051-601 4890, 💻 www.federclimb. it) can put you in touch with mountain-climbing schools, which provide training and organise climbing expeditions for all ages. Even if you have experience, you probably need to hire a guide in an unfamiliar area; these can be found through mountaineering schools or independently at many alpine resorts.

⚠ Caution

Many climbers lose their lives in the mountains each year, often due to inexperience or recklessness. Don't take unnecessary risks, and ensure that you have the appropriate equipment and experience for a planned climb or expedition.

The mountain rescue service, staffed by 7,000 members of the CAI, rescues climbers who are trapped or injured in the mountains, many of whom are inadequately equipped or experienced for the route they're attempting.

Caving

Italy has been an important centre of European caving or spelunking (*speleologia*) for over a century and the sport has enjoyed increasing popularity in recent decades. There are over 10,000 documented caves in Italy, in areas as diverse as Lombardy, Marche, Sardinia and Tuscany, although the greatest number is to be found in Umbria. Umbria was the original focus of caving and includes Monte Cucco, one of the deepest cave systems in the world, and the 'Avenue of the Great Wells' – a series of large underground wells regarded by caving enthusiasts as Italy's most spectacular geological feature. Further north, a popular alpine system is *Pioggia Bella*, which has seven entrances along its 6km (4mi) length.

Those taking part in caving expeditions range from trained members of the various caving organisations in Italy to those wishing to experience a guided weekend adventure in the geological underworld of fossils, rivers and unusual creatures, including bats and cave fish. It's important to have the appropriate training, equipment and conditioning, and to be accompanied by an experienced guide to explore this dark and silent world (best avoided by those who suffer from claustrophobia). Even an 'easy' cave system requires you to scramble over rocks, bend double (possibly for hours) in low passages and squeeze your body through narrow openings. In more difficult caves you may need to use rock-climbing skills and rope systems to cross underground lakes or even to swim under water. Newcomers can attend an introductory weekend, which is arranged in the easier caves, with all equipment provided.

For further information contact the Centro Nazionale di Speleologia, Via Galeazzi, 5, 06021 Costacciaro (☎ 075-9170 400) or the Gruppo Speleologico CAI Perugia, Via Santini, 8, 06128 Perugia (☎ 05-5847 070).

RACKET SPORTS

Badminton

Badminton has only been introduced in the last decade or so, although there are now clubs in most major cities, many of which participate in national tournaments and international competitions. Many clubs offer free use of equipment and coaching for members. Most clubs meet in the evenings at local sports centres, where basic membership starts at around €30 per year plus around €5 per visit to pay for court hire and equipment.

Squash

Squash has a relatively small following in Italy, where there are a small number of squash clubs in major cities (see the *Yellow Pages* under *Squash*), and sometimes facilities are also provided at tennis clubs and sports centres. Specialist clubs may require you to be a member, but often you can hire a court without joining. Squash courses or individual sessions of instruction are usually provided, typically costing around €20 for a 45-minute lesson.

Table Tennis

Table tennis is popular throughout Italy, where tables and bats can be hired for a nominal cost at sports centres and other sports clubs, e.g. tennis and squash clubs, and tournaments are organised at all levels and for all ages. Table tennis tables are also provided in social and other clubs and even on beaches in summer.

Tennis

Tennis is by far the most popular racket sport, and there's a wealth of both public and private courts available. Italian tennis clubs usually operate on a membership basis, so you need to join or be invited as a guest by a member, and membership can be expensive. There are also public facilities in most towns and cities owned by the commune (*comune*), where you can hire (rent) a court by the hour or obtain a season pass (*abbonamento*). Tennis is a popular after-school activity for children and tennis lessons are widely available for all ages and standards, including residential courses. Most courts in Italy are clay (*terra rossa*) or hard (asphalt).

If you want to find a club in a particular area, contact the Italian Tennis Federation, Federazione Italiana Tennis (🖳 www.federtennis.it). Professional tennis enjoys a large following and the country stages a number of top tournaments, including the Italian Open, which is held in Rome in May (on clay) and is the precursor to the French Open. The country has had reasonable success in international events and has a number of top male and female players.

RUGBY

Rugby union (played between teams of 15 players) was introduced in northern Italy by workers returning from France in the late '20s, and it's still strongest in the northern regions. Over the last 20 years or so it has become increasingly popular, aided by government moves to promote the sport. In particular, major tax breaks were provided for companies wishing to invest in rugby clubs and teams. Sponsorship money poured in and the growth of the game was assured – accompanied by an influx of foreign stars to Italian clubs.

At national level, the Five Nations tournament (England, France, Ireland, Scotland and Wales) was expanded in 2000 to become the Six Nations when Italy was admitted. In 2007, Italy (known at home as the *Azzurri*, or blues) won their first away game ever when they beat Scotland, and they capitalised on this by beating Wales the following week in Rome; however, in more recent years they have only managed to win two games – both against Scotland in 2008 and 2010 – and while their success has helped to raise rugby's profile in Italy, it has a long way to go before it rivals football. Most large and medium-size Italian towns boast a rugby club – a total of around 430 teams compete in the country's many leagues and knock-out competitions that take place between September and April.

For information about local clubs, contact the Italian Rugby Federation, Federazione Italiana Rugby, Viale Tiziano, 19, 00196 Rome (☎ 06-3200 036, 🖳 www.federugby.it).

SWIMMING

Not surprisingly given the climate, swimming (*nuoto*) is a popular sport (and pastime) in Italy, although the country has fewer indoor swimming pools (*piscina*) than you may expect. Sea swimming is popular in summer, when the water temperature can reach around 27ºC (81ºF) and a dip provides a welcome break from the blazing summer sun. However, although many Italians get into the water to cool off, this often has more to do with posing than swimming, evidenced by the number of people who take their mobile phones into the sea with them – held carefully above the water level, needless to say! Most beaches are public, the best (white sand) beaches being on the Adriatic coast, where the Lido near Venice is Italy's most fashionable bathing resort. Expect to pay around €1.50 for a beach chair, up to €6 per day to hire a basic lounger and up to €15 per day for an elaborate sun bed with an umbrella.

There are many open-air public pools, some of which are covered and heated in winter. Sometimes you must join a club to use a swimming pool, although there are also many public pools where you pay an entrance fee. Hotel pools are sometimes open to non-residents, but these tend to be expensive. If you join a swimming club, you'll find that there are numerous local and national competitions in which you can take part. Swimming lessons are widely available through clubs and at public pools. In lots of pools you're required to wear a swimming cap, irrespective of how much (or how little) hair you have!

The local tourist or information office can inform you about local swimming facilities. Private clubs with pools are listed under *Impianti Sportivi e Ricreativi* in the *Yellow Pages*. There are a number of water parks (*parchi acquatici*) throughout the country, offering pools, slides, wave machines and games, although these are usually outdoor facilities and therefore open only in summer. They tend to get very busy and aren't ideal for serious swimming, but are good for a family day out.

For more information about swimming, contact the Italian Swimming Federation, Federazione Italiana Nuoto, Stadio Olimpico, Curva Nord, 00135 Rome (💻 www.federnuoto.it).

WATERSPORTS

Given Italy's climate, the length of the coastline and the large lakes in the north, it will come as no surprise to discover that watersports are popular in Italy. Messing about in boats is a favourite pastime and sailing boats, motorboats, canoes and kayaks can be hired at many coastal and lake resorts.

Boating

Sailing (*vela*) in yachts and dinghies is popular throughout Italy, where even small coastal towns often have a marina. Dinghy sailing is also popular on the major lakes, particularly Lake Garda, which often provides better wind conditions than the smaller lakes. Sailing has received a further boost in recent years by the prominent Italian attempts to win the America's Cup. So far, success has proved elusive, but the challenge has raised the profile of the sport in Italy considerably. Motorboats are also popular as they cater for the Italians' love of speed. Many resorts have prominent sailing and yacht clubs, through which boats can usually be hired and courses taken. Generally these require you to be a member and costs vary widely; enquire at a tourist office about the facilities available locally or contact the relevant sports federation (see below). Boating holidays are popular in Italy, both on yachts and on motorboats. You can charter a boat provided you have a licence (*patente nautica*) or are willing to hire a captain (or an entire crew if

Charybdis, Sicily

your budget stretches to it). Before anchoring at a marina in Italy, you must obtain permission from the harbour master (*capitaneria di porto*).

Weekly and weekend sailing courses and holidays are featured in the magazine *Avventure nel Mondo* and advertised in sailing magazines. If you're chartering a boat without a captain, you need a guide to harbours such as the 'Pilot' series (published in England by Imray, Laurie, Norie & Wilson, 🖳 www.imray. com), which includes most Italian ports. A list of sailing clubs and information about courses is available from the Italian Sailing Federation, Federazione Italiana Vela, Piazza Borgo Pila, 40, 16129 Genoa (☎ 010-544 541, 🖳 www. federvela.it). For information about motorboat clubs and racing, contact the Federazione Italiana Motonautica (☎ 02-701 631, 🖳 www. fimconi.it). A boat show (*salone nautico*) is staged in Genoa in October each year. It offers an entertaining day out, if only to marvel at the way a fortunate few live, and is a good place to make contact with sailing organisations and discover the range of boating holidays available in Italy and beyond. Entry is free for foreigners on production of your passport.

Canoeing, kayaking and rowing (*canottaggio*) are also popular in Italy (which is one of the world's leading rowing nations), both on lakes and rivers and along the coast. For information, contact the Italian Rowing Federation, Federazione Italiana di Canottaggio (🖳 www.canottaggio.org) or the Italian Canoeing Federation, Federazione Italiana Canoa Kayak (🖳 www.federcanoa.it), which can provide lists of clubs that hire out equipment and provide training.

Diving

Scuba diving is well established in Italy, where it developed under the auspices of the Italian Federation of Divers. Some of the best scuba diving (*immersioni* or *subacquee*, often shortened to *sub*) in the Mediterranean is in Italian waters, and diving is popular almost everywhere along the coast. However, the best diving areas are in the Ligurian Sea; south of Genoa between the Portofino peninsula and the Cinque Terre;

and around the Italian islands of Capri, Sardinia and Sicily.

The area around the Portofino peninsula has recently been designated a marine nature reserve, with fishing and other activities restricted. The area has a rocky coast and boasts a wide range of interesting marine life (it's particularly noted for its large number of red fan corals), and provides an excellent environment for fish and invertebrate life. However, there are few large fish, due in part to the fact that spear fishing continues to be popular in Italy (outside the marine park), although there's evidence of greater numbers of larger fish in the area since the park was established.

A particular attraction in this area, at San Fruttuoso, is the submerged bronze statue of the Christ of the Deep (*Cristo degli abissi*). This famous statue of Christ with outstretched arms was 'erected' in the bay in 1954 at a depth of 18 metres as a memorial to those who have died at sea. On a calm day the statue can be seen from a boat on the surface, but the view from close up under the water is much more impressive. In August an annual festival takes place at the statue to honour seafarers.

The islands of Sardinia and Capri also offer good diving, with plenty of marine life and several interesting wrecks. Wreck diving is popular in Italy, where even sunken aircraft survive well on account of the weak tides in the Mediterranean. Wrecks suitable for scuba divers include a number of war and merchant ships dating back a few centuries, as well a number of German and British warplanes. If you want to see larger fish and mammals, you should head for Sicily, which has the advantage of being further out in the Mediterranean.

Beginners need to enrol on a diving course, of which there's a wide variety, including those offered by the major training organisations such as PADI, SSI and CMAS. If you're already a trained diver, a local dive centre will ask to see your certification card, after which you'll be able to join them on trips to local dive sites and further afield. If you don't have your own diving equipment, it can be hired at local dive centres.

The water temperature varies around the coast, but can fall to around 14°C (57°F) in winter, rising to 25 to 27°C (77 to 81°F) in summer. Local divers generally wear semi-dry suits in cooler temperatures; while in summer a wetsuit is sufficient (suits can be hired in most areas).

In recent years, independent dive centres have developed all along the coast and on the islands of Elba, Sardinia and the Maddalena archipelago between Sardinia and Corsica, noted for its crystal-clear waters. These tend to advertise in the local press and on roadside posters, and many also advertise in Italian, English and American diving magazines. Information about scuba diving and dive centres can be obtained from the Federazione Italiana Pesca Sportiva e Attività Subacque, Via Tiziano, 70, 00196 Rome (🖥 www.fipsas.it).

Water-skiing & Windsurfing

Water-skiing (*sci acquatico*) and windsurfing are popular, both along the coast and on inland lakes, particularly Lake Garda, whose northern end (around the Riva del Garda) is noted for its strong winds. Equipment and wetsuits – highly recommended at most times of the year – can be rented at resorts. For details of water-skiing clubs contact the Federazione Italiana Sci Nautico, Via Piranesi, 44/B, 20137 Milan (☎ 02-7529 181, 🖥 www.scinautico.com).

SKIING

The country has over 2.5m keen skiers, who are joined each year by millions of foreign visitors from around the world. Both alpine and downhill skiing (*sci alpino* or *lo sci*) and cross-country skiing (*sci di fondo*) are well catered for in Italy (most resorts provide facilities for both), although downhill skiing is far more popular. Italy has some of the best ski resorts in Europe and each year hosts the middle stages of the World Ski Cup.

The best equipped and most famous ski resorts are in the Alps, conveniently situated close to the northern cities of Milan, Turin and Genoa (see below). However, skiing is also possible locally if you live in Rome, Florence or Naples at smaller (and cheaper) resorts in the Apennines (*Appennini*), the Abruzzi (at resorts such as Campo Felice and Roccardo) and even in Sicily, where you can ski on Mount Etna, famous for its active volcano (see below). For snowboard fanatics, the best resort in the area of Rome is Campo Imperatore (L'Aquila).

For more information about winter sports, contact the Italian Winter Sports Federation, Federazione Italiana Sport Invernali, Via Paranesi, 44/B, 20137 Milan (🖥 www.fisi.org).

Alps

The Italian alpine resorts are arranged in a number of distinct geographical areas, each of which has extensive networks of interlinked resorts. The main areas include the Dolomites (Dolomiti) in the Trentino-Alto Adige and Veneto-Friuli regions, the Milky Way (Via Lattea) in the western Alps, and the Aosta Valley (Valle d'Aosta) and Lombardy in the north.

In the east, the Dolomite Superski area is the largest in the world and takes in many popular resorts, including Campitello Matese, Canazei, Cortina d'Ampezzo and Selva. It offers spectacular scenery and includes over 40 ski resorts, some 450 ski lifts, an incredible 1,200km (circa 750mi) of runs (*piste*) to suit all abilities and a large number of ski schools. All lifts can be accessed with a single pass. An unusual ski tour in the Dolomites is the

77km (48mi) Great War Route (*Giro della Grande Guerra*), which wends its way among the most spectacular peaks of Trentino, Alto Adige and Veneto, and explores some of the major First World War battlegrounds where Italian, German and Austrian forces fought. A map of the route is available at tourist offices in Alleghe, Arraba, Cortina D'Ampezzo, Pescul and San Cassiano, enabling skiers to guide themselves along the route, which never exceeds red (intermediate) grade.

In Lombardy, in the north of Italy, the main resorts include Aprica, Bormio, Livigno, Madesimo, Ponte di Legno (one of Italy's highest resorts) and San Simeone (good for beginners). Further west are the Milky Way and the Aosta Valley. The Milky Way, close to the French border, is based on the resorts of Clavire, Sauze D'Oulx and Sestriere, and has over 200km (124mi) of slopes and links with French resorts. The Aosta valley is situated in the northwest of Italy, running from the Mont Blanc tunnel towards Turin, where the main resorts include Cervinia, Courmayeur and La Thuile, among the most fashionable and expensive in Italy. Cervinia is linked to the famous Swiss resort of Zermatt, from Courmayeur you can ski the famous 'Vallée Blanche' (which runs down to Chamonix in France), while La Thuile borders the French ski area of La Rosière, which is included in the ski pass.

There's also year-round skiing on glaciers, which include Marmolada in the Dolomites, Monte Bianco (Mont Blanc) and Monte Cervino (the Matterhorn) in the Aosta Valley. The Italian ski slopes are generally on the sunny south side of the Alps and therefore offer less reliable snow conditions than the northern slopes in other alpine countries, as well as a shorter season. These drawbacks are overcome in many resorts by the use of snow machines, which help keep runs open when the weather doesn't oblige.

☑ **SURVIVAL TIP**

Before booking, it's wise to consult a good ski guide or a travel agent regarding the snow record at the time of year you plan to ski (or, better still, delay booking until you can be sure of good snow conditions).

Mount Etna

The most southerly skiing in Italy is on Sicily's Mount Etna, which rises to over 2,600m (8,539ft). The short season generally runs from January to late March, but the area has become more popular in recent years thanks to its breath-taking views, lack of queues and low prices (the cost of a daily lift pass is only around €20), and it now has nine lifts serving the southern and north-eastern faces of the mountain. Volcanic dust from Mount Etna regularly blackens the snow but doesn't call a halt to the skiing. If the rumbling gets too much for your liking, Sicily's beaches are just 45 minutes away by car, so it's possible to enjoy skiing and sea swimming on the same day.

OTHER SPORTS

The following is a selection of other popular sports in Italy:

Athletics

Most towns and villages have athletics (*atletico*) clubs and organise local competitions and sports days.

Basketball

Basketball (*pallacanestro* or simply *basket*) is a surprisingly popular sport. It was introduced by the Americans after the Second World War, and after Eurobasket 2009 the Italian men's team was ranked 8th in the world. The professional basketball season runs from September to May, and there are amateur clubs in many towns that provide courses for beginners. For information, contact the Federazione Italiana Pallacanestro (⌨ www.fip.it).

Bowls

Bowls (*bocce*) is widely played throughout the country and is the Italian equivalent of lawn bowls. There are *bocce* pitches (*bocciodromo*) in most towns and villages, where frequent competitions are held; indeed for some, predominantly older men, it seems to comprise almost a full-time occupation.

Boxing

Boxing is popular throughout the country, particularly as a spectator 'sport'. Boxing clubs and gymnasiums for budding professionals are common in the main cities.

Foreign Sports

Many foreign sports and pastimes have a group of expatriate fanatics in Italy, including American football, baseball, *boules*, cricket, Gaelic sports (hurling, Gaelic football), hockey (ice and grass), handball, lacrosse, *pelote* and softball. For information, enquire at libraries, tourist and information offices, expatriate social clubs, and embassies and consulates.

Gymnasiums & Health Clubs

Most towns have at least one gymnasium (*palestra*) offering a wide variety of classes, including aerobics, step, yoga, stretching, dance, martial arts and power sculpting. Costs vary tremendously according to the facilities provided and the amount of competition in the area. Many hotels also have fitness rooms.

Horse Riding

Horse riding (*equitazione*) is popular but expensive. There are many riding schools and clubs in rural areas, and you can hire horses from some farms. Many riding holidays are available, either from specialist holiday operators or as part of the 'agri-tourism' (*agriturismo*) scheme, where accommodation and riding facilities are provided on working farms. Information can be obtained from the Federazione Italiana di Sport Equestri (🖳 www.fise.it).

Running

Running is quite popular, although you wouldn't think so from the scant number of joggers seen on the streets. There's an extensive annual programme of competitive races throughout the country, ranging from a few kilometres up to full marathons.

Martial Arts

Unarmed combat such as aikido, judo, karate, kung fu, kushido, taekwon-do and t'ai chi ch'uan, are taught and practised in many sports centres and private clubs around the country.

Rollerskating & Skateboarding

Rinks are provided in large towns, and winter ice-skating rinks may also be used for roller skating (*pattinaggio a rotelle*) in the summer. Much practising is done on the pavements, which can add a touch of excitement (and danger) to a daily stroll.

Ten-pin Bowling

This sport is growing in popularity and there are ten-pin bowling centres in most major towns and cities; however, it's expensive in Italy.

Waterpolo

Waterpolo (*pallanuoto*) is popular both as an amateur and professional sport (the season runs from March to July). Amateur club games take place at local swimming pools.

17.
SHOPPING

Italy is one of the world's great shopping countries and Italian shops are designed to seduce you with their artful displays of beautiful and exotic merchandise. Shopping is both an art form and a pleasure in Italy, particularly food shopping, with most Italians preferring to shop in traditional small family stores (*botteghe*) rather than faceless supermarkets. The major cities, where even the smallest shop windows are a delight, are a shopper's paradise. It's difficult to say which is Italy's finest shopping city; some say Milan or Rome, whose streets are packed with designer boutiques, while others plump for Florence or Venice, with their more traditional shops – each has its unique attractions (see Clothes on page 272).

Italian design has long been internationally acclaimed for its practicality, simplicity and elegance, and Italian products are also synonymous with craftsmanship, quality and style (not to mention expense!). Nowadays luxury designer (*firmato*) products are part and parcel of Italian everyday life, whether they take the form of a gleaming red Ferrari or Lamborghini, a classic Armani suit, a Louis Vuitton suitcase, Gucci shoes or Rayban sunglasses. Legions of foreign shoppers flock to Italy each year to buy top quality Italian labels, particularly those at the forefront of *haute couture* such as Armani, Ferretti, Gucci, Valentino and Versace. Consumerism rates more highly among Italians than in most other European countries and Italians are dedicated shoppers, all aspiring to own luxury goods, particularly designer clothes.

As well as factory-produced designs, Italy is famous for its handicrafts and hand-made goods, and each region has its specialities. Among the best buys are clothing, shoes, luggage, contemporary art, prints, engravings, leather goods, jewellery (particularly gold), perfumes, ceramics, pottery, mosaics, marble, basketwork, straw goods, brass, fabrics, linen, glassware, porcelain, china, furniture, soft furnishings, inlaid wood, carvings, antiques, lace, embroidery and paper goods. Italy is also famous for its food (ham, cheese, pasta, olive oil, etc.) and drink (wines, spirits and liqueurs).

You should try to avoid offering a shopkeeper a €50 or €100 note when you're buying something costing a couple of euros and should also avoid using a credit card to pay for items costing less than around €15 (you may not be permitted to do so anyway). Shop staff vary from cordial and helpful to rude and dismissive, and queuing isn't a practice that's well understood. Getting served is usually a free for all and you must speak up when it's your turn or you'll be trampled by 'sweet' little old ladies! In Rome and other major cities and resorts, where there are many tourists, you must be wary of pickpockets and bag-snatchers. **Never** tempt fate with an exposed wallet or purse or by flashing money around.

There are a number of books for dedicated shoppers in Italy, including Frommer's *Born to Shop Italy* by Suzy Gersham, and *Designer Bargains in Italy* and *Lo Scoprioccasioni* (the bargain hunter's bible in Italian, but easy enough to understand) both written by Theodora van Meurs – the latter two are available from La Feltrinelli (💻 www. lafeltrinelli.it).

SHOPPING HOURS

Italians don't generally 'convenience shop' at
all times of the day and night, and retailing
hours reflect this, although the only law limiting
opening hours forbids retailers from opening
for more than 13 hours daily between 7am and
10pm and on more than eight Sundays annually
(even this restriction is relaxed in resort and
tourist areas). Shopping hours vary according
to the region, city or town and the type of shop.
However, in general, shops open on Mondays
to Saturdays from around 8.30 or 9am to 12.30
or 1pm and from 3.30 or 4pm to 7.30 or 8pm;
although in some cities (particularly in the south)
and during summer months, shops may not reopen until 5pm and may remain open until 9pm:
and afternoon shopping is virtually non-existent
in small towns.

This long lunchtime break (*pausa* or *siesta*)
may come as a surprise to many foreigners. The
pausa makes good sense in the summer, when
it's often too hot to do anything in the middle of
the day, and it allows time for lunch, traditionally
the most important meal of the day for Italians.
However, in winter you find yourself shopping in
the dark, a practice that may seem odd to some
foreigners. In the major cities there's a growing
tendency for shops to stay open all day and
larger shops and department stores open from
9am to 7pm continuously (*orario continuato/no
stop*).

Most shops close on Wednesday or Thursday
afternoons depending on the region, and
department stores and supermarkets may also
close on Monday mornings, although this is
becoming less common in the larger cities. Most
shops close on Sundays throughout the country,
although this practice is changing and many
supermarkets in tourist and coastal areas now
open on Sunday mornings. However, even in
popular tourist areas, many small shops close
for a few weeks in summer; August is the most
popular month, especially around the 15th
(*Ferragosto*).

SALES

Sales (*saldi*) are an important event in the
Italian shopping calendar and, although there
aren't massive queues of shoppers outside
department stores from the early hours of
the morning as in some countries, sales are
nonetheless popular with bargain hunters. There
are three kinds of sale in Italy, all of which are
strictly regulated by local and national laws:

♦ **Annual sales** (*vendite annuali*): The main
sales are held twice a year: between 7th
January and 7th March and between 10th
July and 10th September. Shops don't need
to hold their sales for the whole of these
periods, but sales must start and end within
these periods. Only seasonal products
(including fashion) can be sold at a discount,
and sale prices must be displayed in shop
windows.

♦ **Promotional sales** (*vendite promozionali*):
These can be held at any time of the year,
although clothes, shoes and accessory
outlets cannot hold promotional sales during
the 40 days immediately preceding the main
winter and summer sales. The discount
and original prices must be displayed on all
goods.

♦ **Closing-down sales** (*liquidazioni*): When
a business is closing or moving to a new
address, a closing-down sale is permitted for
a maximum of six weeks, although this may
be extended in certain cases.

As with all purchases, you should choose your
goods carefully before buying in a sale and be
aware of your rights (see **Receipts & Refunds**
on page 278). Bear in mind that you may find
it difficult to pay with a credit card during sales
periods, as many shops refuse to accept them,
although this is illegal if a shop usually accepts
them.

MARKETS

Markets (*mercati*) are a common sight
throughout Italy and are an essential part

of daily life. They're colourful, entertaining and worth a visit even if you don't plan to buy anything. Prices are generally lower than in shops, although much depends on your bargaining skills. You should beware of bargain-priced branded goods, such as watches, perfume, clothes and leather goods, as they're usually fakes.

Some towns have markets on one or two days per week only (usually the same days each week), while larger towns and cities may have a daily produce market from Mondays to Saturdays. There are also Sunday markets, particularly antiques and flea markets, in some places. In major cities there are markets specialising in 'exotic' (e.g. African, Chinese and Jewish) produce and goods.

Markets usually operate from early in the morning to around 1pm on weekdays and all day on Saturdays.

There are three kinds of market in Italy: indoor markets, permanent street markets (*mercati comunali coperti*) and travelling markets that move from town to town on different days of the week. Most cities and towns have indoor or covered markets, sometimes called the 'central market' (*mercato centrale*). A variety of goods is sold in markets, including food, plants, clothes (markets are a

good source of inexpensive clothes), footwear, crockery, hardware, cookware, fabrics, ceramics, CDs and DVDs, carpets, jewellery, watches and leather goods. Specialist markets in Rome and other main cities sell antiques (*mercati dell'antiquariato* – see below), books, clothes, stamps, flowers and animals (for pets). Famous specialist markets include the flower market at San Remo, which caters for wholesalers throughout Europe, the Rialto Bridge market in Venice, which sells fruit, and the Campo de' Fiori in Rome, an open-air food market.

Food Markets

Food markets are extremely popular in Italy and are usually divided into sections for fresh fruit and vegetables; meat, fish, cheese and cooked meats; and olives and olive oil. Produce is always fresh and generally cheaper than in supermarkets, particularly if you buy what's in season and locally produced. You should arrive early in the morning for the best produce, although the best prices may be had at the end of the morning, when stall-holders are packing up and remaining food is sold cheaply.

Produce is usually marked with its price per kilogram and you should order by the kilo (*chilo*), half kilo (*mezzo chilo*) or in multiples of 100g (*ettogrammo*), although some produce is sold by the piece (*parte*). Some haggling over food prices may take place, although usually the marked price prevails. The law in Italy requires market vendors to give you a printed receipt for your purchases and you should ask for one if it isn't forthcoming.

You may be allowed to handle food products, although some vendors may object to this, particularly if the produce is delicate, but you can ask to try a piece before you buy. When buying fruit and vegetables in markets, check that the quality of the produce you're given is the same as that displayed, which isn't always the case. A queue at a particular stall is usually a sign of good quality and value. Local people often sell home-grown produce on the fringes of markets and also by the roadside in rural areas.

Antiques & Flea Markets

Antiques markets (*mercati dell'antiquariato*) and flea markets (*mercato delle pulci*) are common throughout Italy, although you

it's the largest in Europe) and in Florence at the Mercato delle Pulci on the last Sunday of the month. To find out more about antiques markets in your local area, pick up a copy of *Gazzetta dell'Antiquario* (which lists all markets), or enquire at local tourist offices and town halls.

SUPERMARKETS & HYPERMARKETS

Although supermarkets (*supermercati*) are on the increase in Italy, they aren't as prevalent as in America, the UK or even France, and hypermarkets (*ipermercati*) account for less than 10 per cent of the Italian food market (compared with around 50 per cent in France). There are several supermarket chains, including the Co-op, Esselunga, Euromercato, DOC, Pam, SMA, Standa and Unes. Discount supermarkets (*i discount*) have recently sprung up on the outskirts of cities throughout Italy and include chains such as Lidl and In's Discount. Foods sold here are mainly basic, unbranded, non-perishable items that are usually good value. (See also **Food** on page 265.)

Note the following when shopping in supermarkets and hypermarkets in Italy:

♦ Supermarkets and hypermarkets usually provide parking for customers and are open all day without a break for lunch.

♦ Plastic bags (*buste*) aren't always provided free and may cost 5 or 10 cents, therefore it's recommended to follow the Italian custom and take your own bags with you.

♦ Shopping trolleys usually require a €1 coin, which is returned when you take the trolley back to a storage area.

One of the advantages of department stores is that you can browse to your heart's content without feeling obliged to buy anything or being accosted by over-zealous shop assistants.

DEPARTMENT STORES

There are several department stores (*grandi magazzini*) in Italy with branches throughout the country, including Coin, Esselunga, La Rinascente, Metro, Standa and Upim. La Rinascente (🖥 www.rinascente.it), established

shouldn't expect to find many (or indeed, any) bargains in the major cities, where the best items are usually snapped up by dealers. You should never assume that because something is sold in a market it's automatically a bargain, particularly when buying antiques (*antiquariato*), which may not be authentic. You should also beware of buying stolen antiques, the theft of which is widespread.

The most famous antiques markets include those held in the Piazza Grande in Arezzo on the first weekend of the month, the Piazza Bellini in Naples and the Ponte di Mezzo in Pisa, the last two being held on the second weekend of the month. Others include Bergamo (third Sunday of the month), Lucca (third weekend of the month), Milan (last Sunday of the month), Modena (last weekend of the month), Ravenna (third weekend of the month) and Turin (second Sunday of the month). Rome has a permanent antiques market with around 20 stalls at the Piazza Fontanella Borghese.

Italy's best flea (junk) markets are found on Rome's Porta Portese (in the Trastevere quarter) on Sundays (with 4,000 stall-holders, in the early 1900s, is Italy's largest and best department store and has two outlets in Rome and its flagship store in Milan. La Rinascente stocks a variety of goods, including the best and most famous Italian and foreign clothing, accessories, furniture and household goods. It provides an excellent service for foreign shoppers, including multilingual information counters, international shipping and tax refunds, and all major credit cards are accepted. La Rinascente stores have continuous opening hours from 9am to 7.30pm, Mondays to Saturdays.

Coin, Esselunga, Metro, Standa and Upim all have more outlets than La Rinascente and are generally cheaper, although they aren't as stylish or upmarket. They're usually open from 9am to 7pm, Mondays to Saturdays, although some smaller branches may close for lunch.

FOOD

Most Italian cuisine is based on fresh local produce, and shopping for food is a daily ritual carried out with great diligence (not to mention pleasure) by Italian women (mainly). The range and quality of fresh food is far greater than in many other countries, as is the number of specialist outlets from which you can buy food. Italian women are demanding and choosy when buying produce, which tends to be seasonal and locally produced. Traditionally, food shopping has been done in small specialist food shops and at food markets, rather than at large supermarkets. However, as the number of Italian women working outside the home increases, more are shopping in supermarkets.

Italians don't care much for foreign food and are conservative in their taste, preferring simple, fresh (i.e. Italian) ingredients. You won't, therefore, find a huge selection of foreign food in most shops, although larger supermarkets may have a small section and in the major cities there are specialist foreign food shops.

The cost of living in Italy (see page 211) is one of the highest in Europe and the prices of some foods may come as a shock to foreigners, particularly items such as Parma ham and certain Italian cheeses, which are more expensive in Italy than abroad!

Italian Food Shops

- *alimentari*: a general store or grocer's, selling basic foods, fresh bread, dairy products, ham and other cured meats, wine, and usually fresh fruit and vegetables;

- *drogheria*: sells dry goods, foodstuffs and household cleaners;

- *erboristeria*: sells health foods, organically grown produce and wholemeal food, which may also be sold in *drogherie* and chemist's shops. For a list of health food shops, look in the *Yellow Pages* under *Alimentari Dietetici* or *Macrobiotici e Biologici*.

- *gelateria*: sells the world-famous Italian ice cream. For the best home-made ice cream look for the sign *produzione artigianale*.

- *latteria*: sells milk (fresh and long-life) and milk products such as cheese, yoghurt and butter. It may also sell other basic food products.

- *macelleria*: see **Meat** below;

- *negozio del formaggio*: see **Cheese** below;

- *panificio* or *panetteria*: see **Bread & Cakes** below;

- *pasticceria*: see **Bread & Cakes** below;

- *pescheria*: see **Fish** below;

- *polleria*: see **Meat** below;

- *rosticceria*: a good place to buy cooked food such as roast chickens and cold meats, and prepared dishes such as lasagne and pizzas.

- *salumeria*: – see **Meat** below;

- *verduraio*, *fruttivendolo* or *ortolano*: see **Fruit & Vegetables** below.

Generally, meat and fish are expensive, but fruit, vegetables, dairy produce, olive oil and wine are cheaper than in many other countries. If you wish to save money on your weekly food bill, where you shop is as important as what you buy. Generally, it's better to shop at markets, although this is more time consuming than shopping at supermarkets. Obviously it helps if you speak some Italian, but it's easy enough to point to what you want and say *un chilo* (a kilo) or *mezzo chilo* (half kilo). Village shops can be expensive and it may be cheaper to travel to the nearest town to buy food. If you insist on buying imported produce, your food bill will rocket.

Shopping in Italy often involves an Italian idiosyncrasy: you must order what you want from the assistant behind the counter, pay the bill for your purchases at a separate cash desk (*cassa*), and then return to the counter with your receipt (*scontrino*) and collect your shopping (the system was invented by bureaucrats!). This takes some getting used to and involves a lot of queuing, although the time can be profitably spent conversing with your fellow shoppers and improving your Italian!

Each time you make a purchase, ensure that you receive a fiscal receipt (*scontrino fiscale*) – it's illegal for most shops (excluding newsagents, tobacconists and petrol stations) not to give you one and for you not to have one. The tax police (*Guardia di Finanza*) can (in theory) fine you up to €155 for leaving a shop without a receipt, even for a small item such as a can of drink.

Meat

There are several kinds of meat shop in Italy: a *macelleria* sells most kinds of meat, including beef (*manzo*), veal (*vitello*), pork (*carne di maiale*) and chicken (*pollo*) as well as eggs (*uove*); a *salumeria* sells cured, smoked and roast meats and sometimes fresh pork; a *polleria* sells chicken (*pollo*), rabbit (*coniglio*) and game (*selvaggina*); and a *macelleria equina* sells horse meat (*carne di cavallo*).

Veal is generally regarded as the best meat in Italy, which is prepared in numerous different ways throughout the country, the most famous of which is *ossobuco* – stewed slices of veal shin bone with the marrow left in the bone. Pork is generally considered a winter food and isn't widely available in summer; pork products from the north are the best, while roast suckling pig (*porchetta* or *porcheddu*) is a speciality in many regions, including Sardinia and Umbria. Thin slices of rare beef (*carpaccio*) served as a starter with oil or shavings of parmesan cheese is a popular dish, while lamb (*agnello* or *abbacchio*) is popular in the south; you may find the cuts smaller than you're used to. Easter is the main season for lamb and a

speciality is Sardinian milk-fed lamb. Italians, like most Latins, eat a variety of small song birds, including skylarks (*allodole*) and thrushes (*tordi*).

Cooked Meat

Cured ham (*prosciutto*) is the main type of cold meat consumed in Italy and famous throughout the world for its subtle, delicate taste. Ham is cured in many parts of Italy, although the best, *prosciutto crudo* – literally raw ham – comes from Parma. Italians eat it on its own or as a starter with melon. Cooked ham (*prosciutto cotto*) is also popular. Other cooked meats include an infinite variety of sausages (*salsiccia*) and salami, which vary from region to region. Cold meats are sold in a variety of stores, including *salumerie, rosticcerie* and *alimentari* (general grocery stores).

Fish

Fish (*pesce*) and other seafood (*frutti di mare*) are popular in Italy, particularly in Sicily and the south and anywhere near the coast, and most towns have at least one fish shop (*pescheria*). Common seafood includes anchovies (*acciughe* or *alici*), served fresh and usually fried (not salted and from a tin except when on pizzas); clams (*vongole*), a favourite in Naples, where they form part of the famous spaghetti sauce; cod (*merluzzo*); crab (*granchio*); lobster (*aragosta*), usually prohibitively expensive; mackerel (*sgombro*); mussels (*cozze*); octopus (*polpo*); oysters (*ostriche*); prawns (*gamberi*), usually served grilled, particularly in Rome; sardines (*sarde*), served with pasta and a popular dish in Palermo; sole (*sogliola*); squid (*calamari*); swordfish (*pesce spada*) and tuna (*tonno*), both usually cut in thick steaks and grilled. Tinned fish is also popular and a huge variety is available.

Bread & Cakes

Bread (*pane*) is sold in a *panificio* or *panetteria* and is usually baked on the premises each morning. General stores and most supermarkets also have a bread counter. Bread is usually white and similar to a French stick, although wholemeal (*integrale*) bread is also available and there are many regional variations.

> Bread rolls (*panini*) and croissants (*cornetti*) can be bought from a *panetteria*, as can other baked goods, both sweet and savoury. For cakes, pastries and home-made sweets, you must go to a *pasticceria*.

Fruit & Vegetables

Much of the Italian diet is based on fresh fruit (*frutta*) and vegetables (*verdura*), of which there's a huge variety, although most produce is seasonal. Apart from produce that isn't grown in Italy, imported fruit and vegetables are found only in a few delicatessens and specialist food shops. Fruit and vegetables can be purchased from greengrocers' (*verduraio*, *fruttivendolo* or *ortolano*), where you can choose what you want, or from a market or supermarket. In the latter you may be restricted to buying pre-packed, family-sized portions of second-grade (*seconda scelta*) produce and the selection may be more limited, although prices are generally lower. Markets (see page 262) usually offer better quality and value.

Olive Oil

As in all Mediterranean countries, olive oil (*olio d'oliva*) forms an important part of the diet and is the base for most savoury dishes, although in Lombardy butter is used in preference for cooking. Although Italy isn't the world's largest producer of olive oil, it's the world's biggest exporter, the US being its main customer. There are several grades of olive oil, including extra virgin (*extra vergine*) – the finest and a golden-green colour – virgin and plain olive oil. The cheapest olive oils are blends of lower grade oils (called *olio lampante*) that are best avoided. The best oils are cold-pressed (*spremitura a freddo*), low in acidity and expensive.

Fine olive oil is produced throughout the country: Tuscany's oil is widely recognised as among the world's best and is used by many top chefs. Some areas have been awarded a *denominazione d'origine controllata* (*DOC*) quality classification, and a few have the higher *denominazione d'origine controllata e garantita* (*DOCG*), e.g. Montalcino. Olive oil can be purchased direct from the producers, where you can often taste it before you buy. It has varying acidity: low acidity, e.g. 0.4° or 0.5°, is good for salads and odourless in cooking, while acidity of 1° usually means a fuller flavour.

Cheese

A cheese shop (*negozio del formaggio*) sells countless varieties of cheese (*formaggio*) from throughout Italy, Lombardy being one of the largest cheese-making areas. Perhaps the most famous and certainly the most distinctive Italian cheese is parmesan (*parmigiano*), which is eaten grated with most kinds of pasta. Parmesan is made throughout the provinces of Modena, Parma and Reggio Emilia and in parts of Bologna and Mantova (all in Emilio Romagna). The best quality (and most expensive) parmesan comes from Parma and Reggio Emilia and has *Parmigiano Reggiano* stamped on the rind; less expensive parmesans are called *grana padano*. The older parmesan cheese is, the more expensive it becomes, the most expensive being *stravecchione* (very old).

Other cheeses include *burrata*, a buttery cheese from the south; the mild *caciotta*, made throughout Italy; *fontina* from Piedmont, used in fondues (*fonduta*); *gorgonzola*, a piquant, blue-veined cheese that originates from the town of Gorgonzola near Milan and is generally an after-dinner cheese; *mascarpone*, a rich soft cheese used in sweet dishes; mozzarella, a rubbery and delicately flavoured cheese which is usually used as a topping for pizzas or as a stuffing for vegetables; *pecorino*, a hard, strong cheese made with sheep's milk; and *ricotta*, a soft white cheese used in salads and many other dishes and to fill pasta such as *tortellini* (salted ricotta/*ricotta salata* is popular in the south).

Pasta

Pasta is a staple of the national diet and forms part of most Italian meals, although in the north cornmeal (*polenta*) or rice (*riso*) is often eaten instead; a *risotto* is a dish made with rice. Pasta tends to be served before the main course rather than as part of the main course itself, in one of four ways: on its own or 'dry' (*pasta asciutta*) with an accompanying sauce, in soups (*pasta in brodo*), baked (*pasta al forno*), and 'filled' (*pasta ripiena*). There's an almost infinite variety of shapes and sizes of pasta, each with its own name, which may vary from one region to another. Common types of pasta include the universally known *fettucine*, *lasagne*, *maccheroni*, *spaghetti* and *tagliatelle*, along with tube pastas such as *fusilli* (corkscrew shaped) and *farfalle*. Pastas for soup are usually small, e.g. *conchigliette* (shell shaped) or *vermicelli* (literally 'little worms'). Filled pastas include *cannelloni* (cylindrical in shape), *tortellini* (small and circular) and *ravioli*.

Packet or dried pasta is made of durum wheat and water, whereas fresh pasta is made with eggs and flour (*pasta all'uovo*). Egg pasta is usually served with richer, creamier sauces than those accompanying dried pasta. For Italians, cooking pasta is an art: it must be cooked for exactly the right amount of time so that it's firm with a slightly chewy consistency (*al dente*). Different regions have their own specialities and throughout the country the same types of pasta may be served with different sauces. Generally speaking, in the north the sauces are richer, often creamy and are served with red meat such as the world famous *ragù bolognese* from Bologna, while in the south more vegetables and seafood are included.

Further Information

An interesting book (in Italian) for gourmets is *Itinerari del Prodotto Tipico Italiano,* published by Agriturist, C Vittorio Emanuele, 101, 00186 Rome (☎ 06-6852 342, 🖳 www.agriturist.it), which explains the various categories of wine, cheese, olive oil, meat, fruit and vegetables grown and produced in Italy. It also contains itineraries throughout the country where you can sample local produce, which must be one of the most pleasurable ways to discover Italian cuisine. Other interesting books include *Carluccio's Complete Italian Food* by Antonio Carluccio (Quadrille), *Fantastico!: Modern Italian Food* by Gino D'Acampo (Kyle Cathie) and *Italy for the Gourmet Traveler* by Fred Plotkin (Kyle Cathie).

There are numerous websites devoted to Italian cuisine, including 🖳 www.annamariavolpi.com, www.italiana.co.uk, http://italianfood.about.com, www.italianfoodforever.com, www.italianmade.com and www.italyabroad.com (for those who just dream of living *La Dolce Vita*).

ALCOHOL

Drinking forms an essential part of the sweet life and no meal is complete without accompanying wine (*vino*) and a concluding liqueur (*digestivi*). Italy produces a wide variety of alcoholic beverages, including many excellent wines, some good beers, and a huge variety of spirits and liqueurs. Imported spirits and beers are generally available, although considerably more expensive than native drinks. While beer has become an increasing favourite, particularly among young people, Italy remains a predominantly wine-drinking nation, with spirits reserved for special occasions.

Considering the ready availability of alcohol and the frequency with which it's drunk, it may come as a surprise to foreigners that Italians don't have a huge problem with alcoholism or indulge in drunkenness, which is more than can be said for many tourists and foreign residents. In fact, Italians drink far less alcohol than many other Europeans, and drunkenness, especially in women, is much frowned upon in Italian society. Children are introduced to alcohol at an early age and it's common to see them tasting a small amount at social gatherings. However, when Italians go out socially, they rarely overindulge and often order soft drinks rather than alcohol. In contrast, expatriates who like the odd drink (or two) should carefully control their alcohol intake, as alcoholism is prevalent among foreign residents.

Wine

Italy is one of the world's largest wine-producing countries and Italians are justifiably proud of their wine; they find it difficult to believe that any other is better (not that many Italians have ever tasted foreign wine or even wines from outside their local region – like most major wine-producing countries, Italy is extremely parochial). Over 750,000 hectares of farmland (the third-largest area in the world, behind Spain and France) are dedicated to vineyards – more than for food production. Italian wines vary from dry (*secco*) to sweet (*dolce*) and include whites (*bianco*) and reds

(*rosso*). The country produces relatively few rosés (*rosato*) or sparkling wines, although two of the latter are among its most famous wines.

Classification

Italian law prescribes three wine classifications, which must be displayed on labels: *Vino da tavola* means simply 'table wine', which although not known for its quality can be surprisingly good, particularly the Sicilian Corvo reds and whites; *denominazione di origine controllata* (*DOC*) means that a wine has been produced according to certain rules and specifications, although it's no guarantee of quality; and *denominazione di origine controllata e garantita* (*DOCG*) means a wine has met the same specifications as for a *DOC* but has also been approved by government-appointed wine tasters before bottling (nice work if you can get it!). There are only some 50 *DOCG* wines in Italy.

Wine-producing Areas

Virtually no part of Italy (including the islands) is without its local wine producers, which range from among the largest and most sophisticated in the world to small farm plots producing no more than a few hundred bottles per year. The following is a summary of the types of wine produced in each main wine-producing region (see the map in **Appendix E**):

◆ **Campania** has been producing its wines from the volcanic soil of Mount Vesuvius for over 2,000 years, although the wines from this region aren't of particular note nowadays; the most famous include *Lacrima Christi* (literally 'Christ's tear'), a red wine favoured (particularly in Naples) to accompany seafood, *Falerno* and *Gragano*, a dark red.

◆ **Emilia-Romagna** produces the world-famous *Lambrusco*, a sparkling (usually) red wine which can be of poor quality unless it comes from one of the four *DOC* zones. Other wines of note from the region include red *Sangiovese* and *Albana*, a sweet white.

◆ **Lazio** is one of the major wine-producing areas in Italy and produces seven types of wine, including *Cecubo, Colli Albani* and *Frascati,* which are mostly white and dry, and best drunk young. *Frascati*, the region's most famous wine, is also made in a dessert variety.

♦ The **Marche** region on the east coast produces *Verdicchio dei Castelli di Jesi* (characterised by its unique amphora-shaped bottle), a delicate white regarded by some as one of the best wines to accompany fish.

♦ The **Montefalco** area in Umbria produces some excellent *DOC* reds.

♦ **Piedmont** is said to produce the best wines in Italy, including the classy, traditional red *Barolo* and *Barbaresco*, both of which need ageing and are among the most expensive Italian wines. World-famous sparkling *Asti* is also produced here, as is vermouth.

♦ **Puglia** (Apulia) in the southwest produces more wine than any other Italian region, *Castel del Monte* (made in white, rosé and red versions) being the best known.

♦ **Sardinia** produces white *Vernaccia*, which is similar to sherry and comes in two versions: dry, served as an aperitif, and sweet, which is a dessert wine.

♦ **Sicily**, known as the 'paradise of the grape', produces many red and white wines from the volcanic soil of Etna. *Marsala*, a fortified dessert wine, is the most famous of Sicilian wines and is often used in cooking. Other Sicilian wines of note include the red and white *Corvo*, which, although not *DOC* wines, can be quite expensive.

♦ The **Trentino-Alto Adige** region produces more *DOC* wines than anywhere in Italy and its 20 varieties, which are influenced by nearby Austria's wine-making techniques, styles and preferred grape varieties include some excellent whites such as *Riesling*, *Terlano* and *Pinot Bianco*. The area also produces some high-quality reds (*Kalterersee*, *St Magdalene* and *Lagrein Dunkel*) and some outstanding sparkling wines such as *Spumante Trentino Classico*. The rare *vin santo*, a rich dessert wine made from sun-dried grapes (and often served to visitors at all times of day), is also worthy of note in this area.

♦ The red wines of **Tuscany** are justly famous and rate among the world's best. *Chianti* is the best known, although the cheapest can be dreadful; the finest is classified as *Chianti Classico* (with a black cockerel on the bottle). Two other good Tuscan reds (and among Italy's most expensive wines) are *Vino Nobile di Montepulciano*, aged for four years before bottling, and *Brunello di Montalcino*. *Vin santo* (see above) is also produced here.

♦ **Umbria** is known for its dry white wines, of which the most famous is *Orvieto*, although *Grechetto*, a reasonably priced white, is making its mark on the domestic market.

♦ **Veneto** produces a number of world-famous wines, including *Bardolino*, *Soave*, *Valpolicella* and several kinds of cabernets.

Buying Wine

You can buy wine from supermarkets and hypermarkets, where prices are usually reasonable, although there may not be a particularly good range of quality wines and these may be poorly stored.

> In the major cities and wine-producing areas there are wine shops (*bottiglieria*, and the more specialist, *enoteca*), where there's usually an excellent choice and you can often sample wines before you buy.

Most wine is reasonably priced in Italy, a good wine costing in the region of €8 per bottle, although prices rise to over €16 or more for an outstanding vintage. If you want to save money, you can buy wine directly from producers, whose signs 'Vendita Diretta' (direct sales) line the roads in wine-producing areas. At some producers, you can have your own bottles filled with wine, which helps reduce the price, although the wine isn't usually of the best quality. Note that you shouldn't leave wine in a car for long periods during hot weather, as this ruins it.

Wine Festivals & Tasting

Wine festivals are held throughout Italy, where tasting is usually free and wine flows freely. The most notable festivals include Bolzano in late March, Città della Pieve and Panicale in Umbria in April, Orvieto in June, and Tivoli in October. Consult local tourist offices for information. Wine-tasting courses are held in major cities throughout Italy by the Associazione Italiana Sommeliers (known affectionately as Vino Vino, 🖥 www.sommelier. it) or you can sign up for wine-tasting tours organised by wine producers or the Touring Club Italiano (🖥 www.touringclub.it).

Further Information

The Movimento del Turismo del Vino (Italian Wine Tourist Movement – 🖥 www. movimentoturismovino.it/cantine_aperte_ en.html) provide information about over 300 wine producers, many of which cater specifically to visitors. Other interesting websites include 🖥 http://italianwineblackbook. com, www.italianmade.com/wines/home.cfm, www.wine-pages.com/resources/italyexp.htm, www.gamberorosso.it and Wine Intro, which contains descriptions of all the leading Italian wines with an audio guide to pronunciation (🖥 www.wineintro.com/regions/italy/sound. html).

There are many books dedicated to Italian wine, including the *Italian Wine Guide* (Abbeville Press), *Wines of Italy* by Burton Anderson (Mitchell Beazley), *Italian Wines 2010* (Gambero Rosso), *Vino Italiano: Regional Wines of Italy* by Joseph Bastianich & David Lynch (Random House) and the annual *Vini d'Italia* (Arcigola Editore). The latter title is also published in English as *Italian Wines* (or *The Slow Food Guide to Italian Wines*), and is the most comprehensive guide available to Italian wine, rating over 11,000 wines, although you may have to scour second-hand bookshops for a copy.

Spirits & Liqueurs

Before a main meal, fortified wines such as *Campari*, *Cinzano* and *Martini* are popular, often served with soda and ice. These aperitifs cost in the region of €8 for a 70cl bottle. There's also an artichoke-based drink, *Cynar*, often drunk as an aperitif, although it's something of an acquired taste.

Much less in the way of spirits is consumed in Italy than in many other European countries and, rather than have a whisky or brandy after a meal, most Italians prefer home-grown liqueurs, of which there's a great variety, including *Amaro*, *Galliano* and *Strega* (all bitter

Sambuca

and herb-based), *Amaretto* (almond-based and very sweet), *Mistrà* and *sambuca* (aniseed liqueurs usually drunk with coffee), *maraschino* (made from the cherries from which it takes its name), *limoncello* (lemon-based) and *grappa* (the Italian 'firewater', which comes in many varieties and is made from juniper berries, grapes or plums). There are numerous *grappa* outlets in Italy and it's probably Italy's cheapest liqueur, but be warned before you rush out to buy a bottle: it's another acquired taste! As well as being an after-dinner drink, *grappa* is a popular way to start the day, often being drunk with morning coffee (if this doesn't get you going, nothing will!).

All the best known brands of foreign spirits are readily available, plus a number of cheaper Italian brands, although these aren't of such good quality. A bottle of Italian brandy (the main brands are *Stock* and *Vecchia Romagna*) costs around €10, while well-known brands of imported spirits (gin, scotch whisky, rum and vodka) usually cost around €18 for a standard bottle.

Beer

Beer (*birra*) in Italy is usually of the lager type and is sold in 33cl, 75cl and 1 litre bottles. The main Italian brands include *Dreher*, *Moretti* and *Peroni*, all of which are of good quality. As well as lager beer (*birra chiara*), there are also darker beers, called *birra nera* or *birra rossa*, which look rather like British stout or bitter, although they're less malty. Many imported beers are sold in supermarkets, although they cost up to three times as much as Italian beers.

CLOTHES

Italy is renowned for its *haute couture* (*alta moda*), synonymous with elegance and style, and since the Second World War it has vied with France for the number one spot (much 'French' fashion is designed and manufactured in Italy, despite what the label may say). Italian fashion designers rank among the best in the world and include such household names as Armani, Dolce & Gabbana, Fendi, Ferragamo, Ferretti, Gianfranco Ferre, Gucci, Moschino, Valentino and Versace, whose collections attract legions of shoppers annually.

Most Italians have at least a few designer garments and many are even prepared to go without basics in order to have the best in design. Such design excellence doesn't come cheaply and prices are generally very high, but then so is the quality, and an item made in Italy usually lasts for many years (classic design rarely goes out of fashion). Prices tend to be fixed (*prezzi fissi*) and bargaining is usually a waste of time and effort unless you're buying a large number of garments or a particularly expensive item. If you're after bargains, the sales in January and July are a must, as it's possible to make huge savings.

You may see shops with signs saying 'Ingresso Libero' (Browsers Welcome), but in most smart Italian boutiques browsing isn't encouraged; therefore, unless you know exactly what you're after, it's probably better to go to a department store where you can sift through clothes to your heart's content with no risk of disapproving glares from shop assistants.

There are many websites for those interested in Italian fashion, including 🖳 www.modaitalia.net, www.modaonline.it and http://made-in-italy.com/fashion.

Milan

Milan, which in fashion terms is on a par with Paris, dominates the Italian fashion scene and has the largest choice of boutiques, followed by Rome and Florence (see below). Milan is the dynamo behind the Italian fashion industry and it's from here that many of Italy's international designers made their way to fame and fortune. Most Italian and foreign designers have studios and boutiques in Milan, and twice a year (in spring and autumn) major fashion shows are staged in the city: the *Milanocollezioni* and the *Milanovendemoda*. Contact the Milan tourist office (☎ 02-7252 4300) for information.

The heart of the city's fashion scene is found within the shopping area called the Golden Triangle, on the Via Montenapoleone, one of the country's most exclusive shopping streets, where the finest Italian clothes, shoes and accessories are on display in almost every shop window. Window shopping is a delight here (and, due to the prohibitively high prices, it's the only kind of shopping most people do!). Should you be inclined to try something on and you want the shop assistants to take you seriously, you need to look the part; fashion shop assistants in Milan treat you according to how much money they think you're likely to spend!

Poorer mortals go to Corso Buenos Aires, where some 400 shops sell affordable but still fashionable clothes, although you must beware of fake merchandise in some shops. Discount stores (*blocchisti*) sell last year's fashions at reduced prices and you can pick up bargains at stores such as L'Emporio Isola, Gastone Stockhouse and Vestistock Due. Another place to look for bargains in Milan is at wholesale clothing warehouses, mostly based around the Stazione Centrale, some of which offer good prices to retail shoppers.

Rome

Clothes shopping is no less elegant in Rome, where the Via Borgognona and Via Condotti are Meccas for wealthy women from around the world. After you've done your window shopping here, you can find more affordable garments in side streets; discount stores such as Discount System and Labels-for-Less offer both women's and men's clothes for around half their original price. The Castel Romano shopping outlet mall south of Rome has 110 outlet stores, including Valentino and Dolce & Gabbana. The Valmontone Fashion Outlet, also south of Rome, has 200 stores and operates a shuttle bus to and from Rome's Termini station.

Florence

Florence was once Italy's fashion capital, a mantle now assumed by Milan; however, the city still boasts a large number of boutiques and certainly has prices to match those in Milan and Rome. The main fashion boutiques and shoe shops are to be found around the Via dei Tornabuoni, where everyone who's anyone in the Italian fashion industry is represented. Fendi and Dolce & Gabbana have outlet stores outside town (accessible by car), while The Mall, an outlet shopping centre in Leccio-Reggello can be reached by shuttle bus from Florence.

Clothes Shops

La Rinascente department stores (see page 264) stock many top Italian and foreign fashion labels as well as their own line of quality clothing, *Ellerre*, for men, women and children. Other national chains of clothes shops, still of high quality but without the bank-busting prices, include Benetton, Conbipel, Metro (inexpensive clothes for men, women and children), Oviesse (inexpensive men's clothing), Sisley (also sells children's clothes) and Stefanel (for women). Etam and Elena Miro sell clothes for larger women. Many cities and towns have used and new clothes markets, e.g. the Via Sannio in Rome. There are also 'antique' (i.e. second-hand) clothing shops and charity shops in many cities, where you can often pick up bargains.

Clothes sizes in Italy aren't usually uniform and may vary from designer to designer. In general, you may find the sizes smaller than you're used to and women's shoes in particular are manufactured with a small foot in mind. If you aren't the same size as the average Italian and live in northern Italy, it may be worthwhile crossing the border into Switzerland, where sizes tend to be larger. See **Appendix D** for a comparison between European, British and North American sizes.

NEWSPAPERS, MAGAZINES & BOOKS

Newspapers and magazines in Italy are distributed via state-licensed outlets or kiosks (*edicole*), of which there are many, particularly in the major cities. In common with other Latins, Italians aren't generally such avid newspaper and magazine readers as, say, Americans and Britons, although the readership of books, newspapers and magazines is much higher in northern and central Italy than in the south. The average daily newspaper circulation of all newspapers is around 6m, although many Italians read free copies in libraries, cafés and bars.

There's no tradition of newspaper delivery in Italy, other than by post, and you won't see any Italian newsboys or girls.

The press reflects the strong regional allegiances in Italy; there are few national newspapers. The centre-left *La Repubblica* (Rome), centre-left *Corriere della Sera* (Milan) – which includes an English-language section, *Italy Daily* – and *Il Giornale*, a right-leaning daily owned by prime minister Silvio Berlusconi's family are Italy's best-selling and most widely read newspapers. *L'Unità*, the Democratic Left's paper, while not particularly widely read, is considered to be one of the most readable newspapers. Regional newspapers include *La Nazione* (Florence), *La Stampa* (Turin), *Il Messaggero* and *Il Tempo* (Rome), *Il Mattino* (Naples), *Il Secolo XIX* (Genoa), and *La Sicilia* and *Giornale di Sicilia* (Sicily), all of which have large readerships within their own regions.

Italy doesn't have popular 'tabloid' newspapers, the nearest thing to which are the specialist sports newspapers, *Corriere dello Sport* and *La Gazzetta dello Sport*. In Italy, 'sport' is usually a euphemism for Italy's most important news topic, soccer.

The hefty Sunday newspaper complete with colour supplements published in the UK, for example, is virtually non-existent in Italy; many news kiosks are closed on Sundays. English-language newspapers can be purchased in most large cities and towns, although at much inflated prices (sometimes as much as three times their home cover price) and usually a day or so after publication. However, certain newspapers published in Europe such as *The Times*, *Financial Times*, *The Guardian* and the *International Herald Tribune* are usually available on the day of publication.

Italian magazines and periodicals satisfy all tastes and interests – there are some 10,000 to choose from – and often come with gifts, e.g. CDs or videos. International publications such as *Newsweek* and *The Economist* are available at kiosks, and the Italian equivalents, *L'Espresso* and *Panorama*, provide extensive coverage of national and international current affairs. Other quality publications include *Vogue Italia* (fashion), *Domus*, *Arca*, *Bazaar* and *Abitare* (design), *AD* and *FMR* (lifestyle), and *Airone* (nature). Like other Europeans, Italians avidly devour anything concerning the private (or not so private) lives of the famous (not for nothing are freelance photographers who pursue celebrities named after the Italian *paparazzi*), and 'gossip' magazines such as

Oggi and *Gente* are extremely popular. Most major newspapers and magazines have websites.

English-language newspapers and magazines are published in many areas and contain a wealth of information about Italian culture, current affairs, national and local events, restaurants, bars, entertainment, services and shops, as well as providing expatriates with important information. These include *A Guest in Milan* (monthly), *Yes Please* (Milan, quarterly), *Metropolitan* (Rome, bi-weekly), *Time Out* (Rome, monthly), *Wanted in Rome* (bi-monthly), *Where Rome* (monthly) and *Vista* (Tuscany, quarterly).

There's an English-language bookshop in most cities in Italy and a number in major cities. Most, however, are fairly small with limited stock, although they can order any book in print. Bookshops are also a useful source of information for foreign residents: they often have notice boards where advertisements can be placed and distribute leaflets and free publications to the expatriate community. Among the main English-language bookshops in Italy are the American Bookstore (☎ 02-878 920) in Milan and, in Rome, the Anglo-American Book Co. (☎ 06-679 5222, 🖥 www.aab.it) and the Lion Bookshop (☎ 06-32654007). There are also second-hand bookshops in most large towns that buy, sell and exchange second-hand books.

The largest Italian bookshop chain, Feltrinelli, has branches in Bologna, Florence and Rome, which stock a good selection of books in English and other languages. Other Feltrinelli branches usually stock some English-language books and all stores keep English textbooks for language teachers. Book fairs and second-hand book markets for collectors are regularly staged in the major cities. Books aren't particularly expensive in Italy, where a paperback costs around €10 and there's a proliferation of inexpensive paperbacks (*libri economici*) costing from around €5 (although English-language books are more expensive and are best purchased abroad or via the internet).

FURNITURE & FURNISHINGS

Furniture (*mobili*) is generally more expensive in Italy than in many other European countries, although a wide range of modern and traditional furniture is available. Modern furniture is popular and is sold in furniture shops in industrial zones and in hypermarkets throughout Italy; there are few nationwide chains of discount shops. Department stores also sell a wide range of (mostly up-market) furniture. UnoPiu and DuePiu have huge factory outlets north of Rome selling wooden furniture, garden and conservatory furniture (such as rattan and bamboo items), DIY furniture and household goods; they produce beautiful catalogues. Tucano and Oltrefrontiera have a wide selection of furniture and home furnishings, including many products imported from around the world. Inexpensive chain stores include Coin, Habitat, Home Shop, Standee and Upim. At the other end of the scale, a number of international furniture design companies have elegant boutiques in Italy, including English Home and Designers Guild. A mid-range chain is Biggie Best, which has around 25 shops in Italy.

Many regions of Italy have a reputation for quality hand-made furniture, and exclusive modern and traditional furniture is available everywhere, although not everyone can afford the exclusive prices. If you want reasonably priced, good quality, modern furniture, you need look no further than IKEA which has a number of stores in Italy. There are also many good carpet stores although, like most home furnishings, they can be expensive.

☑ **SURVIVAL TIP**

There's a reasonable market for second-hand furniture in Italy and many sellers and dealers advertise in the expatriate and local press, e.g. *Wanted in Rome*.

Italian furniture and furnishing shops often offer design services (which may be free to customers), and stock a wide range of fabrics and materials in patterns and colours ideally suited to Italian homes and the climate and conditions. Most stores make deliveries or loan self-drive vans (or rent them out at reasonable rates).

If you're spending a lot of money, don't be reluctant to ask for a reduction, as most stores will give you a discount. The best time to buy furniture and furnishings is during sales (see page 262), particularly in winter when the prices of many items are slashed. Most furniture shops offer furniture packages for a room or entire home. It's possible for residents to pay for furniture (and large household appliances) interest-free over a year or with interest over a longer period, e.g. five years. It may be worthwhile comparing the cost of furniture in a neighbouring country with that in Italy, although it usually doesn't pay to buy new furniture abroad to furnish an Italian home (particularly as you must usually add transport costs).

If you're looking for old furniture at affordable prices, you may find bargains at antiques fairs and flea markets (see page 262), although genuine antiques are expensive and difficult to find. If you do come across anything worthwhile, you must usually drive a hard bargain, as the asking prices are often ridiculous, particularly in popular tourist areas during the summer. Markets are, however, good places to buy fabrics (e.g. for curtains), bed linen and wallpaper.

Charity shops are an Aladdin's cave of household goods and furniture (and they hold periodic sales). You can also try the classified ads in newspapers such as *Porta Portese* (Rome – named after the city's famous flea market), *La Pulce* (Florence) and

Secondamano (Milan) – there are equivalents in most cities.

DIY MATERIALS

There are do-it-yourself (DIY) hypermarkets in some areas, selling everything for the home, including home-assembly furniture, bathrooms and kitchens, decorating materials and lighting, plus services such as tool hire and wood cutting. Look for the enormous Brico Io and Brico Centre stores, usually located in shopping centres on the outskirts of large cities. There are salvage and second-hand companies selling old doors, window frames, fireplaces, tiles and other materials that are invaluable when restoring an old home or add character to a modern home. Note, however, that many modern DIY supplies and materials aren't as easy to find in Italy as in some other European countries and are more expensive, so you may be better off importing them.

HOUSEHOLD GOODS

Household goods in Italy are generally of good quality and there's a large choice. Prices compare favourably with those in other European countries and bargains can be found at supermarkets and hypermarkets. Not surprisingly in a nation where people spend much of their time in the kitchen (the

rest is spent eating!), Italian kitchenware, crockery, cutlery and glasses can all be purchased cheaply, and the quality and design are usually excellent.

Most Italian kitchens don't come with cupboards or major appliances when you buy or rent a home (unless you agree to purchase the existing kitchen from the previous tenant/owner), so you don't usually need to worry about whether you can fit an imported dishwasher or washing machine into the kitchen. However, you should check the size **and** the latest Italian safety regulations before shipping these items to Italy or buying them abroad, as they may need expensive modifications (see **Power Supply** on page 82). It's recommended to buy white goods (such as refrigerators and washing machines) in Italy, as imported appliances may not function properly due to differences in the electrical supply (it may also be difficult to have them repaired). Italian appliances, such as those made by Candy or Zanussi, have a good reputation for quality and wear, although German brands are generally better (and more expensive).

If you already own small household appliances, it's worthwhile bringing them to Italy, as usually all that's required is a change of plug. If you bring appliances with you, don't forget to bring a supply of spares and refills such as bulbs for a refrigerator or sewing machine and spare bags for a vacuum cleaner. If you're coming from a country with a 110/115V electricity supply, such as the US, you'll need a lot of expensive transformers and it's usually better to buy new appliances in Italy. Small appliances such as vacuum cleaners, grills, toasters and electric irons are inexpensive in Italy and are of good quality. Don't bring a television without checking its compatibility first, as TVs from many countries won't work in Italy (see page 113).

If you need kitchen measuring equipment and cannot cope with metric measures, you must bring your own measuring scales, jugs, cups and thermometers (or refer constantly to **Appendix D**). Note also that foreign pillow sizes often aren't the same as those used in Italy and that duvets are much more expensive in Italy than in some other countries and are therefore worth bringing with you.

TOBACCONISTS

A tobacconist's shop (*tabaccaio*) is easily identified in Italy by a large black '*T*' sign outside. After

Italian unification in 1861, tobacconists were awarded a monopoly on the sale of tobacco, salt and quinine. Nearly a century and a half later, with salt readily available at food shops and quinine no longer made, the sale of tobacco is virtually the only remaining monopoly in Italy – and a thriving business for the state (licensed bars called *bar tabacchi* also sell tobacco products). In addition to the major foreign brands of cigarettes, there's an Italian brand called *MS* (*Monopolio dello Stato*), which is cheaper than imported brands, although less sophisticated. A pack of 20 cigarettes in Italy costs between around €3.70 and €4.10.

Tobacconists are also the official outlet for tax stamps (*marche da bollo*), shown by a '*Valori Bollati*' sign outside, which must be affixed to official documents and application forms. The standard stamp for administrative documents (*atti civili*) costs around €11. Requests for official documents may need to be made on official lined paper (*carta da bollo* or *carta bollata*) with a tax stamp affixed or *carta semplice* (standard white paper to which you may affix tax stamps), both sold by tobacconists. Tobacconists also sell postage stamps, postcards, public transport and lottery tickets, telephone cards, confectionery and ice cream, a few stationery items, photographic film and souvenirs.

SHOPPING ABROAD

Shopping abroad (e.g. in neighbouring Austria, France, Slovenia or Switzerland) makes a welcome change from salivating over all those Italian shops full of tempting and expensive luxuries. It can also save you money and makes an interesting day out for the family. Don't forget your passports or identity cards, car papers, children, dog's vaccination papers, foreign currency and travel insurance. If you're travelling to Switzerland via motorway by car, you need to buy an annual motorway tax sticker at the border (costing around €25). Shopping in Switzerland is popular with Milan and Turin residents, particularly for dairy products and chocolate. Most shops in Swiss border towns accept euros but give you a lower exchange rate than a bank.

Whatever you're looking for, compare prices and quality before buying, and bear in mind that if you buy goods that are faulty or need repair, you may need to return them to the place of purchase.

Since 1993 there have been no cross-border shopping restrictions within the European Union (EU) for goods purchased duty and tax paid, provided all goods are for personal consumption or use and not for resale. Although there are no restrictions, there are 'indicative levels' for certain items, above which quantities may be classified as commercial. For example, those entering Italy aged 17 or over may import the following amounts of alcohol and tobacco without question:

- ◆ 10 litres of spirits (over 22°proof);

- ◆ 20 litres of sherry or fortified wine (under 22° proof);

- ◆ 90 litres of wine (or 120 x 0.75 litre bottles/ ten cases), of which a maximum of 60 litres may be sparkling wine;

- ◆ 110 litres of beer;

- ◆ 800 cigarettes, 400 cigarillos, 200 cigars and 1kg of tobacco.

There's no limit on perfume or toilet water. If you exceed the above amounts, you'll need to convince the customs authorities that you aren't planning to sell any of your purchases. There are fines for anyone who sells duty-paid alcohol and tobacco, which is classed as smuggling.

Never attempt to import illegal goods into Italy and don't agree to bring a parcel into Italy or deliver a parcel in another country without knowing exactly what it contains. A popular confidence trick is to ask someone to post a parcel in Italy (usually to a *poste restante* address) or to leave a parcel at a railway station or restaurant. **The parcel may contains drugs!**

Duty-free Allowances

Duty-free (*esente da dazio*) shopping was abolished within the EU on 1st July 1999 and duty-free allowances now apply only if you're travelling to Italy from a country outside the EU (this includes neighbouring Switzerland).

For each such journey, travellers aged 17 or over are entitled to import the following goods purchased duty-free:

Duty-free Allowances

- One litre of spirits (over 22° proof) **or** two litres of fortified wine (under 22° proof) **or** two litres of sparkling wine;
- Two litres of still table wine;
- 200 cigarettes **or** 100 cigarillos **or** 50 cigars **or** 250g of tobacco;
- 50ml of perfume;
- 250ml of toilet water;
- Other goods, including gifts and souvenirs, to the value of €175.

Duty-free allowances apply to both outward and return journeys, even if both are made on the same day, and the combined total (i.e. double the above limits) can be imported into your 'home' country.

VAT Refunds

If you live outside the EU, you can obtain a VAT refund (20 per cent on most goods) on purchases, provided the value of goods purchased in any one shop (excluding books, food, services and some other items) amounts to at least €154.94, including VAT (shops providing this service usually display a 'Tax-Free' sticker in their windows). Large department stores may have a dedicated counter where non-EU shoppers can arrange for the shipment of duty-free goods. An export sales invoice (or 'tax-free shopping cheque') is provided by retailers, listing all purchases. When you leave Italy, your purchases must be validated by customs (*dogana*) staff at the airport, port or railway station, so don't pack them in your checked baggage. Refunds may be made on the spot at 'tax-free' counters or by post, in which case they're usually made within 90 days of the date of purchase. On-the-spot refunds can take some time, which you should allow for. You can choose to have a refund paid to a credit card or bank account or to receive a cheque.

RECEIPTS & REFUNDS

Receipts (*scontrini*) in Italy are important legal documents; not only is it illegal for a shop not to give you one, it's also illegal for customers not to possess one for the purchases they've made. This practice is supposed to help stamp out tax fraud, a favourite Italian pastime, and the Italian tax police (*Guardia di Finanza*) can fine any customers leaving a shop without a receipt. A receipt is also necessary should you need to return any purchases for exchange or a refund.

Once you've made a purchase, you have eight days in which to return it to the shop, although goods bought in sales are exchanged only if they're faulty or defective, so you should examine any planned purchase carefully. If there's a fault, you must return the goods with the receipt and a written complaint stating the nature of the defect. If you're dissatisfied with the shop's response to your complaint, you should take the complaint to the local police, who have a commercial department (*polizia annonaria commerciale*), or to the local trading standards council (*assessorato al commercio*).

CONSUMER PROTECTION

The law protects consumers' rights to health, quality and security of products and services, and to adequate information and accurate publicity. In order to ensure such protection, legal actions may be brought by individuals and by recognised consumer associations. The foremost Italian consumer protection organisation is called Altro Consumo-Informazione Indipendente per i Consumatori, Altroconsumo (💻 www.altroconsumo.it). You must take out a subscription in order to receive its monthly magazine, which isn't sold at news kiosks.

statue, Esposizione Universale Roma

Angelo Musicanto, Melozzo da Forli

18.
ODDS & ENDS

This chapter contains miscellaneous information (in alphabetical order), including everything you ever wanted to know about tipping and toilets (but were afraid to ask). Most of the topics covered are of general interest to anyone living or working in Italy, although admittedly not all are of vital everyday importance. However, buried among the trivia are some fascinating snippets of information.

CITIZENSHIP

The following laws currently apply to Italian citizenship, but you should check whether these have been amended before making any important decisions:

◆ Any child born of an Italian father or mother is automatically Italian, as is a child born in Italy of unknown or stateless parents, or if the child doesn't obtain the citizenship (*cittadinanza*) of its parents under the law of their country.

◆ A foreigner married to an Italian citizen can apply for Italian citizenship six months after marriage if living in Italy, or three years after marriage if living abroad.

◆ A foreign resident who isn't married to an Italian can apply for citizenship after four years' residence if he is a European Union (EU) national, otherwise after ten years; stateless people resident in Italy and foreigners serving the Italian state can apply after five years.

◆ A foreigner with a parent or grandparent who was an Italian citizen at birth qualifies for citizenship after living in Italy for two years after his 18th birthday or, if born in Italy, at any age.

◆ A child born to foreign parents in Italy doesn't automatically acquire Italian citizenship but may apply at the age of 18. He or she must have continuously resided in Italy from birth to adulthood.

◆ It's not necessary to have to choose between your parents' nationality and Italian, as Italy recognises dual nationality (*doppia cittadinanza*), although anyone with dual citizenship arriving in or leaving Italy must do so with an Italian passport or identity card.

In order to obtain Italian citizenship, you must apply to the Ministry of the Interior (*Ministro dell'Interno*) through the mayor of the commune (*comune*) where you live, or through an Italian consulate abroad. A concession tax must be paid and you must swear loyalty to the republic and that you'll observe Italy's constitution and laws. As with most things involving bureaucrats in Italy, the process of applying for and obtaining Italian citizenship is a long-drawn-out affair often taking years, which will stretch your patience to the limit.

The documents required vary according to your situation and nationality (it's allegedly easier for those married to Italians); up to 12 documents may be required, many of which must be on official paper (*bollo*), translated by an official translator, and must be authenticated or legalised. A list of the necessary documents is available from your local government office (*prefettura*). After you've made an application, the authorities have 18 months to make a decision.

CLIMATE

Italy generally has a temperate climate influenced by the Mediterranean and Adriatic Seas, and the protective Alps encircling the north. Southern Italy and the islands of Sicily and Sardinia enjoy a Mediterranean climate, as does the Italian Riviera. Italy has warm, dry summers and mild winters in most regions, although there's a marked contrast between the far north and the south. Rome is generally recognised as the dividing point between the colder north and the hotter southern regions. The best seasons throughout the country are spring and autumn, when it's neither too hot nor too cold in most regions.

Summers are generally very hot everywhere, and thunderstorms are common in inland areas, with average temperatures in July and August around 24°C (75°F). Summers are short and not too hot in the northern lake areas, while the Po Valley has warm and sunny summers but can be humid. Summers are drier and hotter the further south you go (too hot for most people), although sea breezes alleviate the heat in coastal areas. In the south (including Rome), the *scirocco* wind from Africa can produce stifling weather in August, with temperatures well above 30°C (86°F).

Winters are mild in most areas with some wet spells. However, they're very cold (but usually sunny) in the alpine regions, where snowfalls are frequent. The first snowfall in the Alps is usually in November, although light snow sometimes falls in mid-September and heavy snow can fall in October. Fog is common throughout the north from the autumn through to February, and winters can be severe in the Po Valley, the plains of Lombardy and Emilia-Romagna. Venice can be quite cold in winter (it frequently snows there) and it's often flooded when there's a high tide (*acqua alta*) and

strong onshore winds. Florence is also cold in winter, while winters are moderate in Rome, where it rarely snows. The Italian Riviera and Liguria experience mild winters and enjoy a Mediterranean climate as they're protected by both the Alps and the Apennines (*Appennini*). Sicily and southern Italy have the mildest winters, with daytime temperatures between 10 and 20°C (50 to 68°F).

Rainfall is moderate to low in most regions and is rare anywhere in summer. The north and the Adriatic coast are wetter than the rest of Italy. There's a lot of rain in the central regions of Tuscany and Umbria in winter, although they suffer neither extreme heat nor cold most of the year. There's a shortage of water in many areas during summer, when the supply is often turned off during the day and households are limited to a number of cubic metres per year.

Average daytime maximum/minimum temperatures (in Centigrade) for selected towns are shown below.

A quick way to make a rough conversion from Centigrade to Fahrenheit is to multiply by two and add 30. Weather forecasts (*previsioni del tempo*) are broadcast on television and radio stations and published in daily newspapers.

CRIME

The crime rate in Italy varies considerably from region to region but is generally around average for Europe. Violent crime is rare in most areas, although muggings do occur in resort areas and cities. Foreigners should take care when travelling in the south of Italy, where

Average Min/Max Daytime Temperatures (°C)				
City	Spring (April)	Summer (July)	Autumn (October)	Winter (January)
Brindisi	18/11	29/21	22/15	12/6
Cagliari	19/11	30/21	23/15	14/7
Milan	18/10	29/20	17/11	5/0
Naples	18/9	29/18	22/12	12/4
Palermo	20/11	30/21	25/16	16/8
Rome	19/10	30/20	22/13	11/5
Venice	17/10	27/19	19/11	6/1

highway robbery and kidnappings of foreigners occasionally take place. Despite the fearsome reputation of the Mafia, however, there's **less** violent street crime such as muggings and robbery with violence in most parts of Italy than in many other European countries, and it's generally a very safe place for children. Sexual harassment can be a problem for women in some areas, although most men draw the line at cat-calls and whistles.

Burglary is rife, and vacant holiday homes are a popular target. Many residents keep dogs as a protection or warning against burglars and have triple-locked and steel-reinforced doors. However, crime in rural areas remains relatively low and it's still common for people in villages and small towns not to lock their cars and homes (in some small villages keys are left in front doors).

Theft of and from cars is widespread in cities, where foreign-registered cars are a popular target, particularly expensive models, which are often stolen to order and spirited abroad. Theft of small items such as radios, luggage, mobile phones, cameras, briefcases, sunglasses and even cigarettes from parked cars is especially common. Thieves in the south often take items from cars at petrol (gas) stations, if necessary by smashing car windows, and from occupied vehicles in traffic jams or at traffic lights. It's therefore wise to keep windows closed in cities and major towns, doors locked at all times, and all valuables out of sight. When parking a bicycle, moped or scooter, you should also use as many high-security locks as you can carry. See also **Car Crime** on page 175.

In towns and cities, beware of bag snatchers (*scippatori*), who operate on foot, on scooters and motorcycles or even in cars. Always carry bags slung across your body with the clasp facing inwards; make sure they have a strong strap that cannot easily be cut – if they don't, carry them firmly in your hand. Bags that are worn around the waist ('bum-bags') are vulnerable and should be avoided, as should back-packs, which can easily be cut. One of the most effective methods of protecting your passport, money, travellers' cheques and credit cards is with an old-fashioned money belt (worn under your clothing) or a pouch on a string or strong cord around your neck. It's also

recommended to keep money and credit cards in separate places and a copy of important documents such as your passport in a safe place. Never tempt fate with an exposed wallet or purse or by flashing your money around, and hang on tight to your shoulder bag. Don't carry a lot of cash or expose expensive jewellery, watches or sunglasses when out walking.

Confidence tricksters are also rife in Italy, where it's wise to avoid all strangers trying to attract your attention. Many thieves stage 'accidents', such as spilling something on your clothes (or pointing out something which has been done by an accomplice), in order to distract you and rob you. Be alert to any incident that could be designed to attract your attention and keep strangers at arm's length. Don't accept an offer from someone to take your photograph with your camera (they're likely to run off with it); if you must ask someone to take a photo, ask a tourist or a waiter.

Pickpockets and bag-snatchers are a plague in the major cities, where the street urchins (often Albanians or Gypsies) are highly organised and trained pickpockets (if you get jostled, check for your wallet). They try to surround you and often use newspapers or large pieces of cardboard to distract you and hide their roaming hands. Keep them at arm's length, if necessary by force, and keep a firm grip on your valuables. If you're targeted, shout *va via* (go away) in a loud voice – a loud whistle can also be useful to scare off prospective attackers or pickpockets. Always remain vigilant in tourist haunts, queues, on public transport (particularly on night trains) and anywhere where there are crowds. Thieves on crowded public transport slit the bottoms of purses or bags with a razor blade or sharp knife and remove the contents.

Italy is infamous for its organised crime and gang warfare, which is rife in some areas, although it has no discernible impact on the lives of most foreigners there (particularly in the north of the country). The term 'Mafia' is used to describe five distinct organised crime groups: the original Sicilian Mafia, the *Camorra* in Naples and Campania, the *Ndrangheta* in Calabria, and the *Sacra Corona Unita* and *La Rosa* in Apulia. These groups operate both separately and together, and their activities range from drugs and contraband dealing to protection and gambling rackets and prostitution. They monopolise lucrative contracts in most fields throughout the country and it's estimated that their combined turnover is billions of euros, possibly over 10 per cent of Italy's GNP.

The Mafia holds a death grip on the south of Italy, where business people are often forced to pay protection money (*pizzo*) to the mobsters to ensure their businesses are safe – it's estimated that half the businesses in Naples pay protection money – or are prey to loan sharking (*usurai* – lending money at extortionate rates of interest). Despite many high profile arrests in recent years, rumours of the Mafia's demise or loss of influence are premature and they reportedly have their fingers in every facet of government right up to the Prime Minister's office in Rome!

> In recent years, Albanians, Russians and assorted other foreign gangsters have established their own 'Mafia' in the north, where they're heavily involved in organised crime.

Don't let the foregoing catalogue of crime put you off Italy. You can usually safely walk almost anywhere at any time of day or night and there's no need for anxiety or paranoia about crime. However, you should be 'street-wise' and take certain elementary precautions. These include avoiding high-risk areas (such as parks and car parks) at night and those frequented by drug addicts, prostitutes and pickpockets at all times. You can safely travel on the underground (*metro*) at almost any time, although some stations are best avoided late at night. When you're in an unfamiliar city, ask a policeman, taxi driver or other local person whether there are any unsafe neighbourhoods – and avoid them!

If you're the victim of a crime, you should report it to the nearest police station (*commissariato di pubblica sicurezza*) or to the local *carabinieri* immediately (see **Police** on page 294). You can report it by telephone but must go to the station to complete a report (*denuncia*), of which you receive a copy for insurance purposes. Don't, however, expect the police to find your belongings or even take much of an interest in your loss. Report a theft to your insurance company as soon as possible.

DEFENCE

The Italian armed forces number around 182,200, comprising an army (104,000), air force (43,000) and navy (35,200). Italy also has reserve forces numbering around 60,000. The 113,000 *carabinieri* (see **Police** on page 294) is also part of the army, with control shared between the Ministry of Defence and the Ministry of the Interior. Defence spending is currently around US$35.8bn per year (including the *carabinieri*). Italy, which has no nuclear weapons, is a member of the North Atlantic Treaty Organisation (NATO) and is home to a number of NATO military bases. Mandatory military service ended on January 1st 2005.

GEOGRAPHY

Italy covers an area of 301,245km² (116,319mi²) and comprises a long peninsula shaped like a boot, which is instantly recognisable and tends to give the impression that the country is much larger than it actually is (it covers around the same area as the US state of Arizona or the British Isles). The country is 1,200km (750mi) in length and between 150 and 250km (93 to 155mi) in width. Italy has borders with France (488km/303mi), Switzerland

(740km/460mi), Austria (430km/267mi) and Slovenia (199km/124mi), and encompasses two independent states within its borders: the Vatican City (116acres/47ha) in Rome, established in 1929, and the Republic of San Marino (61km²/24mi²) in the Marche region. The country is divided into 20 regions and 110 provinces, shown on the map in **Appendix E**.

Italy is a land of stark contrasts, including towering mountains and vast plains, huge lakes and wide valleys. It has a wide variety of landscapes and vegetation but is dominated by two mountain ranges, the Alps and the Apennines (almost 80 per cent of the country is covered by hills and mountains – see below). In the north there are large areas of forest and farmland, while the south is mostly scrubland. Lowlands or plains comprise less than a quarter of Italy's total land mass. The largest plain is the Po Valley (bounded by the Alps, the Apennines and the Adriatic Sea), a heavily populated and industrialised area.

The Po is Italy's longest river, flowing from west to east across the plain of Lombardy in the north into the Adriatic. Its tributaries include the Adige, Piave, Reno and Tagliamento rivers. Other major rivers include the Tiber (Rome) and the Arno (Tuscany). A coastal plain (Tavoliere delle Puglia) runs along the Tyrrhenian Sea from southern Tuscany through Lazio into Puglia, while another smaller plain is Pianura Campana near Mount Vesuvius. Italy has a number of great national parks, including Abruzzo in the Apennines and the Alpine Gran Paradiso between Valle d'Aosta and Piedmont.

Mountains

The Alps (*Alpi*) form the country's northern border, stretching from the Gulf of Genoa (*Golfo di Genova*) in the west to the Adriatic Sea (north of Trieste) in the east. The highest mountain peak is Monte Bianco (Mont Blanc, 4,807m/15,770ft), on the border with France. The Alps are divided into three main groups, western, central and eastern, and are at their most beautiful and spectacular in the Dolomites (*Dolomiti*) in the east. The alpine foothills are characterised by the vast Po Valley (see above) and the lakes of Como, Garda and Maggiore.

The Apennines form the backbone of Italy, extending for 1,220km (758mi) from Liguria near Genoa to the tip of Calabria and into Sicily. The highest peak in the Apennines is the Corno Grande (2,914m/9,560ft) in the Gran Sasso d'Italia range in Abruzzo. The Apuan Alps (*Alpi Apuane*) in the northwest of Tuscany form part of the sub-Apennines and are composed almost entirely of marble, which has been mined since Roman times.

In the south, the Gargano and Sila massifs cross the 'spur' and 'foot' of the boot, respectively.

Coast & Islands

The country is surrounded by sea except in the extreme north. The Ligurian and Tyrrenian seas wash the west of the peninsula, the Ionian Sea lies off the coasts of Puglia, Basilicata and Calabria in the south, and the Adriatic Sea in the east separates Italy from the Balkan Peninsula. Italy has a vast and varied coastline of some 7,500km (4,660mi), including its islands, highlights of which include the Amalfi Coast (south of Naples), the crescent of Liguria (the Italian Riviera) and the Gargano Massif (the spur jutting into the Adriatic). Coastal areas vary considerably from the generally flat

Gulf of Naples, while the seven islands of the Tuscan archipelago (off the Maremma coast) are among the most appealing of all Mediterranean islands; they include Capraia, Elba, Giannutri, Giglio, Gorgona, Montecristo and Pianosa. The beautiful island of Elba (where Napoleon was exiled from May 1814 to February 1815) covers an area of 224km² (86mi²), two-thirds of which is woodland, and has some excellent sandy beaches. Other islands include the five virtually unknown Pontine islands some 32km (20mi) off the coast of Lazio.

Earthquakes & Volcanoes

Italy is subject to earthquakes and volcanic eruptions, though it's important to put the dangers in perspective. (There has been a government campaign in recent years to inform people and allay their fears about earthquakes, although it has generally had the opposite effect!) A fault line runs through the centre of Italy from north to south as far as Sicily. Officially, some 3,000 towns out of a total of 8,000 are in constant danger from earthquakes. These contain some 10m homes, at least two-thirds of which aren't earthquake proof (even those that are supposedly 'earthquake proof' often aren't). The highest risk areas are in the south – Calabria and Sicily – where some 70 per cent of the terrain is susceptible to earthquakes. Friuli-Venezia-Giulia, bordering Austria and Slovenia, and Marche and Abruzzo, midway down the Adriatic coast, are also earthquake prone.

The country's last major earthquake hit Messina and Reggio di Calabria in 1908, killing some 85,000 people. More recently, in April 2009, the Abruzzo region was hit by an earthquake measuring 5.8 on the Richter scale in which 308 people died. There have been other earthquakes in Friuli (1976), Irpinia, southeast of Naples (1980) and Umbria (1997). The area extending from Tuscany to Basilicata (with the exception of Puglia) has a medium to high risk, while all other regions are low or low to medium risk.

Italy has a number of active volcanoes, including Mount Etna on Sicily (3,274m/10,741ft), Stromboli (on the Isle of Eolie off the west coast of southern Italy) and Vesuvius (near Naples). Etna, which last

Adriatic coast to the dramatic cliffs of Liguria and Calabria.

The country comprises a number of islands, including Sicily (lying across the Strait of Messina from the 'toe' of the boot), the largest and most densely populated island in the Mediterranean.

The islands of Pantelleria, Linosa and Lampedusa lie between Sicily and Tunisia, and many other small islands surround Sicily, offering spectacular scenery and excellent facilities for scuba diving and underwater fishing. These include the Lipari group of islands (encompassing Lipari itself, plus Vulcano, Panarea and Stromboli), Ustica, Favignana, Levanzo and Marittimo. Italy's (and the Mediterranean's) second-largest island is Sardinia (*Sardegna*), situated in the Tyrrhenian Sea to the west of the mainland and south of the island of Corsica (which belongs to France). It's the country's most sparsely populated region, with a coastline of some 1,300km (800mi), and one of Italy's most unspoilt areas.

Among Italy's most famous and attractive islands are Capri, Ischia and Procida in the erupted in April 2010, and Stromboli are among the world's most active volcanoes, while Vesuvius hasn't erupted since 1944.

GOVERNMENT

Italy was a monarchy from its unification in the second half of the 19th century until 1946, when it became a parliamentary republic following a national referendum. On 1st January 1948, it adopted a constitutional charter, which defines the political and civil liberties of citizens and the principles of government. Italy is headed by a President who appoints a Prime Minister, the elected head of government. The seat of government is Rome, where the President resides in the Palazzo del Quirinale, the Chamber of Deputies sits in the Palazzo Montecitorio and the Senate occupies the Palazzo Madama (see **Parliament** below).

President

The head of state is the President of the republic, who (at least in theory) represents the nation's unity and ensures compliance with the constitution (under the direction of the constitutional court). He is elected every seven years by a college comprising both chambers of parliament and three representatives from each region. The minimum age for presidential candidates is 50. The current President, Giorgio Napolitano, took office in 2006.

The President's duties include appointing the Prime Minister, promulgating laws and decrees, authorising the presentation of government bills in parliament and, with parliamentary authorisation, ratifying treaties and declaring war. He may dissolve parliament (except during the last six months of his term of office), either on his own initiative in consultation with the presidents of both chambers or at the request of the government, and he has the power to call special sessions of parliament and delay legislation. Some of these acts must be ratified by the government. The President commands the armed forces and presides over the Supreme Council of Defence and the Superior Council of Magistrates. Whenever a government is defeated or resigns, it's his duty (after consulting eminent politicians and party leaders) to appoint the person most likely to win the confidence of parliament, although the candidate is usually designated by the majority parties and the President has limited choice.

Parliament

The Italian parliament (*parlamento*) is bicameral, consisting of two chambers or assemblies: the Senate of the Republic (*Senato della Repubblica*) with 315 members (called senators) and the Chamber of Deputies (*Camera dei Deputati*) with 630 members (deputies). The assemblies enjoy equal power and are both elected by universal suffrage. Senators represent Italy's 20 regions whereas deputies come from 26 constituencies, but the most important difference between the chambers is the minimum age required for the electorate and the candidates: 18 and 25 respectively for deputies and 25 and 40 for senators.

Since 2005, both the senators and the deputies have been elected using a party-list proportional representation system. Parliament is elected every five years, although few Italian governments run their course, the average length of office being less than a year. The senators and deputies must declare to which parliamentary group they intend to belong, and any political group consisting of at least 10 senators and 20 deputies has the right to be represented in parliament.

> If at any time the government fails to maintain the confidence of either house, it must resign. Splits in the coalition parties that unite to form a government bring down numerous Italian governments.

The government is appointed by the President and is led by the president of the council of ministers (*il Presidente del Consiglio*), more commonly referred to as the Prime Minister. Although the government carries out the executive functions of the state, in emergencies it also has powers to approve laws by decree. Parliament can be dissolved by the President, e.g. when the Prime Minister loses a vote of no confidence. Ministerial appointments are negotiated by the parties constituting the government majority and each new government must receive a vote of confidence in both houses of parliament within ten days of its appointment.

The most important function of parliament is ordinary legislation. Bills may be presented in parliament by the government, by individual members, or by bodies such as the National Council for Economy and Labour, by various regional councils or communes, and through a petition of 50,000 citizens of the electorate or a referendum. Bills must be approved by both houses before they become law; thus, whenever one house introduces an amendment to a draft approved by the other house, the latter must approve the amended draft. The law comes into force when published in the *Gazzetta Ufficiale*.

Political Parties

From the end of the Second World War to the early '90s, Italy had a multi-party system dominated by two parties, the Christian Democratic Party (Partito della Democrazia Cristiana/DC) and the Italian Communist Party (Partito Comunista Italiano/PCI), with a number of other small but influential parties, ranging from the neo-fascist Italian Social Movement (Movimento Sociale Italiano/MSI) on the right to the Italian Socialist Party (Partito Socialista Italiano/PSI) on the left, while a number of small secular parties occupied the centre. The DC was the dominant governing party in various alliances with smaller parties of the centre and left, and the principal opposition parties were the PCI and the MSI.

The Italian party system underwent a radical transformation in the early '90s as a result of both international and national events. The party system was radically altered by the fall of communism, by a wave of judicial prosecutions of corrupt officials that involved most Italian political parties, and by the fact that in 1991 the Communist Party became the Democratic Party of the Left (Partito Democratico della Sinistra/PDS). The DC, battered by scandal, was replaced by a much smaller organisation, the Italian Popular Party (Partito Popolare Italiano/PPI), which itself virtually disappeared after elections in 1994.

Since the early '90s three new parties began to dominate the political right: Forza Italia (FI), a vaguely neo-liberal alliance created in 1994 by the media tycoon Silvio Berlusconi; the Northern League (Lega Nord/LN), formed in 1991, a federalist and fiscal-reform movement with large support in the northern regions; and the National Alliance (Alleanza Nazionale/AN), which succeeded the MSI in 1994, but whose political platform renounced its fascist past. In 2009, Forza Italia and the National Alliance were joined to create a new party, People of Freedom, led by Silvio Berlusconi. Thus, the Italian political spectrum, which had previously been dominated by parties of the centre, became polarised between parties of the right and left.

Regional Government

For administrative purposes, the country is divided into 20 regions (*regioni*, see **Appendix E**), which roughly correspond to the historical regions of the country. The regions are further divided into 110 provinces (*provincie*, three of which came into being in 2009), which are further subdivided into town councils or communes (*comuni*). The five 'special status' regions (*regioni a statuo speciale*) of Friuli-Venezia-Giuila, Sardinia, Sicily, Trentino-Alto Adige and Val d'Aosta are autonomous or semi-autonomous due to particular ethnic or geographical considerations. They have special powers granted under the constitution, and regional assemblies (similar to parliaments) with a wide range of administrative and economic powers. Italy's other 15 regions have little

Silvio Berlusconi, Prime Minister

autonomy compared with, for example, those in Germany or Spain.

Participation in national government is a principal function of the regions, and regional councils may initiate parliamentary legislation, propose referenda, and appoint three delegates to assist in presidential elections. With regard to regional legislation, the five 'special' regions have exclusive authority in certain fields such as agriculture, forestry and town planning, while the other regions have authority within the limits of principles established by state laws. The legislative powers of the regions are subject to certain constitutional limitations, the most important of which is that regional acts may not conflict with national interests. The regions can also enact legislation necessary for the enforcement of state laws and have the right to acquire property and to collect certain revenues and taxes. Regional and local elections are held every five years.

Communes

The organs of the commune (*comune*), the smallest local government unit, are the popularly elected communal council, the communal committee or executive body and the mayor (*sindaco*). The communes have the power to levy and collect local taxes and have their own police (*vigili urbani*), although their powers are much less than those exercised by the national police. The communes issue ordinances and run certain public health services, and are responsible for such services as public transport, refuse collection and street lighting. Regions have some control over the activity of the communes, and communal councils may be dissolved for reasons of public order or for continued neglect of their duties. The mayor of a commune, in his capacity as an agent of the central government, registers births, deaths, marriages, and migrations, maintains public order (although in practice this is dealt with by the national police), and can, in an emergency, issue ordinances concerning public health, town planning and the local police.

An EU national is entitled to vote in communal elections and stand as a candidate.

Referenda

An important feature of the Italian constitution is that referenda must be held – in order to repeal laws or executive orders (except with regard to anything concerning the state budget or the ratification of international treaties) – at the request of 500,000 signatories or five regional councils. Referenda have been called extensively since the '70s and have resulted in a wide range of institutional and civic reforms. Important referenda held in the past include those on abortion, divorce, nuclear power and electoral reform. Some regions also have a provision for holding referenda. The constitution also provides that 50,000 members of the electorate may jointly present to parliament a draft bill.

European Parliamentary Elections

EU nationals over 18 who are resident in Italy are permitted to vote in European elections for Members of the European Parliament (MEPs). If you wish to exercise your right to vote, you must request an application form from the mayor of the municipality where you're resident not less than 90 days before polling day. You may be required to show your identity documents and give your last address in your home EU country in order to verify that you're an EU citizen. As far as elections to the European Parliament are concerned, you lose the right to vote in your EU country of origin if you choose to vote in Italy.

LEGAL SYSTEM

Italian law is based on Roman law, particularly its civil law, and on French Napoleonic law (itself based on the Roman model). The codes of the Kingdom of Sardinia in civil and penal affairs were extended to the whole of Italy when Italy was unified in the mid-19th century. The revised 1990 penal code replaced the old 'inquisitory' system with an accusatory system similar to that of common-law countries. Besides the codes, there are innumerable statutes that integrate the codes and regulate areas of law for which no codes exist, such as public law. Under the Italian constitution, the judiciary is independent of the legislature and the executive, and therefore jurisdictional functions can be performed only by magistrates and judges cannot be dismissed.

The Italian judicial system consists of a series of courts and a body of judges who are civil servants. The judicial system is unified, every court being part of the national network. The highest court is the Supreme Court of Appeal, which has appellate jurisdiction and gives judgements only on points of law. The 1948 constitution prohibits special courts with the exception of administrative courts and military court-martials, although a vast network of tax courts has survived from an earlier period.

The Italian legal system is inordinately complicated and most lawyers (avvocati) and judges (giudici) are baffled by the conflicts between different laws, many dating back centuries, and EU directives serve to complicate matters further. There are literally thousands of laws, most of which are ignored, and newcomers must learn where to draw the line between laws that are enforced and those that aren't or are only weakly enforced. It sometimes appears that there's one law for foreigners and another for Italians, and fines (multe) are commonplace.

The legal system grinds **very** slowly and it takes years for a case to come to court; the average time between indictment and a court judgement is ten years, and eight out of ten convictions involving prison terms never take effect. This means that you should do everything possible to avoid going to court, by taking every conceivable precaution when doing business in Italy, i.e. obtaining expert legal advice in advance. If things go wrong, it can take years to achieve satisfaction and in the case of fraud the chances are that those responsible will have gone broke, disappeared or even died by the time the case is decided. Even when you have a cast-iron case there's no guarantee of winning and it may be better to write off a loss to 'experience'. Local courts, judges and lawyers frequently abuse the system to their own ends, and almost anyone with enough money or expertise can use the law to their own advantage.

Arrest

If you're arrested in Italy, you have the right to see a lawyer (avvocato) before a hearing before a judge, and the right to notify your local consulate which can provide the names of lawyers who speak your language. You also have the right to silence and need only state your name, date and place of birth, and whether you've been arrested in Italy before. You can be held for a maximum of three days before a hearing, at which you may be required to provide legal representation – this depends on what you're accused of – and if you don't provide a lawyer, one will be appointed by the court. After the hearing, you're usually permitted to go free provided you're deemed unlikely to flee, be a danger to society or destroy evidence.

> In serious cases it can be difficult to obtain bail and you can be held for up to two years without trial!

Lost Property or Documents

If you lose or have something stolen in Italy, you should make a report (denuncia) to the carabinieri (see **Police** on page 294) who are nearest to where the incident occurred, rather than in the town where you live. Making a report is essential if you want to claim on an insurance policy, as the police report constitutes evidence of your loss.

MARRIAGE & DIVORCE

To be married in Italy, a couple must appear before the civil registrar (ufficiale di stato civile) of the town where the marriage is to take place, with two witnesses, and make a declaration of their intention to marry. You must present all necessary documents, which must be translated into Italian and certified by an Italian Consular Officer. These include your passport, birth certificate, a final divorce (sentenza di divorzio) or annulment decree or death certificate (if previously married) and, if either party is under 18, a sworn statement of consent to the marriage by the parents or legal guardians. You also need the inevitable fiscal stamp! You may also need to obtain a 'certificate of no impediment' (nulla osta) from a consulate stating that according to the

Over 75 per cent of weddings in Italy are performed in church. Catholic churches require that both parties are baptised and confirmed Catholics, and attend a church 'pre-matrimonial course'. If a religious ceremony is performed by a Roman Catholic priest, a separate civil ceremony is unnecessary, but the priest must register the marriage with the civil registrar in order for it to be legal. Due to the special requirements that apply to marriages performed by non-Roman Catholic clergymen, however, you must usually undergo a civil ceremony before the religious ceremony in order to ensure the legality of the marriage. A civil ceremony is usually performed by the mayor or civil registrar at the local town hall in front of two witnesses. There's nothing to pay apart from the inevitable fiscal stamp (€11). The authorities require the presence of a translator if neither party speaks Italian.

Family law has seen many reforms in recent decades, including the abolition of the husband's status as head of the household and the legalisation of divorce and abortion. Couples married in Italy must choose between shared ownership (*comunità dei beni*) and separate ownership (*separazione dei beni*) of their worldly goods in the event of divorce or death (which can have important consequences). Foreigners from countries without matrimonial regimes are usually shown as having married without regime or the equivalent of *separazione dei beni*. A wife isn't required to take her husband's name upon marriage and some retain their maiden names. However, some wives append their husband's surname to their own – either in front or behind.

Divorce has been possible in Italy only since 1970. You can be divorced in Italy if your marriage took place there or if one of a couple is Italian or a resident in the country. With the exception of divorce by consent, divorce is a complicated matter in Italy and is best avoided if it can be accomplished abroad, which is possible when one of a couple isn't Italian or you were married abroad.

When two resident foreigners wish to divorce or when only one partner is Italian, foreign law may take precedence over Italian law.

A couple divorcing by consent must wait three years to be divorced but couples not divorcing by consent must wait five years after

laws to which you're subject in your home country, there's no obstacle to your marriage. Presentation of this declaration allows the authorities to reduce the time before a marriage licence is granted from three weeks to around four days.

A divorced woman must wait nine months or obtain dispensation from a local court before she can remarry in Italy, because she could be pregnant by her former husband at the time of the divorce.

After the declaration is made, it's usually necessary for banns (*pubblicazioni matrimoniali*) or an announcement of the forthcoming marriage to be posted at the local town hall (*comune*, sometimes referred to as *municipio*) and church (for a church wedding) for two consecutive Sundays before the marriage occurs, if either party is Italian or resident in Italy. However, banns are waived by the civil registrar if neither party to the marriage is Italian or is residing in Italy. The couple may be married in a civil or religious ceremony on the fourth day following the second Sunday on which the banns are posted (or at any time after the banns have been waived).

fault has been proved. The other difference is the cost; divorce by consent costs little or nothing, while a contested divorce costs many thousands of euros. When a couple decide to divorce, they go before a judge who offers them the choice of reconciliation or a formal separation (*separazione formale*) for one year. Financial matters should also be dealt with at this time. The mother is usually given custody of the children, with access for the father, and once they reach the age of ten they can (within certain guidelines) decide which parent they want to live with. Catholics who no longer wish to be married but equally don't want to get divorced, can obtain a formal judicial separation.

PETS

Although not exactly a nation of animal lovers, Italy is generally tolerant of pets, which are rarely restricted or banned from long-term rental or holiday accommodation (but check when renting an apartment).

The unpleasant aspect of Italy's dog population is abundantly evident on the streets of Italian towns and cities, where dogs routinely leave their 'calling cards'. You must always watch where you walk. Most dog owners don't take their pets on long country walks, but just to a local park or car park or simply let them loose in the streets to do their business. Poop-scoops must be used in some cities and towns, where you can be fined around €30 for not cleaning up after your dog, although most people ignore this law. Although it's of little consolation, it's supposedly good luck to tread in something unpleasant!

Importing Pets

If you plan to take a pet (*animale domestico*) to Italy, it's important to check the latest regulations. Make sure that you have the correct papers, not only for Italy, but for all the countries you'll pass through. Particular consideration must be given before exporting a pet from a country with strict quarantine regulations, such as the UK; if you need to return prematurely, even after a few hours or days, your pet may need to go into quarantine, e.g. for six months in the UK. Since 2000, under the 'Pet Travel Scheme (PETS)', qualifying pets, e.g. cats, dogs and ferrets, arriving from certain countries can enter Britain without going into quarantine.

Under the scheme, pets must be microchipped (they have a chip inserted under the skin in their neck) and vaccinated against rabies, undergo a blood test and be issued with a 'health certificate' ('passport'). **Note that the PETS certificate isn't issued until six months *after* the above have been carried out!** Pets must also be checked for ticks and tapeworms 24 to 48 hours before embarkation on a plane or ship. With a passport, which must be kept up to date abroad, an animal can return to the UK without needing to be quarantined.

The scheme is restricted to animals imported from rabies-free countries and countries where rabies is under control – this includes EU countries, plus a number of other qualifying countries including Australia, Canada, New Zealand, the United Arab Emirates and the US. However, quarantine law remains in place for pets coming from Africa, and much of Asia and South America. To qualify, pets must travel by sea via certain UK ports, by train via the Channel Tunnel or via a number of approved UK airports (only certain carriers are licensed to carry animals). Member countries and conditions change all the time, therefore it's important to check well in advance of travel.

For the latest regulations, contact the Department of the Environment, Food and Rural Affairs, DEFRA, PETS helpline UK (☎ 0870-241 1710, 🖥 www.defra.gov. uk/wildlife-pets/pets/ travel/pets/index.htm). A passport costs pet owners around £200 (for a microchip, rabies vaccination and blood test), plus £60 per year for annual booster vaccinations and around £20 for a border check. Shop around and compare fees from a number of veterinary surgeons and don't leave arrangements too late. Vets in Calais have been known to charge up to €200 for last-minute tick and tapeworm treatments!

There's no quarantine for pets arriving in Italy, but they need a health certificate (bilingual, Italian-English) issued by an approved veterinary surgeon. Dogs and cats need a rabies vaccination not less than 20 days or more than 11 months prior to the date of issue of the health certificate. Animals aged under 12 weeks are exempt but must have a health certificate and a certificate stating that no cases of rabies have occurred for at least six months in the local area. British owners can transfer their pets to Italy – or other EU countries – on a PETS 'passport' (see above). Call the PETS helpline on ☎ UK 0870-241 1710 for the latest information. Animals may be examined at the Italian port of entry by a veterinary officer.

If you're transporting a pet by ship or ferry, you should notify the shipping company. Some companies insist that pets are left in vehicles (if applicable), while others allow pets to be kept in cabins. If your pet is of a nervous disposition or unused to travelling, it's best to tranquillise it on a long sea crossing. Pets can also be transported by air, but a number of conditions apply so contact a pet travel agent for details.

Identification

At the age of three months, a dog must be registered at the local 'dog bureau' (*anagrafe canina*) and some municipalities issue dog tags. Italian regulations require dogs to be tattooed on their body (not just their ear) as a means of registration, although a new microchip identification system is being introduced in 2011 and will replace tattooing. Tattooing must be done by a veterinary surgeon (*veterinari*) or the local health authority (*unita sanitaria locale*), who do it for free.

Dogs and cats aren't required to have identification discs in Italy and there's no system of licensing (a dog tax was abolished because most people claimed their dogs were working animals and refused to pay it).

However, it's recommended to fit your dog with a collar and a tag containing your name, address and telephone number. Lost dogs are taken to the local pound and may be put down if the owner cannot be found. All dogs must be kept on a leash and (if dangerous) muzzled in towns or on public transport, but not in the country.

You must usually pay full fare on public transport for a dog that isn't carried, and large dogs may even be prohibited from travelling on public transport.

Vaccinations

If you intend to live permanently in Italy, dogs should be vaccinated against certain diseases other than rabies, such as hepatitis, distemper and kennel cough, and cats immunised against feline gastro-enteritis and typhus. Pets should also be checked frequently for ticks and tapeworms. There are a number of diseases and dangers for pets in Italy that aren't found in most other European countries, including the fatal *leishmaniasis* (also called Mediterranean or sandfly disease), which can be prevented by using a spray such as Defendog, available from vets and pet shops. Obtain advice about this and other diseases from a veterinary surgeon (*veterinario*) on arrival in Italy.

Insurance & Welfare

Take extra care when walking your dog, as some have died after eating poisoned food laid by hunters to control natural predators. Don't let your dog far out of your sight or let it roam free, as dogs are often stolen or mistakenly shot by hunters.

Health insurance for pets is available from a number of insurance companies (vets' fees are high in Italy) and it's wise to have third party insurance in case your pet bites someone or causes an accident. In areas where there are poisonous snakes, some owners keep anti-venom (which must be renewed annually) in their refrigerator.

The Ente Nazionale per la Protezione degli Animali (💻 www.enpa.it) is the main organisation for animal welfare in Italy and it operates shelters for stray and abused animals, and inexpensive pet hospitals in many cities.

POLICE

There are various police (*polizia*) forces in Italy, most of which are armed (some even brandish machine guns). All police come under the Ministry of the Interior, apart from the *carabinieri*, which come under the Ministry of Defence in certain matters. A 1981 reform was supposed to merge the *carabinieri* with the other police forces, although nothing came of it and there's still considerable duplication of roles. Both *carabinieri* and 'ordinary' police are responsible for public order and security, and you can contact either to report a crime: dial 112 (non-emergencies) or 113 (emergencies) for police assistance. You should report a theft to the *carabinieri* or the *polizia di stato*.

Carabinieri

The *carabinieri* are a special branch of the army (numbering around 113,000), with similar functions to the police, particularly concerning criminal investigation. They deal with national and serious crime, including organised crime, and are Italy's most efficient and professional

police force (and the best-funded). *Carabinieri* officers are distinguished by their dark blue uniforms with a red stripe down the side of the trousers, and white shoulder belts; they also have splendid ceremonial uniforms with long cloaks and 'Napoleonic' hats. They're housed in barracks (*caserma*) in all major towns and cities, drive navy blue cars and also employ helicopters, aircraft and speed boats.

State Police

The *polizia di stato* or *polizia statale* is a national or state police force, with branches responsible for the security of main roads (*polizia stradale*), the rail system (*polizia ferroviaria*) and airports (*polizia aereoportuale*). Officers wear light blue trousers with a thin purple stripe, and a dark blue jacket. They have stations (*questura* or a *commissariati* in smaller towns) in all main towns and cities, and drive light-blue cars with a white stripe and '*Polizia*' written on the side.

Local Police

The *vigili urbani* are municipal or local police, who deal mainly with local traffic control and municipal administration, and consequently aren't very popular (not that any police are popular). Officers wear white helmets and dress in black in winter and blue in summer, drive black and white cars or ride motorcycles or bicycles. Some municipal police speak foreign languages, shown by a badge on their uniforms.

Guardia di Finanza

The *Guardia di Finanza* (numbering around 68,000) is responsible for regulating national and international financial dealings and combating fraud, counterfeiting, tax evasion and smuggling. They're particularly active at border crossings, airports and ports, where they operate fast powerboats to apprehend smugglers. Officers wear grey/green uniforms with an insignia of yellow flames on the shoulders (hence their nickname of *fiamme gialle*). Although it's highly unlikely, you could be stopped by an officer of the *Guardia di Finanza* if you leave a shop without a receipt for a purchase.

POPULATION

The population of Italy was around 60m in mid-2010, roughly the same as the UK and France, with a population density of almost 200 inhabitants per km² (around 500 people per mi²), which makes Italy the fifth most densely populated country in Europe, after the Benelux countries and the UK. As in most countries, however, the population is unevenly distributed and of the 110 provinces, only around 40 have a density higher than the national average, around 70 per cent of the population inhabiting a surface area equal to just one-third of the country. Around two-thirds of Italians live in cities.

From antiquity, Mediterranean peoples had highly developed urban centres. For historical as well as geographic reasons, Italy has never been dominated by one city, each region having its own urban centre. Today, there are two cities with a population of over a million (Rome and Milan), but many cities have a population of over 100,000. Of these, almost half are on or near the sea; a similar proportion are in the north and the rest are in the centre, south, Sicily and Sardinia. A number of cities have, with increased population and industrialisation, merged with neighbouring cities into enormous metropolitan complexes, sometimes called 'mega-cities', such as that surrounding Milan.

> The largest Italian cities are Rome 2.7m, Milan 1.3m, Naples 1m (Portici, a suburb of Naples, is one of the most densely populated areas in the world), Turin 920,000, Palermo 690,000, Genoa 650,000, Bologna 385,000, Florence 380,000, Catania 340,000, Bari 335,000, Venice 300,000, Messina 260,000 and Verona 255,000.

Other heavily populated areas include Liguria, Piedmont and parts of Lombardy, the Veneto and Friuli-Venezia-Giuila. In contrast, many areas, not necessarily mountainous or difficult to reach, are under-populated. The rural population, which at the beginning of the Second World War accounted for practically half the country's population, has been gradually declining. Until recently, Italy's low birth rate (due in part to Italy's prosperous condom industry, despite the Catholic Church's ban on 'unnatural' birth control), at around nine births per 1,000 population (roughly the same as the death rate) and low immigration meant that population growth was practically zero and threatening to go into reverse, but the country's recent economic growth and the expansion of the European Union have seen many immigrants arrive (see below), which has stopped the population from going into decline.

In general, the birth rate and average family size are higher in the south of Italy than in the north, although populations in Basilicata, Calabria and Molise are declining because of migration (northward). The mortality rate is slightly lower in the south than in the north, and in certain northern regions (especially Liguria) populations are beginning to decrease because the birth rate is falling faster than the mortality rate. As regards the country as a whole, life expectancy rose during the second half of the 20th century, reflecting higher nutritional, sanitary and medical standards. The majority of the population is aged between 20 and 70 years old, with a decreasing number below ten and an increasing number over 75, especially women.

Traditionally, Italy has been a land of emigration, as witnessed by the massive flow of Italians to North and South America (mainly to the US, Argentina, Uruguay and Brazil) during the 19th and 20th centuries. Between 1875 and 1925, a total of some 10m Italians left the country (around half eventually returned). There were further mass emigrations to Australia, Belgium, France, Germany, Switzerland and the UK after the Second World War. In this second wave, some 8m people emigrated, of whom roughly half have returned. At the same time, especially in the '50s and '60s, there was a wholesale population movement from the southern and north-eastern regions to the northwest, where industry was expanding.

In recent years, Italy's rapid economic growth has attracted many immigrants to the country, mainly from North and sub-Saharan Africa, but also from the Philippines, China, South America and most recently from Albania and the former Yugoslavia. There are over 4m registered immigrants (*extracomunitari*) in Italy, plus many more living illegally. Illegal immigration has led to tougher immigration rules and a more forceful programme of expulsion.

RELIGION

Italy is a Christian country, some 90 per cent of the population belonging to the Roman Catholic Church, although only around a third of these regard themselves as 'active' in religious terms. The majority of the world's religious and philosophical movements have churches or meeting places in the major cities and resort areas, including the Anglican and American churches. Other religious groups in Italy include over 1m Muslims, 950,000 Eastern Orthodox Christians, 725,000 Protestants, 500,000 Jehovah's Witnesses, 45,000 Jews, and other small groups such as the Swiss-Protestant Baptists in Piedmont, plus a number of Eastern Orthodox Albanian communities in the *Mezzogiorno*. Although the right to freedom of worship is guaranteed under the Italian constitution, some extreme sects are prohibited.

Italy has a unique religious heritage and 2,000 years of Christianity has permeated every facet of Italian life. The Vatican City (covering 47ha/116 acres and with a population of around 900) was established in 1929 and is a self-contained sovereign state (the world's smallest) within the city of Rome. The Vatican is the home of the government of the Roman Catholic Church and of the Pope (*il Papa* or *Supreme Pontiff*), the spiritual leader of the world's Roman Catholics. As well as its own peacekeeping force, the Swiss Guard, the Vatican has its own post office, newspaper and radio and TV stations. It also mints coins (with the Pope's face) and issues stamps.

The Catholic Church enjoys considerable influence, partly by virtue of a historical tradition that has seen the Church of Rome as a constant in government and the organisation of public life. There have traditionally been close relations between the state and the Catholic Church, which remains at the centre of Italian society and political power. However, a concordat signed in 1984 ended the church's position as the state religion, abolished compulsory religious teaching in public schools and reduced state financial contributions to the church.

Every town or village has at least one Catholic church and, although only around a quarter of Italians regularly attend mass, over 95 per cent are baptised, saints' days, first communions and religious festivals remain popular and the majority of Italians prefer to be married in church. Children usually take their first communion – an important day in their lives when they become full members of the Catholic Church – at the age of eight or nine, usually in April or May.

⚠ Caution

When visiting a house of worship in Italy, you should avoid wearing shorts, short skirts or skimpy tops, although you're rarely refused entry or asked to leave (except at St. Peter's in Rome, where both men and women must cover their shoulders and knees).

SOCIAL CUSTOMS

All countries have peculiar social customs and Italy is no exception. As a foreigner you'll probably be excused if you accidentally insult your host, but you may not be invited again. However, Italians are much more formal than most foreigners imagine, and newcomers should tread carefully to avoid offending anyone.

Greetings

When you're introduced to an Italian, you should say 'good day' (*buongiorno*) and shake hands (a single pump is enough). 'Hello' (*ciao*) is used among close friends and young people, but it isn't considered polite when addressing strangers unless they use it first. Women may find that some men kiss their hand, although this is rare nowadays. When being introduced to someone in a formal situation, it's common to say 'pleased to meet you' (*piacere*). When saying goodbye, you should shake hands again. It's also customary to say 'good day' or 'good evening' (*buonasera*) on entering a small shop, waiting room or lift, and 'good day' or 'goodbye' (*arriverderci* or, to be extra polite, *arrivederla*) on leaving (friends say *ciao*). *Buongiorno* becomes *buonasera* any time after the lunch break (around 1pm), although if you choose *buonasera* (or *buongiorno*), don't be surprised if the response isn't the same. Good night (*buonanotte*) is used when going to bed or leaving a house in the evening.

Titles should generally be used when addressing or writing to people, particularly when the holder is elderly. *Dottore* is usually used when addressing anyone with a university degree (*dottoressa* if it's a woman) and employees may refer to their boss as director (*direttore*) or *presidente*. Professionals should be addressed by their titles, such as professor (*professore*), doctor (*dottore*), engineer (*ingegnere*), lawyer (*avvocato*) and architect (*architetto*). If you don't know someone's title, you can use *signore* (for a man) or *signora* (woman); a young woman may be addressed as *signorina*, although nowadays all women tend to be addressed as *signora*.

Kissing

Italian families and friends usually kiss when they meet, irrespective of their sex. If a lady expects you to kiss her, she offers her cheek. Between members of the opposite sex the 'kiss' is deposited high up on the cheek, never on the mouth (except between lovers!) and isn't usually really a kiss, more a delicate brushing of the cheeks accompanied by kissing noises. There are usually two kisses – first on the right cheek, then on the left. It's also common in Italy for male relatives and close male friends to embrace each other.

Lei & Tu

When talking to a stranger, particularly older Italians, you should use the formal form of address (*lei*). Don't use the familiar form (*tu*) or call someone by their Christian name until you're invited to do so. Generally the older or (in a business context) senior person invites the other to use the familiar *tu* form of address and first names. The familiar form is used with children, animals and God, but almost never with your elders or work superiors. However, Italians are becoming less formal and younger people often use *tu* and first names with colleagues. It's customary to use *lei* in conversations with shopkeepers, servants, business associates and figures of authority (the local mayor) or those with whom you have a business relationship, e.g. your bank manager, tax officials and policemen.

Invitations

If you're invited to dinner by an Italian family (this is a rare honour), you should take along a small present of flowers, pastries or chocolates. Gifts of foreign food or drink aren't generally well received unless they're highly prized in Italy, such as single malt whisky. Some people say you must never take wine, although this obviously depends on your hosts and how well you know them. If you do bring wine, it's unlikely to be served with the meal, as the wine will have already been chosen. Flowers can be tricky, as some people associate them with certain things (e.g. chrysanthemums for cemeteries), but a florist will be able to advise you. It's common for Italians to send a small note or gift the following day to thank people for their hospitality or kindness.

Italians say 'good appetite' (*buon appetito*) before starting a meal. If you're offered a glass of wine, wait until your host has made a toast (*salute!*) before drinking. If you aren't offered another drink, it's time to go home. You should, however, go easy on the wine and other alcohol, as if you drink to excess you're unlikely to be invited back!

It's common in Italy to invite people to visit after dinner (*dopo cena*), e.g. from 9.30pm, for dessert and wine.

Dress

Italians dress well and seem to have an inborn sense of elegance and style. Presentation and impression are all-important to Italians and are referred to as *bella presenza* or *bella figura* (literally 'beautiful presentation or figure'). Italians generally dress well and appropriately, tending to be more formal in their attire than most northern Europeans and North Americans. However, although they rarely loaf around in shorts or jogging pants, they also tend not to go to the other extreme of tuxedos and evening gowns.

Italians judge people by their dress, the style and quality being as important as the appropriateness for the occasion. Italians consider bathing costumes, skimpy tops and flip-flops or sandals with no socks strictly for the beach or swimming pool, and not the street, restaurants or shops. (Italians believe that many foreigners are shameless in the way they dress and act in public and have no self-respect.) They also choose the occasions when they wear jeans carefully, as these aren't thought appropriate for a classy restaurant or church.

Bella figura refers not only to the way you look, but also to the way you act and what you say. It's similar in some ways to the oriental concept of 'face', and Italians must look good and be seen in the best light, always appearing to be in control and not showing ignorance or a lack of savoir-faire. It's important not to show disrespect or ridicule an Italian, even if it means biting your tongue on occasions.

Other Customs

You should introduce yourself before asking to speak to someone on the telephone. Although the traditional siesta is facing a battle for survival, it isn't recommended to telephone between 2 and 4pm, when many people have a nap (*pisolino*). If you must call between these times, it's polite to apologise for disturbing the household.

If you have a business appointment with an Italian, he'll expect you to be on time, although he'll invariably be five or ten minutes late. If you're going to be over five minutes late, it's wise to telephone and apologise. Italians usually exchange business cards (*biglietti da visita*) on business and social occasions.

TIME DIFFERENCE

Like most of the continent of Europe, Italy is on Central European Time (CET). This is Greenwich Mean Time (GMT) plus one hour from the last Sunday in October until the last Sunday in March, and GMT plus two hours from the last Sunday in March to the last Sunday in October, i.e. always one hour ahead of the UK. Time changes, which officially take place at 2am, are announced in local newspapers and on radio and TV. The local time is given via the telephone 'speaking clock' service (see your local phone book) and can be displayed on a television set by pressing the 'time' button. When making international telephone calls or travelling a long distance by air, you should check the local time difference, which is shown in phone books.

The time in some major international cities when it's noon in Rome (between October and March) is shown below.

Times are usually written (e.g. in timetables) using the 24-hour clock, with a comma between hours and minutes; for example, 10am is written as 10,00 and 10pm as 22,00. Midday (*mezzogiorno*) is 12,00 and midnight (*mezzanotte*) is 24,00 or 00,00. In Italian, am (ante meridiem) is indicated as *di mattina* and pm (post meridiem) as *del pomeriggio* (from around 1pm to 4pm) or *di sera* (from around 5pm to late pm).

Time Difference					
ROME	NEW YORK	LONDON	JO'BURG	SYDNEY	AUCKLAND
Noon	6am	11am	1pm	9pm	11pm

TIPPING

Italians aren't big tippers, and it isn't usual to tip all and sundry. Many people don't tip taxi drivers, porters, hotel staff, car park attendants, cloakroom staff, shoeshine boys and cinema ushers, although you can give a small tip if you wish or, in the case of taxi drivers, round up the fare to the next euro or say 'keep the change' (*tenga il resto*). If someone expects (or hopes for) a tip, a little basket may be provided. Attendants at public toilets usually have set fees (see below). It's isn't customary to tip a petrol station attendant for cleaning your windscreen or checking your oil. On the other hand, hairdressers or the girl who washes your hair usually receive a tip of between €3 and €5. It isn't necessary to tip a porter, who charges a fixed price per piece of luggage. An apartment block concierge or porter (*portiere*) usually receives a substantial tip at Christmas, e.g. €25 to €50, depending on how helpful he has been and how often you've used his services. He may also receive tips at other times for special jobs. Postmen aren't tipped in Italy. Large tips are considered ostentatious and in bad taste (except by the recipient, who will be your friend for life).

Hotel, restaurant and café prices are inclusive of VAT. Where a cover (*coperto*) and service (*servizio*) charge is included in the price, this is usually shown on the menu as 'all inclusive' (*tutto compreso*). Where cover and service aren't included, restaurants make a small extra charge of around €1-3 per person, listed as *pane e coperto* (bread and cover) – this is compulsory even if you don't eat the bread! Posh restaurants may add up to 10 per cent to the bill.

Italians rarely leave a large tip (*mancia*), although it's customary to leave a few small coins when having a drink standing at a bar. When paying by credit card, a tip is usually left in cash rather than added to the credit card payment. Tips aren't usually left in establishments where you pay at a cash register rather than at the table, or in family-run restaurants where you're a regular customer. The main exception to the tipping rule is in expensive or fashionable establishments, where 'tips' may be given to secure a table (or guarantee a table in future).

If you're unsure whether you should tip someone, ask (Italian) neighbours, friends or colleagues for advice – although they'll probably all tell you something different!

TOILETS

Public toilets are few and far between, although there are modern coin-operated public toilets with soap, hot water, towels and air-conditioning in some cities and resort areas. There may be toilets in department stores, large supermarkets, shopping centres, railway and bus stations, museums and other places of interest, on beaches and near markets, as well as in bars, cafés, restaurants and hotels. Some bars (particularly in Rome) charge customers a euro to use their toilets!

Public toilets vary considerably in their age and facilities, and in addition to some of the world's best, Italy has some of the worst and you shouldn't expect to find toilet paper at most of them (it's recommended to carry some tissues with you). Major tourist sites have the most modern facilities, and there's usually an attendant who may dispense paper (*carta*) and expects a tip of around €0.50.

Toilets may be labelled with a symbol depicting a man or woman or with the letters WC. Sometimes the wording may be in Italian, e.g. *signori* (men) or *signore* (women) – watch that final letter! – or *uomini* (men) or *donne* (women). If you need to ask where a toilet is, you say, *Dov'e' il bagno?*

If a building has a septic tank (*fossa settica*), which many private houses do, certain items must never be flushed down the toilet, including sanitary towels, paper (other than toilet paper), disposable nappies, condoms or anything made of plastic. You should also never use standard bleaches, disinfectants and chemical cleaners in systems with septic tanks (special brands are available), as they can have a disastrous effect on their operation and create nasty smells.

In private residences, you can ask for the toilet (*toilette*) or the bathroom (*bagno*). Most Italian bathrooms have a bidet (*bidé*) in addition to a toilet bowl, which is for 'intimate ablutions'.

Valley of the Temples, Agrigento, Sicily

19.
THE ITALIANS

Who are the Italians? What are they like? Let's take a candid and totally prejudiced look at them, tongue firmly in cheek, and hope they forgive our flippancy or that they don't read this bit (which is why it's hidden at the back of the book).

The typical Italian is courteous, proud, undisciplined, tardy, temperamental, independent, gregarious, noble, individualistic, boisterous, jealous, possessive, colourful, passionate, spontaneous, sympathetic, fun-loving, creative, sociable, demonstrative, irritating, charming, aggressive, self-important, generous, cheerful, cultured, polite, unreliable, honourable, outgoing, impetuous, flamboyant, idiosyncratic, quick-tempered, artistic, a gourmet, ungovernable, elegant, irresponsible, hedonistic, lazy and industrious (contradictory), an anarchist, informal, self-opinionated, corrupt, indolent, flexible, patriarchal, frustrating, inventive, sensual, practical, irresistible, impatient, scheming, voluble, friendly, sexist, musical, sensitive, humorous, garrulous, petulant, macho, noisy, happy, fiery, warm-hearted, a suicidal driver, decadent, religious, chauvinistic, an excellent cook, stylish, bureaucratic, dignified, kind, loyal, a fashion victim, extroverted, tolerant, self-possessed, a tax dodger, unabashed, quarrelsome, partisan, a procrastinator, scandal-loving, articulate, a bon viveur, conservative, nocturnal, hospitable, spirited, urbanised, confident, sophisticated, political, handsome and a football fanatic.

You may have noticed that the above list contains 'a few' contradictions (as does life in Italy), which is hardly surprising as there's no such thing as a typical Italian. Apart from the differences in character between the inhabitants of different regions such as

Campania (Naples), Lazio (Rome), Lombardy (Milan), Sardinia, Sicily and Trentino, the population also includes a potpourri of foreigners from all corners of the globe. Even in appearance, fewer and fewer Italians match the popular image of short, dark and slim, and the indigenous population includes blondes, brunettes and redheads, tall and short, fat and thin people.

Italy became a unified state only in 1861 and most people have more loyalty to their town, province or region than to Italy as a whole, considering themselves Florentines, Milanese, Neapolitans, Romans or Sicilians first and Italians a distant second, summed up by the word *campanilismo* – literally 'loyalty to your bell-tower'. There's long been a north-south divide (gulf), the more conservative northerners dismissing the less inhibited southerners as lazy, lawless, cunning, corrupt and primitive peasants, while southerners consider northerners to be serious, industrious and money-grabbing foreigners who got rich from exploitation.

One of the few things that unites Italians (sometimes in joy, usually in despair, such as their unfortunate dismissal in the first round of the 2010 World Cup after winning it in 2006) is the national soccer team.

Dante's *Inferno* to help pass the time). It's all part of a conspiracy to ensure that foreigners cannot find out what's going on and therefore pay more taxes, fees and fines (or hopefully go home!).

Official inefficiency has been honed to a fine art in Italy, where even paying a bill or using the postal service (which used to be a truly world-class example of ineptitude – it's now more efficient than it was) is an ordeal. Italians are generally totally disorganised (summed up by the word *casino*, which roughly translates as a shambles but also means a brothel!) and the only predictable thing about them is their unpredictability. They seldom plan anything (if they do, the plans will be changed or abandoned at the last moment), as one of the unwritten 'rules' of Italian life is spontaneity. Don't expect workmen to arrive on time (or at all) – when they do finally turn up they probably won't have the right tools or spares anyway – or jobs to be finished on schedule. Italians are dismissive of time constraints and have no sense of urgency, treating appointments, dates, opening hours, timetables and deadlines with scorn (about the only events which start on time are soccer matches). Don't plan on doing anything at all in August, when the whole country goes on holiday and all business (apart from tourism) comes to a grinding halt.

Italy is infamous for its corruption (not to mention the Mafia), which pervades all levels of society, from the government to the humblest peasant. Tax evasion is the national sport and you certainly don't need to be engaged in the hidden economy to be part of it – the 'black' list includes many of Italy's richest and most famous people. In 2008, there were red faces across the nation when every Italian citizen's declared earnings and paid taxes were published online by the government – and removed soon afterwards on grounds of privacy. Fines are always negotiable, particularly if you argue loud and long enough, as is your tax bill if you know someone who works in the tax office. Bribery (*la bustarella*) is part and parcel of everyday life and everything and every Italian has a price: if you have enough money or contacts, you can get anything done; without either it can take aeons to accomplish even the simplest task. There's also one law for Italians and another

Compared with most other European countries of a comparable size, Italy attracted relatively few immigrants in the 20th century (the massive industrial expansion in the north was achieved by the migration of workers from the south) and the country is still trying to come to terms with the huge influx of refugees and immigrants in recent years. Nevertheless, Italians generally live in harmony with their foreign population (*stranieri*) and are among the most tolerant Europeans (particularly when it comes to free-spending tourists).

When Italians and foreigners come into contact, it often results in a profusion of misunderstandings (few foreigners can fathom the Italian psyche), which does little to cement good relations. Italy has the most stifling (and over-staffed) bureaucracy in Western Europe (even worse than France and Spain) and any encounter with officialdom is a test of endurance and patience. Government offices (if you can find the right one) often open for only a few hours on certain days of the week, the person dealing with your case is always absent, you never have the right papers (or your file has been lost), the rules and regulations have changed (again), and queues are interminable (take along a copy of for foreigners – particularly foreigners who don't speak Italian.

Most Italians are anarchists; they generally do what they want when they want, particularly regarding motoring (especially parking), smoking in public places (a 'no-smoking' sign is usually seen as a challenge) and building. Italians (and, it seems, Italian officials) make up their own laws and choose those they wish to obey 'a la carte' (most EU directives are totally ignored). If it wasn't for the large fines for often minor offences, Italians would happily ignore most laws. Most people rely on instinct rather than morals or laws!

Italians are unbridled hedonists and are mainly interested in food, football, sex, alcohol and gambling (especially the men). The main preoccupation of Italians is having a good time and they have a zest for life matched in few other countries. They take childish pleasure in making the most of everything, grasping every opportunity to party, and are at their most energetic when making merry. They're inveterate 'celebrators' and when not attending a feast (*festa*), family celebration or impromptu party, they're to be found in bars and restaurants indulging in their favourite pastime – eating and drinking.

Italians have a passion for food, which consists largely of pasta, pasta and pasta, with lashings of tomatoes, garlic and olive oil. They're committed carnivores and eat anything that walks, runs, crawls, swims or flies – particularly Italy's fast-disappearing wildlife. Like other southern Europeans, they eat most of the objectionable bits that other people throw away, including feet, ears, tails, brains, entrails and reproductive organs (Italians could never be called squeamish). Family celebrations routinely last from dawn to dusk (or even until midnight), with a constant stream of food and wine – if eating was an Olympic event, the rest of the world needn't even bother to turn up! Italians also know a thing or two about drinking, washing down their food with prodigious amounts of wine (though never to the point of drunkenness), and they're one of the world's larger consumers of whisky.

When not eating and drinking (or singing or watching football), Italians are allegedly making love. Italian men have a reputation as great lovers, although their virility isn't supported by the birth rate, which is one of the lowest in the world. Italian women are beautiful (at least until they marry), although what they see in greasy, crooning, smooth-talking mummy's boys who only come up to their knees is anyone's guess. The macho image of Italian men has taken a pounding in recent decades, as women have stormed most male bastions and today are just as likely to be found in the university, office, factory, professions and the government, as in the home or the church.

> Italian men are car fanatics and worship all things automotive (especially if they're red and made in Modena); they have a passionate and enduring love affair with their cars, which are more important to them than their homes, wives (mistresses) and children.

Many Italians are loath to forsake their cars under any circumstances and would rather endure endless traffic jams than resort to public transport. In fact, Italians rarely actually drive anywhere these days; when they aren't in a traffic jam talking on their mobile phones, they're looking for a parking space. Cars aren't

for driving in Italy, but for posing – nothing is guaranteed to draw a crowd in Italy quicker than a blood-red Ferrari or even an exotic foreign machine, provided it looks as if it can do a million kilometres per hour. Italians are among the most ill-disciplined drivers in the world and their frenetic, aggressive driving style is enough to intimidate all but the most battle-hardened motorists. The only way a foreign driver can survive is to drive like an Italian, which means ignoring all signs and road markings, parking restrictions, speed limits and traffic lights, and driving everywhere with their foot to the floor and one hand on the horn.

Enough of this frivolity, let's get down to serious business. Italy is one of the most politically unstable countries in the EU, although this amazingly seems to have little outward effect on the country's economy. There have been numerous changes of government since the Second World War (Italy changes its government as often as some people change their socks), largely due to the country's system of proportional representation, which almost guarantees shaky coalition governments. Italians have no time for politicians (who they blame for all their ills), whose public standing has sunk to record lows in the last few decades following a succession of scandals, including fraud and involvement in organised crime. Not surprisingly, Italians are the most passionate Europeans and firmly believe in a united Europe and the single currency (so would you if you'd had the lira!).

Among the main concerns facing Italians are unemployment, drug addiction, asylum seekers, refugees and illegal aliens, the environment and pollution, pensions, health care, property crime, housing costs and the widening gulf in prosperity between the north and south. However, by far the biggest challenge facing Italy's leaders is how to reform the economy (e.g. debt-ridden public companies and a huge social security deficit) without provoking a revolution.

Despite the country's problems, Italians enjoy one of the best lifestyles and quality of life of any European country, or indeed, any country in the world. The foundation of its society is the family (particularly the mother) and community; Italians are noted for their close family ties, their love of children and care for the elderly, who aren't dumped in nursing homes when they become a 'burden'. In Italy, work fits around social and family life, not vice versa.

The real glory of Italy lies in the outsized heart and soul of its people, who are among the most convivial, generous and hospitable in the world. Italy is celebrated for its simple, relaxed way of life, warm personal relationships and time for others, lack of violent crime (excluding gang warfare), good manners and spontaneity – Italians are never slow to break into song or dance when the mood strikes them. For sheer vitality and passion for life, Italians have few equals and, whatever Italy can be accused of, it's never plain or boring. Few other countries offer such a wealth of intoxicating experiences for the mind, body and spirit (and not all out of a bottle!). Italy is highly addictive, and while foreigners may complain about the bureaucracy or government, the vast majority wouldn't dream of leaving and infinitely prefer life in Italy to their home countries. Put simply, Italy is a great place to live (provided you don't want to do business) and raise a family.

If you're willing to learn Italian and embrace Italy's traditions and way of life, you're invariably warmly received by the natives, who will go out of their way to welcome and help you.

☑ SURVIVAL TIP

Above all, you need to embrace Italy as it is, warts and all (life is so much more enjoyable when you stop banging your head against the wall), and just lie back and enjoy *La Dolce Vita*.

Viva l'Italia! **Long live Italy!**

Alessandro Del Piero

Merano, Trentino

20.
MOVING HOUSE OR LEAVING ITALY

When moving house or leaving Italy, there are numerous things to be considered and a 'million' people to inform. The checklists contained in this chapter will make the task easier and may even help prevent an ulcer or nervous breakdown – provided of course you don't leave everything to the last minute.

MOVING HOUSE

When moving house **within** Italy the following things should be done, if applicable.

♦ Inform the following, as applicable:

- – your employer;

- – your present town hall and the town hall in your new municipality;

- – your social security and income tax offices;

- – your electricity, gas, telephone and water companies;

- – your insurance companies (e.g. health, car, household and third party liability), hire purchase companies, lawyer, accountant, and local businesses where you have accounts; take out new insurance, if applicable;

- – your banks and other financial institutions, such as stockbrokers and credit card companies; make arrangements to transfer funds and cancel or alter standing orders or direct debits;

- – your family doctor, dentist and other health practitioners; health records should be transferred to your new practitioners;

- – your children's school (try to give a term's notice and obtain copies of any relevant school reports and records); if applicable, arrange schooling in your new community;

- – all regular correspondents, publications to which you subscribe, social and sports clubs, friends and relatives; arrange to have your post redirected;

- – your local consulate or embassy if you're registered with them.

♦ If you're renting accommodation, you must give your landlord notice in accordance with your rental contract and have your deposit refunded. Your notice letter should be sent by registered post (*posta raccomandata*).

♦ If you have an Italian-registered car or driving licence and are remaining in the same province, you should return your licence and registration document and have the address changed. If you're moving to a new province, you should inform both your current and new provinces.

♦ Return any library books or anything borrowed.

♦ Arrange removal of your furniture and belongings, or hire a van if you're doing your own removal.

♦ Ask yourself (again): 'Is it really worth all this trouble?'

LEAVING ITALY

Before leaving Italy for an indefinite period, the following items should be considered **in addition** to those listed above under **Moving House**.

◆ Check that your family's passports are valid!

◆ Give notice to your employer, if applicable.

◆ Check whether any special entry requirements are necessary for your country of destination, e.g. visas, permits or inoculations, by contacting the embassy or consulate in Italy. An exit permit or visa isn't required to leave Italy.

◆ Ask whether you qualify for a rebate on your income tax and social security payments.

◆ Make arrangements to sell or let your house or apartment and other property in Italy.

◆ Arrange to sell anything else you aren't taking with you (car, furniture, etc.), and to ship your belongings. Find out the procedure for shipping your belongings to your country of destination. Check with the local embassy or consulate of the country to which you're moving. Forms may need to be completed before arrival. If you've been living in Italy for less than two years, you're required to re-export all personal effects imported duty-free from outside the EU, including furniture and vehicles (if you sell them you may be required to pay duty).

◆ If you have an Italian-registered car that you intend to take with you, you'll need to have it re-registered in your new country of residence and inform the Italian authorities.

◆ Pets may require inoculations or need to go into quarantine for a period, depending on your destination.

◆ Arrange health, travel and other insurance (see **Chapter 13**).

◆ Depending on your destination, you may wish to arrange health and dental check-ups before leaving Italy. Obtain a copy of your health and dental records.

◆ Terminate any loans, lease or hire purchase contracts, and pay all outstanding bills (allow plenty of time as some companies are slow to respond).

◆ Find out whether you're entitled to a rebate on your road tax, car and other insurance. Obtain a letter from your insurance company stating your no-claims bonus.

◆ Check whether you need an international driver's permit or a translation of your Italian or foreign driving licence for your country of destination.

◆ Give friends and business associates in Italy an address and telephone number where you can be contacted abroad.

Buon viaggio!

Florence at dusk, Tuscany

Parma, Emilia Romagna

APPENDICES

APPENDIX A: FURTHER INFORMATION

Embassies & Consulates

Foreign embassies in Italy are located in Rome; many countries also have consulates in other major cities. Note that business hours vary considerably and all embassies close on their national holidays plus Italy's public holidays. Always telephone to check the business hours before visiting. A full list of embassies in Rome is available on the Ministry of Foreign Affairs website (💻 www.esteri.it/mae/doc/lda.pdf). Selected embassies are listed below:

Albania: Via Asmara, 5, Rome (☎ 06-8622 411).

Argentina: Piazza dell'Esquilino, 2, 00185 Rome (☎ 06-4742 551).

Australia: Via Antonio Bosio, 5, 00161 Rome (☎ 06-8527 21, 💻 www.italy.embassy.gov.au/rome/home.html).

Austria: Via G.B. Pergolesi, 3, 00198 Rome (☎ 06-8440 141).

Belgium: Via dei Monti Parioli, 49, 00197 Rome (☎ 06-3609 511).

Brazil: Piazza Navona, 14, 00186 Rome (☎ 06-6839 81).

Canada: Via Zara, 30, 00198 Rome (☎ 06-445 981, 💻 www.canadainternational.gc.ca/italy-italie/index.aspx).

Czech Republic: Via dei Gracchi, 322, 00192 Rome (☎ 06-3244 459).

Denmark: Via dei Monti Parioli, 50, 00197 Rome (☎ 06-9774 831).

Finland: Via Lisbona, 3, 00198 Rome (☎ 06-852 231).

France: Piazza Farnese, 67, 00186 Rome (☎ 06-686 011).

Germany: Via San Martino della Battaglia, 4, 00185 Rome (☎ 06-492 131).

Greece: Via Antonio Stoppani, 10, 00197, Roma (☎ 06-8082 030).

Hungary: Via Messina, 15, 00198 Rome (☎ 06 4424-9938).

India: Via XX Settembre, 5, 00187 Rome (☎ 06-4884 642).

Ireland: Piazza di Campitelli, 3, 00186 Rome (☎ 06-6979 121).

Israel: Via Michele Mercati, 14, 00197 Rome (☎ 06-3619 8500).

Japan: Via Quintino Sella, 60, 00187 Rome (☎ 06-4879 91).

Netherlands: Via Michele Mercati, 8, 00197 Rome (☎ 06-3228 6001).

New Zealand: Via Clitunno 44, 00198 Rome (06-853 7501, 💻 www. nzembassy.com/italy).

Poland: Via Rubens, 20, 00197 Rome (☎ 06-3620 4200).

Portugal: Viale Liege, 21, 00198 Rome (☎ 06-844 801).

Russia: Via Gaeta, 5, 00185 Rome (☎ 06-4941 680/1/3).

South Africa: Via Tanaro, 14, 00198 Rome (☎ 06-8525 41, 💻 ww.sudafrica.it).

Spain: Largo Fontanella di Borghese, 19, 00186 Rome (☎ 06-6840 401).

United Kingdom: Via XX Settembre, 80, 00187 Rome (☎ 06-4220 0001, 💻 ukinitaly.fco.gov.uk/en).

United States of America: Via Vittorio Veneto, 119/A, 00187 Rome (☎ 06-46741, 💻 http://italy.usembassy.gov/mission).

British Provincial Consulates

Bari: Via Dalmazia, 127 (☎ 080-5543 668).

Cagliari: Viale Columbo, 160 (☎ 070-8286 28).

Florence: Lungarno Corsini, 2 (☎ 055-2841 33).

Genoa: Piazza G Verdi, 6/A (☎ 010-5740 071).

Milan: Via San Paolo, 7 (☎ 02-7230 01).

Naples: Via dei Mille, 40 (☎ 081-4238 911).

Palermo: Via Cavour, 121 (☎ 091-3264 12).

Rome: Via XX Settembre, 80a (☎ 06-4220 0001).

Trieste: Via Roma, 15 (☎ 040-3478 303).

Venice: Piazzale Donatori di Sangue, 2/5 (☎ 041-5055 990).

Italian Government Departments

Department of Institutional Reform, Dipartimento delle Riforme Istituzionali, Largo Chigi, 19, 00187 Rome (☎ 06-6779 2751).

Department of Public Function, Dipartimento della Funzione Pubblica, Corso Vittorio Emanuele, 116, 00186 Rome (☎ 06-68991, 💻 www. innovazionepa.gov.it).

Ministry of Communications, Ministero delle Comunicazioni, Viale America, 201, 00144 Rome (☎ 06-5444 2100, 💻 www.comunicazioni.it).

Ministry of Cultural Heritage, Ministero per i Beni e le Attivita Culturali, Via del Collegio Romano, 27, 00186 Rome (☎ 06-6723 1, 💻 www.beniculturali.it).

Ministry of Education, Ministero della Pubblica Istruzione, Viale Trastevere, 76/a, 00153 Rome (☎ 06-5849 1, 💻 www.istruzione.it).

Ministry of the Environment, Ministero dell'Ambiente e della Tutela del Territorio e del Mare, Viale Cristoforo Colombo, 44, 00147 Rome (☎ 06-5722 1, 💻 www.minambiente.it).

Ministry of Foreign Affairs, Ministero degli Affari Esteri, P della Farnesina, 1, 00194 Rome (☎ 06-3691 1, 🖥 www.esteri.it).

Ministry of Foreign Trade, Ministero del Commercio Internazionale, Viale Boston, 25, 00144 Rome (☎ 06-5993 1, 🖥 www.mincomes.it).

Ministry of Health, Ministero della Salute, Lungotevere Ripa, 1, 00153 Rome (☎ 06-5994 1, 🖥 www.salute.gov.it).

Ministry of Infrastructure and Transport, Ministero delle Infrastrutture e dei Trasporti, Direzione Generale Motorizzazione Civile, IV Direzione Centrale, Via Caraci, 36, 00157 Rome (☎ 06-4158 2143 or 06-4158 2144, 🖥 www.mit.gov.it).

Ministry of the Interior, Ministero dell'Interno, Palazzo Viminale, Piazza del Viminale, 1, 00184 Rome (☎ 06-4651, 🖥 www.interno.it).

Ministry of Justice, Ministero della Grazia e Giustizia, Via Arenula, 70, 00186 Rome (☎ 06-68851, 🖥 www.giustizia.it).

Ministry of Politics, Agriculture and Forestry, Ministero delle Politiche, Agricole e Forestali, Via XX Settembre, 20, 00187 Rome (☎ 06-46651, 🖥 www.politicheagricole.it).

Ministry of Teaching, University and Research, Ministero dell'Universita e della Ricerca, Piazzale JF Kennedy, 20, 00144 Rome (☎ 06-58491, 🖥 www.istruzione.it).

Ministry of the Treasury, Ministero dell' Economia e della Finanze, Via XX Settembre, 97, 00187 Rome (☎ 06-476111, 🖥 www.tesoro.it).

Ministry of Work and Social Politics, Ministero del Lavoro e della Politiche Sociale, Via Venato, 56, 00187 Rome (☎ 800-196 196, 🖥 www.lavoro.gov.it).

Prime Minister, Presidenza del Consiglio dei Ministri), Palazzo Chigi, Piazza Colonna, 370, 00187 Rome (☎ 06-67791, 🖥 www.palazzochigi.it).

Miscellaneous Addresses

American Chamber of Commerce in Italy, Via Contù 1, 20123 Milan (☎ 02-8690 661, 🖥 www.amcham.it).

British Chamber of Commerce for Italy, Via Dante, 12, 20121 Milan (☎ 02-8777 98, 🖥 www.britchamitaly.com).

Dante Alighieri Society, Società Dante Alighieri, Piazza Firenze, 27, 00186 Rome (☎ 06-687 3694/95, 🖥 www.dantealighieri.com). Promotes Italy's language and culture, and teaches it worldwide through its network of schools.

European Commission, Information Centre, 8 Storey's Gate, London SW1P 3AT, UK (☎ 020-7973 1992, 🖥 http://ec.europa.eu).

Italian Chamber of Commerce and Industry, 1 Princes Street, London W1B 2AY, UK (☎ 020-7495 8191, 🖥 www.italchamind.org.uk).

Italian Consulate General, 38 Eaton Place, London SW1X 8AN, UK (☎ 020-7235 9371, 🖥 www.conslondra.esteri.it).

Italian Cultural Institute, 39 Belgrave Square, London SW1X 8NT, UK (☎ 020-7235 1461, 🖥 www.icilondon.esteri.it).

Italian Cultural Institute, 686 Park Avenue, New York, NY 10021, US (☎ 212-879 4242, 🖥 www.iicnewyork.esteri.it).

Italian Embassy, 14 Three Kings Yard, Davies Street, London W1Y 2EH, UK (☎ 020-7312 2200, 🖥 www.amblondra.esteri.it).

Italian Embassy, 3000 Whitehaven St, NW, Washington, DC 20008, US (☎ 202-612 4400, 🖥 www.ambwashingtondc.esteri.it).

Italian Federation of Professional Estate Agents (FIAIP), Uffici di Presidenza Nazionale, Piazzale Flaminio, 9, 00196 Rome (☎ 06-452 3181, 🖥 www.fiaip.it).

Italian Government Tourist Board, 630 Fifth Avenue, Suite 1565, New York, NY 10111, US (☎ 212-245 5618, 🖥 www.italiantourism.com). There are tourist offices in a number of other American cities such as Chicago, Los Angeles and Toronto in Canada.

Italian State Tourist Board, 1 Princes Street, London W1R 8AY, UK (☎ 020-7408 1254, 🖥 www.italiantouristboard.co.uk).

Italian Trade Commission, 14 Waterloo Place, London SW1Y 4AR (☎ 0207-389 0300, 🖥 www.italtrade.com).

APPENDIX B: FURTHER READING

English-Language Newspapers & Magazines

English Yellow Pages, Via Belisario 4/B, 00187 Rome (☎ 06-4740 861, 🖥 www.englishyellowpages.it).

Grapevine, Casella Postale 62, 55060 Guamo, LU (☎ 055-334139, 🖥 www.luccagrapevine.com). Monthly English-language magazine for Lucca and the surrounding area.

Hello Milano, Art'Idea srl, Via Lucca 22, 20152 Milan (☎ 02-2952 0570, 🖥 www.hellomilano.it). Free online and printed monthly entertainment magazine.

Italia! Magazine, Anthem Publishing, Suite 6 Piccadilly House, London Road, Bath BA1 6PL (☎ 01225 489984, 🖥 www.italia-magazine.com). UK-published monthly for Italophiles; also publishes a food magazine, *Taste Italia*, and a series of regional guides.

The Informer, Via dei Tigli 2, 20020 Arese, MI (☎ 02-9358 1477, 🖥 www.informer.it). A monthly online magazine for expatriates, with a subscription required to access much of the site.

Ville & Casali, Edizioni Living International, Via Anton Giulio Bragaglia 33, 00123 Rome (☎ 06-96521.600/612, 🖥 www.villeecasali.com). Glossy monthly home magazine containing a catalogue of luxury properties with English summaries of articles and house descriptions.

Wanted in Rome, Via dei Falegnami 79, 00186 Rome (☎ 06-6867 967, 🖥 www.wantedinrome.com). Classified advertisements, jobs, accommodation (rentals, properties for sale, holiday properties), what's on and lifestyle articles.

Where Rome, Via Ostiense 172, 00154 Rome (☎ 06-5781 615, 🖥 www.whererome.it). Monthly entertainment magazine.

The books listed below are just a small selection of the many relating to living or working in Italy. In addition to the general guides listed, there are many excellent regional guides. Some titles may be out of print but may still be obtainable from bookshops and libraries.

Books

Travel

AA Baedeker's Italy (AA Publishing)

Alistair Sawday's Special Places to Stay Italy, Susan Pennington (Alistair Sawday)

Bed & Blessings Italy: A Guide to Convents and Monasteries Available for Overnight Lodging, Anne & June Walsh (Paulist Press)

Cheap Sleeps in Italy, Sandra Gustafson (Chronicle)

City Secrets: Rome, Robert Kahn (Little Bookroom)

Dorling Kindersley Travel Guides: Italy (Dorling Kindersley)

Fodor's Italy (Fodor's)

Frommer's Italy, Darwin Porter & Danforth Prince (Macmillan)

Frommer's Italy's Best-Loved Driving Tours, Arthur Frommer (Macmillan)

The Guide to Lodging in Italian Monasteries, Eileen Barish (Anacapa Press)

The Independent Walker's Guide to Italy, Frank W. Booth (Interlink)

Insight Guide: Italy (APA Publications)

Italian Days, Barbara Grizzuti Harrison (Atlantic Monthly)

Karen Brown's Italy Bed and Breakfast 2010, Clare Brown (Karen Brown)

Let's Go Italy (Griffin)

Lonely Planet Italy, Helen Gillman & others (Lonely Planet)

Michelin Green Guide Italy (Michelin)

Rick Steves' Italy, Rick Steves (Avalon)

The Rough Guide Italy, Ros Belford, Martin Dunford & Celia Woolfrey (Rough Guides)

Property & Living

After Hannibal, Barry Unsworth (Penguin)

Bella Tuscany, Frances Mayes (Bantam)

Buying a Home in Italy, David Hampshire (Survival Books)

Desiring Italy, Susan Neunzig Cahill (Fawcett Books)

The Hills of Tuscany: A New Life in an Old Land, Ferenc Matè (Harper & Collins)

The Hill Towns of Tuscany, Richard Kauffman & Carol Field (Chronicle)

A House in Sicily, Daphne Phelps (Carroll & Graf)

Italian Country Style, Robert Fitzgerald & Peter Porter (Fairfax)

Italian Neighbours, Tim Parks (Fawcett Books)

Italian Villas and Their Gardens, Edith Wharton (Da Capo)
Italy: A Complete Guide to 1,000 Towns and Cities and Their Landmarks (Touring Club Italiano)
Italy: The Hill Towns, James Bentley (Aurum)
The Most Beautiful Villages of Tuscany, James Bentley & Hugh Palmer (Thames & Hudson)
A Place in Italy, Simon Mawer (Sinclair Stevenson)
A Small Place in Italy, Eric Newby (Picador)
Survival Guide to Milan, Jessica Halpern (Informer)
Traditional Houses of Rural Italy, Paul Duncan (Collins & Brown)
A Tuscan Childhood, Kinta Beevor (Penguin)
Under the Tuscan Sun, Frances Mayes (Broadway Books)
A Valley in Italy: The Many Seasons of a Villa in Umbria, Lisa St. Aubin de Terán (Harper Perennial)
Venice: the Most Triumphant City, George Bull
Within Tuscany, Matthew Spender (Penguin)

Food & Drink

The Best of Italy: A Cookbook, Evie Righter (Collins)
Celebrating Italy, Carol Field (Harper Perennial)
The Classic Italian Cookbook, Marcella Hazan (Macmillan)
The Dictionary of Italian Food and Drink, John F. Mariani (Broadway Books)
Eating Out in Italy, Dianne Seed & Robert Budwig (Rosendale**)**
The Edible Italian Garden, Rosalind Creasy (Periplus)
Floyd on Italy, Keith Floyd (Penguin)
Food in Italy, Claudia Gaspari (Rourke)
The Food of Italy, Waverly Root (Vintage)
A Food Lover's Companion to Tuscany, Carla Capalbo (Chronicle)
Frommer's Food Lover's Companion to Italy, Marc & Kim Millon (Macmillan)
Guide to Italian Wine, Burton Anderson (Mitchell Beazley)
Italian Food, Elizabeth David (Penguin)
Italy for the Gourmet Traveler, Fred Plotkin (Kyle Cathie)
Little Italy Cookbook, David Reggurio & Melanie Acevedo (Artisan)
Michelin Red Guide Italy (Michelin)
Slow Food Guide to Italian Wine (GRUB)
A Traveller's Wine Guide to Italy (Aurum Press)
Touring in Wine Country: Northwest Italy, Maureen Ashley (Mitchell Beazley)

A Traveller's Wine Guide to Italy, Stephen Hobley (Traveller's Wine Guides)
Vino, Burton Anderson (Little, Brown)
Walking and Eating in Tuscany & Umbria, James Ladsun & others (Penguin)
Wines of Italy, Burton Anderson (Mitchell Beazley)
World Food Italy, Matthew Evans & Gabriella Cossi (Lonely Planet)

Miscellaneous

Agnelli and the Network of Italian Power, Alan Friedman (Mandarin)
The Architecture of the Italian Renaissance, Peter Murray (Schocken)
Business Italy, A Practical Guide to Understanding Italian Business Culture, Peggy Kenna & Sondra Lacy (Passport)
Contemporary Italy, Donald Sassoon (Longman)
The Crisis of the Italian State, Patrick McCarthy (Macmillan)
D. H. Lawrence and Italy, D.H. Lawrence (Penguin)
The History of the Decline and Fall of the Roman Empire, Edward Gibbon (Penguin)
History of the Italian People, Guiliano Procacci (Penguin)
A History of Rome, Michael Grant (Simon & Schuster)
The Honoured Society, Norman Lewis (Eland)
The Italians, Luigi Barzini (Penguin)
The Last Italian: Portrait of a People, William Murray (Prentice Hall)
La Bella Lingua: My Love Affair with Italian, the World's Most Enchanting Language, Diane Hales (Broadway)
Lives of the Artists, Giorgio Vasari (Penguin)
Lonely Planet: Walking in Italy, Helen Gillman and others (Lonely Planet)
The Mafia, Claire Sterling (Grafton)
Men of Honour: The Truth about the Mafia, Giovanni Falcone (Warner)
The New Italians, Charles Richards (Penguin)
A Traveller's History of Italy, Valerio Lintner (Windrush)
Venice, James Morris (Faber)
Walking in the Dolomites, Gillian Price (Cicerone)
Wild Italy, Tim Jepson (Sheldrake)

APPENDIX C: USEFUL WEBSITES

This appendix contains a list of some of the many websites dedicated to Italy. Websites about particular aspects of life and work in Italy are also listed in the relevant chapters.

Business

Infobel Italy (🖥 www.infobel.com/en/italy). Online business (and residential) telephone directory.

Istat.it (🖥 www.istat.it). Economic and financial data statistics and resource details in Italy.

Italian Foreign Chambers of Commerce (🖥 www.italchambers.net).

Italian Confederation of Trade (🖥 www.italytrade.it/a_166_EN_558_1.html).

Italian Trade Commission (🖥 www.italytrade.com > English).

Italy Business Net (🖥 http://italybusinessnet.com). Directory of resources and trade leads for Italian manufacturers

Italy Business Directory (🖥 www.businesspatrol.com/.../Italy-business-links-directory.html). Business information, links and resources and services in Italy.

WorldBidItaly (🖥 www.worldbiditaly.com). A network of international business-to-business import and export trade leads.

Culture

Culture in Italy (🖥 www.lifeinitaly.com/culture). Festivals, folklore, heritage and la dolce vita.

Guide to Italy and Italian Culture (🖥 www.italiansrus.com). Heritage, traditions and the Italian way of life. Everything from regional guides to Italian home-made wine!

Italian Culture Traditions (🖥 www.romanlife-romeitaly.com/italian-culture-traditions.html). A guide to surviving Roman daily life and Italian culture.

Italy Culture Guide (🖥 www.kwintessential.co.uk/.../italy-country-profile.html). A comprehensive guide to Italian culture, customs, etiquette, language, manners, protocol and society.

Italy From The Inside (🖥 www.italyfromtheinside.com). Real life in Italy – for travellers who want to feel that they're more than just tourists.

My Italy (🖥 www.italiamia.com). A directory of resources about Italy, Italian and Italian American culture.

Government

AGI (⌨ www.agi.it/english-version/italy). A news service on behalf of the Prime Minister's office.

Italian Government (⌨ www.governo.it). The Italian government's website (in Italian), with information about all aspects of life in the country.

Italian Government Sites (⌨ www.worldwide-tax.com/italy/itagov.asp). A comprehensive list of all ministries and government departments, with links.

Italian Local Government (⌨ www.oultwood.com/localgov/countries/italy.php). Italian local government website links, using easily accessible maps and lists.

Italian Ministry of Foreign Affairs (⌨ www.esteri.it). Official website providing information on policies, consular services and economic affairs.

National Institute of Statistics (⌨ http://en.istat.it).

Language

Italian Language (⌨ italian.about.com). Italian language facts, grammar, pronunciation and vocabulary.

Italian Language Schools (⌨ www.applelanguages.com/en/learn/italian.php). Includes intensive teaching courses.

Italian Lessons (⌨ www.italymag.co.uk/italian-lessons). Italian language lessons, from beginners through to advanced levels.

La Bella Lingua (⌨ http://becomingitalianwordbyword.typepad.com). Dianne Hales' information blog on Italian language and culture.

Language Courses in Italy (⌨ www.languagesabroad.co.uk/italian.html). Language schools located throughout Italy, including intensive and business-orientated courses.

Language Overview (⌨ www.orbilat.com/Languages/Italian/Italian.html). General overview of the Italian language origin and history, dialects, phonology, grammar and vocabulary.

Learn Italian (⌨ www.zapitalian.com). Free online Italian language lessons.

Learn the Italian Language (⌨ italian.about.com). An Italian language guide for beginners and travellers, with an audio phrasebook and details of classes.

The Italian Language (⌨ www.italian-language-study.com). An introduction to the Italian language and culture.

Living & Working

AngloINFO Italy (⌨ italy.angloinfo.com). Essential information for expats living in or moving to Italy.

Blog From Italy (⌨ www.blogfromitaly.com). Facts, news, events and expat life in the living museum.

Expats in Italy (⌨ www.expatsinitaly.com).Useful information on living in Italy, dual citizenship, Italian bureaucracy, culture and networking.

In Italy Online (⌨ www.initaly.com). Over 4,000 pages of information about Italy, its regions, places to visit and things to do, along with practical advice about day-to-day living.

Italian Health System (⌨ www.italytravelescape.com/health%20system.htm). Information about Italy's national health service, health insurance, hospitals and medicines.

Italy Forum (⌨ www.italyforum.it/forum.php). Forum dedicated to expats living or planning to live in Italy.

Jobs Abroad (⌨ www.jobsabroad.com/search/italy). A comprehensive directory of international employment opportunities in Italy.

Life in Italy (⌨ www.lifeinitaly.com). Expat views on living and travelling in Italy.

Live in Rome (⌨ www.liveinrome.com). Information and classified advertisements for those living in the Eternal City.

Living in Italy (⌨ www.livinginitaly.com). Help with buying a property, studying or working in Italy and business advice.

Property in Italy (⌨ www.property.livinginitaly.co.uk). Italian property agents directory.

Romebuddy.com (⌨ www.romebuddy.com). A general guide to all aspects of living in Rome and Italy.

Transitions Abroad (⌨ www.transitionsabroad.com). Detailed information on volunteer work, cultural travel, and living and studying in Italy.

UK in Italy (⌨ ukinitaly.fco.gov.uk). The official website of the British Embassy in Italy. Includes help and information for British nationals regarding passports and visas, travel advice, tips for transporting pets and how to stay safe abroad.

Work in Italy (⌨ www.anyworkanywhere.com/jcg_it.html). Temporary and seasonal work in Italy's winter and summer tourist industries.

Your House in Italy (⌨ www.yourhouseinitaly.co.uk). For property seekers.

Media

Corriere della Sera (⌨ www.corriere.it). English language section of well known Italian newspaper. Published daily in Milan.

The Florentine (⌨ www.theflorentine.net). Bi-weekly free newspaper covering news, events, culture and travel around Florence.

In Rome Now (⌨ www.inromenow.com). Online guide to travel, entertainment, shopping, and food and drink in and around Rome.

Italia Online (⌨ www.italia-online.co.uk). Italian news, business, culture and travel.

Italy Magazine (🖥 www.italymag.co.uk). Property, holidays, news and all things Italian.

Life in Italy (🖥 www.lifeinitaly.com). Provides English-speaking people with news and articles about Italy and the Italian lifestyle.

Online Newspapers (🖥 www.onlinenewspapers.com/italy.htm). Comprehensive links (A-Z) to Italian national, regional and city newspapers.

Miscellaneous

Datasport (🖥 www.datasport.it). A comprehensive site dedicated to Italian sport (in Italian).

Dolce Vita (🖥 www.blogdolcevita.com). Dubs itself 'the insider's guide to Italy' and covers fashion, design, cuisine, travel and events.

Education in Italy (🖥 www.euroeducation.net/prof/italco.htm). The Italian education system structure, including information on foreign student applications and admissions.

Italian Automobile Club (🖥 www.aci.it). Italy's leading motoring organisation; the site has plenty of useful information about driving in the country (in Italian).

Italian Football Links (🖥 www.footballinitaly.com/links.html). The Italian football league's official site.

Italian Telephone Directory: White Pages for People & Businesses (🖥 www.paginebianche.it); Yellow Pages (🖥 www.paginegialle.it).

Shopping in Italy (🖥 www.destination360.com/europe/italy/shopping). Advice on buying fashion, jewellery, furniture, glass and leather in all the main Italian cities.

The Vatican (🖥 www.vatican.va). The official Vatican website.

Weather (🖥 www.meteoam.it). Italy's national meteorological service.

Travel & Tourism

Alitalia (🖥 www.alitalia.it). The website of the country's state airline.

BUG Europe: Italy (🖥 www.bugeurope.com). The back-packer's guide to budget travel in Europe. Bus and train travel and driving in Italy; also working in Italy.

Compare Prices (🖥 travel.ciao.co.uk). Special offers and price comparisons and reviews on Italian flights, hotels and restaurants.

Go Italy (🖥 goitaly.about.com). The top ten Italian cities: pictures, maps and sight-seeing information.

A Hotel in Italy (🖥 www.ahotelinitaly.com). A good hotel booking site with no advance payment.

In Italia (🖥 www.initalia.it/en). Comprehensive Italian hotel website.

In Italy (🖳 www.initaly.com). One of the most comprehensive Italian websites containing a wealth of information for residents and visitors alike.

Italian Government Tourist Board (🖳 www.enit.it). Comprehensive travel and tourist information.

Italian Motorways (🖳 www.autostrade.it/en/index.html). Plan you journey using Italian motorways (*autostrade*).

Italian Railways (🖳 www.trenitalia.com/trenitalia.html > English). The website of Italian railways in English, including online booking.

Italy Travel Guide (🖳 www.justitaly.org). Getting around in Italy; maps and general information.

Italy Traveller (🖳 www.italytraveller.com). Luxury and boutique hotels in Italy (with inspiring photos).

London to Italy (🖳 www.seat61.com/italy.htm). Travelling by train from London to Italy.

Slow Travel Italy (🖳 www.slowtrav.com/italy). Independent 'slow' travel in Italy. Renting villas and apartments; hotels, travel notes and reviews.

Travel Italy (🖳 www.travel.it). Information about everything from archaeology to thermal spas to religious tourism.

Travel to Italy (🖳 http://hotels.travel-to-italy.com). A selection of hotels, cruises, sight-seeing tours and package holidays from Rome.

Wikipedia (🖳 http://en.wikipedia.org/wiki/italy). The Wiki pages for Italy.

APPENDIX D: WEIGHTS & MEASURES

Italy uses the metric system of measurement. Those who are more familiar with the imperial system will find the tables on the following pages useful. Some comparisons shown are only approximate, but are close enough for most everyday uses.

In addition to the variety of measurement systems used, clothes sizes often vary considerably with the manufacturer – as we all know only too well! Try all clothes on before buying and don't be afraid to return something if, when you try it on at home, you decide it doesn't fit (most shops will exchange goods or give a refund).

Women's Clothes										
Continental	34	36	38	40	42	44	46	48	50	52
UK		8	10	12	14	16	18	20	22	24	26
US		6	8	10	12	14	16	18	20	22	24

Pullover's												
	Women's						Men's					
Continental	40	42	44	46	48	50	44	46	48	50	52	54
UK	34	36	38	40	42	44	34	36	38	40	42	44
US	34	36	38	40	42	44		sm	med		lg	xl

Men's Shirts										
Continental	36	37	38	39	40	41	42	43	44	46
UK/US	14	14	15	15	16	16	17	17	18	-

Men's Underwear						
Continental	5	6	7	8	9	10
UK		34	36	38	40	42	44
US		sm	med		lg	xl

NB: sm = small, med = medium, lg = large, xl = extra large

Children's Clothes

Continental	92	104	116	128	140	152
UK	16/18	20/22	24/26	28/30	32/34	36/38
US	2	4	6	8	10	12

Children's Shoes

Continental	18	19	20	21	22	23	24	25	26	27	28	29	30	31	32
UK/US	2	3	4	4	5	6	7	7	8	9	10	11	11	12	13
Continental	33	34	35	36	37	38									
UK/US	1	2	2	3	4	5									

Shoes (Women's & Men's)

Continental	35	36	37	37	38	39	40	41	42	42	43	44	45	46	47
UK	2	3	3	4	4	5	6	7	7	8	9	9	10	11	12
US	4	5	5	6	6	7	8	9	9	10	10	11	11	12	12

Weight

Imperial	Metric	Metric	Imperial
1oz	28.35g	1g	0.035oz
1lb*	454g	100g	3.5oz
1cwt	50.8kg	250g	9oz
1 ton	1,016kg	500g	18oz
2,205lb	1 tonne	1kg	2.2lb

Area

British/US	Metric	Metric	British/US
1 sq. in	0.45 sq. cm	1 sq. cm	0.15 sq. in
1 sq. ft	0.09 sq. m	1 sq. m	10.76 sq. ft
1 sq. yd	0.84 sq. m	1 sq. m	1.2 sq. yds
1 acre	0.4 hectares	1 hectare	2.47 acres
1 sq. mile	2.56 sq. km	1 sq. km	0.39 sq. mile

Capacity			
Imperial	**Metric**	**Metric**	**Imperial**
1 UK pint	0.57 litre	1 litre	1.75 UK pints
1 US pint	0.47 litre	1 litre	2.13 US pints
1 UK gallon	4.54 litres	1 litre	0.22 UK gallon
1 US gallon	3.78 litres	1 litre	0.26 US gallon
NB: An American 'cup' = around 250ml or 0.25 litre.			

Length			
British/US	**Metric**	**Metric**	**British/US**
1in	2.54cm	1cm	0.39in
1ft	30.48cm	1m	3ft 3.25in
1yd	91.44cm	1km	0.62mi
1mi	1.6km	8km	5mi

Temperature	
°Celsius	**°Fahrenheit**
0	32 (freezing point of water)
5	41
10	50
15	59
20	68
25	77
30	86
35	95
40	104
50	122

Temperature Conversion

Celsius to Fahrenheit: multiply by 9, divide by 5 and add 32. (For a quick and approximate conversion, double the Celsius temperature and add 30.)

Fahrenheit to Celsius: subtract 32, multiply by 5 and divide by 9. (For a quick and approximate conversion, subtract 30 from the Fahrenheit temperature and divide by 2.)

NB: The boiling point of water is 100°C / 212°F. Normal body temperature (if you're alive and well) is 37°C / 98.6°F.

Power			
Kilowatts	**Horsepower**	**Horsepower**	**Kilowatts**
1	1.34	1	0.75

Oven Temperature		
Gas	**Electric**	
	°F	**°C**
-	225–250	110–120
1	275	140
2	300	150
3	325	160
4	350	180
5	375	190
6	400	200
7	425	220
8	450	230
9	475	240

Air Pressure	
PSI	**Bar**
10	0.5
20	1.4
30	2
40	2.8

David, Michelangelo

APPENDIX E: MAPS

This appendix shows a map of the regions and communications maps showing airports/ports, the rail network, and motorways and major roads. The map opposite shows the 20 administrative regions of Italy, which are listed below with the 110 provinces (and their official abbreviations). A physical map of Italy is shown inside the back cover.

Region	Provinces
Abruzzo (Abruzzi)	Chieti (CH), L'Aquila (AQ), Pescara (PE), Teramo (TE)
Basilicata (Lucania)	Matera (MT), Potenza (PZ)
Calabria	Cantazaro (CZ), Cosenza CS), Crotone (KR), Reggio di Calabria (RC), Vibo Valentia (VV)
Campania	Avellino (AV), Benevento (BN), Caserta (CE), Naples/Napoli (NA), Salerno (SA)
Emilia Romagna	Bologna (BO), Ferrara (FE), Forli (FO), Modena (MO), Piacenza (PC), Parma (PR), Ravenna (RA), Reggio Emilia (RE), Rimini (RN)
Friuli-Venezia Giuila	Gorizia (GO), Pordenone (PN), Trieste (TS), Udine (UD)
Lazio (Latium)	Frosinone (FR), Latina (LT), Rieti (RI), Rome/Roma (ROMA), Viterbo (VT)
Liguria	Genova (GE), Imperia (IM), La Spezia (SP), Savona (SV)
Lombardy (Lombardia)	Bergamo (BG), Brescia (BS), Como (CO), Cremona (CR), Lecco (LC), Lodi (LO), Mantua/Mantova (MN), Milan/Milano (MI), Pavia (PV), Sondrio (SO), Varese (VA)
Marche	Ancona (AN), Ascoli Piceno (AP), Fermo (FM), Macerata (MC), Pesaro (PS)
Molise (Molize)	Campobasso (CB), Isernia (IS)
Piedmont (Piemonte)	Alessandria (AL), Asti (AT), Biella (BI), Cuneo (CN), Novara (NO), Turin/Torino (TO), Verbano-Cusio-Ossola (VB), Vercelli (VC)
Puglia (Apulia/Le Puglie)	Barletta-Andria-Trani (BT), Bari (BA), Brindisi (BR), Foggia (FG), Lecce (LE), Taranto (TA)
Sardinia (Sardegna)	Cagliari (CA), Nuoro (NU), Oristano (OR), Sassari (SS)
Sicily (Sicilia)	Agrigento (AG), Caltanissetta (CL), Catania (CT), Enna (EN), Messina (ME), Palermo (PA), Ragusa (RG), Syracuse/Siracusa (SR), Trapani (TP)
Trentino-Alto Adige	Bozen-South Tyrol (BZ), Trento (TN)
Tuscany (Toscana)	Arezzo (AR), Florence/Firenze (FI), Grosseto (GR), Leghorn/Livorno (LI), Lucca (LU), Massa Carrara (MS), Pisa (PI), Pistoia (PT), Prato (PO), Siena (SI)
Umbria	Perugia (PG), Terni (TR)
Val d'Aosta	Aosta (AO)
Veneto	Belluno (BL), Padua/Padova (PD), Rovigo (RO), Treviso (TV), Venice/Venezia (VE), Verona (VR), Vicenza (VI)

AIRPORTS & PORTS

RAIL NETWORK

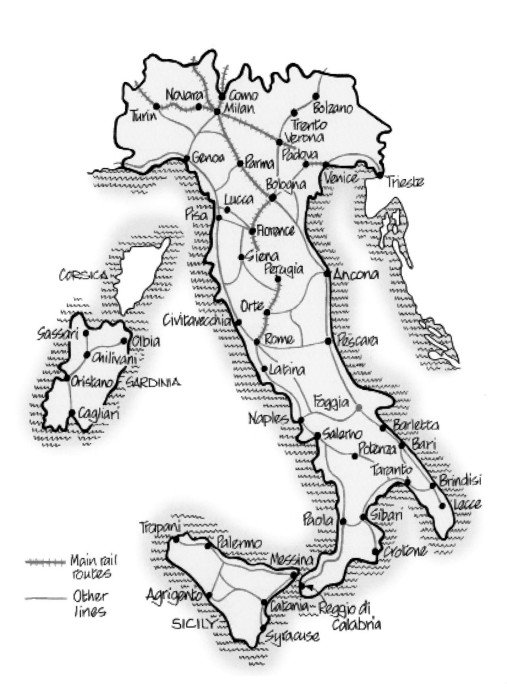

MOTORWAYS & MAJOR ROADS

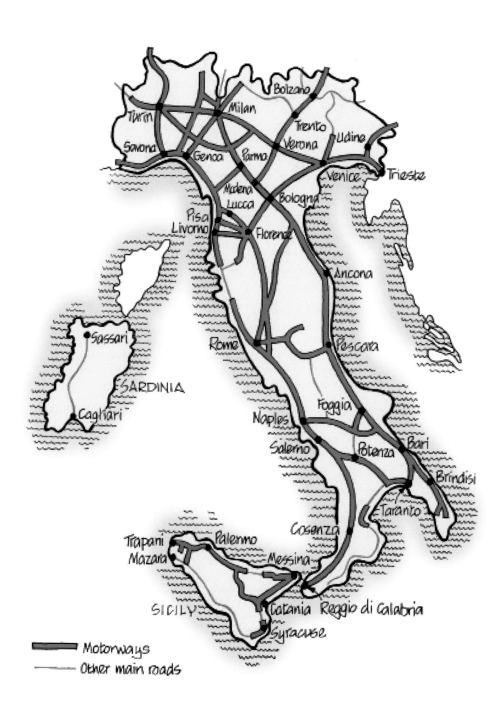

Motorways
Other main roads

INDEX

U

V

W

Survival Books

Essential reading for anyone planning to live, work, retire or buy a home abroad

Survival Books was established in 1987 and by the mid-'90s was the leading publisher of books for people planning to live, work, buy property or retire abroad.

From the outset, our philosophy has been to provide the most comprehensive and up-to-date information available. Our titles routinely contain up to twice as much information as other books and are updated frequently. All our books contain colour photographs and many are printed in two colours or full colour throughout. They also contain original cartoons, illustrations and maps.

Survival Books are written by people with first-hand experience of the countries and the people they describe, and therefore provide invaluable insights that cannot be obtained from official publications or websites, and information that is more reliable and objective than that provided by the majority of unofficial sites.

Our Books are designed to be easy – and interesting – to read. They contain a comprehensive list of contents and index and extensive appendices, including useful addresses, further reading, useful websites and glossaries to help you obtain additional information as well as metric conversion tables and other useful reference material.

Our primary goal is to provide you with the essential information necessary for a trouble-free life or property purchase and to save you time, trouble and money.

We believe our books are the best – they are certainly the best-selling. But don't take our word for it – read what reviewers and readers have said about Survival Books at the front of this book.

Order your copies today by phone, fax, post or email from:
Survival Books, PO Box 3780, Yeovil, BA21 5WX, United Kingdom.
Tel: +44 (0)1935-700060, email: sales@survivalbooks.net,
Website: www.survivalbooks.net

Buying a Home Series

Buying a home abroad is not only a major financial transaction but also a potentially life-changing experience; it's therefore essential to get it right. Our Buying a Home guides are required reading for anyone planning to purchase property abroad and are packed with vital information to guide you through the property jungle and help you avoid disasters that can turn a dream home into a nightmare.

The purpose of our Buying a Home guides is to enable you to choose the most favourable location and the most appropriate property for your requirements, and to reduce your risk of making an expensive mistake by making informed decisions and calculated judgements rather than uneducated and hopeful guesses. Most importantly, they will help you save money and will repay your investment many times over.

Buying a Home guides are the most comprehensive and up-to-date source of information available about buying property abroad – whether you're seeking a detached house or an apartment, a holiday or a permanent home (or an investment property), these books will prove invaluable.

For a full list of our current titles, visit our website at www.survivalbooks.net

Living and Working Series

Our Living and Working guides are essential reading for anyone planning to spend a period abroad – whether it's an extended holiday or permanent migration – and are packed with priceless information designed to help you avoid costly mistakes and save both time and money.

Living and Working guides are the most comprehensive and up-to-date source of practical information available about everyday life abroad. They aren't, however, simply a catalogue of dry facts and figures, but are written in a highly readable style – entertaining, practical and occasionally humorous.

Our aim is to provide you with the comprehensive practical information necessary for a trouble-free life. You may have visited a country as a tourist, but living and working there is a different matter altogether; adjusting to a new environment and culture and making a home in any foreign country can be a traumatic and stressful experience. You need to adapt to new customs and traditions, discover the local way of doing things (such as finding a home, paying bills and obtaining insurance) and learn all over again how to overcome the everyday obstacles of life.

All these subjects and many, many more are covered in depth in our Living and Working guides – don't leave home without them.

The Expats' Best Friend!

Culture Wise Series

Our **Culture Wise** series of guides is essential reading for anyone who wants to understand how a country really 'works'. Whether you're planning to stay for a few days or a lifetime, these guides will help you quickly find your feet and settle into your new surroundings.
Culture Wise guides:

- Reduce the anxiety factor in adapting to a foreign culture
- Explain how to behave in everyday situations in order to avoid cultural and social gaffes
- Help you get along with your neighbours
- Make friends and establish lasting business relationships
- Enhance your understanding of a country and its people.

People often underestimate the extent of cultural isolation they can face abroad, particularly in a country with a different language. At first glance, many countries seem an 'easy' option, often with millions of visitors from all corners of the globe and well-established expatriate communities. But, sooner or later, newcomers find that most countries are indeed 'foreign' and many come unstuck as a result.
Culture Wise guides will enable you to quickly adapt to the local way of life and feel at home, and – just as importantly – avoid the worst effects of culture shock.

Culture Wise – The Wise Way to Travel

The essential guides to Culture, Customs & Business Etiquette

Other Survival Books

The Best Places to Buy a Home in France/Spain: Unique guides to where to buy property in Spain and France, containing detailed regional profiles and market reports.

Buying, Selling and Letting Property: The best source of information about buying, selling and letting property in the UK.

Earning Money From Your French Home: Income from property in France, including short- and long-term letting.

Investing in Property Abroad: Everything you need to know and more about buying property abroad for investment and pleasure.

Life in the UK - Test & Study Guide: essential reading for anyone planning to take the 'Life in the UK' test in order to become a permanent resident (settled) in the UK.

Making a Living: Comprehensive guides to self-employment and starting a business in France and Spain.

Renovating & Maintaining Your French Home: The ultimate guide to renovating and maintaining your dream home in France.

Retiring in France/Spain: Everything a prospective retiree needs to know about the two most popular international retirement destinations.

Running Gîtes and B&Bs in France: An essential book for anyone planning to invest in a gîte or bed & breakfast business.

Rural Living in France: An invaluable book for anyone seekingthe 'good life', containing a wealth of practical information about all aspects of French country life.

Shooting Caterpillars in Spain: The hilarious and compelling story of two innocents abroad in the depths of Andalusia in the late '80s.

For a full list of our current titles, visit our website at www.survivalbooks.net

PHOTO

CREDITS

Living & Working
Series